Governing Taiwan and Tibet

Democratic Approaches

Baogang He

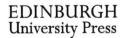

EDINBURGH
University Press

© Baogang He, 2015

Edinburgh University Press Ltd
The Tun – Holyrood Road
12 (2f) Jackson's Entry
Edinburgh EH8 8PJ
www.euppublishing.com

Typeset in 11/14 Sabon by
Servis Filmsetting Ltd, Stockport, Cheshire,
and printed and bound in Great Britain by
CPI Group (UK) Ltd, Croydon CR0 4YY

A CIP record for this book is available from the British Library

ISBN 978 0 7486 9971 1 (hardback)
ISBN 978 0 7486 9972 8 (webready PDF)
ISBN 978 1 4744 0498 3 (epub)

Contents

Photo 1 The author during the 2004 Taiwan Presidential election.

Photo 2 The author with Mao Ying-jeou in 1993, current President of ROC.

Photo 3 The author with Lobsang Sangay, current Kalon Tripa (Prime Minister of the Tibetan government in exile) in 2012 at Deakin University.

Photo 4 Attendees at the three-day deliberative workshop on Tibet in late November 2008 in Melbourne, Australia.

Acknowledgements

I express my sincere thanks to a large number of ordinary Chinese, Tibetans and Taiwanese who shared their thoughts, insights and daily experiences with me during my numerous field trips in Tibet, Xinjiang, Yunnan, Beijing and Taiwan. I would like to thank Louis Henkin, David Chambliss Johnson, Andrew Nathan, Hu Ping and James D. Seymour for constructive criticism of my seminar given at Columbia University in 1993; Anthony Giddens, John Dunn, David Held, Robert Dahl, Ian Shapiro and Juan Linz for their critical comments on my book proposal in 1996; Michael Leifer for his list of writings and his useful suggestions; Onora O'Neill for her comments; Harry Beran for his comments on the early version of Chapter 1; Will Kymlicka for his five or six pages of comments on the minority rights issue and his generous time for our talks in 2012 in Canada; Professor C. L. Chiou for his advice and rich knowledge on Taiwan; Wang Gungwu for his historical perspective of the boundary issue and Michael Bennett for his ideas on the historical development of national boundaries; Alan K. L. Chan, the former dean of the Faculty of Arts at the National University of Singapore, who offered me grants to organise the workshop on Asian multiculturalism; Professor Bruce Tranter and Liu Dongsheng for their assistance in statistical analysis; Peter Boyce, James Cotton, Michael Freeman, Philip Pettit, Barry Hindess, John Dryzek, Jane Mansbridge, James Fishkin, Stephen Bell, Yingjie Guo, Uradyn Erden Bulag, Simon Philpott, Robert Phillipson, Colin Mackerras, Geoffrey Stokes, Peter Larmour, Liu Hong and David Martin Jones for their useful comments and criticisms. I am indebted to Christine Standish, Jackie Hogan, Amy Wheaton, Yingjie Guo, Terry Moore, Lang Youxing, Tennyson Joseph, Zhang Yuehua, Shaw Wang, Nick Thomas, Kingsley Edney and Matt Hood for their research assistance in collecting materials, preparing references and the bibliography, and editing parts of the draft.

The following institutes are acknowledged for their various assistance. The East Asian Institute at Columbia University offered me a visiting fellowship in 1993 to study the secession question. The Faculty of Social Science at the University of Cambridge provided me with an office and library facilities, which enabled me to read a wide literature on the boundary question. The Institute of Asian Studies at

Leiden University and its financial support enabled me to go through most collections of old materials on the identity question in East Asia in 1996. The East Asian Institute at the National University of Singapore offered me a senior researcher fellowship between 2000 and 2004, when I carried out the empirical research on the Tibet and Taiwan question. The Contemporary China Centre at the Australian National University always provides any assistance I need when I travel to Canberra. Finally, the School of Government at the University of Tasmania, the School of Political Science and International Studies at Deakin University, and the School of Humanities and Social Sciences at Nanyang Technological University, Singapore, have been supporting my research work on a daily basis; with special thanks to Beverly Brill, Della Clark, Kate Walpole, David Owen and Helen Andrew.

I would like to take this opportunity to express my gratitude to the Australian Research Council, which not only offered me generous grants (registration numbers A79800910 and H0009804), but also provided the very useful assessment reports from which I learnt a great deal. Thanks also go to Ministry of Education, Singapore (grant number MOE2013-T2-2-025). Special thanks also go to the environment of Australian freedom, within which I can follow and develop my *own* logic of intellectual inquiry free from external interference and self-imposed censorship.

Finally, I would like to thank my wife, Suxing, my daughter, Melinda, and my son, Andrew, for their daily support.

I thank the following publishers and journals for permitting me to reproduce some materials. All are revised and updated substantively with new sections.

Chapter 5, 'The National Identity Question, Nationalism, and Democratization in China and Taiwan', in *Nationalism, National Identity and Democratization in China* (co-author with Yingjie Guo), Aldershot: Ashgate Publishers, Jan. 2000.

'Minority Rights with Chinese Characteristics', in Will Kymlicka and Baogang He (eds), *Multiculturalism in Asia*, Oxford University Press, 2005, pp. 56–79.

'The Question of Sovereignty in the Taiwan Strait: Re-examining Peking's Policy of Opposition to Taiwan's Bid for UN Membership', *China Perspectives*, No. 34, March 2001, pp. 7–18.

'The Power of Chinese Linguistic Imperialism and Its Challenge to Multicultural Education', in James Leibold and Yangbin Chen (eds), *Minority Education in China: Balancing Unity and Diversity in an Era of Critical Pluralism*, Hong Kong: The Hong Kong University Press, 2013, pp. 45–64.

'A Deliberative Approach to the Tibet Autonomy Issue: Promoting Mutual Trust through Dialogue', *Asian Survey*, Vol. 50, No. 4, July/August 2010, pp. 709–34.

Introduction

This book examines the simple but significant idea that ordinary citizens have the right to voice their opinion on the national boundary/identity question and to cast votes on it in a form of referendum. Citizen's voice and public deliberation mechanisms are powerless without a voting device. A vote without citizen's voice and public deliberation is fraught with danger; it escalates conflict rather than solving or managing it. It is necessary to combine referendum and public deliberation: a sort of deliberative referendum (Chapter 11). It is around this idea that this book brings together current work on the normative question of national boundaries with current work on deliberative democracy.

In the long history of human life, the national boundary/identity issue is largely decided by state powers and elites and/or by ruthless military force: 'might' defeated reason with regard to the boundary question. It is also true, historically, that the origins of state boundaries were accidental and that in most cases national boundaries were not made democratically. However, upon the arrival of the Enlightenment Movement and Thomas Paine's *The Age of Reason*, we can discern the beginning of a rational and democratic project.

Changing contemporary conditions make democratic choice increasingly possible. A number of new conditions which were absent, or at least hard to discern, have been created. They include the prevalence of democracy throughout the world, international support for and sympathy with minorities, and sophisticated communication systems which make people aware of minority issues quickly. Deliberative institutions, multiculturalism and the coexistence of multiple identities go a long way towards sustaining these new conditions. Moreover, the effectiveness of force as a means of solving boundary questions has been eroding. There is also a widespread belief that democracy can accommodate multiple identities and demands and can consequently help to manage problems of national identity. Under these conditions, democratic theories in the 1990s thoroughly rethought the boundary question using a new set of democratic ideas and devices, thus challenging the thesis that democracy cannot manage the boundary question. Today, with the deepening process of democratisation around the world, we are able to continue to enrich the great

Enlightenment tradition to solve, settle and manage the national boundary/identity conflict in a rational, peaceful and democratic manner. This book is devoted to a systematic treatment of one of the most pressing problems of our era – the non-violent adjudication of national boundaries.

This book takes the hard case of China as the subject of a thought experiment, to develop and test a theory of democratic governance for it. It presents an analysis of the long-standing political paradox of mainland China's relations with Taiwan and Tibet and explores the possibilities for the development of a democratic approach. The national boundary/identity question has haunted China for more than a hundred years. The dominant political thought on this challenging issue has been nationalism, socialism and Confucianism; and what has been lacking is democratic thought. This book arms to fill this intellectual gap and offers a way forward by articulating a democratic governance project that could address and manage China's national identity/boundary question.

The first part of this book advances a theoretical framework of democratic governance, and then, over two subsequent parts, examines the specific case studies of Taiwan and Tibet through that framework. The framework of democratic governance is further developed into an integrated theory and case studies in the concluding chapter.

PERSISTENT PROBLEMS

China faces national identity problems, that is, sections of the national population such as Tibetans do not identify with the Chinese nation-state in which they live, and endeavour to create their own political identity through the reconstruction of a specific cultural and ethnic identity. China's national identity problem also involves the question of reunification with Taiwan where there is a dichotomy of sentiment. On the one hand, those who do not desire any radical political change in cross-strait relations acknowledge that there are Taiwanese and Chinese identities and encourage the leaderships of both countries to form a strong and constructive partnership as a mechanism for avoiding forceful reunification. On the other side of the spectrum are those who argue that Taiwan is a sovereign nation and should have a state-to-state relationship with the People's Republic of China (PRC). These individuals consider themselves to be ethnically Taiwanese and some want to change the name of the country to the Republic of Taiwan (see, for example, Kuo & Myers 2004: Chapter 9). These people have been led by the Democratic Progress Party (DPP) that has endorsed the independence of Taiwan in its Party's Constitution and refused to reunify with the PRC, yet reunification remains a core goal for the Chinese state and a key part of its national unity vision.

The Tibet and Taiwan issues are different. While Tibet has its unique cultural identity, Taiwan's cultural identity, despite reconstruction in recent years, has been associated with Chinese cultures. Tibet is a 'state' in exile without territory; while Taiwan has had its own state with a clearly defined territorial boundary for more than sixty years. Both, however, share the same concern with the issue of their own independence. Both face similar questions relating to federalism, autonomy, democratic governance and referendum but with different answers. The problems concerning Taiwan and Tibet are different for China, too. For Beijing, Tibet is a case of holding together, while Taiwan is a case of bringing together. They require different treatment in the eyes of Beijing. Beijing's response to the two questions, however, is very much similar in that it refuses to adopt a democratic approach. Such a response, as this book argues, is utterly mistaken and outdated in the modern world. It is also completely against the national interest of China.

AGAINST IMMORAL REALISM

The above-described national identity/boundary problem is contested in China. Chinese officials hold different views ranging from the denial of the existence of such a problem to the recognition of the problem but pointing out different sources of, or different approaches to, the problem. To prepare this final manuscript, I have carried out several informal interviews with Chinese officials whose opinions are very striking. One senior official in charge of foreign affairs from China's Political Consultation Conference, in responding to my question on the Tibet problem, told me immediately and seriously that there is no Tibet problem and if there is, it is invented by the West.[1] One higher officer from the State Council provided his personal view that Tibet and China had a more than one thousand year troubled history. He argued that it is not realistic to 'solve' the problem: what we can expect is to manage the problem and don't let it get out of control.[2] One distinguished professor, who holds an important administrative position in the Central Party School, said that the so-called Tibet problem is the problem of the Lama class that had a privileged life before 1949 but resisted the Chinese communism that destroyed that privilege. He said that it is difficult for Chinese secular culture to persuade Tibetan religious followers not to listen to the Lama. According to the above-mentioned professor, the Chinese government has failed in influencing the Lama through developing the modern ideology of Marxism among the Lama class. Hu Yaobang's relaxation policy in the 1980s offered an opportunity for the Lama class to revive. The government should have cultivated a new class of Lama who would have mastered both the languages of Buddhism and Marxism so that they could have developed a hybrid form of Buddhism and Marxism. However, he argues, they failed to do so. This is the problem.[3] A Chinese diplomat in Australia informed me, 'We were ordered to talk with those who will see the Dalai Lama, and asked them not to see him in terms of respecting China's sovereignty in 2011. We had some success in that Tony Abbott, the leader of the opposition, met him for a few minutes rather than longer.'[4] It is very striking that Chinese diplomats will not address the source of the problem at home but blame the Western support for the 'perpetuation of the Tibet problem'.

It is remarkable that Chinese officials as well as many scholars lack feelings of guilt. In contrast, there has been a deep sense of guilt among intellectuals in Australia and Canada towards the treatment of their indigenous peoples, finally leading to Kevin Rudd's official national apology to the Australian aboriginals in 2008. It is a remarkable divergence that Chinese officials and scholars embrace a paternalistic love, and hold the view that 'we give you [Tibetans] so much aid, but you are still resentful!' It seems that both Confucianism and Chinese Marxism share the same view that minorities are backward and undeveloped, and that the central government should help them and civilise them (see, for example, Duncan 2004).

Here is the politics of the 'problem'. Tibetans say there is a problem, but some officials deny it. Such a denial makes the issue worse. Rather than blame 'Westerners', it is better to acknowledge the existence of this serious problem from the beginning and examine the international and domestic sources of the problem. The 'minority issue' is the worldwide problem; there is nothing unusual in acknowledging the existence of a minority problem like the one regarding Tibet.

Tough control and repression in Tibet and pragmatic compromise and economic integration across the Taiwan Straits characterise current Beijing policies towards Tibet and Taiwan. These policies do not address the sources of the problems, nor do they offer any satisfactory solutions. They only serve to manage the Tibet and Taiwan problems for the time being and to delay the disastrous explosion of potential 'time-bombs'. If the DPP wins the next election, the Taiwan issue is likely to resurface internationally.

Chinese policies towards Tibet and Taiwan lack a decent moral consideration, and there is a dearth of innovative thinking on the Tibet and Taiwan issues. Xi Jinping's new leadership urgently needs to reconsider Beijing's Tibet and Taiwan policies. An examination of the interaction between the concepts of democracy, sovereignty, nationalism and power in a realistic sense is desperately needed.

DEMOCRATIC APPROACH AND ITS PREDICAMENT

Democracy is a modern condition that frames discussions and debates in the contemporary world. Even though Beijing rejects a democratic approach to the Tibet and Taiwan question, it currently has to endorse and appeal to the 'people's will' as a foundation or principle (Chapter 2). Moreover, Beijing cannot overlook the empirical questions of how democracy/democratisation impacts on the Tibet or Taiwan question (Chapter 3). Equally, a simplistic advocacy of democracy without examining the historical and cultural conditions of the Chinese civilisation is also problematic.

Today's Chinese liberals cannot articulate a democratic approach to the issue of national identity, otherwise they will be treated as 'traitors'. Thus, they leave the matter to Chinese nationalists. The political space for Chinese liberals has become increasingly limited as they face the difficult question posed by the national identity problem. The fate of Chinese liberals is predetermined by the national identity question: the ideology of political liberalism is unlikely to produce a satisfactory solution to the national identity question in China. In contrast, the ideology of *economic* liberalism is not only able to dominate China's market economy but it is also compatible with Chinese nationalists who want to build a great China. In the politics of national identity, political liberals are likely to be the losers. They cannot openly challenge Chinese nationalists; they must become a sort of nationalist if they want to say something about the national identity question. In the context of the existing problems of democratisation, Chinese liberal reformers are mainly concerned with political reform and they cannot commit themselves to a tough issue like Tibet. Some liberals deliberately avoid the issue; others think it is important, but postpone it. Worse still, some exhibit illiberal and undemocratic thinking in believing that they are not guilty for the minority issues.

Against the above background, this book adopts a democratic approach, that is, to treat these issues seriously and think of them in democratic terms and ways. I argue that Chinese liberals in fact can offer a democratic approach, defend democratic principles and develop democratic governance. Political liberalism can and should be a constructive force to deal with the national identity question in China.

Chinese nationalists should not be treated as a homogeneous group. There are differences *within* the various groups of Chinese nationalists – not only those within academia, but also those within the Chinese Communist Party (CCP) as well as the 'popular' nationalists. They understand the relationship between democratisation and national integrity in different ways. Among these different nationalist positions, there is a moderate civic form of nationalism which can be compatible with liberalism. This book represents just such a combination of civic nationalism and liberalism.

AIMS OF THE BOOK

A growing literature is examining the Tibet and Taiwan questions, with the majority focusing on the real situation and policy issues. Only some is concerned with the democratic governance or approach. In a special issue of *Asian Ethnicity* focused on Tibet, for example, Yan Sun (2011) compares the cases of Tibet and Taiwan's relations with the Chinese government, but she does not mention the question of democratisation. In the same issue, B. R. Deepak (2011) considers how the Tibetan question affects relations between China and India and also analyses the future of the Tibetan movement, but there is also no mention of democratisation. Virendra S. Verma (2009) writes about the 'post-Dalai Lama situation' but the issue of democratisation does not come into it at all. Whereas Ann Frechette (2007) conducts a detailed examination of democracy in the Tibetan exile community she does not consider the implications for relations with the Chinese government (although her research was published before the 2008 election of the Kalon Tripa). However, there are some scholars and politicians who have been advocating a democratic or human rights approach to the Tibet or Taiwan questions, as will be reviewed and discussed in detail in subsequent chapters. In terms of the national identity question more specifically, Rawski (1996) has detailed the historical legacy of the Qing period and the serious national identity question that today's China faces. Friedman (1994) has discussed the eclipse of anti-imperialist national identity, and the formation of a southern identity based on Chu culture. Both Rawski and

Friedman demonstrate the seriousness of China's national identity question. But such a discussion has not been related to the questions of Chinese democratisation and the fate of Chinese political liberalism. On the whole, despite many discussions on democracy and human rights approaches to the Tibet and Taiwan questions in the form of political commentary, journal articles and book chapters, there is still a lack of systematic study of democratic governance. Such a topic deserves a book, even several books, to deal with each sub-issue of the broad question concerning democratic governance. This book attempts to address these issues in a systematic manner and thus fill an intellectual gap.

Realism has dominated the studies of the political situation and issue of national identity referring to Taiwan and Tibet; and this area is in need of a systematic rethinking based on normative principles. Often the scholarship offers a detailed and sophisticated analysis of history, political events, political parties and institutions but lacks a systematic analysis of democracy and sovereignty. Even when the concept of democracy is deployed, often it is used in a rhetorical sense and the analysis remains superficial. We need to go beyond shallow analysis and explore multiple factors and dimensions of democratic governance.

This book will develop a systematic analysis of different models of democracy and their roles in the politics of national identity. In particular, it develops an analysis of why and how new forms of democratic governance like deliberative democracy are needed for China to address the Tibet and Taiwan questions. It is devoted to a search for democratic governance with regard to the Taiwan and Tibet questions specifically. It problematises the existing hard-liners' realist policies, and examines how and under what conditions democracy can or cannot provide an answer. It examines the different meanings, practices, institutions and various impacts of democracy with regard to the problem of China's national identity. It provides a systematic analysis of different forms of democratic approach and their likely impacts. In particular, it presents the difficulties and obstacles to a democratic approach to the Tibet and Taiwan questions, but it still searches for some political space in which democratic governance can work.

The book examines the advantages and disadvantages of two main approaches, namely, realism and democracy. It investigates the principles and methods of each approach. It develops a 'real utopian' approach to combine these approaches into a mixed policy. When Chinese power reaches the critical point at which the US is likely to make a compromise, and when Beijing adopts deliberative democracy and flexible post-sovereign arrangements, a satisfactory solution to the Taiwan and Tibet question might be found. The book argues that an adjustment to the traditional Chinese practice and international conventional conception of sovereignty is necessary in order to develop a new approach to addressing the Taiwan and Tibet issues.

While four chapters are newly written, this book also includes revised versions of my published work on the Taiwan and Tibet issues. I have been searching for new thinking and new approaches to the Tibet and Taiwan issues, particularly in relation to some normative and theoretical questions, over the last two decades. The first time I engaged with the Tibet question was in 1990–3 when I was writing my PhD thesis in Canberra. In the context of democratisation in Eastern Europe, I was interested in the question of the right to secede claimed by Tibetans. In my first book I developed a liberal normative position that liberal constraint on the exercise of the right to secede can be justified in the Chinese context of democratisation (B. He 1996: Chapter 4). In my second book I explored the role of citizens and civil society in addressing the national boundary and identity question (B. He 1997: Chapter 6; and B. He 2004a). In a third, co-authored, book I examined the clash between state nationalism and democratisation (B. He & Guo 2000: Chapter 7). Following Yan Jiaqi's federalism approach, I have worked on this issue for a long time, finally leading to the edited volume *Federalism in Asia* (B. He et al. 2007). A more philosophical approach was to create a deliberative dialogue on the relationship between Western liberal multiculturalism and Asian political thoughts (B. He 2004b, 2005). I have also published ten refereed journal articles and seven book chapters relating to the Taiwan and Tibet questions. This book has revised and updated these published journal articles and book chapters, representing the culmination of my analysis and thinking to date on the national identity question in China with respect to Taiwan and Tibet.

The intellectual history of my thinking can be characterised as three stages. In the first stage I tried to explore and apply the various democratic approaches to the Tibet and Taiwan issues (B. He 1996: Chapter 4; 1997: Chapter 7; 2001a, 2001b, 2010; B. He & Hundt 2012), and as a result I have encountered many obstacles. I thus moved to the second stage in which I developed a historical and cultural approach to an understanding of the clash between democracy and China's national identity question (B. He 2001a, 2001b, 2002a, 2002b, 2003, 2004c). Such an analysis leads to a realist or empirical approach, which is, however, equally unsatisfactory on normative grounds. Now in the third stage, in the form of this book, I have synthesised different approaches and produced a hybrid analysis, seeking to respond to some of the earlier intellectual and philosophical challenges I confronted. It is extremely enjoyable to rework all of these previous writings, in that I have now developed a more systematic way to deal with my own inner tensions and contradictions.

THE STRUCTURE AND SUMMARY OF THE BOOK

The book consists of three parts. Part One introduces the theoretical approaches; it has three chapters that review and examine democratic theories, present the methodology of the book, and provide an historical examination of empire, democracy and the national identity/boundary question. Part Two is about Taiwan specifically, consisting of three chapters that discuss the impact of Taiwanese democratisation as well as the potential impact of Chinese democratisation on the resolution of the Taiwan question, deliberative referendum and the question of Taiwan's international space with regard to sovereignty. Part Three consists of four chapters about Tibet. These deal with a number of issues concerning democratic governance. They include the theoretical discourse on minority rights, the practice of autonomy, multicultural linguistic policy and deliberative forum. Below is an overview of each chapter.

Chapter 1 serves as a conceptual introduction to the book. It defines the key concepts of the national boundary/identity question and democratic governance (or management, or approach, or solution) related to the national boundary/identity question. It develops an analytical classification of different kinds of national boundary/identity or membership issues, qualifies the project of democratic management, and spells out the concrete components of democratic governance. It explores why democratic management of the boundary issue is desirable, and defends the universal project of democratic governance. This chapter is an intellectual foundation for the quest for democratic governance with regard to the Taiwan and Tibet issues.

Chapter 2 examines two paradigms for, and two approaches to, the Taiwan and Tibet question, namely realism and democracy. It provides a brief account of the general features of each paradigm, characterises what is distinctive about its approach, and outlines the advantages and disadvantages of each approach. It questions some presuppositions of the two intellectual frameworks through which scholars study Taiwan and Tibet and political actors propose various solutions to the Taiwan and Tibet questions. The chapter introduces and employs Eric Wright's 'real utopian' approach, which combines both normative and empirical thinking, and considers the conditions under which various democratic approaches to the Taiwan and Tibet questions are proposed and attempted. Moving back and forth between realism and democracy, a methodologically reflective equilibrium is developed, which continues throughout the book.

Chapter 3 examines the historically-based thesis on empire that argues that the process of evolving from 'empire' to nation-state presents a challenge for China's territorial integrity. It analyses the impact of China's national identity question on Chinese democratisation, and explores why China has difficulty establishing democracy. Through demonstrating the conflictive logic between democracy and state nationalism in the context of China's national identity issue, it provides an explanation or an understanding of, not a justification for, the Party/state's resistance to democracy. The chapter also argues against a strong historical determinism and emphasises the importance of agency. It explores the possible democratic governance mechanisms through which China could avoid the logic of 'the empire thesis'.

Chapter 4 compares nationalism and democratisation in Taiwan and China, and, in particular, seeks to develop an understanding of the rise of Taiwanese nationalism and its impact on democratisation, as well as the impact democratisation has on the politics associated with the national identity question. It examines the effects of democratisation and nationalism that continue to contribute to the outcome in managing the national identity conflicts across the Taiwan Strait.

Chapter 5 focuses on the debate over the resolution of Taiwanese national identity through referendums. It provides a comprehensive historical and political overview of the issues involved, and examines the prospects for future referendums and their policy implications. The chapter traces the initiative and development of the independence referendum proposal by former President Chen Shui-bian. It examines the referendum proposal adopted by the DPP, the referendum law debated in the Legislative Yuan, and the administrative regulation proposed by the Executive

Yuan. The chapter discusses the initially different and later seemingly convergent attitudes towards the referendum proposal by the Kuomintang (KMT) and People's First Party (PFP), and investigates China's policy towards the referendum issue and the Bush administration's opposition to the referendum proposal. The chapter also examines the manipulative aspect of referendum and suggests that a future referendum should follow the guidelines of deliberative democracy to achieve a deliberative referendum.

Chapter 6 argues that the solution to the Taiwan question must take into account Taiwan's desires and its place in international relations, and that to do so, Beijing has to reconsider its Taiwan policy in terms of a new conception of sovereignty. It attempts to transcend nationalist thinking, challenge the traditional concept of sovereignty, and outline an alternative concept of sovereignty. It provides a logical analysis of the impact of the old versus new conceptions of sovereignty on the resolution to the Taiwan question. The chapter does not focus on any immediate practical solution to the Taiwan question, but instead on the long-term intellectual 'solution'. While it is conceded that the alternative idea of sovereignty developed in this chapter may be too 'idealistic' or 'alien' to be accepted by the current leadership in the PRC, it is hoped that the idea may appeal to the next generation of political leaders.

Chapter 7 examines the theoretical sources of current Chinese policies on minority rights. It traces a complex combination of various intellectual inheritances, combining echoes of Confucian ideas of paternalistic guardianship over 'backward groups' or 'younger brothers' with echoes of Marxist/Leninist ideas of ethnic autonomy, mixed with further echoes of liberal ideas of minority rights and affirmative action policies for minority groups.

Chapter 8 examines in detail the current practice of autonomy in China. It first examines current Chinese official practice of autonomy, followed by a discussion of the Dalai Lama's proposal on the Middle Way to achieve genuine autonomy. It then discusses and explains why Beijing rejects the proposals within the Middle Way and offers several explanations for the current deadlock. Finally it makes some suggestions on how to make a breakthrough.

In discussing the erosion of Tibetan language teaching in Tibet, Chapter 9 explores China's long history of 'linguistic imperialism' and asks how it is mediating, and perhaps even undermining, multicultural education in the PRC. It finds that China's linguistic history has been one of linguistic imperialism, in which China's language policies have been shaped by the dominance of the Chinese script and by the state's desire to create and maintain Great Unity. This chapter also offers insight into the probable future direction of linguistic trends of Tibetan language teaching, and suggests several ways in which China can go beyond linguistic imperialism in pursuing a plural and multi-linguistic language policy.

Chapter 10 applies the deliberative approach to the Tibet autonomy issue. It examines the case of a deliberative workshop, including its achievements and limitations. This chapter argues that this deliberative dialogue case appears to have improved knowledge and mutual understanding, enhanced mutual trust and deliberative capacities, and produced moderating effects.

Chapter 11 aims not only to provide a summary of the discussion of democratic approaches in the book, but to develop an integrated theory of democratic governance centred on deliberative referendum. It also develops a synthesis of the theory and case studies in the book.

NOTES

1. Interview on 13 January 2011 in Beijing.
2. Interview on 27 May 2012 in Chengdu.
3. Interview on 15 July 2012 in Beijing.
4. Interview on 10 May 2012 in Melbourne.

PART I

Theoretical Approaches

1 The Idea of Democratic Governance

This chapter serves as a conceptual introduction to the book and provides an intellectual foundation for the quest for democratic governance with regard to the Taiwan and Tibet issues. It first traces the history of democratic ideas and defines the core components of democratic governance related to the national boundary/identity question. It then develops an analytic classification of different kinds of national boundary/identity or membership issue, followed by an investigation of the criteria for choosing national boundaries. It explores the question as to why national boundaries should be a matter of democratic choice, and of whether democracy has the capacity of addressing the issue. It addresses the issue of why democratic management of the boundary issue is desirable and discusses the functions the democratic management entails. Finally it qualifies the project of democratic management with a cautious note.

1.1 THE ORIGIN AND COMPONENTS OF DEMOCRATIC GOVERNANCE

The French Revolution first gave practical effect to the idea that people should have some choice of national boundary/identity. Since the French Revolution was based on the idea of popular sovereignty, it was argued that new rulers should not annex territories without consultation with the inhabitants of those territories (Goodhart 1971: 99). In 1791, the French Assembly rejected the Communes' vote for annexing Avignon, by a vote of 487 to 316, on the ground that there was not sufficient evidence about the freedom of voting. This was the first modern exercise of the democratic principle to resolve national boundary questions (Goodhart 1971: 100–1).

The following is a review of three classical thinkers on this topic in the last three centuries: Immanuel Kant, J. S. Mill and John Calhoun. The reason these writers have been selected is because their theories have far-reaching influence and a strong following in the 21st century.

Kant (1724–1804): perpetual peace and democracy

Kant implicitly and explicitly discussed the boundary question in his famous essay on perpetual peace (1795). Kant's approach to the boundary question was cosmopolitan and democratic, which was evident in his idea of three articles for a perpetual peace. The first definitive article for a perpetual peace is that the civil constitution of every nation should be republican. There are three principles of republicanism: the freedom of the members of a society, the dependence of everyone on a single, common legislation, and the law of the equality of all citizens (Kant 1983: 112). The second article is that the right of nations shall be based on a federation of free states. Through a contract, nations enter into a league of peace, the arrangement of federalism which should eventually include all nations. The concept of the right of nations to go to war is meaningless (Kant 1983: 117). The third article is that cosmopolitan rights shall be limited to conditions of universal hospitality.

For Kant, boundaries are arbitrary and accidental. There is no place for the idea of fixed boundaries, and of boundary-related privileges of peoples. As Kant (1983: 118) said:

> *An alien may request the right to be a permanent visitor, but the right to visit, to associate, belongs to all men by virtue of their common ownership of the earth's surface; for since the earth is a globe, they cannot scatter themselves infinitely, but, must, finally, tolerate living in close proximity, because originally no one had a greater right to any region of the earth than anyone else.

Kant assumed the changeable nature of national boundaries in his vision of a federated world. He laid out the basic principles to deal with the boundary problem; that is, *the principles of freedom, equality, cosmopolitan rights and reason.* Ideally there should be no forceful interference, and no acquisition of nations by inheritance, exchange, purchase or gift.

Kant rejected 'democracy' as a principle to pursue peace on two grounds. First, 'democracy' sets up an executive power in which all citizens make decisions against one who does not agree, therefore it is despotism. Second, the 'democratic' system makes a representative system impossible, for everyone wants to rule (Kant 1983: 114). To better understand Kant, it should be emphasised that what he called a 'republican' system is today's representative democracy; and what he calls 'democracy' is a kind of plebiscitary democracy.

J. S. Mill (1806–73): nationality, assimilation and federation

Mill thought that the boundaries of governments should coincide, in the main, with those of nationalities. 'Where the sentiment of nationality exists in any force, there is a *prima facie* case for uniting all the members of the nationality under the same government' (Mill 1947: 360–1). However, as Mill (1947: 362–3) acknowledged, 'different nationalities are so locally intermingled that it is not practicable for them to be under separate governments'.

Assimilation was favoured by Mill to settle the minority issue, mishandling of which often gives rise to the boundary question. Mill (1947: 363) claimed, 'Experience proves that it is possible for one nationality to merge and be absorbed in another; and when it was originally an inferior and more backward portion of the human race the absorption is greater to its advantage.' In the opinion of Mill, a Breton or a Basque was better off being a member of the French nationality. The same remark applied to the Welsh or Scottish of the British nation. Mill praised the assimilation between the Irish and English peoples. 'There is now next to nothing, except the memory of the past, and the difference in the predominant religion, to keep apart two races [Irish and English], perhaps the most fitted of any two in the world to be the completing counterpart of one another' (Mill 1947: 365). The greatest practical obstacle for the blending of nationalities, according to Mill, is a condition under which the nationalities which have been bound together are nearly equal in numbers and in other elements of power.

In line with Kant, Mill favoured a federal approach and believed that federal arrangements reduce warfare: 'When the conditions exist for the formation of efficient and durable Federal Unions, the multiplication of them is always a benefit to the world.' Diminishing the number of petty states, Mill thought, weakens the temptation to adopt aggressive policies, whether through the direct use of arms, or the exercise of power based on the prestige of superior force (Mill 1947: 373).

In the case of Australia or New Zealand, Mill argued, populations were suitably politically mature for representative government, thus Great Britain ought to consent to their separation should the time come. In the case of so-called 'backward' nationalities, Mill asserted that they must be governed by Great Britain and no separation was allowed, because a foreign but benign government is as legitimate as any other if it facilitates the transition of backward nationalities to a higher stage of civilisation (Mill 1947: 382).

Mill also discussed the effects of despotism, or alternatively the transition to representative institutions, on the national boundary problem. Under a despotic government, in the course of a few generations, identity of situation often produces harmony of feeling, and the different races come to feel towards each other as fellow-countrymen. However, if the era of aspiration to free government arrives before the fusion has been effected, and if the unreconciled nationalities are geographically separate, 'there is not only an obvious propriety, but, if either freedom or concord is cared for, a necessity, for breaking the connection altogether' (Mill 1947: 363). This observation by Mill applies perfectly to the events leading to the disintegration of the Soviet Union between 1989 and 1992.

In summary, to deal with the national boundary question, Mill spelled out the liberal consent principle, the nationalist principle, the assimilation approach, the federal approach and the civilisation argument. Mill's liberal consent principle was met in the case of Australia's separation from the UK; Australian independence was achieved through referendums in 1898, with the support of 67 per cent of voters in four colonies (New South Wales, South Australia, Tasmania, Victoria). This principle is also highly contested in contemporary democratic theories of consent concerning the legitimate source for the national boundary issue, which will be discussed later. Mill's nationalist principle is now followed by David Miller (1995) and his assimilation policy is being attacked by Kymlicka and other neo-liberals.

John Calhoun (1782–1850): a plural executive

Against the background of hostile conflicts between the North and South in the USA, Calhoun, as a member of the United States Senate (1845–50) and a Southern theorist, contended that the states, originally sovereign, had created the Union and, since sovereignty cannot be divided, they retained their sovereign right of secession. Calhoun (1953: 100) saw that 'the restoration of the federal character of the government can furnish no remedy. So long as it continues, there can be no safety for the weaker section.' Drawing on the idea of a dual executive in the history of Sparta and Rome, following the precedent of Timothy Ford's theory of the 'dual contract' (1794), and aiming at maintaining the unity of the USA, Calhoun proposed a plural executive, which has two components. First, the Constitution would be modified so as to give to the weaker section a veto on the action of the government. Second, the executive power should be vested in two, to be elected so that the two should be constituted as the special organs and representatives of the respective sections in the executive department of the government, and requiring each to approve all the acts of Congress before they become law. This could, he thought, avoid hostile geographical parties and would make the Union a union in truth, a bond of mutual affection and brotherhood (Calhoun 1953: 101–4).

Calhoun's institutional design ensures that each interest included in the decision-making process is protected against policy change that would make it worse off. Nevertheless, it faces problems: the problem of identifying the 'major' interest, the problem of inaction, the problem of collective action and inconsistency within veto groups (Herzberg 1992). Calhoun's institutional design was not implemented in the USA, and failed in Cyprus when adopted in the 1960s. A revised version of Calhoun's institutional arrangements can be found in Arend Lijphart's theory of consociationalism.

1.2   CONTEMPORARY DEMOCRATIC THEORIES

'Democracy', as a term, has been used in a variety of ways, and can cause confusion if it is not defined clearly. To develop a clear argument about democratic governance, we need to first clarify the various meanings of democracy being employed in different contexts and identify the different components of democratic governance.

Democratic governance or devices, including referendums, electoral engineering, liberal multiculturalism and consociational arrangements, have been extended to resolve and manage conflicts arising from divided society. Electoral democracy provides a conflict-resolution mechanism through proportional representation for ethnic groups and multi-ethnic-based political parties (Reilly 2001; Fraenkel & Grofman 2006). Liberal multiculturalism (Kymlicka 1989, 1995) has developed a system of minority rights to protect the interests of minorities, consociational democracy (Lijphart 1984) has built up complex power-sharing mechanisms, and deliberative democracy (John Dryzek 2005) offers a talk-centric resolution mechanism and procedure. All reject the use of violence in settling such conflicts. Here I would like to synthesise democratic theories to identify the four components pertinent to the democratic management of the national boundary question (they can be further combined as the idea of participatory and deliberative referendum in the condition of political equality and the respect for minority rights; see the last chapter). These are:

1. Equality
2. Referendums
3. Participation and Deliberation
4. Autonomy and Minority Rights

Equality

In dealing with competing claims over the boundary question, the right to equal consideration in institutional design is a fundamental democratic principle. That is, all people have a right to equality. This is a fundamental respect owed to persons irrespective of the accident of birth or social position. Following this consideration of equal concern a majority should not decide basic interests of a minority. Deriving from this principle, it is assumed that competing claims for territories or statehood between communities cannot be placed in an hierarchical order. In the absence of sufficient reasons to resolve disputing claims, the claims are held to have equal validity; they should be treated as if equal. Claims to a territorial state are only acceptable if they have due regard to, and equal concern for, other claims. The conflicting claims between China and Taiwan, for example, cannot be resolved simply on the basis of one party's claim having more validity than the other. The claims of both sides are deserving of equal regard. The democratic approach therefore provides for an unbiased opportunity for claims to be considered.

The right of state sovereignty and the right of secession are limited by the fact that group A's right to state sovereignty is no more or less valid than that of group B's right to secession. As neither right has precedence, the only solution seems to be an equal reduction in the rights of both parties in order to reach an equal settlement. When rights are in conflict there can be no just settlement unless there is an element of compromise. Therefore democratic management of the boundary question requires compromise, which is ultimately based on the idea of equal concern and respect. A just solution to a boundary conflict involves the right to equal regard and the notion of compromise. Without compromise, democratic management will become empty; and without compromise, there is no solution.

Equal respect and dignity are non-negotiable values in modern times. Within this normative context, any form of hierarchy inherent in the majority–minority relations is dismissed, such as with the Han and Tibetan relations, for example. In this book I deal with questions concerning the equal representation of Taiwan in the UN (Chapter 6); the idea of cultural equality and equality issues in the discourse and practice of minority rights in Tibet (Chapters 7 and 8); and the provision of equal, fair and deliberative forums (Chapter 10).

Referendums

There has been a long tradition of the use of referendums to settle national boundary disputes since 1791, and an equally long tradition of resistance to them. The German lawyers Hotzendorf, Geffker, Stoerk and Lieber dismissed the legitimacy of referendums on the grounds that they subjected the minority to the rule of a simple majority without protection, that they contradicted the organic nature of the state, that they would encourage secession and make the establishment of peace more difficult, and that they were used to ratify fait accomplis (Goodhart 1971: 107–8).

In order to be regarded as democratic, any change in, or refusal to change, national boundaries must be subject to democratic procedures such as referendums, popular vote or the votes of representatives. As Article 2 of the Atlantic Charter states, no territorial changes shall be effected if they do not accord with the freely expressed wishes of the inhabitants of the territories concerned (Christie 1996: 211). In particular, referendums, taken as an important mechanism of voluntary agreement and consent, allow people to cast their ballots over specific boundary questions; thus the referendum can be seen as part of the democratic management of the boundary question.

Referendums have different functions: managing and containing conflicts, ratifying that which has already been decided by an elite's negotiation, or even playing a merely symbolic and not substantial role. It is important to make a distinction between mobilised referendums and deliberative referendums. In the former, the referendum is used by politicians as a tool to mobilise the masses for political gain. Often politicians use hate speech against another group. Such a referendum may lead to and intensify conflicts. In contrast, a deliberative referendum stresses the quality of reason-based argument for or against certain propositions, such as the issue of national identity. It is free of hatred and includes a constitutional provision against ethnic hate speech. It has an independent commission to ensure that balanced arguments are made and all different points of view are expressed. It encourages societal or community deliberation at all levels. The democratic resolution of any question of national identity or national boundaries is based on the consent of the people, whose votes ultimately decide the outcome of the referendum; for this to occur in a democratic way the voting must be free and fair. One noticeable benefit of a deliberative referendum is that no one dies for the cause of 'secession', as demonstrated by the referendum experience in Canada. This book specifically examines deliberative referendum, a combination of electoral and deliberative democracies, as an improvement upon the existing referendums mechanism (Chapters 5, 10 and 11).

Participatory and deliberative democracy

The meanings of democracy include not only periodic elections and rights, but also the participation of people and civil society in the decision-making process.

Under democracy, the general public has its opportunity for meaningful participation in the definition of the state boundary and in the formation of policies about the boundary question. Today, the idea and practice of 'civil society' is playing an increasing role in defining the boundary of political communities. Civil society refers not only to associations of civic groups, but also a number of social conditions, including non-segregation, integration, and people's contact across divided nations or ethnic groups. Such conditions make dialogue and accommodation possible, reduce tension, break down barriers and stereotypes, and promote mutual sympathy and understanding. The tragedy in Kosovo in 1999 shows that without civil society and a civil culture, ethnic cleansing and ethnic conflict are inevitable. The notion of civil society prescribes an ideal model of coexistence between overlapping associations and communities. The notion of civil society challenges the old idea that a unified polity must have a unified ethnic base and that integration requires the subordination of local dialects and regional cultures to a national culture (Gold 1993; B. He 1999, 2002b, 2004a, 2004c).

Departing from the traditional democratic institutions, rules and procedures, deliberative democracy is a talk-centric approach that appeals to the simple idea that conflict resolution must be done through public reasoning. John Dryzek's seminal paper, 'Deliberative Democracy in Divided Societies', explores how inter-communal dialogue at the grassroots level can function as a conflict-resolution mechanism in societies characterised by 'mutually contradictory assertions of identity' (Dryzek 2005).

Different forms of public deliberation such as citizen juries, deliberative polling and inter-community or ethnic-group dialogue are all new democratic devices to improve existing democratic institutions. Chapter 5 of this book will make a strong argument that a deliberative referendum is needed to address the Taiwan question; and Chapter 10 examines how a deliberative forum promotes mutual trust between Han Chinese and Tibetan students. The concluding chapter will return to the synthesised idea of deliberative referendum.

Autonomy and minority rights

A 50 per cent-plus-one mechanism is contradictory to the notion of equal concern. A democratic procedure dominated by majority rule – such as a 50 per cent-plus-one mechanism – may become tyrannical. To overcome this deficiency, democratic management must include a system of minority rights, in particular the right of minorities not to be assimilated by a larger community. Minority rights (Kymlicka 1989, 1995) can be seen as a counterbalance against majority rule, and a set of institutionalised mechanisms within which minorities are protected and represented. A combination of majority rule and minority rights can be seen to be true to the notion of equal concern discussed above. Moreover, minority rights touch upon an internal boundary problem within states, a problem which relates to the genuine protection of the autonomy of minorities. With regard to the Tibet issue, this book features three chapters – 7, 8 and 9 – that deal with theoretical, practical and linguistic aspects of minority rights for the Tibetan people.

1.3   THE CATEGORIES OF NATIONAL BOUNDARY/ IDENTITY PROBLEMS

The concept of the national boundary problem is multi-dimensional – historical, cultural, ethnic and political – and subject to different interpretations and emphases. It sometimes refers to territorial disputes, or it may involve issues concerning changes in the function of a boundary, or transcending boundaries. The term 'boundary problem' may refer to the transformation or evolution of national boundaries, say, from frontiers or natural boundaries such as rivers and mountains, seas and forests, to artificial borders (Boggs 1966; Jones 1967; Kristof 1969; Minghi 1970).

Many boundary problems are not directly pertinent to democracy. These include disputed areas, boundary delimitation and demarcation, offshore or maritime boundaries, boundary disputes over national resources, and international boundaries. Historically, the expansion of national territories always reflected military and political power. The stronger the power, the larger its territory. Changes in territorial boundaries are good indicators of the rise and fall of military and political power. This aspect of the boundary issue does not primarily concern issues of democracy, but is crucially related to power relations. Recently, however, the issues with indigenous access to natural resources in Latin America and Australia's discussion of 'offshore boundaries' are very much related to the idea of democracy and human rights.

The question of the redefinition or redrawing, and the rightfulness, of national boundaries is often associated with the problem of secession or unification. This national boundary problem is a political identity problem. Often it occurs when certain sections of national populations do not identify themselves with the nation-states in which they live, and endeavour to create their own political identity through the reconstruction of cultural and ethnic identities. It also occurs when two separate states want to merge on the basis of shared cultural identity or history. This boundary question, which becomes a question of national identity, also incorporates the problem of control over territories and resources. It can be seen as 'the stateness problem', for it challenges the existence of the state and involves the formation of new nation-states.

This study will focus on this national boundary or identity problem, with the terms 'national boundary/identity problem' used in the sense explained above. The term 'national boundary/identity problem' is sufficiently broad; it can cover the themes of secession, independence and unification, while the more narrow term 'secession' excludes the case of unification, and the term 'identity' alone is too broad, including individual and cultural identities. Take the example of the Australian republican movement, the question concerning the national identity of Australia – whether the head of state of Australia should be the British Queen or its own President. This identity issue does not imply any territorial or boundary implication. The term 'national *boundary*/identity problem' therefore helps to narrow down the broad meaning of identity.

A distinction between the national boundary problem and membership boundary question should be made. The national boundary problem concerning the territoriality of the state and its sovereignty should be clearly distinguished from the membership boundary problem of a political community (Linz & Stepan 1996: 16). In the context of a democratic polity, the membership boundary problem can be understood as relating to questions such as: Who are 'the people'? Who will be granted civil and political rights? Who makes this decision? This final question is of paramount importance, for 'the people' cannot make any decisions until somebody decides who they are (Oklopcic 2012). Nor can democratic theories transcend their home territory of 'normal politics' and provide criteria according to which both con-stitutional changes and the definition of boundaries can be described as more or less 'democratic' (Offe 1991). There is an asymmetric relation between these two prob-lems: changes in national boundaries inevitably lead to changes in the membership of a state, but changes in the latter do not necessarily lead to changed boundaries.

The national boundary problem should also be distinguished from the 'internal boundary problem' within states. This particular boundary problem refers to the issue of internal boundaries: whether they should be drawn in accordance with ethnic, religious or cultural lines within nation-states; or whether the boundaries between internal ethnic or historical communities should be institutionalised in the vein of Kymlicka's theory of minority rights. The internal boundary question con-cerning space or language is related to, or becomes, the national boundary problem when minorities are granted rights to establish their own 'independent kingdom' and when such minorities' rights are used to demand a new state. The internal boundary problem also refers to the spatial issues involved in the institutional arrangements of federalism or decentralisation. The internal boundary question is often related to the issue of multiple identities, that is, how multiple ethnic groups can coexist within a nation-state, or how democratic institutions can accommodate the diverse demands of multiple ethnic groups.

These three problems are analytically separable but empirically related in one way or another. Issues such as autonomy, secession, independence and reunification are inextricably bound up with the national identity/boundary problem. However, each case has its own specific boundary question, and differs from other cases. Looking from different perspectives, we will have different views on a specific boundary ques-tion.

China and Taiwan face different forms of the national identity question. Taiwan has the straightforward question of independence, while China confronts not only secession movements within China, but also the question of reunification with Taiwan. Surely, for Taiwanese nationalism, Taiwan's independence means an internal 'unification' process. That is, a project of nation-state building must incorporate all conflicting social forces into a political entity and develop a new sense of that common entity for all peoples living on the island, regardless of where they originally came from. This is a key process for Taiwan's independence and the political dimension of national identity. In the context of Taiwan, national identity/ boundary questions include Taiwan's national status; its formal independence from Mainland China, a move from *de facto* independence to formal recognition by the international community; its reunification with China; change in the national title; its membership in the World Health Organisation (WHO); and its desire for regain-ing a seat in the UN. Rigger (1999–2000) argues that social scientists and political leaders on Taiwan have erred by conceiving of the national identity issue as a con-flict between independence and unification.

China's national boundary/identity question involves not only maintaining the existing national unity but also reunifying with Taiwan. China, therefore, has a more complex national identity question than Taiwan. Unlike Taiwan, Beijing will likely face a chain reaction in which Taiwan's independence encourages seces-sionism in other parts of China. In the eyes of Beijing, an independent Taiwan will provide political leverage to the separatists of Tibet and Xinjiang. From Beijing's standpoint, preventing Taiwan's independence and achieving reunification is a key to containing other secessionist movements in China. Moreover, Taiwan's national identity question involves no race dimension, because both Chinese and Taiwanese are perceived to belong to the same race. In contrast, China confronts the challenge from Xinjiang where there is a race question, that is, secessionists there are seen to belong to other races. When this author encountered a Uygur man in Xinjiang and asked whether he considered himself Chinese, the man replied, 'Look at my skin, the color of my hair and eyes! Am I a Chinese? No!'

In summary, the following categories are distinguished:

- Identity questions: whether groups seek their own identity and refuse to recog-nise the existing national identity.
- National boundary issues: whether there is a territorial change in national boundary.
- Membership boundary question: whether there is a change in a constituency of people.
- Internal boundary question: whether there is a question concerning autonomy or separate governance within a nation-state.
- Stateness problem: whether an existing state will disappear or a new state will emerge.

A crucial distinction between national and membership boundary issues is made and should be stressed in order to defend the project of democratic management of the boundary issue. The argument made by Dahl (1991), Whelan (1983), Rustow (1970) and others that democracy cannot decide the membership question seems to fail to distinguish between these two kinds of boundary problems in their treatment of the national identity question. If the national boundary issue and the membership issue are confused, one can easily see limits to the democratic management of the national identity problem simply because democracy cannot decide the membership boundary issue. If a conceptual distinction between these two problems is made it then becomes possible to argue that even if democracy cannot decide the question of just who 'the people' are (this is also problematic, as shown later on), democratic institutions can help to manage the national identity issue in practice. Dahl (1998) argues that democracy as the idea of participation and the system of capacity cannot provide a coherent criterion for the question of size and the membership boundary issue. Deliberative referendum, however, certainly provides a means of national boundary conflict resolution.

1.4   THE CRITERIA OF CHOOSING NATIONAL BOUNDARIES

One may argue that national boundaries and identities are seldom chosen: they are our fate, not our choice. Historically, 'in most cases large national territories and common institutions have been formed by kings and statesmen against the will of the peoples' (Hertz 1945: 151–2). Nevertheless, the formation of nation-states and their boundaries often involves many different kinds of choice: the criteria for choosing national boundaries being related to geography, culture, common language, history, nationalism, treaties and actual occupation of territory.

In the past, geographical features like rivers and mountains constituted natural boundaries, but in lands where two or more peoples live, how can the 'rightfulness' of the boundaries of one people be justified? Intermingling peoples, overlapping communities, and historical and current migrations now negate geography-defined territories as a useful criterion for defining 'the people' in a divided society. Today, it is 'demos' that brings territories together. The settlement of the national boundary question is coming to rest upon the free acceptance and free agreement of those immediately concerned.

If one thinks about language as a criterion to define the national boundaries, it too raises many difficulties. As Kedourie (1960: 123) asks, 'First, what is a language, and how is it to be distinguished from a dialect?' 'There is no convincing reason why the fact that people speak the same language should, by itself, entitle them to enjoy a government exclusively their own' (Kedourie 1960: 80).

Nationalists see history as placing antecedent constraints on the decisions that can be taken by current generations. The historical principle attaches no moral or political significance to which group is currently in the majority. National boundaries are to be determined exclusively by historical considerations, with no room for negotiation among present generations. The unique force that nationalists ascribe to history seems to be rather arbitrary. Why should history have so much influence in deciding the fate of current generations?

An historical approach holds that *it is the uniqueness of history that legitimates claims over territories*, and excludes or minimises endless disputes. Shared history and historical national boundaries constitute a collective identity and are important criteria for choosing and maintaining national boundaries. However, if we think seriously about history as a criterion to define the national boundaries, historical boundaries present difficulties. National boundaries have often changed over time in different historical periods. The historical principle cannot answer the question of which period should be taken as a criterion. As Kedourie (1960: 120-1) asks, 'The Polish state at one time expanded to the West, and at another to the East. Which of these historic boundaries should be those of the national state?'

Take another example, that of the reunification of Romania and Moldova. The language of Moldova is, in fact, a version of Romanian; they are mutually intelligible in spoken language, and there is nothing to distinguish Romanian from Moldovan in written form. According to a top Moldovan official, Romania and Moldova have 'a shared thousand year history' (King 1994). In 1940, Stalin annexed the

Romanian province of Bessarabia through the Molotov–Ribbentrop pact. Once under Soviet control, Bessarabia was carved up, with small portions in the north and south going to Ukraine and the largest section joining a newly created Moldovan Soviet Socialist Republic. The Romanian government proclaimed that 'only history' could decide Moldova's fate, and Romanian popular nationalism demanded that every political party must be irredentist in order to survive. In Moldova, it was asserted by the Moldovan prime minister that 'we are brothers, but each has his own home and lives by his own laws' (King 1994). The question of whether Moldova should be reunified with Romania was finally settled by the referendum held on 6 March 1994, in which a reported 95.4 per cent of participants voted for maintaining Moldova's separation from both Romania and Russia. The new August 1994 constitution effectively removed union with Romania as an option. In February 1996, the opposition-dominated Parliament voted down a presidential proposal by President Snegur to change 'Moldovan' to 'Romanian' as the constitutional descriptor of the official language (Banks, Day & Muller 1997: 557).

The criteria discussed above are essentially non-democratic and are often used by nationalists to emphasise the priority of their political community, their culture and their version of history. Nationalists tend to point out the inability of democracy to solve the problem of what constitutes membership of that political community. However, nationalists themselves face the challenging question of how to solve the national boundary question. Different forms of nationalism in China, Taiwan and Tibet offer different answers which frequently conflict with each other (as this book will reveal later on). In short, nationalism cannot provide a satisfactory answer either.

1.5   ARE THE NATIONAL BOUNDARIES THE MATTER OF A DEMOCRATIC CHOICE?

Two theories offer different answers as to whether national boundaries are really a matter of a democratic choice. While one argues strongly for democratic choice as central to the national identity/boundary question, the other forcefully objects to it. Neither is entirely right nor wholly wrong: we must endeavour to get to the root of each argument and discern the truths while rejecting their errors.

The arguments against democratic choice

Robert Dahl (1964: 53–4) holds the view that boundaries are often not open to rational change, because to a large extent everyone must take the boundaries of his or her political world as given by prior tradition and historical events. It was superior force, not adherence to principles of democracy or consent, that enabled the United States to secede from the British Empire and unify the South and North (Dahl 1991: 491–6). Rustow (1970), Offe (1991), Whelan (1983) and Holmes (1988) have all argued that democratic methods have little effect in solving the national boundary problem, which is, they suggest, most frequently resolved through force.

Whelan rejects the consent theory, which suggests that a proper political community is one in which each individual member has freely joined, and consented to the authority of that community. He suggests that the classical theories of Hobbes, Locke, Rousseau and Kant left unresolved the question of the proper method of determining appropriate boundaries. The consent principle, he argues, conjures up the picture of a voluntary association, but this principle cannot apply to nation-states because they are territorial and compulsory associations. Even if the consent principle may establish the composition of groups enjoying local self-government within a federal state, there are problems of arbitrariness, non-democratic origins, manipulation and the difficulty of deciding on the appropriate level within the federal structure for making a particular decision. Consent cannot normally be the basis of the existence of the boundaries of the state in the first place (Whelan 1983).

John Dunn argues that to ask the question of whether democracy can address the national boundary problem is to stretch and distort the concept of democracy. Democracy simply means that people have a free choice of government, and political power is made accountable. It is this simple idea that gives democracy its normative force and appeals to peoples around the world. Dunn argues that if the idea of democracy is expanded to address the complex issue of boundary problems, it will lose its intellectual appeal, because democracy by its nature is incapable of dealing with boundary problems. For Dunn, the democratic choice is a grand rational project coming out of the Western Enlightenment tradition; but, he asks, can the management of the national boundary question ever be rational when it was always irrational and arbitrary in the past?[1]

Arguments for democratic choice

Contemporary contract theorists argue for a democratic approach to the boundary question on the premise that boundaries can be changed for a just society. Baldwin (1992), for example, in applying Rawls's idea of the original position, argues that the parties to the Rawlsian original position will adopt three principles concerning the distribution of natural resources and the determination of territorial boundaries: a principle of self-determination, a principle of self-sufficiency and a historical principle.

The theory of secession (Beran 1998) argues that the idea of liberal democracy, particularly the idea of liberty, entails the right to secede. The right to secede is inherently rooted in the idea of freedom, although theorists differ in their opinions of whether the right to secede derives from individual liberty or cultural community, or whether the right to secede is recognised as fundamental or secondary.

Global statistics show an increasing historical use of referendums to settle the boundary question. A democratic principle has been applied to the national identity issue since 1791 (B. He 2002d). Recently, for example, most countries in Europe, except Germany, decided on whether to join the EU through popular votes. Even in the former Soviet Union, referendums played an important role in settling the issue of the political entity of the Soviet Union and the independence issue of its republics.

The wide use of referendums contradicts the thesis that the national boundary question is not decided by 'the people'. At the crux of this thesis is the single empirical claim that only force can decide boundaries. Such a claim is problematic. History shows that in the politics of national boundary there has been a *slow* transition from a predominance of the use of force to a predominant use of referendums, parliamentary vote, negotiation and international settlement; although force has been, and is still, used as a final resort. If in the twentieth century most nations had been defined and/or created as a result of wars of the previous two hundred years, this is not the case today. Since the third wave of democratisation, procedures rather than wars have played a larger role in addressing boundary problems. Since 1974, twenty new states have been established through referendums, seven by parliamentary vote, nineteen by negotiation (including three by UN settlement), and only around ten through civil or inter-state wars (B. He 2001a). These figures challenge the conventional perception that the boundary issue is always decided by force.

1.6 CAN DEMOCRACY MANAGE THE NATIONAL BOUNDARY QUESTION?

Related to the previous argument, there are two theories that offer contrasting assessments on the capacity of democracy itself. One theory holds that democracy has no competence in addressing the boundary question while the other stresses the changing conditions under which democracy can manage the boundary question. We examine these two arguments in turn.

The argument that democracy itself cannot answer the question of who are 'the people'

For Dahl (1989: 193), it is territory that brings 'demos', rather than the other way around. Dahl (1989: 119–31) argues that the theory of populist democracy does not provide any satisfactory answer to the question of who should be included in the democratic system. Democracy itself cannot resolve the membership issue of who are 'the people', who has the right to vote, and who has the right to decide the boundary of a political community, because national democracy itself logically presupposes the identity of 'the people' as a settled question. Voting presupposes a fixed electorate defined by the boundary of a political community. The people, as Offe (1991) argues, cannot decide until somebody decides who 'the people' are.

Generally it is the state and political elites that make a decision on who is given the right to vote and who is granted citizenship. Membership is also decided by birth, nationality and the length of residency. If non-democratic criteria define membership boundaries, how can democracy decide the issue of political self-determination? One such example is the referendum on Polisario's independence (or autonomy) that was delayed in the 1990s because no final agreement could be reached between Morocco and the Polisario as to who should vote in the referendum.

The argument for democratic capacity

Theoretically, democracy presupposes the existence of 'the people'. In other words, majority rule presupposes the existence of voters. This does not necessarily presuppose an undemocratic method of deciding voters; nor does it assume that the question of 'the people' must be decided undemocratically. The question of who 'the people' are and the right to vote can be made both democratically and undemocratically. There is a distinction between the first order of membership that is presupposed and often made undemocratically and the second order of membership whose decision can be made democratically. In the case of the Australian vote for the voting right of aboriginals, the question of first-order membership was settled: the core member was White. The voting right of aboriginals as a question of second-order membership was made democratically.

The right to vote can be resolved by the procedure of election. Here are several examples: in 1870 Malta had referendums to grant political rights to ecclesiastics, the franchise for women was decided by male votes in the University of Cambridge, and the franchise was granted to Australian Aborigines in 1967 after a referendum in which 90.8 per cent supported the move. In the politics of UN membership, recognition of a state by the UN is dependent upon a two-thirds vote at the General Assembly on the recommendation of at least nine members of the Security Council, including the five permanent members (Shearer 1994: 138–40, 569–71). It is also possible for the UN to use democratic procedures to decide who has the right to vote in a divided society when disputes over membership cannot be settled within the nation-state framework.

The project of democratic governance has encountered strong resistance. The Northern Ireland problem is often cited as an example of the shortcomings of democracy. Northern Ireland failed to agree on a boundary commission in 1922, and thus a proposed referendum over the question of redrawing the boundary between Northern Ireland and the Irish Free State could not be realised at that time. Sinn Fein asserted that all inhabitants of Ireland should vote, while the Unionists of Northern Ireland and the British government asserted that only the inhabitants of Northern Ireland should have a vote. In 1973, the IRA resisted referendums being applied in the resolution of the Northern Ireland problem on the grounds that the pro-Unionist majority had been artificially created through historical immigration, and thus it was unfair for the IRA to accept majority rule. However, the 1988 referendums held in both Northern Ireland and the Republic of Ireland, which were organised successfully and accepted, demonstrates that the membership problem does not preclude the democratic management of the boundary/identity question.

Empirically, most referendums held to decide the national boundary question do not have the membership problem: the national identity question is clear and the question of who should vote is presupposed and defined by other criteria such as history, the existing territories and culture (for example, the three Baltic states including Russian speakers voted to decide the question of independence). Deliberative democracy, most importantly, offers a supplementary approach to the

membership issue. As discussed in Chapters 10 and 11, all sides of historical disputes, including membership dispute, can be addressed through public deliberation.

1.7   WHY DEMOCRACY IS DESIRABLE

Argument from a comparison between animals and human beings

The national boundary question is closely linked to the question of the distribution
of natural resources and lands. When resources become limited or scarce, fighting
over boundaries intensifies. Secession and self-rule ultimately demand exclusive
control of specific territories and resources, and the denial of secession ultimately
is related to the continuation of control over specific territories and resources.
Democratic management is one way to regulate fights over territories and resources.
A balance of majority rule with minority rights attempts to ensure a fair sharing of
limited resources. Without democratic management, the fight for territories and
resources will escalate into war. Democratic management of the boundary question
is an indicator of the great achievement of human civilisation and political modernisation.

We can elaborate this by comparing animals and human beings. Some animals
have a strong sense of territory, and will fight over it. For example, it is observed that
old chickens fight against any newly arrived chickens, and against other potential
invaders of their territory, such as plovers. Human beings have also fought over
territories for centuries, bringing blood, death, violence and warfare. Nevertheless,
human beings, unlike animals, are able to establish borders to maintain and regulate
their existing territories. The advantage humans have over animals is that human
beings have the capacity to establish civilised ways of managing territories and
boundaries. It is in this respect that democratic management of the boundary question can be seen as a civilised manner of regulating and controlling boundaries.
Unlike animals, human beings can establish democratic rules according to which
fighting over boundaries is regulated. While regulating conflict, democratic management also gives people a voice in determining boundary questions and prescribes a
set of fair rules to prevent the use of force. It is here that democratic management
of the boundary question has advantages over other means, such as authoritarian
repression and state violence.

Force had been widely used throughout human history and had tended to
prevail as the final arbiter of boundary settlements. It was responsible for most of
the national boundaries in today's world, many of which are not contested. Force,
however, faces difficulties in ensuring peace, justice and stability. Losers sometimes
will look to future changes in the fluid shifting balance of power: 'Wartime defeat
and cessions of territory were seldom accepted as final' (Lederer 1960: vii). When
Germany suffered considerable territorial losses in the First World War, it seemed
reasonable to expect that it would pursue revisionist policies and resent those territorial losses. To forestall such a possibility, Woodrow Wilson appealed to the principles of national self-determination and democracy to negotiate a just peace, fair to
all sides, in the hope of eliminating the very incentives for war (Lederer 1960: vii).

However, that approach failed. From this failure, one may argue that democracy cannot successfully address the boundary question. It can, however, be argued that the failure was precisely due to the fact that the Allies imposed an unfair settlement by force and refused to employ democratic principles on several occasions. It can be argued further that democracy as a human device does have some deficiencies, but democratic management of the boundary question can be improved and refined in practice. Just as the first contraceptive pill, which had side-effects of the long-term risk of cancer and heart disease, was refined over the years to minimise those side-effects, so the human invention of democratic management of conflicts needs improvement and refinement on the part of democrats to ensure its success.

Argument from a comparison between divorce and secession

Today, individuals certainly enjoy the liberty to marry and divorce. The rate of divorce in the West has increased dramatically, up to 30 or 40 per cent. By contrast, secession, a group right to divorce from a political association, is seldom exercised. Both the right to divorce and the right to secession are based on a fundamental idea of liberty and free choice.

Once, there were intolerant attitudes towards divorce. Today people have gradually developed a tolerant attitude towards it, so that divorce has now become common practice. A similarly tolerant attitude towards secession is, however, still a long way off. War, violence and terrorism are often involved when secession takes place. To reduce war and conflicts, democratic management of boundary issues is necessary and laws need to be established to regulate the activity of secession. We should protect the basic liberty of free choice for political communities, and we must make sure that such a basic liberty is exercised in a democratic way.

At the institutional level, very few constitutions contain articles regarding secession (Chen & Ordeshook 1994). Currently only Liechtenstein, Ethiopia and St Kitts and Nevis have explicit provisions regulating secession in their constitutions. Article 39(4) of the Constitution of the Federal Democratic Republic of Ethiopia of 1995, for example, stipulates that, following a demand for secession by a two-thirds majority of the Legislative Council of any relevant nation, nationality or people, secession can only take place if, within three years, the Council's decision is supported by a majority vote at a referendum (Radan 2012: 16).

Disputable is the existence of any legal right of secession in international law. Within international law 'there is no recognition of a unilateral right to secede based merely on a majority vote of the population of a given sub-division or territory' (Radan 2012: 12). A 'legal stalemate appears to have emerged between the legal claims of secessionists on the one hand, and domestic and international denial of such legal rights on the other' (Seshagiri 2010: 572). There is an inherent tension between the right to self-determination and the right to sovereignty and territorial integrity.

However, Ebai (2009: 635) explains that attempts to claim legal secession (i.e. where secession trumps territorial integrity) can be legitimate if they demonstrate – in the very least – 'that: a) the secessionist are a "people" (in the ethnographic sense); b) the state from which they are seceding seriously violates their human rights; and c) there are no other effective remedies under either domestic law or international law'. Further to this, Qvortrup (2012) argues that international law usually requires two conditions to be met for successful secession: 'the people of the territory must express a wish to secede' and (new) 'countries must be recognised by the international community – based on the Estrada Doctrine that a country should be recognised when it has control over its own territory' (Qvortrup 2012: 2).

If international laws on secession are to be improved, they must take account of minority justice. Seshagiri is right in arguing that 'It is virtually impossible to remove the political equation from secession and there is unlikely to be a singular set of legal criteria that can be applied to separate valid from invalid claims' (Seshagiri 2010: 581).

Moreover, as boundaries have been changing for thousands of years, it is pointless to claim their sacredness. Stability is not sufficient justification for maintaining boundaries. What *is* worthwhile doing, therefore, is to inquire into the moral issues behind boundary changes, and the political regulations dealing with the boundaries.

Argument from complex and overlapping identities in the contemporary condition

In modern societies, there are local, national, regional and global identities; and they overlap. Moreover, the boundary of the state is not identical to the boundary of the nation, the cultural and ethnic people. That is, a nation (an ethnic people or group) does not necessarily deserve a state, and a state does not necessarily require a nation. Furthermore, if growth-oriented industrial society was strongly impelled towards cultural homogeneity within each political unit and engendered nationalism (Gellner 1987: 18), post-industrial society respects cultural difference. Today's states need to promote tourism, which in turn requires and supports multiculturalism, for example the use of different languages, in order to attract overseas tourists. Exclusive nationalism cannot woo tourists. If nationalists want to be respectable, they need new strategies to promote civic and multiple cultures.

Democratic management is urgently required in the contemporary conditions. Political communities are now better thought of as multiple overlapping networks of interactions. Transnational networks, international immigration, refugee seekers, international guest workers, social movements, goods, capital and knowledge flow across territorial boundaries. Transnational and overlapping communities, such as global environmental activist communities, have emerged. It is not exclusive ethnic peoples but overlapping peoples that should be taken as a starting point for democratic thinking about the boundary question. If the intermingling of peoples and the fate of 'overlapping communities' are taken seriously, a democratic accommodation of multiple citizenships, characterised by shared boundaries, minority rights, resistance to the use of force and a civilised approach to the boundary problem, is required. It is not a single national identity but multiple and overlapping identities that require ethnic pluralism and democratic accommodation of multiple citizenships. To be a democratic citizen in the contemporary world, one is required to develop and tolerate complex and overlapping identities, while rejecting the notion of a single national identity. Democratic institutions, such as democratic federalism, should express complex identities and find the way to encourage people to hold complex identities. This will make a difference in settling boundary disputes.

Democracy legitimises national boundaries

In the past, claims to legitimacy for political units were largely based on nationalism, history, common language, treaties and actual occupation of territory. However, nationalist justification of national boundaries on historical and cultural grounds provides no more than provisional legitimacy for the boundary of a political community. Nationalism itself, as Hans Kohn (cited in Emerson 1960: 214) has argued, 'is inconceivable without the ideas of popular sovereignty preceding – without a complete revision of the position of ruler and ruled, of classes and castes'. In Renen's doctrine of 'daily plebiscite', the distinctive principle of boundary definition is voluntary assent, a perpetual plebiscite. In other words, the national boundaries are a choice rather than a fatality (Gellner 1987: 17).

Referendum, public deliberation and the participation of civil society provide legitimacy for national boundaries. However, the referendum provides more legitimacy than civil society, for the former reflects the people's opinion, while the latter may reflect only a fraction of the people's view. Moreover, while a referendum provides a choice of Yes or No, the participation of civil society in defining a boundary question can produce multiple choices, and influence the politics of the boundary and even the referendum question. In short, while the referendum is a kind of democratic procedure, civil society is a crucial actor of participatory democracy. Both provide a sort of legitimacy that nation-states urgently need in different ways.

Generally speaking, one of the greatest virtues of referendums is that they make a political unit more legitimate than those made only by elite officials if a referendum is fair and free from coercion, and both the approval and turnout rates of the referendum are reasonably high but not too high to attract suspicion. A fair and democratic referendum, among other things, constitutes a powerful normative source for the justification of the boundary of a political community. Boundaries based on and legitimated by referendums secure a stable settlement and help ensure the long-term stability of these boundaries. Based on the empirical evidence from all referendums between 1914 and 1933, Wambaugh (1933: 485) argues:

> All but one of the frontiers fixed by vote have escaped any widespread criticism or suspicion, while almost every one of those determined by linguistic or other criteria have been unconvincing.

On the other hand, where referendums, public discussion and the participation of civil society are absent, even a successful unification lacks legitimacy. Habermas (1996b: 12), for example, considers the unification of the two Germanys as lacking legitimacy. He notes a certain discontent in West Germany and a feeling of resentment in East Germany after a reunification which lacked a democratic process. He remarks:

A way of proceeding which permitted broader discussion and opinion formation, as well as more extensive – and, above all, better prepared – participation
of the public, would have included citizens in both East and West in the
eventual responsibility for the process. The allocation of responsibilities for
unwanted side-effects would have been steered from the beginning in a different direction. It would have been the people's own mistakes that they would
have had to cope with.

Democracy is likely to deliver peaceful settlement of the boundary question

When there is dispute over a political boundary or identity issue, that is, when
one group wants to remain in the existing state while other groups want to secede
or join another state, then democratic procedure (a combination of majority rule
with minority rights) is one answer. This is a proper and appropriate way for human
beings to avoid armed conflict over the boundary issue. When applied according to
procedural rules, democracy can provide conditions favourable to the peaceful management of national boundary problems. While it may have flaws, and may not be
best, it is much better than war. Our empirical testing confirms that in confronting
the challenge of independence movements, democratic states are more likely to use
peaceful means to deal with secession, or allow for peaceful secession or independence, than authoritarian states (Goldsmith & B. He 2008).

There is another version of this democratic peace argument. Democratic countries are more likely to negotiate than are non-democratic countries. This is despite
the fact that democracy does not rule out the use of force when dealing with secessionists. Britain, for example, maintained a strong military presence in Northern
Ireland in the past. However, as Qvortrup (2012: 2) highlights, 'referendum results
tend to be respected in democratic countries. And when they are not accepted,
[such as in Bosnia or Croatia], the country secedes anyway.'

The democratic state is likely to secure its long-term stability and unity

In the 1970s the Soviet Union was regarded to 'ha[ve] less difficulty with its national
question than the United Kingdom' (Dunn 1979: 65). However, in the latter 1980s
and early 1990s it was the Soviet Union that suffered disintegration. All the national
boundary changes in the former Soviet Union, Yugoslavia and Czechoslovakia
between 1989 and 1992 happened in non-democratic systems. Although secessionist movements happened in democratic states, for example Corsica in France, the
ETA in Spain, and Quebec in Canada, the scale and number are smaller. There
have been more secessionist activities in authoritarian states, for example Afars,
Tigray, Oromos and Somalia in Ethiopia; Katanga/Shaba and south Kasai in Zaire;
Casamance in Senegal; Azeris and Kurds in Iran; Arakanes, Kachins, Karens and
Mons in Myanmar; Tibet and Xinjiang in China; Kurds in Iraq; and East Timorese,
South Moluccans and West Papuans in Indonesia. Of course, democratic India has
also had secessionist activities in Hyderabad, Nagas, Kashmir, Mizos and Tripuras,
and Sikhs in Punjab. Secessionist movements are likely to persist where ethnic

groups were treated as distinct by colonisers and where the post-colonial regime authoritatively discourages ethnic diversity (Mayall & Simpson 1992). So far none of the secessionist movements in Western Europe, Canada or other well-established democracies has succeeded (Dion 1996). Why is this so? One explanation is that they have developed institutional mechanisms to accommodate minority groups, whereby minority rights are protected, multiculturalism introduced and cultural identities promoted. Here the law of repression and resistance works in the politics of the boundary: the more the repression of secessionism in authoritarian states, the more the resistance to the authoritarian state, and the more secessionist activities will take place. That is why secessionists are first successful when the power of authoritarian states weakens. By contrast, in democratic societies where minorities are not suppressed, but accommodated, the resistance of minorities against majorities is reduced.

Clearly, democratic management can reduce resistance to contain conflicts, and democratic institutions have a greater capacity to maintain existing national boundaries than communist or authoritarian institutions do (Fukuyama & Avineri 1994). Among other things, there is a linkage between the legitimacy of the nation-state and the method through which the boundary is determined. This linkage is demonstrated by the Russian incorporation of the Baltic states into the Soviet Union. Because this was achieved by force and secret treaties with Nazi Germany, the Soviet Union's rule over them could not be morally justified. By contrast, the southerners in the USA, because of their insistence on maintaining slavery, lacked the moral force to secede from the US. One further crucial difference is that the Baltic states did not ratify the Constitution of the Soviet Union, while the southern states did ratify the US Constitution, and thus had less legitimacy to secede from the US.

Another instance is that of Irian Jaya in Indonesia. The people of West New Guinea (or West Irian), today known as Irian Jaya, have demanded self-determination since Indonesian independence was achieved in 1949. In 1969, Indonesia annexed Irian Jaya through the Act of Free Choice, although this 'Free Choice' was not free at all, as all Papuans were denied the right to vote, except for eight representative councils, or consultative assemblies, that comprised a mere 1,026 representatives selected by the Indonesian authorities (Kennedy Memorial Centre for Human Rights 1999). Although these consultative assemblies voted unanimously to remain with Indonesia, such a vote did not provide sufficient legitimacy for the annexation of Irian Jaya by the Indonesian state. The guerrilla struggles for independence in Irian Jaya have continued (Osborne 1985) and a strong independence campaign was mounted during the June 1999 parliamentary election.

1.8   QUALIFICATIONS TO DEMOCRATIC MANAGEMENT

So far we have presented a number of arguments in support of the democratic approach. Some care should now be taken to qualify the forms of democratic management that are consistent with the spirit of the real utopian approach (Chapter 2).

Democracy is not necessarily the best solution to boundary disputes

There are many possible alternatives to managing boundary disputes. Sometimes, international cooperation works, for example the UN intervention in the demarcation of the territorial border between Iraq and Kuwait. Elites' negotiation, which is frequently used, sometimes works better than democratic procedure (Pakulski & B. He 1999). Economic integration and cultural exchange play important roles too. One may argue that there are other options such as authoritarian and corporatist management. Democratic management is only one option.

In addition, democratic management is one of many interacting factors in real politics. Any outcome of democratic management of the boundary issue seems unlikely to last in the absence of some equitable distribution of the world's scarce economic resources. Poor economic conditions and the profoundly unequal distribution of wealth and resources between the rich and poor regions often contribute to the intensification of the fight over limited resources and exacerbate the boundary issue. Wealthy classes in a highly developed economy tend to search for their own identities, be they global, national, ethnic, political or cultural. Moreover, economic factors such as economic integration and increasing international trade are potential forces for the peaceful settlement of the boundary question.

Difficulties in achieving a democratic settlement of the boundary issue

The case of Cyprus demonstrates both the necessity of democratic management and the difficulties involved in achieving a successful democratic settlement of the boundary issue. Cyprus declared independence in 1960 and the Cahounian system, a power-sharing mechanism, was adopted. Executive power was vested in the president and the vice-president, who were members of the Greek and Turkish communities respectively. They were elected by their respective communities to hold office for five years. They also had the right of final veto. This system collapsed in 1963. In 1974, a Greek-sponsored coup attempted to unify Cyprus with Greece. The Turkish army invaded Cyprus in the same year and the Turkish Republic of Northern Cyprus was subsequently established on 15 November 1983. As a result, the island was de facto partitioned into two almost mono-ethnic territories. Negotiations in the 1980s and 1990s were fruitless. In 1983, the then UN Secretary-General, Javier Pérez de Cuéllar, proposed that a federal arrangement with a joint-authority – like the 1960 agreement – should be restored. He also proposed the idea of rotating presidencies and that the two sides should be able to freely express their consent to all arrangements through separate referendums.[2] In April 2004 a referendum, voting on whether the two sides approved of the fifth revision of the UN proposal – the Annan Plan – for reunification, was held. It was opposed by political leaders on both sides and ultimately was approved by 65 per cent of Turkish Cypriots, but rejected by 76 per cent of Greek Cypriots. The turnout rate was high, with 87 per cent and 89 per cent respectively. 'Despite regular leadership meetings, continuous technical level discussions, and five meetings with UN Secretary-General Ban Ki-moon, [they] were unable to find common ground or make enough necessary concessions . . .' (Morelli 2012).

It can be argued that the failure of the power-sharing mechanism was due to the lack of genuine commitment to the democratic principle of equal partnership between the two communities, and to an imbalance between majority rule and minority rights. When the tyranny of the Greek majority prevailed, the minority Turkish community resorted to violence and sought intervention by their parent country. The failure of the referendum and recent negotiations was influenced by the internal politics within the respective constituencies, the internationalisation of the issue, and problems associated with the negotiation process itself (Kaymak 2012).

Democratic redrawing of boundaries is seldom used

Joseph Ernest Renen (1882), a French philosopher, once remarked that a nation is based on 'daily plebiscite' when considering the dispute over the Alsace–Lorraine region. Such a daily plebiscite is problematic because it is practically impossible to ratify the existing boundary through frequent referendums. Democratic redrawing of boundaries is seldom used unless there is great public pressure and the threat of potential chaos. The former UK Foreign Secretary, Douglas Hurd, claims that despite artificial and inconvenient national boundaries, the Organisation of African Unity laid down a wise principle that national boundaries should be respected for the common good. This suggests that considerations of stability should override concerns for justice, when, as Hurd puts it, the 'danger of righting wrongs by meddling with boundaries' is recognised (Mayall 1991: 425).

The above argument is, however, different from the *irreversible* argument that a democratic decision on the national boundary is largely unchangeable, or extremely difficult to change, and even *irreversible*. Losers in the national boundary referendums do not have the chance to win back at a subsequent election; and a minority has no chance to rule in a multinational state. People have no right to 'renew' their contract with the constitution (Holmes 1988: 195–240), nor do they have the right to redefine national boundaries. This is in contrast to the changeable nature of democratic decisions on who constitutes government: losers might be winners in the next election; a minority opposition party might be confident of becoming a ruling party one day in a stable and functional democracy.

The fact that several referendums on national identity questions have been overturned later challenges the assumption that the outcomes of boundary-related referendums are irreversible, and undermines the assumption that only *one* referendum can decide the question. For example, Palau had more than eight referendums to achieve its independence. In 1958, Algeria voted to remain part of France with 96.5 per cent support; it then voted for self-determination in 1961 with 65.9 per cent support. France voted against Algerian independence in 1961, then voted for it in a 1962 referendum with a 99.7 per cent approval rate. New Caledonia voted to stay part of France in 1958 with 98.1 per cent support, then voted for increased autonomy in 1982 with 80 per cent support, and for remaining part of France in 1987 with 98.3 per cent support.

These historical facts demonstrate clearly that referendums over boundary questions, like general elections, can be held several times. If the referendum process is open, the fear of the unchangeable or irreversible nature of boundary-related referendums can be dismissed and minority resistance against referendums can be reduced or removed.

Democratic management is not a final solution to the boundary issue

I do not use the term 'democratic solution' to the national boundary problem, because such a problem exists and will continue to exist in democratic systems. Democracy cannot eliminate the boundary problem. Even if one generation solves today's secessionist problem, it might arise again in the future. Even if constitutional reform replaces a centralised state with a democratic federation, it does not by itself eliminate the problem of secession. The case of the Canadian Federation is an excellent example. In contrast, the term 'democratic *management*' of the boundary question implies ongoing processes with success or failure according to different conditions and timings. More importantly, it indicates that a successful democratic settlement of the boundary problem requires *managerial* skills, leadership and sound democratic systems.

1.9   CONCLUSION

This chapter has outlined a case for considering the democratic approach to managing national identity/boundary issues. It has argued that despite the limitations of applicability in non-democratic entities, practicalities, and complicating factors within real politics, legitimacy of boundary issues cannot be obtained without democratic governance. In discussing the different forms of democratic management, this chapter has highlighted how democracy – and particularly the role of referendums – is fundamental to legitimising national boundaries and in creating lasting conditions of peace.

The following chapter will explore the democratic approach in more detail, contrasting it with a realist approach to managing national identity/boundary issues. Chapter 3 will then highlight the difficulties with democratic governance, utilising the 'empire thesis' as a framework, before exploring several possible successful democratic approaches discussed in the remainder of the book.

NOTES

1. The author had a number of conversations with John Dunn in 1996 when I studied the boundary question at Cambridge University.
2. Source URL: http://www.mfa.gov.tr/f62.htm.

2 The Real Utopian Approach

Two paradigms for, and two approaches to, the Taiwan and Tibet questions can be roughly grouped under the headings of realism and democracy. Analytically, these two are distinctive, but in reality each approach interacts and overlaps with the other. The two paradigms have shaped both political debates and intellectual research.

Over the past decades, realism has dominated in China, while Taipei and Dharamsala have advocated democracy. The US has favoured a democratic principle and supported the democratisation of Taiwan and Tibet communitties in exile, but has to come to grips with the fact that China has become a greater regional power. Different actors in Beijing, Taipei and Dharamsala have different interpretations of and emphases on the paradigms.

When realism and democracy are viewed as oppositional and exclusive, they constitute two closed knowledge systems. They can be considered 'boxes': each approach will be persuasive only to those who look at the issue from the same perspective. Recycling its own ideas, each side has perpetrated paradigms, predetermining opinion and rationality. Chinese realism regards the democracy and human rights language as a disguised attempt to disrupt Chinese unity and order. In contrast, the human rights discourse dismisses Chinese realist thinking as an attempt to maintain the authoritarian system and demand surrender to it. Both paradigms strengthen polarisation, leaving little room to search for a third way, an alternative to address the dilemma that the Tibet and Taiwan questions pose. It is important to develop an intellectual approach to break down closed knowledge production systems and find a way out of this predicament.

This book adopts Eric Wright's real utopian approach as an overriding methodology. Wright's 'Real Utopian Project' seeks to embrace the tension between 'dreams and practice', and is based on the belief that what is possible is not predetermined but is in fact shaped by one's vision. However, it advocates the notion of envisaging utopian ideals that are simultaneously grounded in real possibilities. Thus, the objective is to find radical, yet specific and plausible, solutions to problems (Wright 2010).

A real utopian approach does not endorse immoral realism. It challenges the diminished imagination of realism and calls for a more democratic imagination in addressing the Tibet and Taiwan questions. It takes democracy as central in addressing the Tibet and Taiwan questions. It holds that a utopian way is not wishful thinking, nor is it an intellectual luxury. Instead, it is an imaginative, creative, normative and philosophical form of thinking aimed at changing the world and persistently searching for a just world. It is a dream done intelligently and wisely.

The real utopian approach combines both normative and empirical thinking. The normative centrality of the democracy approach is the notion of people. The democracy paradigm stresses the democracy principle, the will and consent of the people, as well as the democratic mechanisms, such as referendums (as was discussed in detail in Chapter 1). Central to any democratic analysis is an empirical question of how democracy, democratisation and the non-democratic regime impact on the definition and emergence of the Taiwan or the Tibet question. It also considers the conditions under which various democratic approaches to the Taiwan and Tibet questions are proposed and attempted.

This chapter provides a brief account of the general features of each paradigm, characterises what is distinctive about the approach, and outlines the advantages and disadvantages of each. After questioning some presuppositions of the two intellectual frameworks, the chapter utilises the real utopian approach to combine the two paradigms of realism and democracy. Moving back and forth between them, the book develops a methodologically reflective equilibrium, which continues throughout the whole book.

2.1   REALIST PARADIGM

The analytic centrality of a realist paradigm is power. Power is viewed as a sum of economic, political, military and moral forces of one political entity, and the capacity of one to interfere, constrain and influence the behaviour of others. According to realism, it is power that matters, power that decides Taiwan and Tibet's fate, and power that settles the Taiwan and Tibet questions.

A power-centric approach holds that the Taiwan and Tibet questions are about power relations. Domestic power relations in the US, China and Taiwan matter, and they are the sources of changing foreign policies.[1] Moreover, US–Sino power relations hold a key to solving the Taiwan and Tibet issues. In the eyes of Beijing, Taiwan and Tibet are the most important and sensitive issues for Sino–US relations. It is the US's support for Taiwan that prevents China from reunifying with Taiwan.

Realist thinking about the Taiwan issue

A realist holds that a dyad analysis of power relations between Beijing and Taipei is simplistic. The Taiwan question needs to be put in the context of the power relationship between China and the US. Taiwan is only a minor player, and merely a consumer and recipient of international norms. Increasingly China is becoming a shaper in the regional order. Due to the US's superpower position, a peculiar triangular relationship exists between Washington, Beijing and Taipei. Both Beijing and Taipei ask the US for help and interference in different ways. While Beijing has asked Washington not to support a referendum on the independence question, Taipei asked for the sale of modern military fighter jets to protect its security. Currently both the US and China have accommodated each other with regard to the Taiwan question, so that they have successfully prevented the Taiwan issue from dominating the agenda. The US has adopted a strategic ambiguity policy towards the Taiwan question. While it supports the one China policy,[2] it also protects Taiwan's security and democracy. The Reagan administration, for example, issued the 'Six Assurances' for Taiwan. A realist holds that only military balance can ensure peace across the Taiwan Strait. The Pentagon therefore sells military weapons to Taiwan to maintain East Asian peace. Currently the US accommodates the rise of China, and Taiwan has to adapt to this accommodation policy to adopt a more conciliatory policy. If the US changes its Taiwan policy and, say, uses Taiwan to contain China, Taiwan will be more resistant to China.

A Chinese realist would hold the view that even if China embarks on a democratisation process, as long as China remains a regional power in East Asia the conflict between China and the US will remain. A Chinese realist holds the view that it is impossible for China to rely on Taiwanese votes for reunification. A realist therefore strongly believes that democratic unification is too idealistic to achieve. Beijing believes in the power of economic interdependence. Economic integration across the Taiwan Strait does not favour Taiwan's independence if Taiwan's economic development relies on China completely. In the first half of 2011, for example, Taiwan's exports to China (including Hong Kong) accounted for 40 per cent of its total exports (Lin 2011). And according to the American Chamber of Commerce, China also accounts for 80 per cent of Taiwan's overseas direct investment (Lin 2011).

A Chinese realist would hold the view that the source of the Taiwan and Tibet questions is American support for Taiwan and the Dalai Lama; and that the US will adopt a more practical approach towards the Taiwan question if China becomes more powerful in the next two decades. Zbigniew Brzezinski, former US national security adviser, commented on the Taiwan question in March 2012, 'That's not going to wait indefinitely.' Nor, it is argued, can the US continue to be the source of weaponry for Taiwan without negative consequences for the relationship (Omestad, Saferstein & Harper 2012).

A Chinese realist would also hold that China, as an increasing great power, can build a 'bird cage' to contain Taiwan's independence and set its agenda for dialogue with Taiwan; that the idea of political equality is irrelevant to settling the Taiwan question. In the eyes of a Chinese realist, China's increasing power is the best way to ensure its territorial integrity, prevent Taiwan from gaining its independence, and therefore resolve the Taiwan question.

Conflicts of two empires and maintenance of the status quo

The key to Washington–Beijing–Taipei trilateral ties is the US–Sino relationship, the essence of which is that between two empires. In providing global security, the US empire or primacy can intervene in the sovereignty of other countries but not the other way round. Stephen Peter Rosen (2002), a former National Security Council (NSC) and Defense Department staff officer, a full endowed professor and head of the Olin Institute for Strategic Studies at Harvard University, elaborates the US's primacy well. He argues that the US is a global power, the only one in the world without rival. Its military spending exceeds that of the next six or seven most powerful countries combined. It is militarily dominant around the world and inter-venes in the internal affairs of other countries. The US is an empire in the sense that it has overwhelming superiority in military power, and uses that power to influence the internal behaviour of other states. It is, however, an indirect empire since it does not seek to control territory or govern the overseas citizens of the empire.

According to Rosen (2002), the American goal is not combating a rival, but maintaining its domination in the Asia-Pacific regional order. He argues that American strategy should focus on preventing the emergence of powerful, hostile challengers to the empire. In this regard, 'China is not yet powerful enough to be a challenger to the American empire, and the goal of the United States is to prevent that challenge from emerging.'

In contrast, China's policy on Taiwan aims to bring back the Qing Dynasty's imperial territories. As a historical mission, the reunification of China with Taiwan is seen as a restoration of the Chinese empire. The Chinese empire is restora-tive. It does not aim to expand its territories nor does it want to overstretch its power, a lesson it learnt from the collapse of the Soviet Union (Wang Gungwu 1996).

The two empires are very much concerned with maintaining their power and are struggling for influence and their national interests. China is concerned with becoming a regional power. China's reunification project constitutes a threat to US primacy in Asia and a potential challenge to its domination in East Asia and beyond. At the same time, the US is worried about a rising China and is determined to prevent China from becoming a serious challenge.

In this regard, Professor Wang Gungwu proposed an interesting thesis of 'two nightmares'.[3] According to Professor Wang, it is unrealistically ambitious to the hawkish American neo-cons to keep the US as the eternal superpower and to avoid the decline of the US empire. Beijing also has an unrealistic ambition to search for the permanent domination of the Chinese Communist Party (CCP). Despite the fact that no party can maintain a one-party domination forever or avoid its decline, Beijing is still hoping to achieve the impossible task of maintaining the longevity of the CCP.

In the eyes of those who support realism, maintaining the status quo in Taiwan is in the best interests of both the US and China. The perfect outcome for the US is the independence of Taiwan, but China would not agree to it. The best result for China is the reunification of China and Taiwan, but the US is likely to resist it powerfully. As a compromise, the status quo is the second-best option. All political forces work towards such a position. Wallace (2007), like many other authors, emphasises the interests of each party (US, China, Taiwan) in maintaining the status quo. According to Lieberthal (2005), the role of the US would be to facilitate international support and adherence to the agreed-upon framework and commit to supporting confidence-building measures for each country. He once called for the Bush administration to move quickly in laying the groundwork for an agreed framework based on the brief window of time available to work and warned of the dire consequences of miscalculation on either side of the Strait. A 2012 survey by the Mainland Affairs Council, seen as a barometer for Taiwanese opinion on cross-Strait relations and the issue of unification, found that 32.4 per cent supported 'maintaining the status quo and making a decision later', 29.9 per cent supported 'maintaining the status quo in perpetuity', and 15.7 per cent wanted Taiwan to 'maintain the status quo and declare independence later', compared with 8.2 per cent who supported 'maintaining the status quo and seeking unification at a later date' (Su 2012).

Realist approach towards the Tibet issue

Policy-oriented studies on Tibet have been informed by the mainstream paradigms of realism (Kolas 2003; Makley 2003; Kolas & Thowsen 2006). The politics of Tibet has been analysed through an examination of the political relations among major powers (Cuevas & Schaeffer 2003; Goldstein 1995; Anand 2009). The Dalai Lama's policies and strategies have been adapted to shifting international power relations (B. He & Sautman 2005–6; Brahm 2005: A4), while Beijing's Tibet policy is certainly based on its constant assessment of and adjustment to great-power relations (Norbu 2001). Despite the recommendation by many that its officials should talk to the Dalai Lama directly (Thurman 2008; Schell 2001; Knaus 2003: A13), Beijing has adopted an ever-tougher policy. Its intention appears to be to isolate and silence the Dalai Lama completely: time is on Beijing's side as China rises and the Dalai Lama ages.

In recent years Chinese authorities have acquired a stronger power base both politically and diplomatically in the Himalayan region (Mathou 2005). Beijing's realist policy towards the Dalai Lama is best summarised by an official on the Nationalities Affairs Committee of State Council: *Qiangqi* (capture the moral high ground), *suozhu* (lock in), and *tuokua* (wear down) (Huang 2009).

Three measures are adopted by Beijing towards the Tibet issue. First, it has used force to crush any rebellion in Tibet, and employed divide-and-rule tactics to control the Tibetan elite. This approach has, however, failed to neutralise the secessionist movement, instead driving it underground, so that it is likely to re-emerge if political and military control is weakened. The second measure has been to financially 'buy off' secessionists with promises of wealth and the provision of funding. For example, in recent years the Chinese government has funded fifty development projects in Tibet. The third measure is to accommodate secessionist claims by offering a kind of semi-autonomy coupled with an affirmative policy towards minorities.

An affirmative policy towards minorities must prevent minorities from forming a privileged social group that may undermine the unity of the state. In the eyes of Chinese state nationalists the art of ruling consists of employing all three methods.

Realist approach towards sovereignty

China has adopted a power perspective of sovereignty and treats it as absolute and indivisible. To challenge China's national sovereignty is to challenge its national power. The Chinese government believes that the best way to defend China's national sovereignty is to maintain and develop its military power.

China and Taiwan have adopted different – and competing – paradigms in their efforts to gain legitimacy through international recognition. China's approach is based on the Westphalian notion of sovereignty. In this form, legitimacy is secured and strengthened through the recognition of a state's sovereignty by other legitimate states. By attempting to deny international recognition to Taiwan, China employs this Westphalian approach to delegitimise Taiwanese claims to independence. If a state is to gain independence through this approach it must win the recognition of other states as sovereign. By pressuring states to deny Taiwan recognition, China hopes to prevent Taiwan from achieving full sovereignty. In contrast, Taiwan has favoured the promotion/development of legitimacy through democracy, which will be addressed later.

Weakness of the power approach

What constitutes 'real' is always contested. Chinese realist denial of democracy ignores the *reality* of the twenty-first century, in which democracy has increasingly played an important role in redefining and addressing the national boundary question (Chapter 1). When they overlook the reality of human rights discourse and the spread of democracy in the world, they are becoming 'anti-realist'. The 'four modernisations' paradigm of China ought to include the modernisation of the political system and the governance approach towards the Tibet and Taiwan questions. The real issue is that any meaningful governance with regard to the Tibet and Taiwan questions must rely on the consent of the people. A nationalist rejection of democracy is 'unrealistic' and morally wrong because of its absence of consent and the presence of coercion.

One weakness of the power approach is that it does not pay sufficient attention to democracy. Although Chinese and American policy-makers care about power, they operate under different political systems. Consider the strategic competition of the two empires discussed earlier. The cost of maintaining US primacy in Asia would be enormous. The attitude of the American population and their preferences are crucial. If the Americans do not care and even resist the idea of the US empire, they will send their message to elites through periodical elections. The American democratic system will influence and change the US policy. In short, the power of the US is constrained by democratic institutions. By contrast, China's restorative empire is not controlled and constrained by its people, but may be subject to popular nationalism.

The structural element of the realist power approach overlooks agency, perception, cognition and value change. American scholar Amy Mountcastle (2006: 100) elaborates this well:

> To dismiss human rights by relegating them to some unattainable, pie-in-the-sky, idealistic fantasy land, and to thus depoliticize the issues represented by the human rights discourse, or to criticize those who engage in the human rights discourse for the unseemly politicization of a set of ideals (two sides of the same realistic paradigm), is to deny political agency to people. It is to forget that for many people, human rights are not ideals, but a matter of survival. It is to allow political discourse to be controlled by state authorities and members of privileged groups.

The failure of Beijing's realist policy

Chinese realist policy towards Tibet leads to dirty politics, perpetuates the Tibet problem, leaves normative issues out, and fails to provide any moral ground for China. Wang Lixiong (2002) was an outspoken person who has openly and critically exposed the dark reality of Tibet to Chinese audiences through his literature and political writing. Through the democratisation of the exiled Tibetan community, exiled Tibetans have defeated three realist tactics of *Qiangqi* (capture the moral high ground), *suozhu* (lock in) and *tuokua* (wear down), discussed previously. The democratisation process offers Tibetan exiles a high moral ground and helps them gain international legitimacy, despite the fact that they do not have judicial control over Tibet. Rather than *suozhu* (lock in), the Tibetan resistance movement is getting stronger and has taken root in democratic countries like Australia, Canada and the US. In opposition to *tuokua* (wear down), the Tibetan exile movement will be sustainable and even stronger with support from voters. The democratic election of Lobsang Sangay in 2011 as the Kalon Tripa indicates the separation of politics and religion. This separation of religion and politics means that if the Dalai Lama passes away, the new Kalon Tripa will continue to lead the Tibetan struggle, which will grow stronger given it has been empowered by elections.

Take another example of the realist economic approach towards the minority issue in Tibet. What we witness is the fact that the minority question cannot be answered by economic development alone. It seems that economic 'sweeteners' cannot squash secessionist aspirations. Nor can economic integration deflect the demand for political and cultural identity by Tibetans (Liu 1966). Tibetan secessionism is not a matter of economics but one of politics.

To encourage economic development in Tibet, Beijing had exempted Tibet from the general rule that one must be a permanent resident of a given area to start a business there. The result was that Tibetan cities, Lhasa in particular, were inundated with a so-called 'floating population' of Han Chinese from other provinces. Typically possessed of better linguistic and technical skills than the locals, the Han Chinese tended to take business away from native Tibetans. There was also a widespread feeling that it was the Han Chinese, and not the local people, who profited from tourism (Dreyer 1989: 282). As Lobsang Sangay (1999: 27) (now Prime Minister of the Tibetan government in exile) put it when he was a PhD candidate in Harvard University:

> Tibetans have felt increasingly marginalised in their own territory and see themselves as mere observers of an economic development benefiting others. This has made the ethnic 'us vs. them' sentiment all the more concrete, since it is usually the Han Chinese who reap the profits of change.

In short, the limits of realism highlight the need to take normative issues and democracy seriously, in particular to search for an alternative thinking and approach.

2.2   DEMOCRACY

Taipei's democracy approach

Taiwan's approach to the 'Taiwan question' is, in contrast to China, rooted in the democratic approach. As such, Taipei holds that the authoritarian system of China is the primary source of the so-called Taiwan question, that China's policy towards Taiwan failed to take Taiwan's democratisation into account, and that the China–Taiwan relationship is fundamentally a question of democracy. The democratisation of China is a precondition for reunification. A democratic Taiwan will not, cannot, reunify with an authoritarian China. Many people in Taiwan would not oppose reunification were China to democratise. For example, then Premier Tang Fei was quoted in 2000 as saying, 'If, in the future, there is a new, prosperous, and democratic China, I doubt we would have any reason to reject unification' (*Lienhebao*, 5 July 2000: 2).

Taiwan promotes the democracy paradigm for its international legitimacy. From this perspective the basis for international recognition of Taiwan's legitimacy is its democratic political system. This approach involves a number of components. Taiwan attempts to use its democratic status to establish, join and generally support democratic international organisations that use ideological affiliation as a membership requirement. In this way it can participate in the international community and gain international recognition and legitimacy. At the same time, Taiwan uses this democratic approach to highlight the fact that the People's Republic of China is not democratic and therefore does not represent the Chinese people. Taiwan, in contrast to the Mainland, can at least claim to have a system of government that is representative and participatory. This democratic approach is underscored by the US's desire to maintain the status quo, to protect a democratic Taiwan, and to encourage healthy diplomatic relations between the PRC and the Republic of China (Taiwan) (Wallace 2007). Democracy is seen as the best guarantee of Taiwan's security.

Tibetan democracy and the human rights approach

The Tibetan government in exile has adopted a human rights approach and democracy among its members in exile. The human rights discourse engages normative issues and criticises Chinese policies on Tibet from a moral position. In 1959, the US counselled Tibetan exiles that they could get more political mileage by emphasising human rights rather than sovereignty (Roberts 1997). This had little impact at the time. Since 1987, however, the use of human rights language has been actively advocated and accepted by a number of international non-governmental organisations (NGOs). Nowadays, discussion on the Tibet issue in the West is predominantly framed by human rights. Michael Davis, for example, drew on the new UN Declaration on the Rights of Indigenous Peoples in recommending a change in China's policy towards Tibet by establishing a more genuine system of autonomy there (Davis 2008).

The Dalai Lama has advocated referendum as a democratic mechanism to address the Tibet question. It was planned that a referendum be held in 1997 to discover the nature of Tibetan political goals, but this was called off because the Tibetan government in exile feared that the Middle Way policy might not be the preferred choice and that Tibetans in exile did not have the right to make a decision on which the six million Tibetans inside Tibet had no say (Ardley 2003: 356). The Dalai Lama has imagined a federal system in which Tibetans can elect their leaders within China (see Chapter 8 for a detailed discussion). Of course, other factors have also influenced Tibetan democratisation, including the democratic nature of the host country of India, the secularisation brought by China, and the democratic faith of the Dalai Lama (Boyd 2004).

Like Taiwan, the Dalai Lama promoted democracy aimed at 'an international audience to emphasize the progressive nature of the contemporary polity compared both with old Tibet and modern China' and has hoped that 'his government is to be taken as legitimate by the West' (Ardley 2003: 357).

Realising that there is no way to progress the resolution of the Tibet problem during his lifetime, the Dalai Lama has moved towards an elected political leader in exile to address the issue of how the Tibetan community will continue the struggle in the event of his death (Ardley 2003: 358). The Tibetan government in exile has transformed through elections. In 2011, the Dalai Lama transferred his authority to Lobsang Sangay by passing down to him a traditional seal, the symbol of power more than 260 years old. Lobsang Sangay won the election in 2011 through his platform of the Middle Way.

In his inauguration speech on 8 August 2011, Kalon Tripa Dr Lobsang Sangay promised to work towards the goal of restoring freedom to 'occupied Tibet', and creating the Dalai Lama's vision of a 'truly secular democratic society'. He claimed that the Tibetan election among those in exile sent a strong signal to the world that Tibetans are committed to universal democratic principles. He stated that the struggle was against the hardline policies of the Chinese government, not the Chinese people themselves, and that there was 'ongoing political repression, cultural assimilation, economic marginalisation and environmental destruction' in Tibet.

He insisted that there is colonialism in Tibet, rather than socialism. He stated the Tibetan movement's commitment to non-violence and the Middle Way policy of 'genuine autonomy' within the People's Republic of China. He emphasised that the Dalai Lama's political power had been devolved not to him personally as the Kalon Tripa, but rather to all Tibetans through the democratic process. He also stressed that unity is vital if the Tibetan cause is to be successful (Sangay 2011).

Now Tibetan leaders must consider and take seriously the concern of their 'constituents'. Every five years there is an election. Tibetan exile politics is moving towards an unclear, unstable and increasingly radicalised position. The democratisation of Taiwan witnessed the growth of the Democratic Progress Party (DPP), which has endorsed the independence stance in its party constitution; whether a similar process will take place, that is, whether a more radical party movement will be born from the democratisation of Tibetans in exile, remains to be seen. Lobsay Sangay, in conversation with the author on 25 June 2012 in Melbourne, admitted the possibility that a movement towards radicalisation similar to Taiwan's DPP is in the making now among exiled Tibetans.

China's half-hearted democracy approach: *minxin gongcheng*

For a long time the Chinese resisted the democracy approach to resolving the Taiwan question. This rejection is based on the following reasons: that democracy cannot solve the national identity question; that democratisation might break down the domination of the CCP and lead to the fragmentation of China (for a detailed discussion, see Chapter 3). Recently, however, there has been a shift in the Chinese approach and the leadership has started to recognise the role of the Taiwanese in their quest for reunification. This is what is called *minxin gongcheng*, that is, Beijing's initiative to win the hearts and minds of the Taiwanese for the reunification cause; implicitly Beijing recognises that in the end the Taiwanese people matter. Hu Jintao has expressed this as *yi min wei ben* (taking people as fundamental) (Sina 2006).

To implement this new policy, Beijing has reduced Taiwanese student fees and taxes for products imported from Taiwan. It has also allowed Taiwanese airlines to pass over Chinese airspace, making travel much easier. It has changed its approach to diplomacy, engaging in a much less hostile way. It seems that the CCP is confident that the Taiwanese people will slowly warm to the idea of reunification. There is an understanding that this will take time so timetables have been scrapped and the CCP seems committed to slowly working for the people.

This *minxin gongcheng* can be conceptualised as a half-hearted democracy approach. This is because the Chinese leadership does not have any intention of allowing the Taiwanese to determine whether or not unification takes place. It does, however, show a change in tactics on the part of the Chinese. The CCP still inhibits public debate in China on the Taiwan issue. If this approach fails to convince the next generation that reunification is in their best interest, will the leadership revert to their old tactics? It is vital to remember that the current approach is using democratic elements as a means to reunification, not as an end in itself. If the Taiwanese continue to support independence, will the PRC respect this wish or begin to curtail freedoms?

Two diplomats from Taiwan with whom I had an interview on 25 April 2012 in London provided a negative assessment of the *minxin gongcheng* policy. They felt that even if Beijing offers material benefits, it is for short-term gain and the middle class does not have an obvious sense of any direct benefits. Moreover, Taiwan is still excluded from participating in many international organisations, and even when it was allowed by Beijing to participate in the World Health Organisation (WHO), for example, its status was secondary as 'China's Taipei'. In this process, according to Taiwanese diplomats, the dignity of Taiwan is disrespected, making Taiwanese people feel insignificant despite the material benefits Beijing has offered. Taiwanese diplomats argue that unless Beijing changes its policy to allow Taiwan more international space and respects Taiwan's dignity in the world community, the so-called 'winning people's hearts' project is unlikely to generate the influence which Beijing expected. The US think tank Centre for Strategic and International Studies reports the results of a poll conducted in August 2011 whereby only 30.8 per cent of Taiwanese people considered that their president 'safeguards sovereignty and secures Taiwan's interests and peace across the Strait' (Glasner & Billingsley 2011: 4). In recent years the *minxin gongcheng* strategy has struggled to win over the Taiwanese public. From 2007 the number of people in Taiwan who self-identify as only Taiwanese surpassed for the first time the number who see themselves as both Taiwanese and Chinese. In recent years the support for maintaining the status quo indefinitely has increased from 18.4 per cent in 2007 to 27.4 per cent in 2011, while support for moving towards unification or 'maintaining the status quo now and making a decision later' has decreased slightly over the same period. This has been explained in different ways. Some see this as a tactical response by voters to warn the Ma administration not to get too close to the Mainland, while others see this as a more permanent ontological shift. According to the latter interpretation, some Taiwanese view moves to improve economic ties as involving a relationship between businesspeople and not something that increases their identification with the Mainland, or even see it as a Mainland conspiracy to create a united front. While the former interpretation is not a major concern for the Mainland's *minxin gongcheng* strategy, if the latter interpretation is correct it is more problematic because it represents a more permanent shift away from reunification (ChinaReviewNews.com 2012).

Related to *minxin gongcheng* is the Chinese government's advocacy of 'democratisation of international relations'. China attacks the hegemonic power of the US because it is unjust. China sees the virtue in giving small and middle powers a voice (Ni & Wang 2002; Guo 2000). Yet this idea is very hypocritical. Considering China's own internal political situation, calling for global democracy lacks legitimacy if it is coming from within an undemocratic state. If China is really committed to changing the current US-unipolar system and democratising international relations, China must carry out democratic reform internally, and treat Taiwan as equal. China cannot continue to discuss the democratisation of international relations while failing these tests.

Democracy and Sino–US relations

Chinese democracy and human rights are a source of cooperation and conflict between Washington and Beijing (He 2013). While village elections in the latter 1990s were a renewed source of cooperation, the 1989 crushing of the democratic movement was a cause of conflict. The 4 June 1989 events shattered hopes for friendly ties within months of George H. W. Bush's assumption of office. Literally overnight, Suettinger (2003) writes, the relationship between Washington and Beijing went from 'amity and strategic cooperation to hostility, distrust, and misunderstanding'. In the succeeding years, bilateral relations never evolved 'beyond Tiananmen'.

According to the democratic approach, China's democratic reform is the best means to improve Sino–US relations. It will narrow the political system gap across the Strait and between the US and China. It is believed that the democratisation of China will constrain China's political behaviour; hopefully China will renounce its intention of using force against Taiwan. Rosen (2002) argues, 'If Chinese political reforms are successful, and the Chinese government ceases to be a dictatorship, it is likely that there will be a large-scale movement of power away from Beijing toward the provinces or regions that have their own ethnic or religious identities. The government of China will concentrate on improving the lives of its own people, and participating in the world order led by the United States' (Rosen 2002: 3). Rosen, however, might be too optimistic as the democratisation of China may lead to China not wanting to participate in a US-led world order if that is what the Chinese people wanted.

Democratic thinking needs to take realism seriously

To advocate democracy one cannot abandon realism. The operation of democracy must rely on real forces on the ground. The right questions are under what kind of power conditions will China embark on democratisation, and under what conditions can Chinese democratisation avoid China's territorial disintegration and prevent military conflicts from occurring?

A simplistic human rights discourse has its own problems. To argue that the source of the Tibet issue is a failure to protect human rights is a kind of normative thinking that transforms complex Tibetan issues into human rights issues. Often it plays up moral issues, overlooks the complexity of politics, and offers little in the way of realistic policy alternatives (B. He 2005). The case of the Tibetan language issues, explored in Chapter 9, provides an example of this.

Democracy is a way of regulating power, in particular the power struggle over the boundary/identity question, and actual power relations influence the implementation of the democratic approach and constrain the democratic principle and approach. The boundary/identity question ought to be analysed through a power perspective. It is the power struggle between the centre and minority groups, between ethnic groups, or between classes within an ethnic group. The key issue is how to lead the power struggle through democratic channels. Power analysis is needed to supplement democratic analysis, a key methodology throughout this book.

Power and power structure can explain why democracy is adopted as a solution or not. A realist power approach helps to explain why referendum was adopted in Taiwan where power distribution was in favour of the Taiwanese, and why it was constrained due to geopolitics (Chapter 5). A realist power approach helps to explain the change in sovereign practice, for example why Taiwan was excluded from the United Nations (UN) but both North Korea and South Korea have seats there (Chapter 6).

The paradigm of democracy needs to take Chinese realist assessment, and in particular Chinese fear of disintegration, seriously. We need to recognise the danger of democratisation. For China, the logic of democratisation indeed may lead to national disintegration. Politicians often play the ethnic card of national identity in elections so as to intensify conflicts and polarise the politics in Taiwan. Newly established democratic institutions that are immature are not able to contain conflicts and constrain radicals and populists. Comparatively speaking, the US is a mature democracy with a high level of stability as well as a certain level of predictability. China is an authoritarian regime within which certain predictability can be assumed as long as the leadership is stable and united. Taiwan is an immature democracy, as evidenced by the series of events in the 2004 presidential election during which an unexpected event of shooting changed the campaign and voting behaviour. The ongoing democratisation process is full of uncertainty and unpredictability; this uncertain process constitutes a crucial unstable element in the triangular relations among Washington, Beijing and Taipei. Before the democratisation of Taiwan, Washington, Beijing and Taipei were committed to the one China policy. Even today, Beijing, Washington, the Kuomintang (KMT) and the People First Party (PFP) are committed to the one China policy, with different interpretations and emphases. The Democratic Progressive Party (DPP), however, has adopted a creeping independence strategy and rejected the one China policy. Nevertheless, the changing policy of the DPP should not be excluded if China adopts a compromising and conciliatory attitude towards it. Among DPP leaders Chen Shuibian once talked about one future China. Xie Changting (谢长廷) said that they do not exclude reunification. Lin Zhushui (林蠋水) acknowledged the possibility of the cooperation between multiple states within a *huaren* (Chinese) world (华人世界). If China were to embark upon democratisation, the predictable element of authoritarianism would be reduced and a great uncertainty would be expected. This needs to be kept in mind when arguing against the realist approach.

2.3 THE REAL UTOPIAN APPROACH

I have so far examined realism and democracy paradigms and evaluated the advantages and disadvantages of each approach. Now I will argue for a real utopian approach; an approach that attempts to take advantage of realism and democratic thinking while overcoming some of the problems associated with each of the paradigms.

The real utopian approach enables an exploration of the Tibet and Taiwan

questions in both normative and empirical ways. It is empirically informed normative thinking; and it is normative-guided empirical research. It studies a historical trend, which helps to see the future possibility. It is not merely realism; nor is
it pure philosophical meditation either. The real utopian approach is based on
multi-disciplinary social science research. It is situated somewhere in the middle
ground between pure normative thinking and sole empirical study. It moves the
position back and forth from normative thinking to real politics, and from real
politics to normative thinking. Utopian thinking takes account of real conditions
and mechanisms. It works out a normative position that has empirical grounds and
support.

The real utopian approach is the basis of the analysis throughout this book. All
of the chapters of this book move back and forth from realist thinking to normative
thinking or from normative thinking to realist thinking. When realism turns out
to be 'ugly and cruel', I move back to normative thinking to balance against realist
thinking. When normative thinking becomes too far away from the real world, I
move back into the real world to balance against excessively wishful democratic
thinking. Such processes repeat many times in all chapters, although the stress of
each chapter is different, with some leaning more towards normative thinking while
others focus more on empirical enquiries. Nevertheless, all chapters attempt to
achieve a balanced and reflective equilibrium.

As such, all chapters of the book exhibit the feature of the real utopian approach.
Several chapters largely engage and develop normative thinking and argument. For
example, Chapter 1 addresses and defends the democratic governance approach.
At the same time, it qualifies the democratic approach in an empirical world, and
acknowledges the limits of democratic governance in some situations. Chapter 6
challenges the Chinese realist policy towards Taiwan's international recognition
and advocates a new normative rethinking of post-modern sovereignty. It, however,
returns to the real world and explores how it is possible to adopt post-modern sovereignty. Chapter 11 develops a normative argument about deliberative referendum,
and then engages an empirical investigation of the conditions under which referendum can be successful.

Most chapters take an empirical study. Chapter 3 examines the impact of Chinese
democratisation on Chinese restorative empire. While it examines how the logic of
democratisation disfavours the empire heritage, it does not accept the claim that
China should reject democracy. On the contrary, it also explores how democracy
can be introduced to address the national identity issue. In contrast, Chapter 4
examines the other side of the question: how Taiwan's democratisation empowers
the opposition party that has advocated Taiwanese national identity and its independence. While it addresses how Taiwan's democratisation impacts on the definition of and resolution to the Taiwan question, it also speculates on how Chinese
democratisation might provide a solution to the Taiwan question, as well as how
Chinese democratisation might generate an impetus towards the federalisation of
the Taiwan Straits.

A realist approach is employed to examine the politics of referendum in Taiwan
in Chapter 5. It provides a realist assessment of the situation in which the Bush

administration was very prudent not to support the referendum proposal by former president Chen Shuibian. Such a realist study, however, does not preclude the search for democratic governance. The last section of Chapter 5 thus returns to the normative issue of deliberative referendum as a corrective to manipulative referendum.

An analysis of the changing political discourses regarding minority issues in China is developed in Chapter 7. In particular, it examines the Chinese realist argument that the current autonomy system and policy failed, and that a second-generation ethnic minority policy, a sort of more traditional assimilation policy, is needed. These second-generation ethnic policy scholars follow the USA melting pot model as a solution to the challenges of resolving ethnic minority issues, but ignore the point that such a melting pot model is only relevant to migrants, and usually does not work for historical homeland peoples. This chapter again returns to a normative analysis and provides a liberal critique of both Confucian and Marxist discourse on minority rights.

In discussing the national identity issue, one fundamental question is about the CCP. Comparatively speaking, a multi-party system in a liberal democracy is beneficial. Minority-based parties can appeal to a large community and if they go too far, the public can express its dissatisfaction by not voting for them. In an ideal situation, minority people can express their voice and make a rational choice without being restricted by constraints within a system of one-party domination. Given the domination of the CCP and the likelihood that it can maintain its power for the foreseeable future, a realist option has to explore autonomy under this one-party system. The Dalai Lama has been advocating the Middle Way; an autonomy option in the current Chinese political system. How realistic is this Middle Way policy? The political reality poses the question of how it is feasible and realistic for the Dalai Lama to ask for political autonomy in Tibet when the CCP's power extends everywhere. How can we pursue democratic governance under this condition? While it is not an ideal solution, as it rules out many issues, it is nevertheless a sensible and realistic question. Chapter 8 explores the Tibetan autonomy question within the current environment of tough constraints.

While I concur with the European moral position on linguistic issues, I also develop a historical approach to trace the history of the Chinese language situation and linguistic policy in Chapter 9. Such a history-based empirical study provides a key to understanding current educational and linguistic policies in Tibet, and offers an insight into the likely future direction of linguistic trends. While the chapter engages with this historical examination in detail, it returns to normative thinking by asking the question of how China can move beyond its history of linguistic imperialism.

Chapter 10 discusses how deliberative democracy can address the national identity conflict issue. It engages an experimental study of how deliberative forums really impact on the resolution of the national identity question. While defending and developing the deliberative approach, the chapter also acknowledges the limits of deliberative democracy.

In summary, there are internal tensions between realism and normative thinking, and between the stress on democracy and the emphasis on governance. To reduce these internal tensions, the book has applied and developed the real utopian approach throughout, and moved back and forth between empirical realist study and normative thinking.

2.4   CONCLUSION

This chapter has examined two paradigms for the study of the Taiwan and Tibet questions and outlined the strengths and weaknesses of each paradigm. The power approach comes to terms with the real world, no matter how ugly and cruel it is. It is too cruel in the sense that it accepts ugly reality to the point that it lacks political imagination and moral decency. It is also dominant and prevailing among politicians and scholars in China. Think tanks in Beijing endorse different versions of the realist paradigm. However, it does not offer a groundbreaking solution to the Taiwan and Tibet questions. The power analysis that a realist embraces is not only an incomplete solution but also the partial source of problems. It is also unstable because the status quo is changing. It overlooks democracy that constrains power.

The democracy paradigm offers innovative mechanisms and procedures. Democratic actors fight against a dreadful and brutal world with a political imagination of how the unjust and cruel world would be replaced by a more equal, free, humanitarian and peaceful world. Nevertheless, the democracy approach must not ignore the issue of power. The leadership in Beijing does not accept the democracy approach. The US adopts a pragmatic attitude towards the democratic approach and even makes a compromise with democratic values in dealing with China. Democracy is also an incomplete solution and also the partial source of problems; in particular, democratisation might worsen the situation and lead to further conflicts.

This chapter therefore advocates the real utopian approach. At a minimum, a better understanding of one paradigm from the other one would lead to a more sophisticated appreciation of issues. Each paradigm seems to be providing a partial account of the forces at work or capturing partial dimensions of the Taiwan and Tibet questions. Considerable promise may lie in a creative, but not crude, synthesis of the two. The solution lies in an imaginative combination of the two paradigms; in particular, how power-holders use the democracy paradigm to address the Tibet and Taiwan questions. A normatively decent and satisfactory resolution to the Taiwan and Tibet questions ultimately requires changes in power relations and China's move towards democracy.

NOTES

1. They deserve a lengthy discussion. However, due to the focus and scope of this book, I will not pursue the issue further here.
2. Both Clinton and Bush endorsed the Three Nos policy: no support for Taiwan's independence,

no support for a two-China policy, and no support for Taiwan's membership of international organisations on the basis of statehood.

3. Professor Wang Gungwu's remark in an informal meeting at the East Asia Institute, National University of Singapore, on 4 May 2004.

3 The Empire Thesis and its Critics

This chapter comprises seven sections. Section 3.1 raises the question of the impact of democratisation on the national identity issue and political unity. Section 3.2 proposes several theoretical hypotheses. Section 3.3 undertakes a historical test of a controversial 'empire thesis' through an historical overview of China's national identity question, in particular an historical account of the various episodes when Chinese nationalism has clashed with democratisation over the national identity question. Sections 3.4 and 3.5 examine further the clash between democratisation and nationalism in today's China, with a particular focus on Taiwan and Tibet. Section 3.6 argues against a strong historical determinism by formulating an anti-empire thesis, and explores the possible democratic mechanisms through which China could avoid the logic of 'the empire thesis'. Section 3.7 is a short conclusion.

3.1 THE IMPACT OF CHINA'S NATIONAL IDENTITY QUESTION ON CHINESE DEMOCRATISATION

The Chinese leadership is now reluctant to initiate large-scale democratisation at the national level in China. Indeed, Chinese state nationalists oppose democratisation, which they see as threatening national unity and control of the territories. In particular, the break-up of the former USSR and the separation of East Timor from Indonesia have reinforced Beijing's fear and resistance to democracy, while China's successful reunion with Hong Kong and Macau has strengthened Beijing's belief that power, not democracy, can unify China.

In contrast, Chinese liberal dissidents, such as Yan Jiaqi, Wei Jingsheng and Hu Ping, call for democratic federalism to resolve the questions of Taiwan and Tibet. It is argued that through federalism, a grand-coalition government and genuine autonomy, China might be able to maintain its size and unity while also becoming democratic. This view is contested by this empirical study of Chinese modern history and the effect of the national identity question on democratisation.

This chapter attempts to analyse the impact of China's national identity question on Chinese democratisation and to explore why China has difficulty in establishing democracy. Shaohua Hu (2000) has used historical legacies, local forces, the world system, socialist values and economic development to explain China's difficulty in establishing democracy. This chapter focuses on the national identity question and examines the conditions in which Chinese nationalism can be said to constitute an obstacle to democratisation. It will seek to demonstrate the logic of the conflict between democracy and state nationalism in the context of China's national identity issue.

This analysis, however, aims to provide an explanation or an understanding of, *not a justification for*, the Party/state's resistance to democracy. Regardless of how strongly the Party/state is hostile to democracy, a section of the Chinese people still demand democracy as their inherent right; a right which cannot be denied. Within this tough environment, democracy advocates are still searching for democratic governance. We should be cautious to leave room for possibilities that are not reducible to the theoretical formulas discussed below. The historical argument and structural argument should not exclude the role of agents.

The Party/state has appropriated the nationality question and framed the problem in terms of the way that democratisation will affect China's boundaries, because democratisation threatens the unity of the PRC. While this chapter demonstrates the logic of such a view, it also examines the post-empire thesis that the democratisation of China might provide a solution to China's national boundary question. It argues strongly that the national boundary question should not be used as an excuse to delay democratisation. Of course, it should be acknowledged that democratisation only plays a part of roles; and there are many other factors that have impacted on the process and outcome. Here we focus on the effect of democratisation.

3.2   THE EMPIRE THESIS AND ASYMMETRIC EFFECT

The process from 'empire' to nations often involves ethno-nationalism, which is said to lead inevitably to the proliferation of smaller and more ethnically homogeneous states. I therefore formulate the first theoretical proposition of the 'empire thesis'. The core idea of the empire thesis is that *the democratisation of empire is likely to undermine or break up its political unity*. In such a circumstance, democracy is seen as a useful tool to break down the empire system because it enables multi-ethnic groups, or nationalities, to be empowered.

There are different versions of the empire thesis. Victor Louis, a member of the KGB, presented his version of the empire thesis as a rationale intended to justify a Soviet 'war of liberation' against the People's Republic of China in 1979. Louis (1979: 186) outlined three key ideas of this thesis. First, the Chinese leadership, continuing the traditional imperial expansionist line, was laying claim to vast areas of the Soviet Far East, Siberia and Central Asia. Second, for several decades the people of the outlying regions of China, all along the Sino–Soviet border, had been waging an unrelenting struggle for their national self-determination and independence. Third, the solution, according to Louis, was to grant independence to the people of Manchuria, Mongolia, Eastern Turkestan and Tibet. For him, this was a just solution of the national identity problem (in his terms, the 'nationalities question'), and would largely remove the threat of Chinese expansion towards the adjacent territories. Louis (1979: 187) predicted that future developments would show how soon the national aspirations of the Manchu, Mongols, Uyghurs and Tibetans could become reality.

Zhuang Wanshou, a Taiwanese scholar, presents another version of the empire thesis. He argues that Taiwan's independence movement is historically determined by the inevitable breakdown of the Chinese empire (Shih 1994: 276–7). Former Taiwanese leader Chen Shuibian adopted the China empire thesis. In his interview with Japanese journalist Yoichi Funabashi in May 2004, Chen said: 'So long as the Beijing leadership continues to run a Chinese empire that is a far cry from democracy, none of us will see unification during our lifetime. The people of Taiwan will never agree to become one with the Chinese empire.'[1]

Similarly, it is often said that Tibetan independence should be seen as a just and ineluctable outcome of this same historical trajectory. It is often said too that China annexed and colonised Tibet. Although China modernised Tibet with a flow of central financial and technological support, the colonisation or de-colonisation experience shows that rapid modernisation invariably empowers indigenous people who will demand their autonomy and independence. On the other hand, if modernisation fails, indigenous people tend to blame the failure on the colonisers' policy. Modernisation thus works in both ways against colonisers. Viewing Tibet in such a way, whatever Tibet has achieved, it is argued a 'golden cage' is still a cage; and the best option is for China to pull out.

Let us now test this empire thesis. After a period of expansion during the fifteenth and sixteenth centuries, Ottoman domination was extended over much of Central Europe, the Balkans, the Middle East and North Africa. The empire underwent a lengthy period of contraction and fragmentation. In July 1908, the constitutional monarchy was instituted and democratisation started. The election of November/December 1908 led to the success of the Unionists, who attempted to transform and rescue the empire. However, the Ottoman empire collapsed and its territorial question was resolved as a result of the internal struggle between military and civil forces and between fundamental and secular forces, the demand for independence from non-Muslim and non-Turkish communities, and a disastrous alliance with Germany in the First World War. During Mustafa Kemal's rule, a process of Turkey-nisation occurred, so that the old Ottoman identity was replaced with a new Turk identity. Elections were held in 1946 and the People's Party was replaced by the Democratic Party in 1950 (Ahmad 1993).

In Portugal, opposition parties were legalised in 1969, the new constitution came into effect on 25 April 1976 and an election to the Assembly of the Republic was held the same day. In 1974, the military government of Vasco dos Santos Goncalves recognised the right of the Overseas Territories to 'self-determination' with all its consequences, including independence. Guinea-Bissau gained its independence in 1974, Mozambique in 1975 and Angola in 1976. Portugal's initial refusal to grant independence provoked fighting and guerrilla warfare (Banks, Day & Muller 1997: 682).

The Sovietisation of the Russian centre retained and expanded the territories of the Russian empire in the wake of the Second World War. However, the Soviet empire underwent imperial decay in the 1980s and 1990s, finally breaking up when democratisation began (Skak 1996). The emergence of ethnic nationalisms played a decisive role in generating centrifugal forces to tear the Soviet Union apart (Wang & Yi 1996). According to S. N. Eisenstadt (1992), given the centre–periphery relations in the former USSR, the collapse of the Soviet empire was inevitable. Historically, a highly active Russian centre exercised centralised control over a politically passive periphery. However, during the Soviet period the political centre mobilised the periphery and activated it socially and politically to such a degree that it changed the balance between the centre and the periphery. The totalitarian regime maintained effectively tight controls, forbidding the formation of autonomous sub-systems, but legitimating national cultures within a universalistic framework. Once the totalitarian controls weakened, ethnic tensions were enhanced by the rise of ethno-nationalism, leading to the breakdown of the empire system (Harmstone 1997: 92). As another example, East Timor gained its independence through referendum and international intervention in 1999 following the democratisation of Indonesia.

The empire thesis can be further supported by the second theoretical proposition. *If democratisation is regarded as an independent variable, and the national identity question as a dependent variable, the impact of democratisation on secession and unification is asymmetric* (B. He 2002c). Precisely, *democratisation – other things being equal – plays a bigger role in facilitating independence than it does in encouraging reunification* in the context of the global trend towards independence, and the marginalisation of reunification. The asymmetric effect offers us a deepening understanding of why China does not favour democratisation as a solution to its national identity question.

Empirically, democratisation is associated with far more political divorces than marriages. Among the forty-seven new member states in the UN since 1974, twenty-six have won independence while their 'parent states' were democratising. By comparison, among those states which have successfully achieved reunification since 1974, such as Vietnam, Germany, Yemen and China–Hong Kong, only the unification of the two Germanys and the two Yemens was related to democratisation. China's reunification with Hong Kong was through diplomatic negotiation, while the reunification of Vietnam was achieved through war, following the surrender of the southern government on 30 April 1975.

In the case of East Germany, it could be argued that democratisation broke down the Communist state, thereby facilitating its reunification. In the case of the merger of the former Yemen Arab Republic and the Marxist People's Democratic Republic, a Yemen Council, embracing the two chief councils, and a Joint Ministerial Council were established in 1981, promising to submit a draft constitution for a unified Yemeni Republic to referendums in the two states. The constitution was ratified by the respective parliaments in 1990. It should be noted that the reunification took place in 1990 prior to the national election in 1993, and this sequence of events should not lead us to overestimate the role of democratisation in promoting unification in Yemen. In the case of Taiwan, its democratisation has resulted in a virtual abandonment of the project of reunification with China, and thus a de facto independence. Also of note is the fact that while the democratisation of Moldova supported its independence from the former Soviet Union, it did not enable its reunification with Romania.

These two empirical-based theoretical propositions can be used to help understand the predicament of China. *China is the last empire and the democratisation of China is likely to undermine or break up the political unity of China's empire.* The rise and persistence of ethnic nationalism and independence movements in Taiwan and Tibet can be deemed part of the logic of the breakdown of the world's 'last empire' into several nations. In order to maintain the unity of its territorial integrity, China is likely to resist the kind of democratisation that will break it up.

The difficulty associated with establishing democracy in China is historically embedded; that is, Chinese democratisation challenges the territorial basis of the Qing empire, and the business of nation-building in China confronts this historical legacy. *When the empire thesis is combined with the structural argument (that democratisation does not favour reunification), the national identity problem makes it difficult to introduce democracy in China.*

There are more tensions between nationalism and democracy, in the process of nation-state-building in those countries where three basic conditions (the past history of empire, the multinational state, and large and territorially concentrated ethnic minorities) are present, than in those where these conditions are absent. Also of importance is the particular situation of how democratisation relates to the form of the national identity question. For instance, there are more tensions between nationalism and democracy in the case of China's unification with Taiwan than there are in the case of Taiwan's independence because Chinese democratisation produces uncertainty for its reunification while Taiwan's democratisation has assisted its independence cause.

The tensions existing between nationalism and democracy illustrate the tragic fate of Chinese democracy. This tragedy, concerning the transition from 'empire' to nation-state, has been played out throughout China's history. As ethno-nationalism has threatened to break down the 'empire', pan-Chinese nationalists have attempted to maintain it at the cost of democracy. For Chinese state nationalists to be patriotic they must support an authoritarian state. This is a major problem for contemporary China and if it cannot be resolved it will be difficult for democracy to flourish. This is the crucial connection between democracy and the question of national identity, and between democracy and the existence of the Chinese nation-state. Democratisation threatens the very existence of the Chinese nation-state.

The clash between pan-Chinese nationalism and democracy derives from China's unique position as a multi-ethnic country with a historical legacy as an 'empire'. Pan-Chinese nationalists are born only in China and are driven to defend their nation even at the cost of democracy if it threatens to break up China. The logical tension between nationalism and democracy can be seen as a 'historical accident'. It is 'accidental' in the sense that the historical circumstance of each country, as a starting point, is highly contingent. Australia as a new nation-state was formed through referendums and parliamentary vote, because of the influence of the British democratic tradition and the nature of its immigrant society. Taiwan is now a semi-independent state and can win full independence without having to worry about its disintegration. China, like the former Soviet Union, has an historical burden as an 'empire', and its state was formed through wars. It is difficult for China, therefore, to reconstruct a new nation in accordance with democratic procedure. In short, the special context and circumstances of China do not favour the adoption of demo-cratic procedure in order to settle the national identity question by any Chinese nationalists. Chinese nationalists' commitment to the historical principle (China as a nation is entitled to claim its territories on historical grounds) is understandable, and such a commitment has contributed to the tension between nationalism and democracy.

In such a context, it is difficult to be both a democrat and a patriot in China. This is because the liberal and democratic camp appears to be fundamentally opposed to Chinese nationalism. This is why this group is 'unpopular' with the nationalist camp. Equally, it is difficult for Chinese democrats today to overcome the tensions between democracy and nationalism. Indeed, some contemporary Chinese liberals face a dilemma in their attitude towards the USA. While they favour the political institutions of the USA, they are opposed to its Tibet and Taiwan policies. If they do not exhibit an anti-American stance on these questions they are likely to be criticised as 'traitors'. In particular, if Chinese democrats do not support reunifica-tion with Taiwan, they would lack legitimacy for introducing democracy in China in the first instance.

Of course, we have to acknowledge that Chinese nationalists will not venture to openly reject the principle of democracy. This is because the age of modern nation-alism is one linked to the modern idea of 'the people'. The people, that is, the mass of ordinary human beings, are believed to have a sense both of their own worth and of their rights. Indeed, Chinese nationalist leaders from Sun Yat-sen, Chiang Kai-shek, Mao Zedong and Deng Xiaoping to Jiang Zeming have, for the purposes of political mobilisation, been forced to use some form of democracy and speak in the name of the people.

3.3   HISTORICAL TRAJECTORY

China's national identity problem has to be understood in historical terms. In this regard, Rawski's discussion of Qing history gives us an excellent explanation of how Qing history influences today's Chinese politics. The territory of today's China is a product of the Qing empire, from the long historical interactions of Inner and East Asia. China was incorporated into the Qing empire that spanned Inner Asia and East Asia. The Qing was the most successful of China's dynasties in terms of its territorial expansion. Under the Qing empire, ethnic minorities were colonised. Xinjiang became a province in 1884. But neither Mongolia, Qinghai nor Tibet was ever converted into a province during the Qing. When the Qing was overthrown in the 1911 Revolution, the Provisional Law of the Republic (1912) specifically identified Mongolia, Tibet and Qinghai as integral parts of the nation. However, loyalty to the Qing dynasty did not automatically translate into loyalty to the Republic of China; for example, the Mongols never considered themselves part of a *Zhongguo* (China) (Rawski 1996: 840). Even today, the Dalai Lama claims that the Qing dynasty is not China; and the relationship between Tibet and Manchu is not the relationship between Tibet and China (Xu 1999: 122–3).

It should be noted that China's suzerainty over Tibet was not modern sovereignty, nor was Tibet's autonomy independent. In the context of nation-state-building, as Harald Bockman (1998: 317) observes,

> former barbarian buffers like Mongolia, Xinjiang, and Tibet had to be either excluded or included. Faced with different imperialist designs, late Imperial, early Nationalist, and Communist leaders went for the second option: the vast ethnic regions of the former Empire were transformed into inalienable parts of the motherland.

In the republican period, China struggled to retain all the Qing territories in the new nation-state. Like its predecessors, the People's Republic of China worked hard to retain the inherited Qing territories through the consistent repression of independence movements in Tibet, Xinjiang and Inner Mongolia. In the process of modern nation-building, China successfully defeated the attempts by Tibet, Manchu and Uygur to establish their statehood but failed to defeat the Republic of Mongolia. China also successfully reclaimed its sovereignty over Hong Kong in 1997 and Macau in 1999. Nevertheless, China still confronts a secessionist movement in Tibet and Xinjiang, and the Republic of China (Taiwan) has coexisted with the People's Republic of China since 1949.

Behind China's national identity question is the thorny task of nation-state-building. As John Fitzgereld (1996) argues, China has a state but lacks a nation, which is still developing. For Harald Bockman (1998: 332), China is still an empire-state and a new Chinese nation based on citizenship has not yet formed. Bockman even concludes 'The country is not a nation-state in the regular sense of the term, and it probably never will be.' These two views suggest that China is far from developing into a modern nation-state.

The basic problems associated with China in building a modern nation-state are: What is an effective and normatively persuasive way to define state boundaries? What are the sources of the legitimacy of the territories of the nation-state: historical or democratic? What is an appropriate form for the state: unitary or federal? What is the social base of the nation: Han Chinese, or a modern Chinese citizen comprising all peoples living in the PRC?

China has been working hard to build a modern nation-state along with other nation-states in the world. Liang Qichao and some of today's Chinese intellectuals have proposed a pan-Chinese nation. There are two opposite processes in building the Chinese nation-state. One involves the retention of territories of the former Qing 'empire' while building a new, modern nation-state. In such a move, super- or pan-nationalism employs visions of a broad political community binding together different ethnic groups and nationalities, and preventing the disintegration of the nation. Liang Qichao invented a pan-Chinese identity in order to retain the Qing peripheries. As Rawski (1996: 841) points out, 'Only a definition of the nation that transcends Han identity can thus legitimately lay claim to the peripheral regions inhabited by non-Han peoples, since these claims rest on the empires created by the Mongols and the Manchus.' To strengthen Chinese national identity, local identities have been reconstructed in terms of vertical hierarchy rather than vertical relations so as to discover and defend the national significance of the local identities (Finane 1994). The Party/state has done its best to redefine and homogenise Han Chinese images of national minorities as a way to gain more control over the Han majority (Gladney 1994).

A critical question therefore is, can democracy/democratisation settle China's national identity question in favour of China's unity? The answer is 'difficult'. Democracy is after all about power. When the process of democratisation faces a national identity question, it is difficult for nationalities to compete and compromise on matters of political power, thus making the process of democratisation difficult. Also, democracy needs a civic culture. China's traditional culture is characterised by centralised power, the idea of great unity, and a long tradition of an appointment system from above, making it difficult for China to adopt federalism to deal with the national identity question.

The logic of democratisation will undermine the Chinese starting position that China's territory is fixed and closed off forever. Democratisation empowers minorities and ethno-nationalism, and may break up the unity of the old 'empire'. Democratisation gives rise to an immediate and divisive question of who 'we' and 'the people' are. Democratisation challenges the political entity in a unitary form, and opens a window to a federal China, which is promising but also dangerous. Most importantly, democracy challenges those who control power, and in particular challenges the image the Chinese Communist Party presents of itself as a unifying force maintaining China's territorial integrity, hence the equation that the CCP = Nation = State.

In China's case, it is the process of evolving from 'empire' to nation-states that challenges China's territorial integrity. China's 'family' union was achieved under the Qing empire and has been maintained by the CCP. The question is, will it break up as a modern state if it is democratised? The idea of the empire thesis implies that the empire has to break up if democracy is established.

Chinese nationalists certainly dislike the empire thesis. We have seen some Chinese argue that Tibet is not a Chinese colony and that China did not colonise Tibet because Tibet was a part of China for several centuries. It is also argued that Han immigrants bring their culture and create a cultural fusion.

Unlike the above historical narrative, Chinese history texts stress that all Chinese people have suffered from the Western imperial invasion and expansion during modern Chinese history. They state that all the people unified to struggle against Japanese imperialism and its invasion. Mao Zedong claimed that the self-determination of China's nationalities was decided, once and for all, by their common revolutionary struggle and voluntary incorporation into the PRC (Smith

1990: 78). One may also argue that the Qing empire had already been broken up in 1919, and that therefore the empire thesis does not apply to today's China.

One may disagree with what has been said about the empire history of China and raise the question of whether the concept of 'empire' can be applied in China. Wang Gungwu (1995: 55), a renowned historian, elaborates this well: 'China's concept of historical empire was unlike that of the Persians, Greeks, or Romans, that of Asoka, Tamerlane, or Babur, or in modern times, that of the Ottomans, the British, the French, or tsarist Russia. These were empires by conquest.' By contrast, 'with the exception of the short Mongol period of 90 years, when China was itself part of the world empire of the Mongols, no armies marched out of traditional Middle Kingdom (*Zhongguo*) lands.'

For some people and commentators, and in particular for those who struggle for independence inside or outside China, despite differences between Western and Chinese empires the empire thesis still holds. China faces the national identity question simply if secessionist minorities think that China was an empire and those in the former Chinese tributary states claim their own independence.

In the context of the national identity question that China has faced, a democratic approach to the national identity question has been advocated but never put into practice. In 1924, Sun Yat-sen addressed the national identity problem, writing in the manifesto of the 1st Chinese Nationalist Congress:

> The Kuomintang solemnly declares that the right of self-determination is recognised for all the nationalities inhabiting China; following the victory of the revolution over the imperialists and militarists there will be established a free and united (formed on the basis of a voluntary union of all nationalities) Chinese republic. (Cited in Louis 1979: 114)

Later this policy of self-determination was completely abandoned, both in theory and practice, by the Kuomintang. Sun Yat-sen also advocated a federal system that would curb the power of the central government and grant autonomy to the provinces and minority regions. This was abandoned by Sun himself when he witnessed the rise of regional militarists (*geju*). Chen Duxiu, a radical Marxist, also discredited the idea of federalism. Chen, who had originally favoured self-government and federalism, realised that the circumstances of feudalistic politics meant the self-governing movement was doomed to become a pawn in the game of the militarists. If federalism was built upon the aspirations of regional militarists, it could, he concluded, never achieve national unity and strength (Duara 1990: 12).

From 1934 to 1935, the national identity and unity issue again rose to prominence. This time there was heated debate among Chinese intellectuals over the 'democracy versus dictatorship' question. In rejecting 'military unification', Hu Shi favoured 'political unification' – which involved the establishment of a national congress where people from different provinces would be invited to take part in national politics. This, he believed, would cultivate the centripetal force that would help to build a strong national identity (Cheng Yishen 1989: 88–91). By contrast, Jiang Tingfu and Chen Zhimai expressed a preference for an authoritarian leadership that could unify China by force. They asserted that the political reality of China was such that the parliament could be closed down by a few soldiers. For them, even though a few representatives were sent to central governmental organisations, those who did not favour unification were considered untrustworthy, as it was felt they might use parliament for political purposes. Here, the problem of fostering national identity was intertwined with the problem of choosing a political system. For liberal intellectuals, democracy was seen as the best means to overcome local division and develop a national identity, while anti-liberal intellectuals saw dictatorship as the best option. In the end, rather than adopting the idea of democratic national identity and unification, Chiang Kai-shek opted for an authoritarian one-party government to combat the warlords and Communists. The Chiang regime had an outward parliamentary form that made no attempt at revolutionary translation of power to the masses. Moreover, when the Japanese army invaded and occupied northern China, most Chinese liberal intellectuals and democrats gave up the democratic enterprise and became nationalists in defence of China's national unity.

The Chinese Communist Party initially entertained the idea of self-determination. In 1945, Mao Zedong wrote, in 'On a Coalition Government', that the future People's China would 'grant nations the right to be their own masters and to voluntarily enter into an alliance with the Han people'. 'All national minorities in China must create, along voluntary and democratic lines, a federation of democratic republics of China.' Revealingly, in the later edition of Mao's *Selected Works* that passage had vanished, the original words 'granting of the right to national self-determination to all national minorities' being replaced by the phrase 'the granting of the right to national autonomy to all national minorities' (Louis 1979: 115). In the early 1950s, Soviet-style federalism was also rejected by the CCP, on the grounds that it would enable various nationalities of China to form separate states and thus allow the national autonomous regions to secede (Louis 1979: 116).

In conclusion, China has confronted the national identity or unity problem and among the various options for dealing with it both nationalist and democratic approaches have been advocated. Ideas of self-determination and federalism, that is, elements of the democratic approach to managing the national identity problem, were adopted by both the nationalist and Communist parties but abandoned immediately after they became powerful. It can be argued that when they came to power, they had an obligation to maintain the unity of China and used the political unity as a basis for their political legitimacy.

The building of a democratic nation-state was advocated by democrats in the later Qing period, and by liberal-minded intellectuals in the 1930s, but it was not taken seriously and never implemented. The winners were always the nationalists, authoritarians or centralists. This was because it was perceived that democracy would undermine the unity of China in the historical circumstance of Japanese invasion. It would seem, therefore, that the fundamental statist traditions override all the differences between the nationalists and Communists.

Any fighting over national territorial integrity is likely to alter the direction of democracy because, as a general rule, whenever the unity of China has been threatened the course of democracy has changed. In the case of such a conflict the drive for national unity is sure to subordinate the claims of the individual, and liberal democracy would give way to an authoritarianism in which the actual and diverse wills of the people are replaced by a leader who, in some mystical fashion, is able to express the national ethos.

The initiation of democratisation in China not only requires the monopoly of power to be broken up, it also needs the national identity issue to be addressed. If Chinese democratisation is seen to threaten the unity of China, history may repeat itself so that democracy is sacrificed in the higher interest of saving the nation-state. We can say, therefore, that state nationalism and democracy are in an intrinsic state of constant tension and contradiction. This inherent tension creates an ominous prospect for democratisation in China.

Rising nationalism during the 1980s and 1990s has revived the debate over democracy versus neo-authoritarianism in modern history. In particular, the national identity question raises a difficult issue for Chinese democrats: through democracy how can they maintain China's unity and reunify Taiwan with China? The next two sections give consideration to the impact of the national identity question on contemporary Chinese democratisation, and analyse the tension between Chinese nationalism and democracy in the contexts of Tibet and Taiwan.

3.4   THE TIBET QUESTION

The problem of fixing the boundary between Tibet and China is not a new one; rather it has a considerable history. With the collapse of the Qing dynasty, the Dalai Lama declared independence from China. The Dalai Lama's idea of Greater Tibet claims thousands of square kilometres of territory in the province of Qinghai, Gansu, Sichuan and Yunnan that have been under Chinese administration and jurisdiction since 1949 and is regarded by Beijing as a challenge to its territorial integrity. The idea also challenges the founding principle of the Chinese modern state, in which all territorial issues are closed off. If the Dalai Lama's idea of Tibetan territory is accepted, it would create a precedent that other nationalities may follow.

The Chinese state's fear of the disintegrating effects of democratisation has resulted in resistance to implementing true autonomy in Tibet. The break-up of the Soviet Union and 'peaceful evolution' in Eastern Europe were alarming precedents for Chinese leaders who mischaracterised these events. Chen Kuiyuan, Party Secretary of the Tibet Autonomous Region (TAR) (1992–2000), explained China's tough policies towards Tibet by referring to international changes in the post-Cold War era: 'Especially under the influence of the international macro-environment, separatist activities have intensified in Tibet and the situation of the anti-separatist struggle has sharpened. These factors are causing political instability' (Karmel 1995: 494). China's official press also claimed that the Dalai Lama's supporters harboured 'a hidden motive': 'They want to take advantage of [turmoil] to split China. To be frank, they want to bring about another "Bosnia-Herzegovina" in China! But China is not Yugoslavia' (cited in Karmel 1995: 494).

The CCP has little faith in democracy and believes that it is democracy and human rights discourses that have brought down the USSR. Its monopoly on political power makes it difficult to accept a solution based on the devolution of power. The CCP also resists any type of federalism that would result in a transfer of political power from the centre to localities. Unlike the Indonesian government, which is willing to grant concessions to East Timor and Aceh, since Han Chinese have the predominant position and bargaining power, they are reluctant to make concessions to Tibet. The rise of China as a world power may make it even more unwilling to accept a democratic procedure based on compromise and power-sharing. Moreover, China's self-righteousness about its control of Tibet, and its sense of having suffered under Western imperialism, exclude any democratic thinking on the Tibet issue.

Furthermore, the CCP does not recognise the right to self-determination nor does it allow for the right to secede. In China, only the state has the right to define territorial boundaries, and it does so through diplomatic efforts rather than through democratic mechanisms, as shown by China's settlement of the Hong Kong issue. Chinese leaders strongly believe that the state has the right to suppress any secessionist movements by whatever measures (carrot and stick). The argument against secession is grounded on communitarian (or collectivist) claims that are supported by state-sponsored nationalism. Individual consent has little value in this regard and is, at best, a supplement to the power of the state. In the Confucian tradition, secessionists will lose their appeal if their claim is grounded on material considerations. What has happened in the Baltic republics would be quite inconceivable in China. It would be regarded as selfish, and secessionists are not able to mobilise people on such grounds. For this reason, the disparity between rich and poor regions may not lead to support for secession, but may undermine the unity of the state by changing the power balance between the centre and local regions.

In comparison, Tibetan nationalists demand democracy because they believe it will support their cause. The separation of Tibet from China, they argue, will not damage China's integrity, because it has no legitimate claim over Tibet in the first place. Some Tibetan nationalists cherish the idea of a 'Greater Tibet', one autonomous region that extends into three provinces in China. This radical faction of Tibetan nationalism has been committed to a pan-Tibetan identity since 1959 and is on a collision course with Chinese nationalists over the sensitive internal boundary question.

In contrast, some more moderate Tibetans[2] argue that Chinese nationalism actually has much to gain from democratisation, because it will serve to legitimise the Chinese state and make secession difficult. They maintain that as human rights violations decrease, so the moral force for secession will diminish accordingly. If Tibet enjoys freedom, why should it continue to demand secession? If, despite democratisation, it still wanted to secede, this would be seen as little more than a political power struggle among the Tibetans, which would be unlikely to attract international support. If so, radical Tibetans argue, the most favourable timing for Tibetan secession would be before Chinese democratisation, not after it.[3]

3.5   THE TAIWAN QUESTION

In approaching the Taiwan question, Chinese nationalists appeal to common traditions, history and Chinese culture, because it is the shared history and culture that legitimates Chinese claims over the territories of Taiwan. Thus, Chinese nationalists insist that the fact that Taiwan was historically a province under the Qing empire's rule cannot be denied. Tang Guoqiang, a spokesperson for the Ministry of Foreign Affairs, said clearly: 'No matter what kind of election is to be held in Taiwan, no matter what the outcome of any election, it cannot change the fact that Taiwan is a part of China and a province of China' (*China Times*, 4 December 1997: 9).

Beijing considers a democratic approach to the Taiwan issue unfeasible and undesirable. Qian Qichen, then Minister of Foreign Affairs, for example, said it is illegitimate, fruitless and pointless to declare Taiwan's independence through a referendum (*The People's Daily*, overseas edition, 29 January 1999: 1).

Beijing denounced the referendum held in Tainan in 1998 as the work of a few extreme separatists in favour of Taiwan independence. If a referendum had been held in Taiwan, it would have gone against unification, for Taiwanese nationalism and a democratic spirit have already developed. For Chinese nationalists, the 'One China' policy will never be compromised by democracy or anything else. They see the unification of Mainland China and Taiwan as a primary task in building a strong nation-state. The rationale is that 'Taiwan was an inalienable part of China, thus any self-determination process that might result in a permanent separation was totally unacceptable' (Chiou 1986: 480). In the eyes of Beijing, the One China policy presupposes the membership of the political community of China and the precedence of Chinese national identity over the democratic enterprise. For Chinese nationalists, when there is a dispute over what constitutes 'the people', Chinese nationalism provides the answer. It is a guiding principle for unification that overrides the ideological competition between socialism and the three principles of the people (Zhao 1988: 54–5).

By contrast, a democratising Taiwan increasingly recognises the important role of the people, civil society, public opinion and referendums in settling the Taiwan question. Importantly, Taiwan witnessed the establishment of the Promoting Referendum Foundation on 25 July 1990, and the Association for Promoting Referendum on 17 November 1991. Some members of the DPP have been advocating the idea of establishing an independent state of Taiwan through a referendum. After the DPP suffered a setback in the 1998 election, many party members advocated dropping phrases such as 'establishment of a Republic of Taiwan' and 'determined by referendum'. This proposal was rejected in early 1999 (Lu 1999a: 2). Hsu Hsin-liang, a former party chairperson, also described prospects for a plebiscite on the future of Taiwan as a 'frightening' scenario that would 'bring disaster' to Taiwan (Baum 1999: 28). Both the KMT and the New Party opposed a referendum on independence on the grounds that such national votes could stir up disputes over national status, erode social cohesion, invite China's intervention and threaten the status quo (Lu 1999c: 1). On 24 May 1999, the Ministry of the Interior of the ROC gave its approval to a draft of the initiative and referendum law. This law enables the public to vote on local issues and national policy matters but excludes any vote on national territory and sovereignty, and changes to the name and flag of the country. These powers continue to reside with the National Assembly (Lu 1999b: 2).

On the other hand, Taiwan's democratisation makes it difficult for one party or government to make a promise not to become independent because such a promise cannot be made against the will of the people. Since the democratisation of Taiwan, any significant change with regard to the national identity question cannot take place without consulting the people. As Tien Hungmao (1994: 190) remarked, 'Democratization helps open up the debate over legitimacy of the ROC identity, defined by the KMT ruling elite but increasingly challenged by the advocates of an independent Republic of Taiwan'. Neither can the diplomatic negotiation model of Hong Kong be applied to Taiwan, for diplomacy alone cannot decide its status.

By comparison, because it lacks democratic legitimacy the Chinese leadership is to a large degree dependent on the Taiwan issue for its survival. As Wang Gungwu (1996: 2) points out:

> The theme of reunification is at the heart of restoration nationalism. Restoration is not only an essential part of the structure of legitimacy, the supremacy of continental interests. It is also the best defense against other threats to the sanctity of China's borders. The tense developments of 1995–1996 in cross-straits relations testify to the emotional force that this view of its destiny can still generate.

Beijing insists on military options as a preventative measure against Taiwanese independence, that is, it will not use force to conquer Taiwan, but rather to prevent it from gaining independence. China will use force, according to the White Paper released on 21 February 2000, under three circumstances: (1) a Taiwanese declaration of independence; (2) foreign intervention; and (3) if Taiwan indefinitely refuses peaceful reunification through negotiations. Liu Huaqing, Vice-Chairperson of the Central Military Commission under Jiang Zemin, said clearly that if Taiwan moves towards independence, China will use force to defend its sovereignty (*Cheng Ming*, September 1994: 24). Beijing believes only military force can deter an independence movement in Taiwan. In terms of Machiavellian politics, Beijing does not need to please the 'enemy' by renouncing the use of force. For Beijing, force is a necessary resort (Lin Gang 1996).

Moreover, Chinese politics of national identity operate within the framework of nationalism, where '[a]ny leader who is perceived as soft on this issue [Taiwan] and fails to protect Chinese sovereignty and territorial integrity would be regarded as another Li Hongzhang, a diplomat in the later Qing and discarded by the people' (Chen 1996: 1059). In fact, Jiang Zemin was accused of adopting a soft policy on Taiwan and, in 1994, a tough stance was demanded. Containing Taiwan's independence was, and is, a major task for Chinese nationalism, for no one dares to let Taiwan go. Chinese leaders would not survive if they could not prevent Taiwan from achieving independence. In light of this nationalist framework, therefore, political actors are likely to become more radical and adopt more extreme policies in order to combat Taiwan's independence movement.

Two other factors contribute to a clearer understanding of the conflict between Mainland China and Taiwan. First, both are concerned with identifying the agents which deal with the Taiwan question. The authoritarian state of China recognises only the right of the state to deal with the national identity problem; while a democratic Taiwan increasingly recognises the important role of the people, civil society, public opinion and referendums. The statist solution to the Taiwan question clashes with the belief, held by some members of the DPP, that referendums should decide the question of Taiwan's international position. It should be pointed out that the key issue here is not so much the CCP's slow recognition of, or passive reaction to, democratic development in Taiwan, but more concerned with the nature of political regimes and the ways in which they gain legitimacy.

Second, the conflicting logic is also revealed in the difference in attitudes towards democracy in respect to the Taiwan question. A Chinese nationalist must be a unionist in the sense that she or he must be committed to the cause of unification with Taiwan. For Chinese politicians, the unification of China with Taiwan is a fundamental aim, while democracy is merely a potential means. The Chinese nationalists take an instrumentalist view of democracy: if it can promote unification, they might introduce it; if not, they will reject it. The fact that Beijing talks about unification without mentioning democracy indicates that, in its eyes, democracy is incompatible with unification. When Beijing realises that, in effect, the logic of democratisation favours Taiwan's independence, it will choose to push for unification at the cost of democracy within China. The fact that the DPP talks about both independence and democracy indicates that, in the eyes of Taiwanese nationalists who attempt to establish a republic of Taiwan, democracy is compatible with, and can assist, independence. The DPP therefore intends to declare or maintain *de facto* independence through democratisation and referendums. No wonder Li Jiaquan, a scholar of Taiwan-related affairs at the Chinese Academy of Social Sciences, warns that Taiwan should not use public opinion or democratisation to pursue its independence cause (*The People's Daily*, overseas edition, 23 March 1996).

Zhang Wenmu (2002), a scholar in China's Institute of Contemporary International Relations, argues further that the rise of China as a great power depends on the development of its naval capabilities. Zhang further contends that the Taiwan question is essentially about China's naval right to access the sea. He argues that peace across the Straits will only come from Chinese power and might, not words or good will. In dealing with the Tibet question, Zhang puts forward a strong statist argument for non-secession: when all the nationalities joined the Chinese nation-state, they transferred their right to self-determination to the Chinese state, and as such have no right to withdraw from China's union. In Zhang's eyes, America's promotion of democracy in China is designed both to divide China and to weaken Chinese competitive ability.

3.6   THE ANTI-EMPIRE THESIS ON DEMOCRATIC MECHANISMS

So far I have examined all kinds of arguments against the utility of democracy in confronting the national identity question. In particular, I have tested the empire thesis against the modern Chinese experience, examining the cases of Tibet and Taiwan respectively. Now I would like to propose an anti-empire thesis that the breakdown of China is avoidable when it embarks on democratisation.

Despite the clash between democratisation and China's national identity issue, it is still possible to embark along a path of democratisation and avoid the logic of breakdown at the same time. We should not assume an outcome based on historical determinism; there are roles for human agency. Through democratisation we can address the legitimacy issue of the CCP and address the national identity question. China may prove to be an exception in that it may avoid breakdown when it embarks on democratisation. There are a number of reasons for this scenario, as explored below.

Firstly, contemporary China has become a post-empire state in the sense that China has built a modern form of the state with imperial legacies. The political structure in China, with its foundation in the Qing empire, has transformed dramatically; today's China has witnessed the centralised political system with autonomous regions, the blurring of ethnic boundaries (Chapter 8) and the overwhelming spread of *Putonghua* (Chapter 9). Using its new political language, Beijing never describes present-day China as an 'empire'; instead, it refers to the country as 'a socialist country' or 'modern China'. It aims to deal with the imperial past through this reconstruction of language. With this understanding, China is no longer the 'last' empire, but rather a new modern state or a sort of post-empire state.

More importantly, China can take advantage of the positive legacies of its imperial history. China has built its modern state not within a 'one nation-one state' framework, but rather created it within its implicit imperial framework and history. Due to the imperial history, different ethnic groups have migrated and lived in different areas in a mixed configuration. This makes it difficult for one ethnic group to exclude others. They have to live together. In addition, China can learn lessons from the past experiences of other empires and invent new mechanisms to deal with the challenges. Importantly, therefore, China, which has learnt a great deal from the collapse of the Soviet Union, will do its best to avoid the same fate.

Secondly, China has a modern history of avoiding the breakdown of its territories. From the later Qing to the Republic of China, despite being in a weak position, China was able to hold its Qing territories – with the exception of Outer Mongolia, which was successful in achieving independence. In the 1990s, both Hong Kong and Macau returned to China. This reunification contrasts with the disintegration of the former Soviet Union. China's history of unity and China's capacity to recover and to rebuild a strong state are deemed remarkable in world history and will arguably help China to maintain the unity of the Chinese modern state. There are many factors that have contributed to the maintenance of nationality unity, including the impact of a majority Han ethnicity, and the role of linguistic imperialism, which will be discussed in detail in Chapter 9. In addition, Chinese leaders are unified in their approach to dealing with the national identity question.

Thirdly, the dramatic rise of China with its impressive economic development may modify the logic of the empire thesis because a rising power is unlikely to experience disintegration. A Greater China economic zone precludes the possibility of secession, and increases the chances of Tibetans deciding they will be better off staying part of China. Economic development is now making China more attractive to potential secessionists on the peripheries. Many Mongols and Uyghurs who left China and went to the Republic of Mongolia and to Central Asian countries are now returning to China because of its high standard of living. During a visit to China by Tibetan exile officials in 2003, they were overwhelmed by China's economic development, thus strengthening the idea that Tibet is better off staying in China than seeking independence.[4] As the Dalai Lama said, 'the best guarantee for Tibet' is to 'remain within the People's Republic of China', and 'more union, more cooperation is in our best interest' (Tibetan Bulletin, September–October 2003: 24). Of course, economic development and migration of Han Chinese has also increased the tension between the Han and Tibetans. Economic development does not provide a final and safe solution (Chapters 2 and 8).

Fourthly, the rise of China and its increasingly influential global position limits the ability for external actors to press for territorial change. China's fundamental position within the global marketplace arguably serves to strengthen its national unity. For example, if the USA's policy towards China aims to maintain the unity of China because it doesn't want to pay its high cost of dealing with the negative consequences of a collapse of China, it will create the condition of the absence of external threats from a super-power. China's democratisation will likely be able to develop much more easily when not simultaneously responding to a disintegration of the Chinese state.

Fifthly, the most important fact is that democracy can offer a solution to deal with the dilemma of the empire thesis. Democratisation cuts two ways when dealing with the national boundary question. On the one hand, democratisation processes make independence or secession much more likely to succeed. Democratisation has facilitated successful secession in contexts such as the former Soviet Union, Pakistan,[5] Ethiopia and Yugoslavia. On the other hand, democratisation can strengthen the unity of states. Spain, the Philippines, South Africa, St Kitts and Nevis, Papua New Guinea, Nigeria and Turkey, for example, have all been democratised in the third wave of democratisation, and have maintained the unity of their states. Democratisation helps them to contain secession problems and maintain the unity of states. (Of course, other factors, such as the stability of a democratic regime, international relations and diplomatic efforts, also come into play.) This is because national elections legitimise the political unit and support the regime's claim to legitimacy. Democratic packages, such as de-centralisation and regional autonomy, have also accommodated secessionist demands.

Take for example the democratisation experience in Spain where statewide elections, in 1976 and 1977, provided the state with legitimate power to restructure the polity and negotiate with separatists. As a result, '*none* of the important state wide interest groups or parties engage in *system blame*' (Linz and Stepan 1996: 99) and the percentage of the population demanding independence in Catalonia and Pais Vasco-Navarra dramatically dropped after the 1979 Referendum on Devolution of Power to the Autonomies. Moreover, elections provided a political contract and legitimacy for the unity of the Spanish state. The statute of Basque's autonomy was approved by the voters in the affected region with 94.4 per cent of the 57 per cent of eligible voters favouring the proposed statute (Clark 1989: 22). This referendum can be interpreted as a contract, which the Basque region signed with the Spanish state, under which the Basque region was granted autonomous powers in return for recognising the unity of Spain. Nevertheless, this does not mean that democratisation offers a final 'solution' to the national identity problem. A small section of the Basque people still demand independence despite the decrease in public support for the terrorist organisation ETA (Linz and Stepan 1996: 105).

Sixthly, for further democratisation to successfully occur in China, while still maintaining China's territorial integrity and thus catering to the concerns of Chinese nationalists (and the CCP), a number of safeguards should be established. These could include – but are not limited to – establishing a sequence of elections, with national elections conducted first followed by provincial elections (B. He 2001a), and introducing the process of conciationalism (to be examined in Chapter 8). China could also adopt measures that have been successful in other countries, such as Indonesia's experience of emphasising loyalty to the nation-state through banning violence, but protecting the freedom of speech; banning one ethnic-based party and allowing only multi-ethnic parties; and banning political parties that advocate secession but making it permissible for individuals to write about it. The case of Canada where the system balances between the right to referendums and the right to consultation could also provide useful inputs for China.

3.7   CONCLUSION

An analysis of the centrality of the national identity problem, and its impact on Chinese democratisation, demonstrates the reasons why nationalism has prevailed and democratisation has been delayed in China. The prediction that rapid democratisation would follow in the wake of Deng Xiaoping's death has not been realised. On the contrary, post-Deng Xiaoping China has witnessed the very slow progress of democratisation. This is because, fearful of repeating the Soviet experience, Chinese leaders have delayed full-scale democratisation in order to enhance the strength of the nation's identity and thus avoid the potential threat of disintegration.

The Party/state has now taken advantage of the national identity question and appropriated it as part of what might be called a 'crisis management programme'. Chinese leaders seem to propagate the idea that democracy threatens the unity of China and undermines the pan-Chinese national identity project. State nationalists disseminate the view that the USA's promotion of democracy is a conspiracy aimed at China's disintegration. Leaders convince people that China faces the possibility of breaking up. They have invented an equation that the CCP equals China: if the

CCP collapses, China will break up. Such a formulated idea has penetrated into people's minds and many people think that the CCP is the only organisation that is able to maintain the unity of China. The Party/state seems to be dependent upon such an argument as a basis of its legitimacy and thus constructs anti-democratisation as the basis of power.

The official view above may prove a source of problems, as it adopts the denial approach to the national identity problem and a rejection of the role of democracy. An alternative is to develop an anti-empire thesis that explores how democracy can help to address the national identity question. A variety of democratic mechanisms is available to China to democratically manage the national identity problem. These will be explored further in the proposition of a federalism solution to the Taiwan question (Chapter 4), use of the referendum mechanism (Chapter 5), movement towards political representation and equality (Chapter 6), opportunities for dialogue and engagement between Confucianism and liberalism (Chapter 7), the development of genuine autonomy in Tibet (Chapter 8), development of the multi-linguistic policy (Chapter 9), and the proposition of a deliberative approach towards Tibetan autonomy (Chapter 10).

NOTES

1. http://www.asahi.com/english/opinion/TKY200405110126.html, accessed 12 May 2004. Thanks to Dr Lam Peng-er for this information.
2. The author's conversation with Lobsang Sangay at Harvard University in March 2008.
3. The author's conversations with Professor Samdhong Rinpoche, then Speaker of the Tibetan Parliament in Exile and Director of the Central Institute of Higher Tibetan Studies in Hobart on 20–21, 24 and 28 April 1998.
4. The author's conversation with Lodi Gyari in Singapore in 2003.
5. In the case of Bangladesh secession, it was a long process. Bengali became an official language together with Urdu in the 1950s. Bangladesh demanded a level of autonomy in the 1954 'Twenty-one Points', then a loose federal system in the 'Six Points' in 1966, and finally secession in 1971 in the wake of the Awami League's victory, with a 75 per cent vote, in the 1970 December election.

PART 2

On Taiwan

4 Nationalism, Democratisation and the Taiwan Question

This chapter aims to develop an understanding of the rise of Taiwanese nationalism associated with Taiwanese democratisation, and the impact of Taiwanese democratisation on the politics of the national identity question. It will also examine the possible effects of Chinese democratisation on the resolution to the national identity conflicts across the Taiwan Strait, and the relationship between democratisation, federalism and the resolution of the conflict between Taiwan and the Mainland.

The chapter begins with a discussion of the national identity question in Taiwan and the rise of neo-nationalism in Taiwan. It then investigates the impact of democratisation on the Taiwan national identity question, in particular the hypothetically possible and plural impacts of Chinese democratisation. The chapter develops several hypotheses concerning the impact of Chinese democratisation on the resolution of the Taiwan question. The idea of federalism, as a super-national arrangement which could manage national identity conflicts, its limits and resistance to it, is also discussed, with the suggestion that the PRC should be renamed Huaxiang Guo.

4.1 THE NATIONAL IDENTITY QUESTION

Taiwan possesses a number of unique historical, political and social characteristics that differentiate it from the Chinese Mainland. Taiwan's colonial history includes half a century of Japanese colonial rule from 1895 to 1945, during which time the introduction of the Japanese education system and language had a major effect on Taiwanese culture (Copper 2003: 16). Not only did Taiwan possess unified and modern systems of law, administration and education, but Taiwanese who had grown up under Japanese rule had also been introduced to a worldview in which Taiwan, as part of the Japanese empire, was superior to China (Chu & Lin 2001: 112). In the second half of the twentieth century, Western culture also became much more influential in Taiwan than on the Mainland. Political development has also taken a completely different path to that of the Mainland. After early decades under the control of the Kuomintang (KMT) government of Chiang Kai-shek and then his son Chiang Ching-kuo, from the late 1980s Taiwan began to move away from a system of government that claimed to represent the whole of China and towards a stand-alone democracy. In 1996 the first direct presidential election was held and since then rule of the country has changed hands between the KMT and the Democratic Progressive Party (DPP), indicating the consolidation of Taiwan's democratic system (Copper 2005). Unlike on the Mainland, where traditional family relations and many feudal customs were suppressed by the Communist Party, in Taiwan these customs and traditional relationships continued for much longer, although traditional family relations were challenged as modernisation and nation-building gained pace in Taiwan (Copper 2003: 70). Religious observance and religious tolerance has also flourished on Taiwan in the absence of the kind of official control and even persecution that has existed on the Mainland (Copper 2003: 82).

Despite these differences, it has been argued that Taiwan and the Mainland share a common cultural heritage and Taiwan 'has no clear national identity but rather an unresolved national identity dilemma' (Dittmer 2005: 85). The question of Taiwan's independence did not arise during the Chiang regimes because both the KMT and the CCP shared an imagined community and reunification that was taken for granted. Despite holding different ideological positions, both Mao Zedong and Chiang Kai-shek held the same view about the future of the Chinese nation-state: that it should include Mainland China and Taiwan. In this sense, both were Chinese nationalists beyond their ideological differences.

Under Chiang's regime, there was no national identity question except the 'provinces problem'. People in Taiwan were classified into two groups: *benshengren*, the people from the province of Taiwan; and *waishengren*, the people from other provinces of China. The 'provinces problem' referred to the sensitive relations between Taiwanese and Mainlanders. It involved, for example, the issue concerning the fair distribution of public office positions among the two groups. It should be noted, however, that there also were and still are significant differences and even conflict between the Taiwanese *benshengren* from Hakka and Fujianese backgrounds (Copper 2003: 72).

Since the beginning of democratisation, in 1978, the unification forces have gradually eroded, while the pro-independence forces have increasingly grown in Taiwan. The DPP now challenges the assumption of reunification, which was previously unquestionable on Taiwan and remains sacrosanct on the Mainland. Huang Xinjie (Huang Hsin-chieh), former chairperson of the DPP, for example, asserts that the presumption of reunification is due to Chinese psychology.[1] The DPP has challenged the assumption that Taiwan is simply one province of China, and has refused to use the concepts of *benshengren* and *waishengren*, so that the so-called 'provinces problem' has now disappeared, at least for Taiwanese nationalists. It has now transformed into Taiwan's national identity question; that is, Taiwan is one unique nation and is entitled to have its own independent state. Today, Taipei is ruling out the issue of Taiwan's unification with China, and reunification ceased to be an electoral issue in the 1996 presidential election in Taiwan. Meanwhile, independence, from *de facto* independence to formal recognition by the international community, has become an important issue.

It is difficult to categorise Taiwan's national identity question in terms of ethnicity. Arguably, most people are perceived to belong to the same race and use the same written language while speaking different dialects (however, this view is now challenged by the DPP). Mainlanders and the Taiwanese are best regarded as sub-'ethnic' groups. The group who came to the island prior to or during the 1895–1945 period of Japanese rule, and speak Hokkien or Hakka, are usually referred to as the 'Taiwanese', who make up the majority of the population. The remainder are Mainlanders who fled to Taiwan, after 1945, and their descendants. By the mid-1980s, however, less than 6 per cent of Taiwan's population was born on the Mainland and most of the 'Mainlanders' were in fact born in Taiwan (Copper 2003: 15). The focal point in the national identity issue in Taiwan is the relationship between Taiwan and China. While those deeply attached to Chinese culture and tradition tend to identify themselves as Chinese, pro-independence Taiwanese are more inclined to take an active part in the construction of a new Taiwanese national identity. Independence has far more supporters among the Taiwanese than among the Mainlanders. Copper has pointed out that many Taiwanese who trace their origins to Fujian only see themselves as Chinese in the sense that European Americans might regard themselves as European (Copper 2003: 74). According to a 1992 survey, 39.5 per cent of Taiwanese respondents supported independence, compared to only 18.5 per cent of Mainlander respondents (Wu 1993: 48). However, sub-ethnic conflicts in Taiwan's politics have been successfully contained as a result of the intermingling of Mainlanders and Taiwanese; the Taiwanisation of the KMT; the abolition of register systems, which has eradicated the official categories of 'Mainlanders' and 'Taiwanese'; cross-political support (Taiwanese support for the KMT, and Mainlander support for the DPP); and the cooperation between the DPP and the New Party in the Legislative Yuan. Over time, ethnic differences between Mainlanders and Taiwanese are disappearing and will likely continue to decrease in importance (Copper 2003: 76).

The national identity question of Taiwan is a political question, rather than a cultural or ethnic one. Although aboriginal culture had some influence over the development of Chinese culture in Taiwan, Chinese culture is dominant at both regional and national levels (Copper 2003: 16). Professor Shih Cheng-Feng, Taiwanese scholar, acknowledges that, culturally and ethnically, the Taiwanese may be considered Chinese, or more properly Han. But the issue is that people sharing the same cultural heritage do not have to accept the same political entity, as shown by the case of Australia and England (Shih 1997: 25).

4.2 INVENTING A NEW NATION

It should be acknowledged that Taiwan's nationalism is still in the making and there are different versions and evaluations of it. Here we only outline the main elements and the ways in which it facilitates the construction of a new nation.

Reinterpretations of people, history, culture and language are the main methods used to construct a neo-Taiwanese nationalism.

The rise of Taiwanese neo-nationalism has been associated with the DPP, which has invented and promoted Taiwan's identity as distinct from Chinese identity.[2] A distinctive Taiwan identity is also expected by other countries in the international system: if Taiwan wants to be a member of the international community, it must give up its claim as a genuine representative of China. The rise of Taiwan's nationalism can be understood with reference to the international system. Taiwan lost its seat in the UN in 1971; and currently it is only recognised by twenty-three countries. China remains firmly opposed to Taiwan's admittance to the UN, on the grounds that this would constitute dual membership for a region which is already a member by virtue of being a Chinese province. Beijing has been trying to force Taipei into accepting China's terms for reunification by marginalising it internationally through diplomatic manoeuvering. Ironically, such efforts have prompted Taiwan's ongoing search for international status and for a distinct national identity of its own (Dittmer 2005). Taiwan is compelled to expand its international status in a world order divided into states, lest it be pushed out of the international community into isolation. Taiwan, therefore, has much to gain from *de jure* or formal independence, and international recognition for its separate political entity, but little to lose except an increasingly ludicrous dream by some to retake the Mainland.

History also provides some clues to the issue of Taiwan's emerging nationalism. Taiwanese nationalism has been developing since the process of anti-alien resistance in the seventeenth century (Shih 1994, 2000). Taiwan was first a colony of Holland, then was under the rule of Zheng Chenggong (military general under the Ming Dynasty) between 1662 and 1683; Qing rule 1683–1893; Japanese rule 1895–1945; and the KMT's authoritarian rule from 1945 until the 1990s. As the first colony of Japan, it was deemed a symbol of Japanese imperialist power and was thus elevated as an example of cooperation with the New Order in East Asia. The Japanese ruled the island with due consideration of its socio-political traditions, although Taiwanese were discriminated against and did not enjoy the benefits of full Japanese citizenship, despite officially being Japanese subjects (Chu & Lin 2001: 106). Taiwan had civil government, while Korea had a Japanese military government (Jeon 1992). Taiwanese ethnic consciousness began clearly to emerge under Japanese rule, although it did not yet reach the status of a major nationalist movement (Chu & Lin 2001: 108). Further, the KMT's killing and suppression of indigenous Taiwanese, in the wake of its occupation in the 1940s, sparked hatred towards the KMT and created an impetus for self-rule by the Taiwanese.

The history of Taiwan has also been reinterpreted by Taiwanese nationalists. They reject the view that Taiwan shares a 5,000-year history with China, and declare that Taiwan is only about 400 years old, beginning with Holland's colonisation but developing fast under Japanese colonisation. To some degree, Taiwanese nationalism is pro-Japan and considers Japan's colonisation as positive and constructive for Taiwan's economic development. At the same time it regards the KMT's rule as ruthless, negative and exploitative.[3] Cheng-Feng Shih (1994, 2000) argues that Chinese influence on the Taiwanese nationalist movement was 'negligible', while Japanese liberal impacts were surprisingly more crucial. It is argued further, that after fifty years of Japanese colonisation, the Taiwanese must have, unintentionally or intentionally, gained certain Japanese cultural characteristics, ranging from customs to housing, food, clothing and language. The Taiwanese were even proud to join the Japanese imperial armed forces. As supporting evidence, Shih (2000) cites the example of Li Yuan-che, a Taiwanese-American and a 1986 Nobel Prize winner, who recalled one time that he had never felt he was Chinese, even when Taiwan was returned to China in the wake of the Second World War. Shih (2000), however, notes that Han culture had been used as a symbolic weapon to rally nationalist support in order to counter alien Dutch, Manchu and Japanese culture in Taiwan. While some Taiwanese elites tactically emphasised their status as Japanese citizens to push for equal rights during the colonial period, others emphasised their distinctiveness to argue Taiwan should have its own parliament, and Han identity remained strong for most people (Chu & Lin 2001: 108, 111).

An excellent example of rewriting history is a series of textbooks for some 350,000 junior high school students that caused heated debate in Taiwan. On 22 June 1997, new Party Legislator Lee Ching-hua charged that the volumes on history and society promoted Taiwan independence and were loaded with pro-Japanese and anti-Chinese sentiments. According to Lee, the two volumes seemed to glorify Japan's 1895–1945 colonisation of Taiwan, and the two textbooks did not use the terms 'Chinese' or 'the Chinese people' at all. Instead, the term 'Taiwanese' was used (Sheng 1997: 4). Moreover, the reference to Sun Yat-sen as the 'founding father' was removed.

The DPP, with its nationalist reconstruction efforts, has resisted the use of Mandarin, a cultural symbol of Chinese identity. Instead, Taiwanese nationalists have used a distinctive Min-Nan dialect. Cheng-Feng Shih argues that the term 'dialect' blurs the exact extent of the linguistic differences and is somewhat misleading, since 'dialect' may only suggest differences in pronunciation and tone for the same word. Shih (1998, 2000) asserts that the differences between Hoklo/Hakka and Mandarin are even more marked, including not only different pronunciation and tone, but also distinctive grammar features and different lexical items. The prevalence of Hoklo and Hakka-Taiwanese is noticeable during election campaigns, when Hoklo and Hakka are deemed imperative to attract native Taiwanese voters (Sheng 1997: 5). The revival of Taiwanese folk literature is basically a movement to translate spoken Taiwanese into a written form in the hope of consolidating a Taiwanese national identity against a Chinese one (Shih 1998, 2000).

The promotion of Taiwanese language is not only concerned with the construction of a new Taiwanese national identity, but also with the distribution of power and cultural resources. In the past, and even today, some Taiwanese have perceived that speaking 'properly', that is, speaking Mandarin, is the only way to become upwardly mobile, and therefore have consciously adopted Mandarin exclusively at home. However, for the Taiwanese masses entangled in the structure of the vertical division of labour, Hoklo or Hakka-Taiwanese is their main media of daily communication, as long as they do not seek a job in government institutions (Sheng 1997: 5). To demand Hoklo or Hakka as the official and national language is to empower Hoklo or Hakka speakers and to diminish the domination of Mandarin and its associated elite class.

Chen Shui-bian's administration took a number of symbolic steps while in office to emphasise the uniqueness of Taiwan's national identity. This included in 2003 adding 'Taiwan' (in roman letters, not Chinese characters) to the cover of the Republic of China passport, renaming parks and streets to emphasise Taiwan's distinct history, and promoting textbooks that take a Taiwanese perspective (Dittmer 2005: 84). Some official documents and national monuments were changed under Chen's administration to refer to Taiwan rather than the ROC (Chang & Holt 2007: 141), although some were later changed back following the 2008 KMT victory. A process of cultural Taiwanisation took place under the DPP, with the promotion of the academic field of 'Taiwan Studies', a Taiwan-centric school history curriculum, and the promotion of Taiwan's distinct aboriginal culture for tourism and 'branding' purposes (Chang 2004).

Taiwan nationalism is criticised by scholars and writers from China, Taiwan and overseas. Yin Wan-Lee argues against the view that Taiwan, as a nation, is based on its unique language by pointing out that Fujianese (Fukienese) originates from the southern region of Fujian (Fukien) Province in China and continues to be a dialect in that region. It is also identical to Mandarin in writing, in grammatical structure and most of the vocabulary. As spoken dialects, there is no greater difference between Fukienese and Mandarin than, for example, between Cantonese and Mandarin (Yin 1995). Many people in Taiwan still think of themselves as both Chinese and Taiwanese. One survey conducted since 1992 has found that the percentage of respondents who see themselves as both Taiwanese and Chinese has fluctuated between a high of 49.3 per cent, which was reached in 1996, and a low of 39.6 per cent, which was reached in 1998 and again in 2012 (Election Study Center–National Chengchi University). This constitutes a challenge to *exclusive* Taiwanese nationalism which focuses on difference: for example, 'We are Taiwanese, and you are Chinese!' A radical proposal by exclusive Taiwan nationalists is that national treasures, displayed in Taiwan, should be returned to Beijing in order to cut off the cultural link with China.

Since Ma Ying-Jeou took over as president in 2008, his administration has shifted away from the strong promotion of a distinct Taiwanese identity, although Ma has also tried to avoid appearing too close to China. Economic ties with the Mainland have deepened through the introduction of the Economic Cooperation Framework Agreement (ECFA), while cultural ties have also been strengthened by taking steps to increase interaction between the two sides, such as the administration's decision to open Taiwanese universities to students from China. Although the ECFA was controversial, during the campaign for the 2012 presidential election the DPP leader Tsai Ing-wen promised that her party would not repeal the agreement or other links established with the Mainland under Ma's administration (Chen 2012: 74–5).

4.3   NEO-NATIONALISM IN TAIWAN

Taiwanese neo-nationalism is a popular phenomenon, coming from below, originating in the 'local' and the public, and building on a genuine sense of Taiwanese identity. A quantitative indicator of the 'popularity' of Taiwanese nationalism can be found in the results of six surveys conducted in 1998, which found that around 38 per cent of the respondents saw themselves as Taiwanese. The proportion of the population identifying as Taiwanese has increased steadily since then. In 2012, 53.7 per cent saw themselves as 'Taiwanese', 39.6 per cent as 'Both Taiwanese and Chinese' and only 3.1 per cent as 'Chinese'.[4] For Taiwanese nationalists, Chinese state nationalism, whether the Mainland Chinese or orthodox KMT version, is not genuine; only the sentiments of the Taiwanese people can provide the foundations of an authentic nationalism. Contemporary Taiwanese nationalism criticises the Republic of China, and its state nationalism, for suppressing Taiwanese nationalism and the discourse of independence (Chun 1994: 69). Taiwan's nationalists have challenged the official nationalism, envisioning the Taiwan of the future as an independent state, built on an indigenous (pre-Japanese, pre-KMT) history.

Taiwanese popular nationalism has undermined the old state nationalism of the KMT. The KMT's old state nationalism in Taiwan, linked to the project of unification, has become weaker, and its anti-Communist identity has faded into history. Moreover, the KMT cultivates an indigenous image, with its indigenous wing seeking the recognition of Taiwan as a sovereign entity. The Taiwanisation of the KMT, an increasingly free and assertive mass media, and an awakening electorate, all have challenged the assumption that the Mainlander–KMT elite can impose its vision of unification on the remaining segments of Taiwan's relevant political strata (Tien 1994: 189).

The concept of the 'New Taiwanese', advocated by former President Lee Teng-hui in December 1998 (or earlier in 1995), indicates that Taiwanese nationalism has already developed into a kind of neo-state nationalism. Over the years, steps have been taken to instil, within the younger generation of Mainlanders, the notion that they too are Taiwanese. In his later years, Chiang Ching-kuo frequently remarked that, having lived in Taiwan for so long, he considered himself to be both Chinese and Taiwanese (Yu 1998: 6). There is considerable evidence that Mainlanders, living in Taiwan, will increasingly consider themselves Taiwanese. Surveys have found that the proportion of the population who consider themselves 'Chinese' fell from 25.5 per cent in 1992 to 3.1 per cent in 2012, while the proportion who consider themselves 'Taiwanese' increased from 17.6 per cent to 53.7 per cent over the same period (Election Study Center–National Chengchi University). This means that those who consider themselves only Taiwanese now make up a majority of the population, although the percentage who consider themselves both Taiwanese and Chinese remains significant, at 39.6 per cent.

The notion of the New Taiwanese was used by the opposition DPP in calling upon Mainlanders living in Taiwan to relinquish what it called their 'greater China' mentality (Yu 1998: 6). It was not adopted as official ideology until President Lee presented the idea of the New Taiwanese as a means of promoting national harmony during campaigning for the 5 December 1998 legislative, mayoral and city council elections (Chang 1998: 1). Lee appealed to voters to support his party's candidate for Taipei mayor, describing the candidate, Ma Ying-jeou, as a 'New Taiwanese'. The concept of New Taiwanese aims to nurture a common identity among the various sub-ethnic groups and to unite all citizens in the pursuit of political reforms. Ma's subsequent victory, and the victory of the KMT in a solid majority of seats in the Legislature, indicate that the New Taiwanese identity had taken shape (Chang 1998: 1). A survey of Taipei city citizens, conducted by the *United Daily News* in the wake of the December 1998 election, found that 68 per cent of the respondents agreed with the New Taiwanese concept promoted by the ruling party (Chung 1999: 13). Even the New Party recognised the concept of New Taiwanese. The consensus on the new Taiwanese, reached by main political parties, albeit with different interpretations, indicates the formation of a civic and territorial notion of Taiwan's identity.

Although a discourse of New Taiwanese has become an element of state nationalism, there are at least two differences between this neo-state nationalism and radical popular nationalism. First, radical Taiwanese nationalists emphasise the exclusive nature of Taiwanese nationalism; from this perspective, Taiwanese are not Chinese. By contrast, Lee's understanding of New Taiwanese does not exclude the notion of a Chinese identity, for he envisions that New Taiwanese will become 'New Chinese' once a free and democratic system is established in Mainland China (Yu 1998: 6). Eminent dissident, Wei Jingsheng, supports the use of the term 'New Taiwanese', although he insists that Taiwanese people are also Chinese people. As he put it, 'A white horse is still a horse' (*Free China Review* 1999). Second, the concept of New Taiwanese implies a civic and territorial definition of Taiwan's identity; that is, people living in Taiwan should identify with the Taiwan Island as their home. By contrast, radical nationalists advocate a cultural or ethnic notion of Taiwanese identity; that is, Taiwanese are seen as a nationality with a unique culture, history and ethnicity.

Taiwanese nationalists argue that the government of Taiwan should not concern itself with the suffering of overseas Chinese in Indonesia because they are not Taiwanese; and that the government of Taiwan should not encourage the teaching of Chinese overseas. Taiwanese nationalism challenges the fundamental assumptions of overseas or borderless Chinese nationalism. For example, they think the description of Taiwanese democratisation as 'the first Chinese democratization' (Chao & Myers 1998) is inappropriate. Taiwanese nationalism demands a new constitution, which is, above all, a question of the political community, its territoriality and people, and its political structure. Taiwanese nationalists perceive the idea of popular sovereignty as the foundation for a new independent state. In 1994, the DPP convened a 'people's constitution conference' calling for a new national flag (*Central Daily News*, 27 June 1994). In the 1996 election, there was a consensus that Taiwan's president must be Taiwanese. And, moreover, the DPP aims to solve the national identity problem through a referendum on gaining formal independence from Mainland China.

Although holding different visions of Taiwan's future, Chinese pan-nationalists and Taiwanese nationalists share the view that the independence of Taiwan means the failure of China's reunification project, and China's reunification with Taiwan implies the failure of the DPP's independence project. This kind of nationalist thinking leads people across the Taiwan Strait to think that this is a zero sum game in which one side must lose so that the other can win, and consequently compromise over the national identity question is thought to be difficult, if not impossible. However, it is worthwhile drawing attention to another way of thinking whereby we can see the old boundary/identity problem in a new light. The idea of 'ambiguity about boundaries' suggests that some boundary questions can be pursued in an ambiguous way so that boundaries are not clearly demarcated, and exclusive authority over boundaries is not established. An example is the 1998 referendum in Northern Ireland, which was not clear about whether to pursue reunification with Ireland or maintain unity with the UK. This may be positive and beneficial in that it helps to avoid conflicts and clashes. Such ambiguity is a key component of the tolerance of liberal-democracy.

4.4   THE IMPACT OF DEMOCRATISATION ON THE NATIONAL IDENTITY QUESTION

The effects of democratisation on Taiwan's national identity question are complex. People have different notions of 'positive' or 'negative' effects depending on their political positions. One may argue that the democratisation of Taiwan has facilitated unification, and made exchanges across the Taiwan Strait possible. The business sector has made use of the opportunity provided by democratisation to transfer its surplus capital and technology to Mainland China, despite restrictions imposed by Taiwan's government. Such increasing exchanges and economic interdependence could facilitate unification. Nevertheless, the democratisation of Taiwan has strengthened forces for independence more than those for unification. Democratisation, combined with other factors, such as a growing native nationalism in Taiwan, a history of Japanese colonial rule and the KMT's suppression of the Taiwanese, the isolation of Taiwan in international relations and the Mainland's blockade policy, has contributed to the independence movement.

The effects of democratisation on the independence movement can be analysed through the themes of protection of political and civil liberties, political competition among parties, and political elections, and their impact on the strategies of political parties over Taiwan's national identity question.

Taiwan's democratisation has made it possible to discuss and construct Taiwan's national identity. The democratisation of Taiwan has provided the protection of political and civil liberties, and the relaxation of political controls on mass media and individual expression. Under Chiang's regime, those who openly discussed the independence of Taiwan were heavily punished. Today, people can openly speak about independence without fear. Furthermore, since democratisation, opposition parties have been allowed to exist and expand to the point where they have won major victories in national elections.

Democratisation has redistributed political power and resources between Mainlanders and Taiwanese in favour of the latter. The influence and power of pro-unification groups have decreased, while pro-independence forces have gained increasing influence and power. The legislative and political changes in Taiwan in 1991, the DPP's influential seats in the National Assembly, and its successful demand for transparency in Mainland policy have put any secret deal with Beijing out of the question. It was rumoured that secret negotiations across the Taiwan Strait were undertaken under Chiang Ching-kuo's instruction. After Chiang's death, in January 1988, Beijing hoped that Lee Teng-hui would continue the process and send a five-man group for a secret visit to negotiate for reunification. Such a thing did not happen because of dramatic political changes in Taiwan (Sheng Lijun 1998: 69).

Under democratic conditions, political parties have used the national identity issue to shore up political power. To preempt the DPP's ability to exploit sub-ethnic cleavages and the identity issue, President Lee introduced the Taiwanisation of the KMT. This has changed the image of the party from an externally-imposed Mainlander institution to a Taiwanese-controlled party. The Taiwanese component of the party has risen steadily from 15 per cent, in 1976, to 35 per cent in 1988, and again to 54 per cent in 1993. At the same time, the Central Standing Committee's Taiwanese membership rose from 19 per cent, in 1976, to over 60 per cent, in 1993 (Tien 1997: 145). The KMT is now portraying itself with an indigenous image. Its anti-Communist identity has faded into history. The indigenous wing of the KMT is also seeking the recognition of Taiwan as a sovereign entity separate from China. The KMT is using the unification process to create conditions for greater autonomy, or eventual independence (Johnston 1993: 15). Taiwanese KMT elites and some second-generation Mainlanders do not share the vision of unification with Mainland China. As a result, Taiwan has decided to abandon the idea of conquering the Mainland; its idea of nationalism has much less to do with unification than with independence. In the July 1997 fourth round of Constitutional revision, the KMT and DPP worked together to freeze the Taiwan provincial government, which was seen as a symbol of Taiwan's subordination to China.

The electoral results between 1995 and 1998 in Taiwan revealed opposition to both unification and independence. The majority of voters did not take an extreme position, but favoured the middle ground, namely, maintaining the status quo. Arguably, this result is due to a lack of consensus on basic security questions regarding the threat from China, and to the growth of the middle class and its calculation of strategies and choices. In the 1995 parliamentary election, Zhang Shijie, who urged voters to 'Use "One Nation Two Systems" to Save Taiwan', received only 855 votes. The other candidates of the pro-China Labour Party received only 498 and 510 votes respectively (Jacobs 1997: 25). The New Party, a pro-unification party, failed to gain even one post in the 1997 November election for city mayors and county magistrates. In the 1996 Presidential election, the pro-independence DPP won only 21.3 per cent of the vote, and the newly formed Taiwan Independence Party failed to win a single post. As an editor of *The Free China Journal* (5 December 1997: 6) put it: 'The fact that it only garnered 0.19 per cent of the total vote is an unmistakable indication that its secessionist campaign platform has little appeal to Taiwan's increasingly sophisticated voters.'

The outcomes of elections have had an impact on the strategies of the DPP with regard to the independence question. Since electoral support for the DPP decreased partially, due to its independence position, in 1996, a major faction of the DPP has become pragmatic, adjusted its radical independence policy, and moved towards the middle ground. During the campaign period for city mayors and county magistrates, in November 1997, the DPP reoriented its objective. Stepping back slightly from the independence platform, the party channelled its campaign energies towards social welfare issues in Taiwan (Moon & Robinson 1997: 8). Hsu Hsin-liang, the DPP's chairperson, and his Formosa Faction also advocated negotiations with Mainland China on trade, and postal and transportation ties, the so-called 'three direct links'. The strategy paid off at the polls for the DPP, which won an unprecedented victory by taking twelve out of the twenty-three county magistrate and city mayor posts, while the KMT gained only eight. Significantly, at the DPP's symposium in 1998, a pragmatic and progressive consensus was reached. Despite the division within the DDP,[5] it was agreed that Taiwan should be viewed as enjoying independent sovereignty, and that cross-Strait talks should resume first with discussions on economic ties, civilian exchanges and technical issues, and eventually proceed to government-to-government negotiations (V. Sheng 1998b: 1; 1998c: 7). The DPP is becoming much more pragmatic than it was with regard to the independence issue. Some members even suggest that Taiwan should not waste taxpayers' money by maintaining diplomatic relations with a few small countries. The Formosa Faction also urged a bold step to fully open trade relations with the Chinese Mainland on the western side of the Taiwan Strait.

While the DPP took seventy seats in the December 1998 Legislature election, which was seen as a defeat for the party (Lu 1998: 1), the KMT secured 123 of the 225 seats in the new Legislature, representing a solid majority. Moreover, the former Justice Minister, Ma Ying-jeou, of the KMT unseated the DPP's Chen Shui-bian to become the new mayor of Taipei in the December 1998 election. Many party members of the DPP have speculated that advocacy of independence could be frightening away any voters who prefer either the status quo in Taiwan's relations with China or Chinese unification (Lu 1999a: 2). It should be noted that Chen Shui-bian, in his election campaign, insisted that 'the biggest threat to Taiwan's security lies in its national identity', and that 'if Taiwan cannot free itself from the myth that it is part of China, it will have no future' (V. Sheng 1998a: 2). In early 1999, many party members of the DPP argued that phrases such as 'establishment of a Republic of Taiwan' and 'determined by referendum' should be revised but this proposal was rejected (Lu 1999a: 2).

When Ma won the presidential election in 2008, breaking the DPP's eight-year control, cross-Strait relations became much less contentious. The KMT had been making overtures towards Beijing in an attempt to sideline Chen and negate his influence over the relationship. Beijing certainly seemed much more comfortable dealing with the KMT than with Chen and the DPP. It could also be argued that the cross-Strait relationship had already shifted somewhat in the years following Chen's 2004 election victory, with more economic integration between the two sides and more Taiwanese living on the Mainland (Ross 2006). According to Ross, who cites opinion polls that claim 90 per cent of Taiwanese oppose an immediate declaration of independence, although the independence movement gained greater international visibility during Chen's presidency, within Taiwan itself the trends were actually running against confrontation and in favour of stability (Ross 2006: 2). Ross points to KMT victories in the December 2005 municipal and local elections as evidence that Taiwanese prefer pragmatic diplomatic and economic ties over a risky push for independence, and claims that Chen's election victories were aberrations rather than accurate indications of the popularity of independence among Taiwanese voters.

From Ma's new policy against Chen's independence stand, it seems that democratisation itself does not decide the direction of unification or independence. Comparatively speaking, democratisation is associated with forces of unification in South Korea but is associated with independence forces of the DPP in Taiwan. This fact illustrates that we cannot make the general claim that democratisation inevitably gives rise to independence movements. The relationship between democratisation and the shift towards independence or unification in Taiwan and Korea is influenced by other factors.

Firstly, historical experience plays a different role in Taiwan and Korea. The particular colonial history of Taiwan and Korea has influenced the development of national identity in each place. In Taiwan, the contrast between the Japanese colonial period, which was often perceived as benign, and the KMT's brutal suppression of local Taiwanese following the handover to Chinese control served to strengthen anti-Chinese feeling and encourage pro-independence movements. In Korea, however, the history of Japanese military rule instead served as a unifying force that fed the development of a pan-Korean nationalism. Rather than dividing North and South Korea, this shared experience helps to foster a common cross-border national identity.

The second factor is the different level of ethnic diversity in Korea and Taiwan. Ethnicity is almost homogeneous in Korea and the two sides share a common culture and language, which constitutes a basis for unification. Taiwan, however, is made up of a range of different ethnic groups, including indigenous Taiwanese. This has helped to create a situation where some groups have stronger cultural links to the Mainland and tend to be more positive towards unification, while others have no ties to the Mainland at all and are more closely aligned with the independence forces.

Thirdly, the international institutional context is quite different. The institutional arrangement whereby both Koreas have their own seat at the United Nations creates conditions that actually facilitate unification. They have a framework within which to interact with one another and each is seen as a legitimate representative of the Korean nation in international affairs. In Taiwan's case, where the UN seat is held by Beijing and Taipei is excluded from participating in international institutions, the impossibility of Taiwanese representing China internationally has resulted in an attempt to create an alternative identity as Taiwan, which does not require sharing the claim to represent China with the Mainland.

The fourth factor relates to the alignment between economic prosperity and political control. In the German reunification, West Germany was willing to offer economic help to the East because it was in a position to take a dominant role in political reunification, while East Germans were willing to give up their political system in order to obtain the economic benefits of reunification. In the Korean case, the South is much more likely to assume political control of the North and is affluent enough to bear the economic costs. In Taiwan's case, however, it is more affluent than the Mainland on a per capita basis but also much smaller and is unlikely to be able to assume political control of all of China. If unification were to occur under these circumstances then Taiwan might become less well off in a material sense while also losing political control, which is an outcome that holds little appeal for Taiwan's people.

Finally, there are different conceptions of self-determination in Korea and Taiwan. Both Taiwanese and Korean nationalism is related to the struggle for self-determination, but this manifests in different ways. In Korea, self-determination is related to the struggle against foreign intervention and for national unification. In Taiwan, however, the idea of self-determination is linked to the ongoing struggle against the Chinese empire and the desire to be independent of Mainland control. If the conception of self-determination is modified in a way that aligns with a post-modern form of state sovereignty where independence is not a crucial question, then this will change the dynamics and effect of democratisation. If a democratisation programme exists in the absence of the desire for ethnic self-determination, then democracy will be more likely to support unification.

All the above factors interact with democratisation. The result has been that democratisation has pushed Taiwan towards independence through empowering a growing Taiwanese nationalism, which defies the Chinese unification policy, while it pushes South Korea towards unification. In conclusion, the impacts of democratisation on Taiwan's independence movement rely on history, international relations, the nature of the power relationship between the two sides, the strategies of the parties, and people's ideas and beliefs. Without taking these conditions into account, it is naïve to claim that Taiwan's democratisation causes its independence movement. The effects of democratisation occur in a broader social and political context.

While it is clear that democratisation has aided the independence movement, we can only cautiously conclude that democracy provides an institution in which independence and reunification forces can compete with each other and that this competition can lead in different directions. In Taiwan, all major parties have moved towards the middle in order to attract votes. In the future, democratisation might lead in different directions, depending on other factors such as the economy or the positions of China or the US.

4.5   CHINESE DEMOCRATISATION AND THE TAIWAN ISSUE

What if China embarks upon democratisation? Will unification be achieved? Or will Taiwan gain its independence in the process of Chinese democratisation? Now let us turn to various hypotheses on the likely impact of Chinese democratisation on the Taiwan issue.

The democratisation of China would create political systems and institutions compatible with those in Taiwan, and thereby facilitate unification. Sheng Lijun (2001: 221) claims that competition from a democratic Taiwan may even be a driving force that helps push the Mainland towards better human rights and democratic governance. It is likely that the democratisation of China will help China win a positive international reputation and improve its relations with the USA. Arthur Waldron (2004) argues that were China to democratise, it would reduce its military spending in favour of domestic welfare and would change its foreign policy to be friendlier to countries that provide the most economic benefit, like the US, Japan and Taiwan. It is likely that the democratisation of China would both intensify pro-unification pressure on Taiwan, as it would reduce the differences between political institutions, and increase confidence in a peaceful solution among Taiwanese people. Tien (1994: 192–5) asks the question whether the PRC must democratise in order to appeal to newly democratic Taiwan, or whether real negotiation requires prior democratisation or federalism on the Mainland. In 1990 a survey conducted by a Taiwanese newspaper found that 42 per cent of respondents supported independence if the CCP's authoritarian system continued, but only 5 per cent supported independence if the Chinese Communists 'practice democracy and freedom' (cited in Wachman 1994: 231). A democratic China, with decentralised powers and perhaps a confederation, will foster a trust between China and Taiwan. Moreover, elected leaders in Mainland China would push unification further, if they had an electoral mandate.

The democratisation of China is insisted upon as a precondition of China's reunification if it is not an excuse for postponing and resisting reunification. To take one example, when Jiang Zemin reiterated that 'one country, two systems' would 'set an example for the final solution to the Taiwan question', former Premier Lien Chan argued, 'Taiwan is governed by a democracy, and no one in Taiwan wants to live under Communism. Hence the government has to respect the wishes of the people' (Chou 1997: 35). Koo Chen-fu, Chairperson of the Strait Exchange Foundation, reiterated in his meeting with Jiang Zemin, Qian Qichen and other Chinese leaders during his trip to China in October 1998, that the democratisation of China is a precondition for unification. In response to Taiwan's insistence on democracy as a precondition for unification, Jiang Zemin cited village elections as an example of China's democracy. It looks like Jiang does not reject the idea of *democratic* unification. In contrast, Tang Shubei, Vice-President of the Association for Relations Across the Taiwan Straits, asserted that democracy is not an essential question and that democracy should not constitute an obstacle to the negotiation on the reunification question. He stressed that Taiwan should not impose democracy on China, nor should China impose socialism on Taiwan (*The People's Daily*, overseas edition, 28 January 1999: 5).

Here I would like to propose a hypothesis concerning the relationship between the pattern of Chinese democratisation and the resolution of the Taiwan question. If the democratisation of China is prompted by popular mobilisation, Taiwan is more likely to gain its independence, as shown by the case of the successful secession of Mongolia from Qing, when the Manchu rulers' resistance against democratic reform led to a revolution from below. This is because popularly mandated democratisation weakens the power of the centre and creates an opportunity for independence. If, on the other hand, the democratisation is imposed from above, through elite negotiation, Taiwan would not have a favourable opportunity to declare independence. Democratisation from above can boost the legitimacy of the government and may even strengthen state power.

China would have a chance to unify with Taiwan if it were to follow Linz and Stepan's (1996) model of *sequential* democratic reform: statewide election precedes provincial election, followed by the negotiation of an autonomy statute with Tibet and a confederal arrangement with Taiwan. China would risk disintegration if the first competitive election were at the provincial, not nationwide, level. In the USSR, democratisation started with the Baltic states, not with the centre. Thus the centre and Gorbachev had no legitimate authority to manage the boundary problem; and democratisation in the republics assisted secession. The result was disintegration (Linz & Stepan 1996; Stepan 1997: 17). In fact, Chinese leaders seem to have already learnt a lesson about this sequence. In 1993, 'multiple candidate' elections were held for provincial leaders, by ballots in regional 'parliaments', in a few provinces, including Zhejiang and Guizhou, where officially designated candidates for governors were voted down. For fear that they would lose control of provincial leaders as a consequence of elections, the central leaders decided that multiple candidate elections for provincial leaders should be stopped.

Moreover, one immediate effect of Chinese democratisation would be that Chinese dissidents, particularly those who do not care about the Taiwan issue or who would even willingly let Taiwan gain independence, could freely express their views. Thus the myth that there is an indisputable consensus on unification might be shattered. Once democratised, Mainland China may not favour reunification, as the value of national reunification may not be the top priority of a ruling party. This is because an election grants the ruling party political legitimacy. In these circumstances the importance of reunification as a source of legitimacy is likely to be reduced and the ruling party will rely less on unification as a mode of legitimacy.

Democratisation would introduce competitive political parties, and the emergence of pro-Taiwan and anti-Taiwan parties or social groups. The value of this competitive party system is that it provides a check against extreme views. For example, in Scotland the Scottish National Party can articulate its stance in favour of independence, but when it goes too far it suffers an electoral loss. A democratic system offers citizens a weapon against parties taking extreme political positions. A Mainland political party that supports Taiwan's independence could also be punished by the electorate. The dominant party would likely be a pro-unification party. Under plural and competitive politics, it might be speculated that either some democrat members, or some members of the government, might strike a political deal with Taipei that would support its independence claim in exchange for certain support from Taiwan. If this were done quickly and wisely, peace would be assured. Historically, Sun Yat-sen made such a secret deal with Japan over Northern China in the 1910s (Jansen 1967), and Boris Yeltsin supported and encouraged the Baltic states to secede in order to gain power over his rival, Gorbachev, in 1991.

4.6   DEMOCRATISATION, FEDERALISM AND THE TAIWAN ISSUE

I will discuss first a general question of how democratisation facilitates federalism, then the case of China.

How does democratisation facilitate and improve federalism?

Since the end of the Second World War, and particularly since the late 1970s, federalism has increasingly become a paradigmatic practice. There are now twenty-one federations with about two billion people (40 per cent of the world's total population) (Elazar 1995, 1996). Moreover, federalism has contributed to the restoration of democracy in Argentina and Brazil, to the extension of democracy in Venezuela, and to the slow transition from a one-party to a multi-party polity in Mexico (Elazar 1995: 16). Spain and South Africa, when embarking on democratisation, have undertaken a transformation from a unitary to a federal state.

In today's world, democratisation and federalisation are linked in various ways with different forms. The way in which a federal or confederate arrangement is established must involve a democratic process. A unifying federalism must listen to public opinion, appeal to ratification by both parliaments, and finally rest upon referendums. Such a process will provide legitimacy for an emerging federal or confederate system. Moreover, the federal or confederate arrangement may contain several democratic elements. First, the two political entities would equally share the pool of sovereignty. Second, federalism would place constitutional constraints both on central government and on the governments of sub-units. And third, the autonomy of sub-units would be fully guaranteed. These democratic elements are necessary incentives and safeguards for Taiwan in coming to terms with a federal or confederate arrangement.

In addressing the question of how democratisation facilitates federalism, the existing federal states need to be distinguished from non-federal states because each requires a different approach in regard to the federalism project. In the case of non-federal states like Sri Lanka, Burma, Indonesia, the Philippines and China, the question is whether democratisation will facilitate the introduction of federalism. In the case of existing federal states such as India, Pakistan and Malaysia, the question is whether democratisation will help to improve or reform the existing federalism.

The fact that the Philippines and Indonesia have embarked on a road towards federalism clearly demonstrates the effect of democratisation on the process of federalisation. While revolution has the logic of strengthening the central authority and developing a unitary state, democratisation offers a different normative order and logic in favour of federalist development. The effects of democratisation on federalisation can be grasped in the following ways.

Pressure for federalism comes from the process of democratisation in which the idea of human rights dominates political debates, giving rise to an extension of rights awareness to minorities. In the politics of national identity, nation-states tend to stress all peoples as one common people, and don't treat minority nationalities as a separate people, while minority groups see everything through the eyes of distinctive ethnicity. The process of democratisation provides an opportunity for minority groups to challenge the state's discourse of people, and to fight for their separate identity. Empowered by human rights discourse and institutions in the process of democratisation, minorities have enthusiastically demanded their cultural identity and rights. They openly criticise the state's undemocratic measures for a homogeneous cultural domination that threatens cultural liberty and diversity. In particular, some minorities who have had historical experience of self-rule have been advocating and demanding a federal system in which the sub-units are granted certain powers to control their own affairs. Democratisation empowers minority groups and increases their bargaining power in the process of federalisation (B. He 2002c).

Public debate and open advocacy for federalism have been closely associated with, and encouraged by, the process of democratisation. With freedom of speech and freedom of association, NGOs can oppose the official line of autonomy and advocate federalism in Indonesia and the Philippines (B. He 2004c). In Taiwan and South Korea there are numerous proposals on federalism or confederation (Hwang 1994: 293). The impact of democratisation on federalism can be illustrated by the lack of democratisation and its impact in China and Myanmar, where public debate over federalism is banned by the authoritarian states; using Allan Smith's phrase, federalism is 'not on the radar' in Myanmar; and the debates over federalism for China and Myanmar can only be heard overseas.

Party competition in the process of democratisation contributes to policy options with regard to federalism. For example, in Taiwan, Zhou Yanshan (1995), a former legislative member of the New Party, suggested the model of a Chinese Commonwealth as a solution. The KMT considered federal or confederate arrangements as a way to achieve unification; the DPP opposed it in the 2000 general election. Public debate and party competition will eventually lead to debate over federalism in the parliament, for example in the Philippines, where the senators have been arguing for a federal solution to the Mindanao secession or autonomy problem. The 2004 general election in Indonesia strengthened the central government, which was then able to make a deal with regard to self-government in Aceh. The function of federalism requires that all parties are committed to democracy; in particular, the political forces in the constituent units of federalism must be subject to the democratisation process so as to achieve federalism. If the democratic element is absent, military forces are likely to be used to suppress other rivals.

Huaxiang Guo: a federation of Mainland China and Taiwan

Overseas Chinese intellectuals, such as Yan Jiaqi, propose federalism as a solution. Wang Pengling (1997), a Chinese philosopher in exile in Holland, proposes constructive nationalism, which advocates the reunification of the two separate sides of the Taiwan Strait through a constitutional democratic state. Federalism, as a supernational arrangement, is always called for to manage the national identity conflict. As Friedman (1996: 180) said clearly:

Beijing cannot insist on coercively imposing unification and Taipei cannot insist on absolute independence. That is, democratic confederation is the projected content of a greater Chinese (Zhonghua) nationalism that can contain all of China's challenging diversity.

Federalism can meet autonomy demands in Tibet and Xinjiang, and secure unity through diversity. Federalism offers not only a much better alternative to the current Chinese authoritarian control over secessionist regions, but also a means to achieve China's unification with Taiwan. Gerald Segal (1996: 20) considers a federal system to be 'the only way to democratically govern a country as large and as disparate as China', and argues that federalism is the only way to deal with the issue of Taiwan. Steve Tsang (2000) proposes a 'Chinese Union' or 'United States of China' as the basis for negotiations between the two sides. In fact, both sides of the Taiwan Strait have discussed some aspects of a federal or confederate solution to the Taiwan issue. So have both sides of the Korean peninsula (Hwang 1994: 293). Moreover, Hong Kong's special status has already weakened the traditional unitary model. China is now a semi-federal state, in the sense that Hong Kong has its own currency and independent financial and legal systems.

Deng Xiaoping's proposal of 'one nation two systems' entails federal elements. Under Deng's proposal, Taiwan would enjoy a high degree of autonomy, consisting of administrative and legislative power, judiciary power including final judgement, the power to keep its own army, and certain powers in foreign affairs, such as signing commercial and cultural agreements with foreign countries (Chen 1996: 1056). Taiwan would also have the power to issue its own currency. But only the PRC would represent China in the international arena; Taiwan would recognise the sovereignty of China; and its military arm would not constitute a threat against China. Deng Xiaoping's notion of 'one nation two systems' is interpreted by Yan Jiaqi as a federal solution with confederate characteristics, for the larger federal power of China would have a constitutional connection with the smaller federal state of Taiwan, which would maintain more autonomy than in normal federal-state relationships (Yan 1992; China's Constitutionalism Newsletter, No. 2, June 1994: 24). This notion is innovative in the Chinese context, in the sense that China would move away from a unitary notion of state and go towards a federal idea of nation-state. In fact, China has to accept and develop such notions and arrangements in order to meet complex contemporary political conditions. The concession made in the notion of 'one nation two systems' reflects the fact that China's national identity can be negotiated through bargaining. As Deng reportedly said, federalism could be considered if it was acceptable to Taiwan. Jiang Zemin went further by saying that so long as the principle of one country is upheld anything else can be negotiated.

In the eyes of Taipei, Deng Xiaoping's idea of 'one nation two systems' is inadequate in addressing the Taiwan issue (Chiou 1986). It can be argued that Beijing may consider dropping the term 'one nation two systems' and adopt common international terms such as federalism and confederation, so as to avoid confusion and come close to international standards. Taiwan proposes 'one country, one culture, two governments', under which Taiwan would not only maintain its present system but also enjoy equal status with the PRC in international affairs (for example, dual UN representation). This latter model is closer to a confederation, where each state maintains its own sovereignty and right to secede, than a federation, where sovereignty resides in the federal government and there is collective national defence and international diplomacy (Hao 2010: 129).

Both Taiwan's 'one country, two governments' formula and China's 'one country, two systems' proposal have retreated from the idea that reunification be accomplished under a single government and with one socio-economic system. Former Taiwanese premier Lien Chan (Lian Zhan) considers federal or confederate arrangements as a way to achieving unification. Beijing has previously considered a federal proposal to unify China with Taiwan (*China's Constitutionalism Newsletter*, No. 2, June 1994: 24). Federalism, if attempted, seems likely to be successful, as it would be based on a shared cultural affinity, as are other successful federations like Australia and the United States (Hao 2010: 136–7).

The idea of federalism, no matter how attractive, faces resistance from both sides. In Mainland China, Beijing tends to emphasise the self-defeating nature of federalism and its unanticipated consequences, namely the proliferation of autonomy across China and the escalation of conflicts. According to Beijing, the central governing body would find such changes difficult to resist, and would eventually be forced to accommodate local demands. Modern Chinese history shows that federalism once gave rise to regional militarists (*geju*). If federalism was built upon the aspirations of regional militarists, it could never achieve national unity and strength (Duara 1990: 12). There are other arguments against federalism for China and Taiwan. Federalism is a political model with its roots in Western political systems, where China's tradition has been more unitary. Within Asia, federalism has a negative image and the variety of different federal models can be somewhat confusing.

In Taiwan, it is often said that Taiwan is bigger than Singapore, and if Singapore has its own nation-state, then why doesn't Taiwan? The desire for an independent nation-state is strong in Taiwan, and, moreover, Taiwan does not meet certain conditions for federalism. Among other things, one necessary condition for federalism is that one state should not be so powerful as to be able to rely on its individual strength for protection against foreign encroachment (Mill 1947: 367). A combination of the economic, military and political powers of Taiwan; the history of Taiwan's semi-independence; the democratisation effect on the Taiwan question; and the worldwide secession/independence tendency, make it extremely difficult for federalism to be accepted by Taiwanese nationalism. A looser form of confederation, where each state maintains its autonomy and is able to secede, is more attractive to the Taiwanese side but unlikely to be accepted by the Mainland. For this reason, Zhidong Hao (2010: 132) suggests a hybrid of federation and confederation, which maintains most of the characteristics of a confederation, such as separate national defence, diplomacy, tax and legal systems, but does not allow unilateral secession. Hao argues that this form of relationship might be acceptable to both sides because it is similar to Deng Xiaoping's formulation but, unlike 'one nation two systems', it does not imply that there is only one central government and that the other components of the grouping are only local governments (Hao 2010: 132).

Yujen Chou (1997) argues for confederation in which the PRC does not swallow the ROC, nor does the ROC swallow the PRC. Putting aside the complex issue of what and how federal or confederate institutions should be adopted, federal or confederate arrangements must contain democratic elements. One condition necessary to render a federation advisable, in the opinion of J. S. Mill (1947: 366), is that there should be a sufficient amount of mutual sympathy among the populations. Chinese democratisation can create an opportunity to meet this condition. Among other things, Chinese democratisation is a precondition to establish a confederate or federal structure, in the sense that it would build trust and good will, and reduce political and ideological differences. Within the current Chinese authoritarian system it is impossible to establish a federal system.

Federalism and other proposals, such as 'one China, two governments' or 'one nation, two systems', adopt and continue to reinforce the framework of the nation-state system. Under such a system, since nationalism in China and Taiwan share features such as the exclusion of other forms of state, or other orders of state, or the intensification of national identities, there is no peaceful solution to the Taiwan question. One alternative is 'Confucian China' or 'cultural China', the key idea being that a 'cultural China' can allow the existence of plural political entities. In this context, it is proposed that the name of PRC should be changed to Huaxiang Guo.

4.7   CONCLUSION

This chapter has examined the various ways in which democratisation in Taiwan and China will impact on the resolution to the Taiwan question. Taiwan has gone through different stages as its national identity question has been shaped by its unique history and by the political changes that have come with democratisation. The KMT's old state nationalism based on reunification has been largely replaced with a neo-nationalism that reduces the distinctions between the different sub-ethnic groups living in Taiwan. While democratisation cannot be seen as the sole cause of a shift towards a more independent national identity for Taiwan, it has combined with other factors to allow this change to occur.

If the democratisation of China is prompted by popular mobilisation, Taiwan is more likely to gain its independence through the opportunity provided by the weakening of the power of the centre. If, on the other hand, democratisation is imposed from above, through elite negotiation, Taiwan would not have a favourable opportunity to declare independence. Federalism is a viable option for solving the conflict between Taiwan and the Mainland, but the Mainland would need to become more democratic for this to occur.

NOTES

1. The author's conversation with him on 23 July 1991 in Taipei.
2. Qianfeng Publisher, for example, has published thirteen series and around 178 books on

Taiwan. The topics in the series include a Collection of Taiwan's Writers, a Study of Taiwan's Literature, a Collection of New Taiwan, a Collection of New Taiwanese, Taiwan's Literature and History, Taiwan's Winds and Clouds, Taiwan Studies and the People of Taiwan's Nation. For recent books on nationalism, see Shih 1994, 1998.

3. Similarly, through an emphasis on Japanese influences in Taiwan, the Japanese scholar Mitsuta contends that 'the assumption that Taiwan is nationally a part of China is nothing more than a conceptual one'. Wan-Lee Yin, however, comments that Mitsuta's account 'left out centuries of cultural heritage preserved by Chinese settlers in Taiwan. In the result, he almost managed to posit a state of nature for the islanders prior to Japanese occupation.' Yin (1995) also argues that Mitsuta's account does injustice to history, truth and reason.

4. Election Study Center–National Chengchi University, http://esc.nccu.edu.tw/main.php, accessed 20 July 2014.

5. The New Tide Faction promoted a strategy similar to President Lee Teng-hui's 'no haste, be patient' policy, and said there is no need for cross-negotiations because the US will protect Taiwan. And Hsu Yang-ming, of the Justice Alliance Faction, urged Taiwan to abandon its so-called One China policy and use its name when it bids for membership in the United Nations: see V. Sheng 1998d: 2.

5 Referendum and the Taiwanese National Identity

The controversial referendum proposals and the first island-wide referendum on 20 March 2004 were a crucial aspect of the emergence, growth and acceleration of the conscious effort by President Chen Shui-bian and the Democratic Progressive Party (DPP) to articulate and redefine a distinct Taiwanese national identity. The controversial issues concerning Taiwanese national identity and the referendum have drawn much attention from policy-makers and scholars in Taiwan, Mainland China and the US. Yet a substantial study of the intrinsic and complex multi-relations between Taiwanese national identity and the referendum question has not been undertaken.

This chapter focuses on the important topic of the debate over the resolution of Taiwanese national identity through referendums. The previous chapter provided the political background against which the impact of Taiwanese democratisation on the national identity question and the politics of referendum took place. Through a case study of the referendum in 2004 in Taiwan, this chapter shows how the proposed referendum was manipulated and watered down. While it points out the limits of referendums in general and the flaws of the Taiwanese referendum in particular, the chapter still favours referendums as a conflict-resolution mechanism, and argues for increasing the deliberative component of such referendums.

The chapter begins by outlining the party-political origins of the referendum and then examines the influence of outside actors on the process. It then describes the process of political struggle and negotiation between the pan-Blue and pan-Green camps and assesses the outcome of that struggle before finally arguing in favour of deliberative over mobilised form of referendum (Chapter 1).

5.1 REFERENDUM: PRINCIPLES AND PROBLEMS

Today, national groups are seen to have a right of secession, that is, a right to leave the existing state and to take over control of the territory that they currently occupy. The legitimacy of state boundaries is thought to be conditional upon the popular vote. There is a growing consensus that state boundaries are legitimate only if the state protects the peoples within them *and* the people assent to remaining within those boundaries. If these conditions are not met, peoples are increasingly able to divorce themselves from the political unit and take their land with them. The settlement of the national boundary question thus depends upon the free decision of those immediately concerned. This represents perhaps the strongest argument for democratic management of the boundary question. In Renen's doctrine of a 'daily plebiscite', the distinctive principle of the boundary definition is voluntary assent. In other words, the national boundaries are a choice rather than a fatality (Gellner 1987). Beran (1998: 32–59) sees referendums on the national boundary question as an important mechanism of voluntary agreement and consent. He also imagines an ideal world order in which referendums can settle any dispute over boundary questions, in particular the question of secession.

A referendum is arguably the only reliable means of ascertaining the will of the people. In the words of Hungarian delegate Count Apponyi following the First World War: 'The plebiscite *alone* would establish beyond dispute the will of the peoples in question' (Goodhart 1971: 116). Wambaugh (1933: 9) offered a convincing argument along similar lines:

> There is, however, no perfect method of establishing national boundaries. The problem is one of alternatives, a choice between methods varying in imperfection. To allow questions of sovereignty to be settled by conquest, or by a group of Great Powers gathered at a Peace Conference, resorting for their method of determination at one time to strategic considerations, at another to languages statistics, or to history, or to geographic or economic criteria – such methods are even less satisfactory to democratic principles. Therefore it seems certain that we shall keep the plebiscite as a tool in the workshop of political science.

But the referendum in its current form is not without its own limitations as a conflict-resolution mechanism. It may offer a quick resolution, but not always a satisfactory and sustainable one. If all relevant actors do not accept the process as legitimate then those on the losing side of a referendum might simply refuse to accept the result. If some groups deny the need for a referendum, feel they have not been adequately consulted, or perceive the formulation of the question or the organisation of the vote as biased then this can fail to resolve the question peacefully. In the real world, referendums have been known to exacerbate ethnic conflicts and lead to civil war and unrest. Take for example the former Yugoslavia. In February 1991, the Croatian Assembly, in conjunction with that of neighbouring Catholic Slovenia, issued a proclamation calling for secession from Yugoslavia and the establishment of a new confederation which would exclude Serbia and Montenegro. Concerned at possible maltreatment in a future independent Croatia, Serb militants announced secession from Croatia and proclaimed the formation of the Serbian Autonomous Region of Krajina in March 1991. In May 1991, a referendum was held in which 90 per cent of those in Krajina supported remaining with Serbia and Montenegro in a residual Yugoslavia. A week later, Croatian electors voted by a 94 per cent margin for independence within a loose confederation of Yugoslav sovereign states; and in June 1991, the Croatian government, in conjunction with the Slovenian government, issued a unilateral declaration of independence. The conflicting results of the two referendums were used to support claims for both union with Yugoslavia and independence from Yugoslavia in Croatia and Bosnia-Herzegovina. Following the two referendums, there was an escalating conflict between Croatian government forces and the Serb-dominated Yugoslav army, and civil war between Serbs and Croats within Croatia. Arguably the misuse of referendums and the tyranny of majority rule contributed to Yugoslavia's degeneration into ethnic war.

In Taiwan the referendum also had the potential to trigger conflict with the Mainland and even between China and the United States. Although direct conflict was ultimately avoided, the process by which the referendum was initiated and carried out was problematic and unsatisfactory.

5.2   PARTY-POLITICAL ORIGINS OF THE REFERENDUM

The referendum originally emerged as a party-political issue; although there was ongoing debate and eventually some compromise, these partisan origins hampered deliberation and limited the ability of the referendum to resolve national identity issues. Although there was a constitutional basis for holding referendums, in the 1990s the issue of holding a referendum on national identity came to be associated with the DPP and Chen Shui-bian. According to Article 136 of the ROC Constitution, a new law should be enacted for the people's exercise of the rights of initiative and referendum. Legislator Trong Chai first suggested the idea of a referendum law in 1992 and introduced the referendum bill in 1993. The Bill was defeated on 16 March 1994. In the July 1997 fourth round of Constitutional revision, the KMT agreed to a long-time DPP demand to incorporate provisions for popular initiatives and presidential referendums into the Constitution. It was agreed that the exercise of the rights of initiative and referendum must be prescribed by law. At the same time, there was a debate over whether a referendum should be employed to decide on the national status of Taiwan. While a section of the KMT rejected it, the DDP pushed for it.

In 1998, the DPP was confronted with the question of whether the issue of referendums should be dropped. On 9 May 1999, Article 5 of the Resolution on Taiwan's Future, which was passed at the 8th meeting of the Second DPP Convention, demanded that the KMT speed up the legislative process to enact a referendum law so as to institutionalise popular sovereignty. On 24 May 1999, the Ministry of the Interior gave its approval to a draft of the initiative and referendum law. This law enabled the public to vote on local issues and national policy matters but excluded any vote on national territory and sovereignty or any changes to the name and flag of the country. These powers continued to reside with the National Assembly (Lu 1999b: 2).

In his inauguration address in March 2000, President Chen Shui-bian made the pledge that he would not promote a referendum to change the status quo in regard to the national identity question. This pledge, however, did not prevent Chen from leading the debates over how to conduct a referendum and what issues should be included or excluded.

In the context of the 2004 presidential election, Chen's strategy was to use the referendum issue to weaken the electoral support for opposition parties. If the Kuomintang (KMT) and People First Party (PFP) were adamant about their opposition to referendum, this could help the DPP win the 2004 elections by undermining the KMT and PFP's democratic credentials. If the KMT and PFP were to change their position, Chen would be able to claim that he was successful in 'luring' opposition parties to support the referendum, thereby demonstrating his leadership and paving the way for a future referendum on Taiwan's national identity.

Chen avoided the sensitive issue of a referendum on independence, which could have provoked direct conflict with the Mainland, by arguing that Taiwan was already an independent sovereign state and therefore did not need a referendum on this question. In response to Jiang Zeming's Eight Points, Chen suggested that a referendum should be held on the reunification question (*The Independence Daily*, 29–30 January 2000: 10). A bi-partisan group also proposed that a referendum on reunification be held every four years if China did not use force against Taiwan (*United Daily*, 6 October 2000: 2).

In 2001, Chen promised a referendum on a fourth nuclear power plant. In May 2003, Chen called on a popular vote to show Taiwan's determination to gain a seat in the World Health Organisation (WHO) when the People's Republic of China (PRC) blocked the SARS-stricken island's efforts to attain observer status in the WHO (*Taiwan News*, 28 May 2003). Chen also advocated a referendum that aimed to reduce the size of the legislature.

Chen called for a 'defensive referendum', that is, if Taiwan were attacked by China, Taiwan would declare independence quickly through a referendum. In a situation of crisis, the president has the right to initiate a referendum, which is examined by the Executive Yuan, and voted for by the people.

On 28 September 2003, at the DPP 17th anniversary celebrations, Chen said that the DPP and the 23 million people of Taiwan would jointly push for a new Constitution in 2006. On 10 October 2003, Chen told the PRC to quit the One China framework and called on all the people of Taiwan to 'accelerate the birth of a new constitution that will allow Taiwan to become a normal, complete and great democratic country'. On 25 October 2003, more than 100,000 people took to the streets in Kaohsiung calling for a referendum law and New Constitution. Vice-President Annette Lu led the march, saying referendums would give Taiwan the opportunity to establish Taiwan's sovereignty; to establish Taiwan's national name; and to give Taiwan a completely new identity.

In 2004 the electoral strategy of the DPP was to play up the national identity issue and raise the referendum question to distinguish the DPP from the pan-Blue Lien-Soong alliance. In the DPP's anti-China and anti-KMT message, the KMT is represented as equivalent to China, while 'democracy' is linked to Taiwanese nationalism. The DPP used the language of colonialism and imperialism to portray China's claims of sovereignty over Taiwan. Taiwanese nationalism or 'indigenisation' is, indeed, a powerful weapon in mobilising the Taiwanese. It was also the best strategy to demoralise the KMT, which did not make a full commitment in its campaign to a separate Taiwanese national identity. Without a comparative advantage over the DPP on this issue, it could only adopt reactive strategies to counteract the DPP's attack. The DPP strategy is not new; it has been widely used by nationalists in Eastern Europe and Southeast Asia. The use of the referendum as an electoral strategy meant that the deliberative component of the referendum process was undermined, however, when the KMT responded by questioning the legitimacy of the referendum and calling for a boycott.

5.3   INVOLVEMENT OF EXTERNAL ACTORS

Chen's advocacy caused controversy outside Taiwan. It led to American 'concern' and Chinese warnings. Defying opposition to his referendum proposal from both inside and outside Taiwan, Chen insisted that referendums are a standard feature of democratic systems. He argued that holding a referendum is a basic human right that cannot be deprived or restricted, saying that he wanted 'to sincerely urge and encourage everybody to seriously consider the importance and urgency of passing legislation on a referendum'.[1] DPP legislator Parris Chang said, 'We hope that the United States will not violate its democratic and human-rights principle to obstruct Taiwan's movement to launch the referendum' (*Taipei Times*, 24 June 2003). Some members of the DPP asserted that the DPP must listen to people's opinion and reflect people's interests and demands and that it couldn't always follow the US line. Despite these views, the US and China played a key role in shaping the kind of referendum that was eventually held.

China was one of the main players in the politics of referendums in Taiwan. It constrained options available to the Taiwanese and shaped the framework of any referendum. The US, KMT, PFP and even some members of the DPP accepted the red line defined by China, that is, China cannot tolerate any referendum concerning national identity, title or status. The threat from China's willingness to use force compelled the Chen Shui-bian government to adopt a cautious approach to any referendum over the national identity question, because a rash referendum was likely to generate a crisis. Nevertheless, some radical DPP members and the Taiwan Solidarity Union (TSU) challenged China's red line and its definitional role.

For Chinese nationalists, a referendum will never compromise the One China policy. The rationale is that Taiwan is an inalienable part of China, thus any self-determination process that might result in a permanent separation is totally unacceptable. Zhang Fengshan (1997: 9), a research fellow at the Institute of Taiwan Studies from the Chinese Academy of Social Sciences, offers a systematic critique of the referendum proposal to resolve the Taiwan national identity question. First, Taiwanese are culturally, racially and historically Chinese, and they are therefore not a unique ethnic group that is entitled to the right to self-determination. Second, it is undeniable that Taiwan was historically a province of China under Qing rule, and it therefore should come under Chinese sovereignty. Third, there is one China, and

China is the only sovereign entity. Rule over one particular area does not equate to sovereignty. More importantly, popular sovereignty belongs to all Chinese people.

Zhang Mingqing, spokesman for the Taiwan Affairs Office of the State Council, said that a referendum would be illegal and invalid; and that Taiwan's legal status as part of the Chinese territory had been explicitly stated in both domestic and international laws. Zhang stressed that Taiwan belongs to all 1.3 billion Chinese people including Taiwan compatriots: 'So the future of Taiwan should also be determined by all 1.3 billion" (*China Daily* 2003). In contrast, according to Liu I-chou's (1998: 10) survey, for which respondents were asked who had the right to determine the future of Taiwan, 75 per cent of Taiwanese respondents said only Taiwan residents had that right, while just 11 per cent said residents of the Mainland should be included.

On 25 June 2003, Li Weiyi, the spokesman of the State Council's Taiwan Affairs Office, refuted the Taiwanese attempts to conduct referendums on a number of issues, calling it a separatist move to create tensions across the Taiwan Straits. Li said the Taiwan authorities' support for referendums issues like the nuclear power plant, Taiwan's entry into the WHO, and the addition of the word 'Taiwan' to passports were an attempt to promote the 'gradual independence of Taiwan' and a split from the motherland.[2]

Chinese scholars saw Chen Shui-bian's referendum proposal as embarking on a course that would eventually lead to Taiwan's creeping independence. They regarded it as a trick to deliberately anger China and invite Chinese hostile reactions, and at the same time arouse Taiwanese nationalist feelings that would bolster Chen Shui-bian's electoral support. Lee and Chen used this strategy successfully respectively in 1996 and 2000. In 2003–4 and subsequent elections, China was cautious to avoid overreaction. Beijing did, however, take action to formalise its opposition to any potential referendum on independence by passing an anti-secession law in 2005, which commits the Mainland to military action should Taiwan formally secede.

Beijing distinguished referendums over national identity issue from those over concrete social policies. China could live with policy referendums, given reassurances from the US that Taiwan would not go beyond public policy issues and use a referendum to change Taiwan's status (Rigger 2003). Instead of using military threats, Beijing adopted a strategy of relying on the US to keep radical populist Taiwanese politicians in check. Yu Keli, director of the Institute of Taiwan Studies at the Chinese Academy of Social Sciences, called for cooperation between the US and China to fight Chen's referendum proposal (*People's Daily Online* 2003). The leadership in Beijing focused on economic development, solving social problems, and refraining from disturbing the existing peaceful environment. It did not treat China's reunification with Taiwan as an urgent priority.

The United States also played a part in influencing the referendum, although, unlike China, there was some disagreement within the government over whether to support or discourage a referendum. James Lilly, the former US ambassador to Taipei, supported the referendum proposal to solve Taiwan's national status (Lin 1991: 44). In 2002, more than a hundred members of the House of Representatives formed a Representative Taiwan caucus. In September 2003, ten senators founded a Senator Taiwan Caucus. Senator George Allen, a Republican and one of the two co-chairmen of the caucus, said that the senate caucus would initially concentrate on such issues as Taiwan's participation in the WHO.

The George W. Bush government, in contrast, did not support any referendum proposal. Doug Paal, Director of the American Institute in Taiwan, in his meeting with President Chen in Taipei on 20 June 2003, expressed that the US was opposed to all forms of referendum in Taiwan. In a Foreign Press Center Briefing on 1 August 2003, Philip T. Reeker, Deputy Spokesman of the Bureau of Public Affairs, Department of State, stated, 'We have made clear our position about referenda. . . . What President Chen said in his inaugural speech back in May of 2000, that he would not promote a referendum to change the status quo with regard to the question of independence or unification. We appreciate that pledge and we take it very seriously.'[3] On 16 October 2003, National Security Advisor Condoleezza Rice in Washington stressed that 'nobody should try unilaterally to change the status quo'.

In November 2003, President Bush in a meeting with Chinese Premier Wen Jiabao at the White House condemned Chen for certain unspecified 'comments and actions', and for making 'decisions unilaterally to change the status quo, which we oppose'. According to senior national security council official James Moriarty's interpretation, Bush opposed Chen's plan to hold a referendum in March 2004. He even sent a letter to urge Chen to reconsider holding the planned referendum.

When Chen announced his watered-down version of the referendum on the procurement of military hardware in the face of China's missile threat and equal negotiation with Mainland China on the establishment of a peaceful and stable framework, the United States softened its opposition. Washington saw no plausible reasons for Taipei to hold a referendum.

The Bush government recognised the reality of China, in particular Beijing's denial of the referendum principle. It badly needed China's support for its international campaign against terrorism. The Bush administration was unhappy with Chen Shui-bian for using the referendum issue to destabilise Sino–US relations. The democratic principle should not be used by Chen to advance his narrow electoral interests.

Nevertheless, the seeming 'alliance' between the US and China in opposition to Chen's referendum proposal should not blind us to the fundamental differences between the two countries. China rejected the referendum principle because it was against China's national interest and nationalist principles. In contrast, the Bush government expressed its 'concern' over Chen's referendum proposal because a referendum on national identity would be politically unwise. The Bush government acknowledged that referendums are a tool of democracy that Taiwan has the right to use. It would honour its duty of protecting a democratic Taiwan if attacked by China. It insisted on the consent principle, that is, the solution to Taiwan's national status must have the consent of the Taiwan people. Following American democratic traditions, the Bush government should have supported Chen Shui-bian's referendum proposal. But a realist assessment of the situation showed that the Bush administration was prudent not to support the referendum proposal and, in Michael D. Swaine's (2004: 49) words, this was 'a step in the right direction'.

Despite strong opposition to the planned referendum from the United States and especially from China, Chen went ahead with his referendum on 20 March 2004. The postponement of the planned referendum could have been seen as a sign of weakness that would have damaged Chen's election campaign. Chen interpreted China's 496 missiles targeted at Taiwan as an immediate threat, thus providing justification for revoking Article 17 to hold a defensive referendum. Nevertheless, to move away from his previous referendum proposals on the national identity question, he proposed a watered-down version which did not aim to declare independence or address the Taiwanese national identity question. For Chen, the purpose of the referendum was to 'prevent China from using force against Taiwan and therefore, unilaterally changing the status quo' and to 'increase people's awareness of and readiness for such [that is, China's] threats'.[4]

The two questions of the referendum were: 1. The people of Taiwan demand that the Taiwan Strait issue be resolved through peaceful means. Should Mainland China refuse to withdraw the missiles it has targeted at Taiwan and to openly renounce the use of force against us, would you agree that the Government should acquire more advanced anti-missile weapons to strengthen Taiwan's self-defense capacities? 2. Would you agree that our government should engage in negotiation with Mainland China on the establishment of a 'peace and stability' framework for cross-Strait interactions in order to build consensus and to look into the welfare of the people on both sides? Chen calculated that these two questions were likely to be easily approved by voters and would win the support of the US. This is because the approval of the first issue would mean the purchase of anti-missile weapons from the US.

5.4   NEGOTIATION AND POLITICAL STRUGGLE

While the issue of the referendum was split largely along party lines, it was not simply a matter of one side pushing for a referendum and the other opposing it. The discussions became more complex as both sides tried to use the issue for their own political advantage. During the period 2000–4, the KMT used its control of the Legislative Yuan to hamper Chen's efforts as president to hold the kind of referendum he wanted.

In the past, the KMT opposed holding a referendum on independence on the grounds that such national votes could stir up disputes over national status, erode social cohesion, invite China's intervention and threaten the status quo (Lu 1999c: 1). KMT Chairman Lien Chan and PFP Chairman James Soong initially regarded the DPP's referendum motion as 'unconstitutional'. They were of the view that the question of reunification and independence should be excluded in the referendum. However, the KMT and PFP changed their tune quickly when Chen played up the referendum issue to gain electoral support. They proposed that the legislature should examine the referendum law; that the fourth nuclear power plant issue and the national identity issue should be decided by one referendum; and that the referendum and the 2004 presidential election should be separated.

This shift was due to changes within the pan-Blue camp, the movement of public opinion in favour of independence, and an electoral strategy designed to outmanoeuvre the DPP. Taiwanese KMT elites and some second-generation Mainlanders no longer share the Chinese vision of unification with the Mainland. As Qi Dongtao (2012) has shown, support for Taiwanese independence has become distinct from support for the DPP; since Chen became president in 2000 there has been an increase in the number of Taiwanese nationalists from the KMT and PFP. Public support for the referendum also placed pressure on the pan-Blue camp to reconsider its stance. A *United Daily News* survey found that 59 per cent of Taiwanese supported the idea of holding a referendum on the question of formal independence or unification with China, although 54 per cent thought there was no need to do so at present.[5] Afraid of the adverse effects of objecting to the referendum law in terms of electoral votes, the KMT was 'forced' to follow the ruling DPP on the issue. Finally, both the KMT and PFP played a complex strategic game. They first aimed at forcing the DPP to express its official view on the referendum. If the DPP rejected Chai Trong's proposal, it would lose its grassroots support. If it supported it, it would go against Chen Shui-bian's pledge made in 2000. KMT legislators even attempted to vote for Chai's proposal after it was amended to exclude a referendum on Taiwan's national status. They knew the DPP's caucus would oppose the measure. They hoped to use the DPP's votes against Chai's referendum bill to argue that the DPP was inconsistent in its support for referendum (Rigger 2003). Nevertheless, at a crucial moment when Chai asked the KMT legislators to endorse his referendum proposal, they refused while the DPP legislators signed it.[6]

In April 2002, the Cabinet sent a draft of the initiative and referendum bill to the Legislative Yuan for review, but law-makers were deadlocked over the issues a referendum should cover. In March 2003, the TSU vowed to push for a referendum law that could be applied to all issues, including politically sensitive subjects related to national identity. The TSU's initiative won the backing of Chai Trong, the DPP legislator who was most committed to passing a referendum law. However, the DPP legislative caucus did not endorse the initiative. In June 2003, the TSU proposed that referendum should be used to decide national status. This proposal was again defeated in the Legislative Yuan.

It was extremely difficult to pass the referendum law or to hold a referendum through the Legislative Yuan. To circumvent the normal legislative process, the Chen administration stated its intention to create enabling rules through administrative means.

In June 2003, the Executive Yuan drafted a measure that allowed the government to hold a referendum. This was called an 'administrative regulation', which, in contrast to an 'administrative decree', does not require the approval of the legislature (Ko 2003: 3). In July 2003, the KMT and PFP called for a special legislative session considering enabling rules. Chen's government issued its guidelines in early August 2003, including that the Cabinet would promulgate the referendum issues within ten days of their passage in a Cabinet meeting. The voting date must be arranged within two months from the day of the issues being made public. Debates and seminars must be held during that two-month period.

On 5 August 2003, 300 local township chiefs, most of whom were KMT supporters, threatened to oppose or thwart the government's 'administrative regulation'. With the backing of KMT Chairman Lien Chan and PFP Chairman James Soong (Soong Chu-yu), the grassroots administrators threatened to boycott any referendum held before legislation was enacted to regulate such plebiscites.

In response to the threat, on 6 August 2003 Cabinet spokesman Lin Chia-lung said that local governments did not have the right to hold up the central government's plan to hold referendums. The enforcement measure was drawn up in case legislation governing referendums could not be passed by the Legislative Yuan in time for the administration to fulfil its pledge to hold a plebiscite on or before the day of the next presidential election.

On 27 November 2003, Chai Trong's proposal of allowing referendums on changing the national status, formal title and national anthem was defeated with only 14 approving votes and 175 abstaining votes in the Legislature Yuan. Instead, the Legislature Yuan adopted a watered-down Referendum Law. Article 2 confines the issues of referendum to laws, major policies and the revision of constitution, and excludes any referendum on national flag, anthem and title, remaking of a new constitution, and Taiwan's participation in the World Health Organisation. Nevertheless, Article 17 states that the president may call for a referendum on 'national security' through a resolution by the Executive Yuan in the case of an external threat to the nation that may alter the nation's sovereignty and erode Taiwan's territorial integrity.

Eventually, President Chen used Article 17 of the Referendum Law to hold a defensive or peace referendum on 20 March 2004, the day of the presidential election. Chen's approach bypassed the endorsement of the Legislative Yuan and undermined its power. It has damaged the existing power-check mechanism, caused political division between major parties on the defensive referendum, and set a precedent for using administrative power to appeal to popular will without the support of the Legislative Yuan.

5.5   REFERENDUM ON 20 MARCH 2004

The referendum and national identity issues drew emotional and passionate responses from the electorate and divided the island. While the DPP and TSU called for Taiwanese support for a referendum, the KMT and PFP boycotted it. Southern Taiwan is a strong base of the pan-Green camp, a coalition of the DPP and TSU, which is attempting to build up a 'Republic of Taiwan'. Northern Taiwan is the pan-Blue camp's stronghold; it is a coalition of the KMT and PFP, and is attempting to defend the 'Republic of China'. It is thus not an exaggeration to say that the 2004 presidential election, in essence, represented a struggle between the 'Republic of China' and the 'Republic of Taiwan' conceptions of Taiwan.

Despite Chen's anti-China campaign, the referendum failed to garner sufficient votes. The low turnout of 45.17 per cent disqualified the referendum and was a blow to Chen. The legitimacy index of the referendums was only 41.46 per cent for the anti-missile question and 41.53 per cent for the question of peace dialogue, much lower than 68.48 per cent, the mean legitimacy index of fifty-two referendums for independence conducted between 1791 and 1998 (B. He 2002d: 78–9). The failure of the referendum was largely due to the call for a boycott by the Lien–Soong alliance and opposition from China, the US, Europe and Japan. The argument that the threshold was too high is not convincing because it should be high, perhaps even higher at 75 per cent.

Chen, however, interpreted the result of the referendum as a victory because the majority approved the two issues, without mentioning the disqualification of the referendum. Chen blamed the lower turnout on the pan-Blue boycott campaign.

The result of the presidential election was a victory for Chen Shui-bian, the DPP and Taiwanese nationalism. The votes Chen gained increased from 39.3 per cent of total votes in the 2000 election to 50 per cent in 2004. Chen captured Taizhong city and county, widening the gap between the pan-Green vote and the pan-Blue vote in southern Taiwan, and narrowing the gap in Taipei. The political map of Taiwan changed substantially. Despite the DPP's loss in presidential elections in 2008 and 2012, and Chen's imprisonment for bribery, the DPP has succeeded in pushing national debate over Taiwan's identity and shifting the pan-Blue camp further towards the DPP's position on referendums. The result of the KMT's acceptance of referendums, however, has been to further politicise the referendum process along party lines. Chen's introduction of the national referendum in this election led to four further referendum questions held on two separate occasions in 2008 – two initial questions on transitional justice and corruption and two later questions on Taiwan's goal of membership of the United Nations. In each of these referendums one of the questions was supported by the KMT and the other by the DPP, although they were all invalidated due to low turnout. Rather than using referendum questions to discover the people's will, the referendums were used as tactical political tools by either side and were largely boycotted by the public.

5.6   CONCLUSION

The process by which the referendum was held under Chen can be seen as a sort of mobilised form of referendum. It limited its democratic legitimacy. Referendums that are manipulated by politicians to provide backing for a particular political group's territorial claims cannot help to resolve the question of national identity or national boundaries. In Taiwan's case, both internal and external political factors tarnished the freedom and fairness of the process. Internally, the referendum was the subject of a major political struggle between the DPP and the pan-Blue camp. Rather than try to obtain the outcome that would resolve the issue, both sides expended a great deal of effort trying to shape the referendum to their own advantage and to mobilise their own supporters (Mattlin 2004). The referendum appeared driven by electoral politics rather than the desire to enhance democracy, despite claims to the contrary from the DPP (Kao 2004). This politicisation damaged the legitimacy of the vote. Externally, the threat of war with the Mainland and the pressure from the US inserted an element of coercion into the process and made it more difficult for the referendum to be designed in a way that would determine the views of the Taiwanese public on the issue of national identity.

Despite its flaws, Taiwan's referendum was an important first step towards a democratic approach to Taiwan's national identity problem. Referendums have the potential to assist in the resolution of conflict over Taiwan's national identity. Even though its restrictive rules prevented a clear resolution of the national identity issue, the 2004 referendum gave the Taiwanese the opportunity to express their identity (Huang 2006: 173–4). The issue is not whether referendums should be held on Taiwan but rather how best to implement the referendum mechanism so that they achieve a positive outcome. From this perspective there are a number of lessons to be learned from the process that occurred under Chen. In particular, future referendums in Taiwan need to be more deliberative in order to avoid the divisiveness that can accompany such public discussions of national identity. This hybrid combination of deliberation and referendums will be fully examined in the final chapter.

NOTES

1. CNN, 3 August 2002; copy available at http://www.taiwandc.org/cnn-2002-04.htm.
2. http://en.chinacourt.org/public/detail.php?id=2834.
3. http://2002-2009-fpc.state.gov/22985.htm.
4. President Chen's televised statement of the peace referendum on 20 March, accessed 26 November 2012: http://english.president.gov.tw/Default.aspx?tabid=491&itemid=17897&rmid=2355.
5. United Daily News Public Opinion Survey Center, 5 August 2002. The survey was based on interviews with 885 adults. An additional 307 people declined to be interviewed. The sampling error is under 3.3 per cent at a 95 per cent confidence level. The survey was based on a random sample of residential phone numbers in Taiwan.
6. The above episode was commented on by Mainland Chinese scholars as a political joke with a sarcastic tone: http://tw.people.com.cn/GB/14811/14869/1982527.html>; http://tw.people.com.cn/GB/14811/14869/1984588.html, accessed November 2003.

6 Sovereignty and the Taiwan Question

To find a solution to the Taiwan question, policy-makers and scholars have discussed the proposal of the interim (or peace) agreement across the Taiwan Strait (Chang 1999b; White 2000; for a critique of White, see Dittmer 2000). Nevertheless, the proposal does not address the underlying question of sovereignty, and misses the key issue of Taiwan's place in international society.

This chapter aims to fill this gap. It argues that the solution to the Taiwan question must take into account Taiwan's desire and place in international relations; to do so, Beijing has to reconsider its Taiwan policy in terms of a new concept of sovereignty. Beijing's rigid approach to sovereignty has led to Taiwan's attempts to take the alternative route of trying to generate international legitimacy by emphasising democracy (Larus 2006). This chapter examines ways to move beyond these diverging approaches and bring China and Taiwan back into a shared framework that reduces the likelihood of conflict and meets the needs for international recognition of both sides.

The notion of sovereignty is a key concept in the normative thinking and strategic policy on the Taiwan question, yet it appears illusory, ambiguous and problematic. It lends political leaders forceful justification for their actions on the one hand, and traps them in a fixed way of thinking without policy innovation on the other. Currently the One China policy means recognising only 'one China', the Mainland, as legitimate. And the membership of the UN means international recognition as a sovereign state. In this normative conceptual imperative, Taiwan is excluded from the UN.

To deal with the Taiwan question, Professor Wang Yizhou (2000) from the Academy of Social Sciences of China has called for a search for a new concept of sovereignty which is capable of defending the core element of the sovereignty principle while at the same time providing greater flexibility. Wang, however, does not propose a concrete idea. The chapter attempts to transcend nationalist thinking, challenge the traditional concept of sovereignty, and outline an alternative approach to international recognition for China and Taiwan. It will provide an analysis of China's conceptions of sovereignty, the Taiwanese response, and options for bringing these diverging approaches back into a shared framework for international recognition. The chapter does not focus on any immediate practical solution to the Taiwan question, but on the long-term intellectual 'solution'. While it is conceded that the alternative ideas developed in this chapter may be too 'idealistic' or 'alien' to be accepted by the current leadership, it is hoped that the ideas may appeal to the next generation.

Sovereignty can be classified as internal and external. Internal sovereignty denotes a state's entitlement to control the population and border, its ability to set the agenda in policy-making, and its capacity to control exchange rates and taxation policy with legal jurisdiction within its national territories. External sovereignty covers representation in international organisations, establishing diplomatic relationships with other countries, and negotiating and signing international treaties (Krasner 1999). This chapter will focus on various aspects of external sovereignty and argue that external sovereignty can be shared between China and Taiwan.

6.1 CHINA'S OPPOSITION TO TAIWAN'S BID FOR UN MEMBERSHIP

The Republic of China (ROC) government launched its seventh bid to join the UN on 12 August 1999. Twenty nations supported its proposal to the UN steering committee. However, the number of countries that opposed Taiwan's bid increased from 40 to 48. In particular, the USA, UK and France, which had chosen to stay away from the issue in the past, stood against the proposal in 1999. The ROC launched its eighth bid to join the UN in August 2000. On 3 August 2000 only twelve UN members submitted a joint proposal to the UN Secretary General requesting the inclusion of the proposal for considering the ROC seat as a supplementary item in the agenda of the 5th plenary session of the General Assembly in September 2000. The US and other major powers continued not to back Taiwan's quests for recognition (Carpenter 2005: 5). The annual bids for UN membership continued under President Chen Shui-bian, including applying under the name of 'Taiwan' rather than 'ROC' in 2007. This unsuccessful result led to the inclusion of a referendum on the 'UN membership' issue as part of the 2008 Presidential elections; however, it was declared invalid due to low turnout. After President Ma came to office, Taiwan announced in 2009 that it would not seek to join the UN. This was the first time in seventeen years that the ROC did not bid for membership, and was part of President Ma's efforts to improve cross-Strait relations.

Beijing saw Taipei's bid as a separatist action and stood firm against the move (*The Free China Journal*, 20 August 1999: 1; *The Free China Journal*, 23 September 1999: 2; *The People's Daily*, overseas edition, 17 September 1999: 1). China's blockade of Taiwan's bid for UN membership is understandable in light of general perceptions of the UN as an intergovernmental organisation of sovereign states. UN membership is an international criterion for independent statehood. In this context, it is understandable for Beijing not to allow dual seats for China in the UN. For Beijing, only Mainland China can represent China's national sovereignty.

It is also easy to understand China's opposition to Taiwan's entry to the UN in the light of the deep-rooted Chinese ideal of Great Unity, which holds that there can be but one sovereignty, just as there is one sun. Thus, as far as China is concerned, there is only one China that can only be represented by one seat in the UN (*The People's Daily* 1999).

There is another important reason why China is against Taiwan's UN membership. It might be thought of as a mentality, a centre–province mentality. To China, Taiwan is but a province, and as such it cannot join the UN separately. This mentality, however, ignores the historical fact that Taiwan has not been under China's jurisdiction for more than sixty-five years. The PRC has to realise that (however politically incorrect it may be to admit it publicly) Taiwan is politically, economically and militarily as independent as any other nation-state, whose populations and land areas may be smaller than Taiwan's.

China's blocking of Taiwan's involvement in sovereignty-based international organisations extends beyond the UN General Assembly. For example, even after Taiwan was allowed to join the World Health Organisation (WHO) in 2009, the ROC was forced to change its continued referencing of itself as 'China (Taiwan)' on the WHO website. In addition, the UN has refused to recognise the Ma administration's ratification of the two UN human rights covenants and, more substantially, the ROC was blocked from participating at the UN Framework Convention on Climate Change meeting in Copenhagen in December 2009 where a WHO-like arrangement could have applied. Accordingly, Taiwan's participation in the WHO cannot be considered a breakthrough in terms of the expansion of Taiwan's international space.

6.2   DEADLOCK

Given Taiwan's political, military and economic power, it is not certain whether China would succeed in preventing Taiwan from joining the UN in the long term. Taiwan's UN membership will repeatedly present itself in the twenty-first century as a thorny political issue. So far Taiwan is recognised by twenty-three countries. It has never stopped expanding its 'living space' by establishing flexible, substantive international relations. It is only logical that Taiwan will continue to push this agenda as its economic strength grows. Nevertheless, the tacit agreement between China and Taiwan in 2009 that they would not seek to take each other's allies led to the absence of changes in diplomatic recognition since late 2008. A different government in Beijing or Taiwan may change this, of course.

Although economic interdependence helps to contain conflict, territorial considerations are more important. The desire to preserve the economic benefits of trade and investment between Taiwan and the Mainland would not be sufficient to prevent conflict were Taiwan to declare independence. This is partly because the territory of Taiwan is itself of great economic benefit to the state that controls it. Additionally, the greater interests of Chinese power-holders in going to war to prevent Taiwan's independence would most likely outweigh the broader economic interest in maintaining peace in the Taiwan Straits.

The potential for war between China and Taiwan comes from the contradiction between the democratic and authoritarian logic. The democratic logic in Taiwan is that Taiwan's democratisation makes it difficult for one party or the government to make a promise not to seek independence because such a promise cannot be made without consulting the will of the people. Since the democratisation of Taiwan, any significant change with regard to the national identity question cannot take place without the people being consulted. As Tien Hung-Mao (1994: 190), a professor of political science and the former Minister of Foreign Affairs of ROC, remarked, democratisation helps open up the debate over legitimacy of the ROC identity, which was in the first instance defined by the KMT ruling elite but has been increasingly challenged by the advocates of an independent Republic of Taiwan.

Neither can diplomacy alone decide the status of Taiwan. The model of diplomatic negotiation used to settle the Hong Kong question does not apply to Taiwan because the resolution of Taiwan's national identity has to be subject to popular approval, and democratisation makes it even more difficult or impossible for any ruling party to reach a deal with Beijing without the consent and consensus of the people, social groups and parties in Taiwan. An assertive media has also expressed its concern over the 'secret mission' between Beijing and Taipei (*China Time* 22 July 2000: 2). By contrast, the authoritarian logic in China (given the lack of need for democratic legitimacy for the leadership) is that the Taiwan issue is an important source of legitimacy for the survival of the leadership.

Underlying these two contrasting logics is the presupposition of national sovereignty shared by both Mainland China and Taiwan. Both sides seem to be reluctant to make any concession on the sovereignty question. Their rigid commitment to the idea of exclusive sovereignty is an intellectual source that may contribute to violence and war. In China, at an 'enlarged' meeting of the Central Military Committee (CMC) on 17 December 1999, President Jiang Zemin called for 'mobilising the armed forces to settle the Taiwan issue and accomplish the great reunification cause of the motherland'. A working group would be established directly under the politburo. Beijing then drew up new budgets for the fiscal years 2000 through to 2003, with plans that were specifically targeted at Taiwan accounting for 52 per cent of the military budget, instead of the previous 32 per cent (BBC 2000).

However, the Hu Jintao leadership dramatically changed China's Taiwan policy (though not the underlying objectives) through promoting a policy of conciliation and economic interdependence, and, in effect, giving up on the idea of immediate reunification. This policy included the expansion of economic ties, the launching of direct shipping, air transport and postal services, and the allowance of tourism from the mainland; a 'people first' policy. As Chinese scholar Xin Qiang (2009: 59) puts it, Hu's policy in effect amounts to 'no independence, no immediate unification, but develop together peacefully'.

In the United States, on 1 February 2000, the House of Representatives voted overwhelmingly to strengthen the US's commitment to Taiwan's security by voting 341–70 for the Taiwan Security Enhancement Act. The Act calls for increased training opportunities for Taiwan's military officers and seeks the establishment of direct security communications between US and Taiwanese forces. More importantly, it strengthens US policy that any determination of the ultimate status of Taiwan must have the express consent of the people of Taiwan. In a response on 4 February, a spokesperson of the People's Liberation Army warned the United States not to mistake China for Yugoslavia (*Reuters*, 4 February 2000). At the same time, however, successive US administrations have made it clear that they 'oppose any unilateral decision, by either China or Taiwan, to change the status quo of Taiwan's relationship with the mainland' (Zhao 2005).

6.3 TAIWAN'S RESPONSE

Currently, twenty-three states officially recognise Taiwan as an independent state (Wines 2008). While at times there has been vigorous competition between the PRC and Taiwan for diplomatic recognition (see, for example, Payne & Veney 2001; Stringer 2006), since the election of Ma Ying-Jiu in 2008 this competition has eased somewhat. Diplomatic recognition is not the only way Taiwan competes for international legitimacy, however. Over the last ten years, Taiwan has attempted to promote international democratic organisations. By promoting such organisations, of which there are now five, Taiwan automatically is able to gain membership in an international grouping while enhancing its legitimacy by emphasising its democratic credentials (Larus 2006).

The Taiwan Foundation for Democracy (TFD) <www.tfd.org.tw> was set up in 2003 and was the first national democracy assistance foundation established in Asia. Focusing primarily on the Asian region, the TFD provides grants to NGOs that promote democracy and human rights. The Democratic Pacific Union (DPU) <www.dpu.org.tw> was established the following year and aims to safeguard human rights, democracy and the rule of law, ensure the peaceful resolution of regional disputes and the protection of human security, promote maritime culture and sustainable development in the Pacific region and encourage the development of cooperation in industry, trade and technology. Its broad membership of twenty-eight countries includes a range of states in Asia, Oceania and the Americas, including Russia, the US, South Korea, Japan, Malaysia, Indonesia, Canada, Australia, Chile and Peru. In 2005 Taiwan established the World Forum on Democratisation in Asia (WFDA) <www.wfda.net>. The goals of this organisation are to support Asian democracy activists in their struggles against autocratic regimes, increase public focus on and participation in democratisation in Asia, marshal international support for Asian democratisation and support existing democratisation mechanisms in the region. The Initiative and Referendum Institute-Asia (IRI-Asia) also came into being in 2006, tasked with advancing constitutional reform in Taiwan and supported by the Taiwan Foundation for Democracy, and in 2007 the same Foundation established the Global Forum on New Democracies (GFND) to provide a platform for the leaders of new democracies to share their experiences and find solutions to problems of democratic governance.

Taiwan's democracy approach to international legitimacy was influenced by the position of the United States during the George W. Bush administration, which largely overlapped with Chen Shui-bian's time as president. Neo-conservatives in the Bush administration pushed for democratic expansion, sometimes through military means, as a way to increase US security and global stability. If faced with a crisis over Taiwan, these neo-conservatives would be likely to support action to defend Taiwan in order to protect the democracy from an authoritarian threat. Their support for Taiwan is increased by their shared democratic values and institutions, and is based on the desire to construct and defend an international community of democracies. There is some risk involved for Taiwan in aligning its quest for legitimacy with this neo-conservative view, however, because it may overestimate the US commitment to the expansion of democracy, and relies on the neo-conservatives being in power.

Taiwan's current strategy is a response to being excluded from the international community. Originally the government on Taiwan sought to claim international legitimacy through its identity as the Republic of China. After this failed, the ROC identity became weaker over time, replaced by Taiwanese identity. Rather than compete directly with the PRC over who could legitimately represent China, the strategy is instead to promote a state with a distinct Taiwanese identity in the international arena.

6.4   THE NEED FOR INSTITUTIONAL INNOVATION: UN MEMBERSHIP

It is now useful to look at an alternative mode of thinking to prevent a potential war from occurring. This involves institutional innovation. A peace agreement put forward by scholars has proposed that if Taiwan promises not to declare independence within fifty years, Mainland China will relinquish the use of force against Taiwan (Chang 1999b; White 2000). However, what is missing in the proposal is Taiwan's position in the world. Although Taiwan has already been a member of the Asian Development Bank and APEC, a peaceful unification policy requires Beijing's agreement to Taiwan's UN membership and intergovernmental cooperation.

Territorial communities like Taiwan have come to enjoy considerable international status. Taiwan has diplomatic relations with twenty-three countries. Does the reunification with China mean that Taiwan should break off its diplomatic relations with these countries? If yes, what would be the incentives for Taiwan to reunify with China? Beijing offers to allow Taiwan to retain its army, currency and political system but Taiwan has to surrender its sovereignty in the international community. This seems to be a modern version of Chinese traditional suzerain arrangement whereby the Qing court controlled the foreign policy of Tibet but allowed it to govern its internal affairs by itself. The suzerain arrangement was a sort of semi-sovereign system, under which a political unit enjoyed autonomy internally but did not have sovereign power externally. Such a model seems inapplicable to today's Taiwan, which in fact has already enjoyed considerable external sovereignty.

If the unification means a loss of external sovereignty for Taiwan, Taiwan would find it more difficult to accept.

To make reunification possible, China has to make a big concession by granting more international space for Taiwan. Then external sovereignty has to be flexible enough to accommodate Taiwan's demand for a seat in the UN. As Michael Davis (1999: 135), Professor of Law at the Chinese University of Hong Kong, argues,

> Beijing should recognize that affording an autonomous constituent community a substantial degree of international participation would help to gain its trust in any agreed arrangement. For a confederal Taiwan, this might even include participatory rights normally enjoyed by states. Taiwan's leaders will be reluctant to agree to anything less.

The inability to participate in international organisations is a major cause of anti-China feeling in Taiwan, so the Mainland should shelve political differences and work pragmatically with Taiwan internationally; this would also help establish mechanisms for dealing with crises and contradictions when they arise (*Chinareviewnews.com* 2012).

Taiwan could take three steps to re-enter the UN. Taiwan may first become an observer in the UN, as have twenty other states or organisations (including Palestine). Next, Taiwan may obtain associate membership. Finally, Taiwan may gain a seat in the UN under the name of China-Taiwan, similar to the arrangement of China-Hong Kong in APEC. The UN system does provide such institutional flexibility. For example, San Marino as a sovereign state associates with Italy but controls its own foreign policy and has UN membership. Liechtenstein as a sovereign state has agreed to share a limited number of powers with neighbouring Switzerland.

Even in the UN, there might be an asymmetric relation between China and Taiwan, that is, Mainland China as a member of the Security Council enjoys more power and rights than Taiwan would in the UN. If Taiwan were back in the UN, it should also be allowed to establish a sort of quasi-diplomatic relationship, for example, general consulate, with those who have already established formal diplomatic relationships with Mainland China. Again, this would be asymmetric: while Mainland China enjoys full diplomatic relationship with countries, Taiwan only enjoys the status of general consulate, as Ya-Chung Chang (1999b), a Taiwanese scholar of Mainland origin, suggests.

It should be stressed that China's support for Taiwan's UN membership would be conditional on Taiwan's commitment to an eventual union and a form of unification that would be under way. China should maintain its right of revoking the agreement if Taiwan is not on the reunification track in the first 10–20 years. This is a safeguard for Beijing, in case Taiwan's UN status emboldens it to move further away from reunification.

The proposal of UN membership as a possible solution to the Taiwan problem might sound 'unrealistic', because it is unlikely that current Chinese leaders will accept the idea of democratic federalism, or the idea of a separate UN seat for Taiwan. The current Chinese leadership rejects such a liberal or democratic line of thinking. Tang Shubei, Vice Chairperson of the Association for Relations across the Taiwan Strait in the 1990s, has asserted that democracy is not an essential question and that democratic reform should not constitute an obstacle to negotiations on the reunification question (*People's Daily*, overseas edition, 28 January 1999: 5).

Nevertheless, such a proposal is certainly not far removed from reality. In the mid-1990s it was reported that top leaders in Beijing did actually consider the recognition of Taiwan's political entity (*Central Daily News*, 28 May 1994). In an initiative of political dialogue, Beijing has promised that it would not appoint senior Taiwan officials as it does those of Hong Kong and Macau; also Taipei may maintain some quasi-diplomatic functions and the unified country need not be called the People's Republic of China (*South China Morning Post*, 5 January 2000).

Therefore, the proposal for Taiwan's seat in the UN is feasible in the future if we take account of the international practice of dual seats in the UN, the costs and benefits of the recognition of Taiwan's seat, the changes in Chinese practice of sovereignty, and the development of post-modern state sovereignty.

6.5   DESIRABILITY: A COST–BENEFIT ANALYSIS

Taiwan's UN membership is both desirable and feasible. There are numerous potential benefits if China agrees to Taiwan's UN membership. First, it can ensure peace across the Strait in the twenty-first century. In particular, it can break the cycle of tension and relaxation across the Strait, and reduce the possibility of military conflicts. It will also reduce the motivation of Taipei to buy military airplanes from the US for defence.

Second, the financial cost for both sides can be greatly reduced or saved as the need to compete for diplomatic recognition is removed (*The Australian*, 22 July 1999: 6). It would be far more beneficial to the people of Taiwan and the Mainland if the money consumed in diplomatic wars were wisely used on cross-Strait relations.

Third, Taiwan's UN membership might be helpful to reunification in the long run. If China welcomes Taiwan to the UN, then the two can create an economic union. This can in turn provide a foundation for political union. From a comparative perspective, dual seats did not prevent the final unification of the two Germanys (bear in mind that they had separate seats in the UN for seventeen years) and the two Yemens. It is the political arrangements based on mutual recognition, as in the case of the two Germanys, that have actually promoted the final unification. In the case of the two Koreas, since both are members of the UN, independence is a non-issue. For them, the only issue is reunification.

Among many reasons, one reason why independence is on Taiwan's agenda is that it is deprived of UN membership. If Taiwan were to become a UN member, the remaining question would be reunification. This would be beneficial to the improvement of cross-Strait relations. To achieve a final reunification, the sequence of action is important. The rigid view that any action taken must not be seen as a step in moving away from the goal of reunification is unhelpful. It might be a better sequence to allow Taiwan to join the UN and be autonomous before pursuing reunification. This would be 'dialectic' politics to realise China's reunification despite supporting a seemingly 'independence' policy that welcomes Taiwan into the UN. Reunification, like a marriage, should be a voluntary bond. Reunification is less likely if goodwill in Taiwan is damaged as a result of political pressure from the Mainland. Moreover, as a result of China's threat towards Taiwan, Taiwan's unification advocates cannot speak out strongly, otherwise they would be regarded as 'traitors' to Taiwan. However, they could develop into a more dynamic force for unification if Taiwan were admitted to the UN.

A fourth benefit of China being more positive about Taiwan's UN membership is that a contradiction between economic *convergence* and political *divergence* can be resolved. While economic contact and exchange are increasing between Taiwan and the Mainland, Taipei and Beijing are drifting further apart politically and emotionally. The diplomatic blockade by China aimed at hurting the Taiwan government politically and diplomatically also hurts the feelings of the Taiwanese people. As a result of Chinese pressure exerted in the name of reunification, the very notion of reunification is losing its appeal to many Taiwanese (Jacobs 1997: 25). China's recognition of Taiwan's UN membership will repair the emotional relations between the two sides. Beijing's respect of Taiwan's dignity and its compassion will do a great service for its reunification cause.

Fifth, China's recognition of Taiwan's UN membership will win international respect for itself. When China treats Taiwan unequally and violently, it invites international condemnation. If China respects Taiwan as an equal partner, it would be highly respected by the international community.

What is the cost of the recognition from the perspective of Beijing? First, the greatest cost is Taiwan's independence. Two seats for China's sovereignty means the reduction of one party's claim of sovereignty over the other. Moreover, a substantial cost in the eyes of the Chinese military is that Taiwan's independence poses threats to China's sea power and to China's domestic politics, for it sends a signal for secessionists in Tibet and Xinjiang. However, complete independence should be distinguished from the form of 'independence' implied in the proposal for Taiwan's seat in the UN. As stated above, the recognition of Taiwan's UN seat is a special arrangement that will require Taipei's commitment to reunification in return. In reality, to Taiwan, this is 'nominal independence', since Taiwan is already politically autonomous. Moreover, what Beijing would really like to have is only 'nominal reunification', as Beijing has promised that Taiwan would maintain its army, currency and government if unification materialises. Essentially Beijing will not have the right to control Taiwan's people and land, nor can it impose taxation. If that is the case, China should not stick to its rigid position opposing Taiwan's move for international space.

The second cost for Beijing is the loss of legitimacy upon which the CCP's political authority relies. In Chinese nationalist thinking, the Taiwan question is a potential and actual source of legitimacy for the government (Wu 2004). However, if the government can reduce the tension, lower the diplomatic cost, and benefit both the Taiwanese and Mainlanders, this will bolster the government's legitimacy.

The third cost for Beijing is the reduction of China's standing in the UN. Until now the exclusion of Taiwan has helped China to maintain its status and privilege in the international community. Don Feder, clearly a staunch supporter of Taiwan's efforts to secure UN membership, however, argues that excluding Taiwan does more harm than good because it undermines the UN's own principles. He argues that Taiwan is economically integrated with the world and democratic, and that excluding it from the UN denies Taiwanese the human rights that the UN is dedicated to upholding. It also exposes the undemocratic power politics at work in the UN (Feder 2003, 2004, 2006).

To consider the balance of costs and benefits, Beijing must consider the greatest cost of all, a potential war against Taiwan's independence, which would seriously damage the domestic economy, evoke opposition from Asian countries and the West, and delay its modernisation process. The cost of war outweighs the cost of making concessions to Taiwan's international demand. Of course, there are other perceptions of costs and benefits. Some military officers in China may see great benefits in war against Taiwan.

The above analysis contains a rationalist account, which sees the Chinese politics of UN membership in a new light. It stresses that membership is merely a political 'commodity'. China is on the supply side. To allow Taiwan a seat in the UN would not cost China anything; rather it returns enormous benefits. Could sovereignty then be traded for interests? A pragmatic approach would take such a trade-off seriously. Some countries sell membership or national licences to gain economic interests. Conversely, Beijing has used economic incentives in allowing some countries access to China's market in order to secure China's 'integrity', that is, to get these countries to promise that they respect Beijing's One China policy.

Can economic logic influence sovereignty? In so far as territorial sovereignty is concerned, Beijing has always maintained its rigid thinking: 'We won't make any compromise over sovereignty over Taiwan.' For Beijing, unification is the goal; and rhetorically, Beijing insists on no compromise in sovereignty. As Qian Qichen, former PRC vice-premier, said, 'We have never compromised in the least on a major issue of principle', and 'We have always stuck to our word' (Lim 2000). All in all, the key issue here is sovereignty. In its Taiwan policy, the Chinese government consistently attempts to defend its sovereignty.

Nevertheless, Beijing is flexible enough to adjust its practice of sovereignty, though it often rhetorically insists on the sacredness of sovereignty. The Chinese government has demonstrated considerable flexibility on some practical issues in its cross-Strait relations. For instance, Beijing negotiated a treaty with Taipei as a way of dealing with the hijacking and rerouting of numerous Chinese airplanes to Taiwan. While the negotiations initially foundered on issues of sovereignty, such as whether Taiwan has the jurisdiction to decide whether hijackers are to be sent back to Mainland China, Beijing ultimately compromised and agreed to an unwritten agreement on the handling of hijackers (*Central Daily News*, 20, 22 December 1993).

Another example is that in past years Beijing always emphasised the recognition of the One China policy as a prerequisite for any talk about 'three mini-links' of communication, transportation and direct flight. At the same time, former President Chen Shui-bian refused to recognise the Mainland's One China policy. 'Three mini-links' remained a roadblock. However, in 2002 Beijing suggested that three links, being seen as a technical and economic question, be negotiated and carried out without *a priori* resolving the dispute over the One China consensus. Now the issue is whether Beijing is flexible enough to allow Taiwan to have a seat in the UN, in effect allowing China's sovereignty to be represented by dual seats.

6.6   FEASIBILITY: COMPARATIVE LESSONS

China's current opposition to Taiwan's UN bid is predicated on the assumption that UN membership means independence for Taiwan. This does not seem a well-grounded assumption. When there is dispute over the national identity question, or the question of divided nationhood, the UN allows for dual representation.

From a comparative perspective, the two Germanys were admitted to the UN in 1973 and unified in 1990. The Yemen Arab Republic joined the UN in 1947, the People's Democratic Republic of Yemen became a UN member in 1967, and the two Yemens merged in 1990. It was also proposed that UN membership be granted to the two Vietnams, but this did not occur due to the formal unification of Vietnam in 1976.[1] Both the Democratic People's Republic of Korea and the Republic of Korea became UN members in 1991. Moreover, 189 countries have established official diplomatic relations with the South, and 165 with the North, as of the end of 2012.

One of the most important things that these cases tell us is that the UN system allows for dual representation to deal with the question of divided nationhood and that state sovereignty does not have to be represented by one seat in the UN. In 1945, the sovereignty of the Soviet Union was represented by the Soviet Union, Ukraine and Belarus, when the Soviet Union demanded two extra seats for its republics in order to increase its influence in international affairs. Today, Korea – the cultural motherland of the Korean nation – is represented by both South Korea and North Korea. It is clear now that Beijing's notion of one-sovereignty-one-seat does not equate with the way in which sovereignty is construed in the cases of the two Yemens, the two Koreas, the two Germanys and the Soviet Union, Ukraine and Belarus. China's opposition to Taiwan's UN membership might be justified historically in the sense that Taipei and Washington had successfully blocked Beijing's bid for UN membership in the 1950s, but finds little support from comparative politics.

One, however, may present an alternative interpretation, that is, legally speaking both East and West Germany were separate sovereign states when they were admitted to the UN. Nevertheless, West Germany thought the relationship between East and West was not that of 'foreign countries', rather a special state–state relationship. West Germany thought the two belonged to one mother country. According to this line of thinking, politically speaking, the two Germanys can be seen as sharing sovereignty in the UN when they joined the UN.

If the two Germanys, the two Koreas and the two Yemens could have dual seats in the UN, why is a similar arrangement denied to Taiwan? Many answers to this question can be found. Chinese scholars and officials often point out the differences between the China–Taiwan case from other cases. One of these differences is that the partition of the two Germanys and subsequently their dual seats in the UN was the result of an international deal. By contrast, the Taiwan issue is the result of civil war and therefore the two Germanys model does not apply to China. The two Germanys were two separate sovereign states under international law. But crucially, the precondition for both sides being UN members and each recognising the independence and sovereignty of the other was that neither would regard the other as a foreign country, sharing a common identity and living under the same roof, namely in a German cultural community. Such a precondition does not exist across the Taiwan Strait. The DPP aims to be independent and to create its own cultural and political identity. It doesn't even recognise the existence of the One China consensus said to be reached during the Wang-Gu dialogue held in Singapore in April 1993. The DPP's rejection of one country consensus makes a dual-seat arrangement difficult to achieve. When China cannot achieve a consensus on the One China principle across the Straits, it tries to create and strengthen this consensus within the international community, demanding that other countries declare Taiwan a part of China when signing treaties with China.

Another explanation is the asymmetric power relations between China and Taiwan. China as a greater power in East Asia is able to block Taiwan's bid to enter the UN, while North Korea was in no position to block the South's entry to the UN in spite of its initial objection to the idea of dual UN seats (Cough 1978). Here, it is China's greater power that renders the idea of dual seats improbable (Cooper 2009: 229). For this reason, it can be argued that it is imperative (as a precondition to the settlement of the Taiwan question) that China uses its greater power wisely. It must be pointed out that it is this asymmetric power situation that has brought in the power of the USA as a balancing force, thus creating a kind of power equilibrium and the current stability in the region.

6.7 PHILOSOPHICAL FOUNDATION: AGAINST ABSOLUTE SOVEREIGNTY

The old idea that one sovereignty enjoys only one seat is counterproductive in dealing with the Taiwan question. The new idea is that one sovereignty can be represented by two asymmetric seats in the UN. This flexible arrangement is capable of satisfying Taiwan's desire for international space, and yet is in line with China's One China policy. That is, Taiwan would still be a part of China, while at the same time enjoying special status in the UN.

Questionable is the tendency to regard territorial integrity as sacred and place it ahead of human rights, people, economic interests and culture. Sovereignty in the modern world is not sacred, but a commodity that has an exchange value. Sovereignty can be used in bargaining. Compromises on sovereignty can be made for the sake of economic interests. Here, what is required is political pragmatism, which is found in Deng Xiaoping's policies with a functional emphasis. A thorough political pragmatism contains the notion that economic interests can override symbolic sovereignty. In other words, symbolic sovereignty can be traded as a commodity for economic benefits. In the South Pacific, for example, symbolic sovereign right to issue national postage stamps was sold to overseas collectors (Pitcairn Island funds 20 per cent of its budget in philatelic sales). Today, Tonga licenses other countries to use the geostationary satellite slots it controls as a member of the International Frequency Registration Board. Tuvalu has leased out its internet domain code: tv.

It is useful to refer back to Mencius, who said that 'minweigui, sheji cizhi, junweiqing' ('The people are the most important element in a nation; the land and grain are the next; the sovereign is the lightest') (Fung 1952: 113). If this ancient idea of the people is married with the idea of democracy, it amounts to the principle that the people should be given priority in the cross-Strait bickering and that they should have a say. If the first priority is the interests of the people on either side of the Taiwan Strait and if peace is in the best interests of the people, then territorial integrity and state sovereignty can and should be negotiated. Sovereignty cannot be detached from the interests of the people. The use of force is certainly not beneficial to the people. Flexible policies in a spirit of magnanimity will better serve the interests of the people.

For this purpose, the nationalist idea of absolute sovereignty must be rejected. A nationalist approach justifies the power of the state to do whatever is necessary to preserve the integrity of national boundaries, and endorses the use of force to defend the superiority of national interests and the national territory. As British sociologist Hertz (1945: 150–1) remarks:

> The idea of the national territory is an important element of every modern national ideology. Every nation regards its country as an inalienable sacred heritage, and its independence, integrity, and homogeneity appear bound up with national security, independence and honor. This territory is often described as the body of the national organism and the language as its soul.

If Mainland China regards its right of sovereignty as absolute and maintains it over dissident Taiwan, and if a pro-independence group in Taiwan asserts an uncompromising right of self-determination on the part of any community that calls itself a nation, no peaceful solution is possible. In such a case, the politics of exclusion and the A-B-C paradox, pointed out by Morgenthau, take place: nation B invokes the principles of nationalism against nation A and denies them to nation C, in each case for the sake of its own survival (Morgenthau 1957: 481). It seems that the idea of absolutist national sovereignty must be abandoned in order to find a peaceful resolution to the Taiwan question.

Independence groups must not view the right to self-determination as absolute. To do so assumes egoism without taking account of the impact of independence, which is by no means simply a national identity question. At the present, the independence force will not entertain the idea that they should give up their effort to build an independent Republic of Taiwan as an incentive for Beijing to consider a renouncement of using military force against Taiwan. With regard to this matter, independence groups must consider the self-restricting strategy: to limit their claims on sovereignty so as to make a peace treaty possible.

If Beijing were to make such a move, a crucial precondition for the resolution of the Taiwan question would be some concession by Taiwan to its claim of sovereignty. Independence-related activities must consider the interests of China and the feelings of the Mainland Chinese people. The key issue is whether Taiwanese nationalists will exercise self-restraint on the right to self-determination and popular sovereignty with regard to the national identity question (Lu 1999a: 2). This has been a controversial question within the DPP. Some members of the DPP suggest that Taiwan should not waste taxpayers' money by maintaining diplomatic relations with a few small countries. The Formosa Faction also urged a bold step to fully open trade relations with the Chinese Mainland, on the western side of the Taiwan Strait. In early 1999, many party members of the DPP proposed that phrases such as 'establishment of a Republic of Taiwan' and 'determined by referendum' should be revised but this was rejected (M. Lu 1999a). In the ninth general meeting of the DPP in July 2000, the party insisted on its independence stance and that the national status of Taiwan must be finally decided by the Taiwanese people (*Lianhe Zaobao*, 17 July 2000: 22).

If Taiwanese nationalists insist on popular sovereignty as a final moral authority to settle the Taiwan question, Chinese nationalists will stress the necessity of the use of force against Taiwan's independence. An exclusive notion of sovereignty, be it national or popular, seems to be an intellectual source of conflict. To settle the Taiwan question peacefully, both sides of the Taiwan Straits need to pool together their sovereignty to form a loose federation and share their sovereignty in the UN. Both sides can learn valuable lessons from the European Union shared sovereignty arrangement.

6.8   COMPARATIVE LESSONS: US FEDERALISM AND EU SHARED SOVEREIGNTY

The experience of the United States offers China and Taiwan a federal model of sovereignty. This model attempts to balance the rights of the individual states against the sovereign power of the federal government. In this system the states have certain rights, such as the right to raise their own taxes, pass laws and administer their territory. The states recognise the sovereignty of the federal government and do not question the supremacy of the President, Supreme Court and Congress, although at times they may also use the court system to test the limits of federal powers under the Constitution.

Officials in China and Taiwan are familiar with this federal system. Many of them have personal experience with the US system because they have studied at American universities. When these individuals return to their home countries their experience can play a part in shaping policies.

The value of the US model to Taiwan and China is questionable, however. For Taiwan, the US experience that led to independence and the federal model is not a positive model because of the violent conflict that was a fundamental part of that experience. Not only did the US colonies fight a war of independence to establish their federal system, they later also had to fight a civil war to maintain the union. The Spanish–American war also played a part in the expansion of the United States. From a Taiwanese perspective this experience does not provide a viable framework for the peaceful end to the question of independence. The US offers Taiwan a model based on self-determination, but how to achieve this without violent conflict is unclear.

The experience of the US is also problematic for China's efforts to find a path to peaceful reunification. The US had used military power to defeat the southern separatist force. Chinese officials look to the US experience as a justification for military force against Taiwan, not as a model for peaceful unification.

In the process of 'unlearning' and 'relearning', it is important for China to learn the new practice of sovereignty from the European Union (EU) rather than the USA. The USA seems to lag behind the EU in developing new ideas and practices with regard to the sovereignty issue. Nationalist thinking still predominates in US foreign policy. When the two sides on the Taiwan Strait are both influenced by American nationalism, there seems very little hope for either side to get out of the messy trap of exclusive sovereignty.

From a normative perspective the US experience cannot provide lessons for either of the two actors across the Strait. Because so much US territory was claimed using force, the US experience is relatively unhelpful in finding a peaceful framework for solving the problem of reunification. The USA, unlike the EU, does not have complex arrangements with regard to sovereignty. It is still committed to the idea of one sovereignty and one seat.

A new model is required to inspire the political imagination on both sides. Governments in Taipei and Beijing can instead learn from the European experience. The EU certainly offers rich intellectual resources regarding the multiple possibilities of sovereignty arrangements. Western Europe has been peaceful since the end of the Second World War and the EU has been able to produce a flexible arrangement that is very attractive to its members. EU members see this arrangement as highly beneficial, to the extent that they are willing to give up a degree of their national sovereignty in an effort to ensure cohesion, stability and peace. The EU shows humankind the possibility of escaping the ashes of war and appalling human destruction, and of creating collaborative institutions across nation-states. A best case is the successful resolution to the territorial boundary problem in Alsace and Lorraine, a region over which France and Germany have shed much blood, and which now houses the European Parliament and the European Court of Human Rights.

From the Chinese perspective there are a number of barriers to accepting this EU model. The first difficulty is the common Chinese argument that Europe cannot be a model for China due to its vastly different history and culture. In addition, if China were to support a form of regional multilateralism along EU lines then it would also have to be willing to accept that it would not have the final say on many regional issues. As the strongest regional power, China would have to surrender some of its own power to allow regional middle powers to play a greater role. It is also possible that China's authoritarian political system makes it less likely to accept democratic decision-making and power-sharing at the regional level. Another difficulty of the European model is that it requires a strong degree of trust. States need confidence in each other in order to surrender some of their sovereignty and create a regional order. As Zhao (2005: 237) explains, 'agreement requires mutual trust, and to develop that trust the two sides must sit down and talk'. Once this initial unity and cohesion is achieved, then states can assert their sovereignty over certain areas and make adjustments to the conditions of the union, but a regional union needs an initial period of confidence in which to build unity before this can occur.

In a multilateral regional organisation each member must recognise the sovereignty of the others. Even if a regional multilateral union along EU lines that included China were to be established in Asia, there it is questionable whether China would be willing to recognise Taiwan's sovereignty and accept it as a member (deLisle 2002: 744). Another relevant question is whether there would be any consequences for China wishing to exclude Taiwan from such a regional block. Historically Taiwan has been part of the Chinese empire and has not had autonomy, while in more recent times China has had a track record of attempting to exclude Taiwan from international organisations.

From the Taiwanese perspective the EU model holds considerable attraction. Former President Chen has raised the possibility of the EU integration model being applied to Taiwan and China, although he stressed that it was based on principles of sovereignty, democracy, peace and equality (Ko 2006). Firstly, democracy is a precondition of membership in the EU. Taiwan could use its democratic credentials as justification for its membership in a similar organisation in Asia. Membership is largely open to regional states that can demonstrate the required qualities. Membership, once achieved, confers equal status with other members of the organisation. Additionally, and importantly, this kind of organisation is rooted in a post-modern idea of sovereignty, where states are willing to give up some of their sovereignty and attempt to create a transnational identity in order to obtain the benefits of close association. Finally, the EU model is useful because it began with economic integration and then moved towards political integration as economic links deepened. Taiwan's economic links with the Mainland and with other regional states provide a strong basis upon which to build along these lines.

If the EU model is to provide a framework for the relationship between Taiwan and the Mainland, then both sides need to demonstrate a certain amount of political imagination. They will need to be willing to abandon their preconceptions and view the conflict with fresh eyes. Regionalisation could offer a model for unification that satisfies both parties, but it is important to recognise that regionalisation can take different forms.

One possible form of regionalisation could involve Taiwan being left out of the formal organisation. In this case it would be vital that Taiwan consider what it means to be independent. China could use the benefits of membership to try to convince Taiwan to reunify and thus be included in the regionalisation process. It is possible in this scenario that the benefits of membership provide Taiwan with the impetus for reunification but it would depend on whether the Taiwanese view the opportunity of membership as something they are willing to forgo to retain their current status. Another possibility is that Taiwan could attempt to form its own regional body.

An EU-style model would also reduce the urgency and lower the political stakes surrounding unification for both sides. It would also provide an opportunity to rebuild a common identity across the Taiwan Strait (Chang 1999a). By taking practical steps to increase the processes of regionalisation and therefore bring Taiwan and China closer together, the issue of reunification could become somewhat redundant. In the European case, Gibraltar's push for reunification with Spain became less of a priority after Spain and Britain entered the EU and national borders became less important.

The EU model opens up the possibility of new thinking. The EU model provides a basic blueprint to which new ideas can be added. This framework allows the members to be creative and to work around their problems. Even within the EU itself the model is still developing and states must continue to work together to solve problems. Importantly, the EU model is not a stark choice between two options, such as reunification or independence, or peace or conflict. Instead it presents many different paths and invites all sides to think creatively about how to solve the issue. There are many different approaches to integration within the EU. Chih-Mei Luo (2011) has argued that the most appropriate models for Taiwan's integration with China are either the best-case Finnish model, which matches the approach of the pan-Blue coalition, or the worst-case UK model, which better fits the pan-Green coalition's approach. Applying the Finnish model would mean treating integration as being in Taiwan's national interest, but first focusing on economic and trade policy and developing a full economic community before considering political or security issues such as a political union. Applying the UK model would mean taking advantage of integration for economic gain while maintaining Taiwanese sovereignty, and focusing on the issues connected with the economy while rejecting any issues that might impact on sovereignty (Luo 2011: 285).

The flexibility of the EU model is part of its strength, but putting it into practice requires political imagination and long-term efforts. Policy-makers and politicians need to make adjustments to the basic blueprint in order to customise it to suit the circumstances. Other actors such as diplomats, academics, cultural figures and business leaders can also play a role in suggesting ways to adapt the model. Broadening the discussion in this way creates opportunities for new thinking. At the same time, the role of military officials is likely to decline under this model.

In the early stages of the development of the European Economic Community, the predecessor of the EU, the first areas of industry that the reformers focused on were the coal and steel unions. As a basis for building peace in Europe this strategy made sense, as it is very difficult to fight a war without coal and steel. What can we conclude from the economic integration that is occurring in Asia? The deep integration going on across the Taiwan Strait is significant. Could regionalism in Asia begin with economic integration and eventually provide a peaceful solution to the question of Taiwan's status?

The key to resolving the conflict is political imagination. Those most likely to make substantial contributions to this effort to rethink the dispute are the diplomats, economists, intellectuals and others who are committed to peace. In addition, a major issue for China is the cost of learning. If China can adopt flexible policies towards Taiwan, the cost will be lower; refusal to adapt to the post-modern notion of sovereignty is likely to cost China dearly. It would be tragic for both sides of the Taiwan Strait to learn the necessity of a post-modern notion of sovereignty and find cooperation only through war.

6.9   CONCLUSION

In the context of cross-Strait relations, both Mainland China and Taiwan hold the view that sovereignty is indivisible.[2] Both advance the position that sovereignty has no meaning if it is not located at a single source, and therefore that the ultimate choice for any cross-Strait settlement with regard to the determination of the sovereignty issue is essentially binary – Taiwan's incorporation into the PRC (under a credible separation of powers arrangement) or sovereign independence for the regime on Taiwan. With regard to the territory of Taiwan, either the Republic of China has sovereignty, or the People's Republic of China has sovereignty. They cannot both have sovereignty at the same time. Both share the presupposition of absolutist national sovereignty and are reluctant to make any concession on the sovereignty question. In such a context, no peaceful solution is possible. Absolutist national sovereignty excludes the possibility of establishing a federal or confederate system. The idea of absolutist national sovereignty cannot provide a solution to the Taiwan question. The Taiwan question can be resolved only if national sovereignty is compromised, negotiated and shared. Some sort of shared sovereignty arrangement could possibly provide for a feasible solution to the cross-Strait dispute (R. C. Bush 2005; L. Jakobson 2005).

The post-sovereign paradigm is an attempt to transcend nationalist thinking, challenge the traditional concept of sovereignty, and outline an alternative concept of sovereignty. It offers a pioneering solution but moves away from the reality of politics. It is unrealistic and alien to the current leadership in Beijing, but may, hopefully, appeal to the next generation of Chinese leadership. If political forces across the Taiwan Strait try to find a novel idea, the post-sovereign paradigm would be a qualified candidate. Taiwan's UN membership would be a more immediate way for both sides to take action to share sovereignty in a multilateral forum and a concrete step prior to the more radical idea of European-style regionalisation. Sharing sovereignty in a multilateral forum is one critical element of democratic governance structure.

NOTES

1. On November 16, 1976, the United States used its veto in the Security Council to prevent the admission of the Socialist Republic of Vietnam. However, Washington dropped its objection to Vietnamese membership in July 1977.
2. For a persuasive argument regarding the logical incoherence of notions of divided sovereignty, see Morgenthau 2006.

PART 3

On Tibet

7 Confucian and Marxist Theoretical Traditions of Minority Rights and Beyond

China has a long history of dealing with minorities, and a long tradition of theorising about ethnic relations, based largely on the Confucian tradition, and supplemented with Marxist belief in the twentieth century. These two very different traditions are still influencing the Chinese practice of minority rights and multiculturalism. They both stand in some contrast to the Western liberal model of minority rights. With the growing influence of liberalism in China, it is important to see how traditional Chinese political thought will respond to Western liberal ideas of multicultural citizenship, and how the Western liberal model of minority rights will impact on China's ethnic minority policy.

The above different theoretical traditions constitute paradigms through which we can think about the Tibet issue and the future of Tibet. Currently, the dominant Western theoretical paradigm is a liberal-democratic one with several features like self-determination, referendum and autonomy. While I subscribe to this theoretical paradigm, I think that it is necessary for us to look at different theories of autonomy which offer different answers and scenarios. One possibility is the Confucian notion of *ronghe*, a kind of civilisational intermingling or integration between peoples and different religions.

The above three theoretical traditions are difficult to reconcile, and create theoretical tensions and difficulties in addressing the autonomy question in Tibet. Currently Beijing's Tibet policy is a mix of Confucius' assimilation, Karl Marx's classless society, and Adam Smith's market force which will diminish the importance of ethnicity. The critical question is to explore areas of convergence to help reduce the theoretical gaps, and also to assess how Beijing can go beyond the Confucian and Marxist traditions.

This chapter examines the theoretical sources of current Chinese policies on minority rights. It will trace a complex combination of various intellectual inheritances, combining echoes of Confucian ideas of paternalistic guardianship over 'backward groups' or 'younger brothers' with echoes of Marxist/Leninist ideas of ethnic autonomy, mixed with echoes of liberal ideas of minority rights and affirmative action policies for minority groups.

The structure of this chapter is as follows. It begins with a brief introduction of the competing views of autonomy so as to highlight how different theoretical traditions offer different solutions to the Tibet issue, followed by an examination of both Confucian and Marxist discourse on minority issues and minorities' rights. After the theoretical review, it then engages with a theoretical debate between Confucianism and liberalism. It first articulates a Confucian view of *ronghe* in rejecting liberal multiculturalism, followed by a liberal critique of Confucian practice. The conclusion examines the limits of Confucianism, and calls for a democratic governance with regards to China's minority policy.

7.1   COMPETING CONCEPTIONS OF AUTONOMY

There is an intrinsic divergence between the concept of autonomy as understood by China and by the Dalai Lama and his supporters in the West (Yang 2009). The Chinese official conception of regional autonomy derives from Marxist principles. Both Mao and Deng conceptualised autonomy in a different and contrary way from current liberal theories of autonomy. The Preamble to the National Regional Autonomy Law (1984) states:

> Regional national autonomy means that the minority nationalities, under the unified state leadership, practise regional autonomy in areas where they live in concentrated communities and set up organs of self-government for the exercise of power of autonomy. Regional national autonomy embodies the state's full respect for and guarantee of the right of the minority nationalities to administer their internal affairs and its adherence to the principle of equality, unity and common prosperity for all its nationalities.[1]

By contrast, the Dalai Lama's *genuine* autonomy proposal draws on liberal principles of autonomy. The international campaigners for Tibet and the International Human Rights Law Group, for example, adopt Hurst Hannum's *liberal* definition of autonomy, which denotes a locally elected legislative body, a locally elected chief executive, an independent local judiciary, and joint authority over matters of common concern (International Campaign for Tibet and the International Human Rights Law Group's report 1994: 6–7).

The Chinese concept of autonomy plays down the role of local elections within autonomy, and sees autonomy as a product of political expediency (thus it can be changed when situations change) rather than as a consequence of inviolable rights. In the view of the Chinese state, autonomy does not involve an ontologically privileged right to self-determination. Rather, because the power of the centre cannot be denied or limited, it is fundamental, first, direct and unlimited, while autonomous powers are secondary, indirect, deriving from the centre and limited. It is the centre that delegates power to autonomous regions and determines autonomous powers and rights, and these are limited mostly to economic and cultural issues.

Being based on a liberal framework, however, the Dalai Lama's proposal of autonomy is characterized by local elections, self-governing power which the centre cannot unilaterally change, political and administrative control of the population, and a fixed internal border. This view is illustrated by Orville Schell (2001): 'After all, this is an era of self-determination. Most colonies and territories have been granted independence. Quebec is regularly allowed to vote on secession from Canada. Scotland holds referendums on autonomy from Great Britain. Why should Tibet not have the right to determine its future relationship to China?' This view does not in any way coincide with the view of regional autonomy held by the Chinese leadership.

The profound difference is the theoretic orientation and disposition towards the intermingling of different ethnic groups. While Confucianism prefers *ronghe* as a satisfactory solution to the Tibet issue, Tibetan leaders in exile, however, feel overwhelmed by the encroachment of Han Chinese and they prefer an internal boundary against the influx of Han Chinese into minority areas.

7.2   CONFUCIAN HERITAGE

The political philosophy of Confucianism has had a rich experience in dealing with minority issues. It accumulated substantial knowledge about them, as, particularly during the Yuan and Qing dynasties, China was invaded by minorities from the north and west. The questions of how to effectively control minority areas and how to deal with minority rule over China had to be confronted. Ironically, contemporary Confucian scholars have said very little about the ethnic minority question and minority rights. A library search for a combination of 'Confucianism' and 'minority rights' finds little in several data sources. No article is devoted to the topic of minority rights in de Bary & Tu (1998); and J. Chan's (1999) work has also seldom touched upon the minority issue. This is quite understandable as Confucianism is primarily a doctrine of morally regulated family–state relations; and the current scholarship on Confucian political philosophy focuses on good governance, rulers and moral leadership.

Despite the above limitations, the Confucian doctrine of five relations (ruler–subject, parent–child, husband–wife, older–younger brother and friend–friend) is useful in addressing the minority question even though it does not specifically aim to deal with the relationship between a majority and minorities. Within a Confucian culture, with its emphasis on family, minorities are seen as younger brothers, sometimes as occasionally disobedient ones. Confucian obedience involves minority groups conforming to Confucian norms, maintaining unity and correct relations. Importantly, Confucianism gives priority to the state. In the state-dominated framework, the value of minorities is seen as instrumental in serving and strengthening the state; and minorities do not have an ontological status of autonomy; nor do they enjoy equal status with the majority, as will be discussed below.

The dominant framework within which Confucian scholars have dealt with the question of minorities is the Yi-Xia doctrine. In the Confucian order, Xia (Han Chinese or Zhongyuan) are the rulers while Yi (barbarians, outsiders or minorities) are the subjects; Xia is the centre, while Yi are the peripheries; Xia consists of insiders and fellow country people, while Yi consists of outsiders and strangers; and Xia is superior while Yi is subordinate. The idea of Yi-Xia supports the Middle Kingdom and the central power of China.

Confucius' approach to minorities is premised on the moral principle of *ren* (compassion), or the assumption that Xia embodied this moral principle; if the minorities conform to it, all under Heaven can coexist peacefully. It was expected that Yi would not disrupt Xia (Liu 1999: 98–102). Mencius held the view that Xia could cultivate or civilise Yi, but not the other way round. Writing after the fall of the Mongol Yuan dynasty, Fang Xiaoru (Fang Hsiao-ju), a great Confucian scholar in the Ming dynasty, asserted: 'to elevate them [barbarians] to a position above the Chinese people would be to lead the world to animaldom. If a dog or a horse were to occupy a human's seat, even small boys would be angry. . . . Why? Because the general order would be confused' (cited in Fincher 1972: 59). Fang insisted on the importance of the distinction between Chinese and barbarians and asserted that a barbarian should not hold the Chinese throne. In Chinese history, many Confucian scholars and officers ruthlessly ordered the killing of minorities, like Wang Yangming in Guangxi in the Song dynasty and Zuo Zhongdang in Gaishu in the Qing dynasty, for example. Their actions were deemed justified by the implicit idea that Yi was treated as a sort of animal. In the Chinese language, the names of many minorities are closely related to animals.

Not all Confucian scholars agreed on how to interpret the Yi-Xia relationships. For example, Hao Jin, a Confucian scholar who lived in the Yuan dynasty, developed a new interpretation of the Yi-Xia doctrine. The essential argument of his interpretation was that Yi can rule China if they follow Confucianism. In this interpretation, Confucianism has gone beyond ethnicity – it does not necessarily belong to Han Chinese – and ethnic groups can also cherish and develop Confucianism. The rulers of China can be anyone committed to Confucianism, regardless of their ethnic backgrounds. Through this interpretation, Han Jin recognised and legitimised minority rule, and the right of (Yuan dynasty) Mongol to rule China if Confucianism were followed (Liu 1996: 457–73).

While the Confucian Yi-Xia doctrine typically privileged the Han Chinese, in practice ethnic minorities enjoyed a degree of autonomy, institutionalised in the *tusi* (土司) native chieftains system. *Tusi* – the product of imperial expansion – was the official native system of appointing minority hereditary headmen during the Yuan, Ming and Qing dynasties. In such a system a headman was appointed by, or inherited his position through the confirmation of, central authority. Headmen enjoyed a number of autonomous powers, such as the right to tax and the right to have their own culturally regulated laws (Jiang 1990: 138–45). As Dreyer (1976: 10) explains, '[this] hereditary elite was responsible for the taking of censuses, the collection of taxes, and the keeping of the peace. The tendency was to avoid interfering with local affairs unless developments directly threatened imperial control of the area.' These practices, which lasted for several hundred years, can be seen as customary rights in the sense that they are customary practice and have to be followed and cannot be broken. While customary rights are not absolute, they are important for safeguarding the right of minorities to defend their way of life.

Building upon the Yuan dynasty's system, the Ming dynasty under Emperor Zhu Yuanzhang used the *tusi* system as its fundamental policy for governing the southern minorities. The Ming dynasty's *tusi* were divided into two kinds – civilian and military. *Tusi* were conferred by the Ming court with seals, official dress and talismans as tokens of their office. Regions even legally held armies and weapons. There was a joint system of inherited *tusi* and appointed Han officials; a kind of co-governance between locals and outsiders. There were two forms of the joint system. In regions where *tusi* power was comparatively strong, *tusi* took a principal position, with the outside Chinese official as deputy. This was the fundamental situation in the Guangxi *tusi* area, for example. In regions where *tusi* power was weak, however, the outside official took a principal position, with the *tusi* as deputy.

The *tusi* system confronted a number of practical problems under the Yongzheng regime in the Qing dynasty. Minority areas had witnessed internal struggles over the level of taxes and other issues. This led to some minority people going to the Han area and asking for arbitration and justice. At the same time, some Han criminals escaped to minority areas in order to benefit from minority laws. All of this caused tensions between minorities and the Han, and raised questions concerning political and legal unity.

Under Emperor Yongzheng's rule (1722–35), a debate took place over whether the *tusi* system should be ended. Confucian scholars held the view that it should be continued while Yongzheng and his supporters initiated the *gai tu gui liu* policy to end the autonomy system and to establish a unitary political system. Confucian scholars also preferred a moral persuasion approach to military force, and urged minorities themselves to demand the reform of the *tusi* system.

Gai tu gui liu (改土归流) was a policy of replacing native chieftains with state officials; it involved abolishing *tusi* in many frontier regions with large ethnic minority populations in favour of a system of limited-tenure official titles and the same Confucian culture and the written system of *hanzi* (Xu 1998). It has been the dominant policy since the Ming and an administrative force that has consolidated Chinese linguistic imperialism. *Gai tu gui liu* converted the law and cultural customs of any minority into a unitary system of administrative control. In particular, the policy encouraged the elite and even ordinary people of ethnic communities to study Chinese and sit for the imperial examination, so that they could become Chinese officials. In the process of *gai tu gui liu*, some minority languages were gradually eroded and Chinese Han language slowly became dominant. Today, in the contemporary *neidi Xizang ban* and *Xinjiang ban*, the dislocated boarding school policy seems reminiscent of Chinese Ming and Qing historical practice (Chen Yangbin 2014).

After a transformation from the *tusi* system to the unitary system, Confucian schools were established, and minorities, who had been banned from taking examinations by their chiefs, were encouraged to take examinations for official posts. They had to learn the official language within eight years as a prerequisite for their imperial examination. Clearly, despite the initial opposition of Confucian scholars to the unitary system, Confucianism played a significant role in the process of assimilation.

Yongzheng's forced reform led to rebellion in Guizhou. As a result, when

Qianlong became emperor, he granted tax exemptions for the Guizhou area and the right of the Miao minority to follow their traditional laws. It was no longer up to the central government to settle disputes taking place in the Miao community in accordance with central laws (Feng 1992: 386–99). Nevertheless, the trend of *Gai tu gui liu* continued into the Qing dynasty era.

Despite the fact that Confucianism was heavily criticised and discarded in the May 4th Movement in 1919, Confucian legacy is still important. *Gai tu gui liu* embraced a different political language of Marxism. The so-called 'democratic reform' in Tibet in the 1960s can be seen as a revised modern version of *Gai tu gui liu*, as will be discussed in more detail in Chapter 9. The difference was that Marxism was employed to reform so-called 'feudal' Tibet in the 1950s and 1960s, and Marxism was established as the official ideology while Confucianism was heavily criticised during the Cultural Revolution. However, both Confucianism and Chinese Marxism endorse the idea that minorities are 'backward' and need to be civilised by the 'more advanced' cultures of either Confucianism or Marxism.

7.3   THE MARXIST HERITAGE

In the twentieth century, the Confucian tradition has been supplemented, and to some extent supplanted, by Marxist ideas. However, like Confucianism, Marxism has been interpreted in various ways in terms of the status of minority groups.

For Marx and Engels, the historical forms of human identity, as expressed in inherited cultures, should not be viewed as authentic (Gray 1993: 159–60). They expressed a preference for strong, centralised states that assimilate smaller minorities. Marxist historical materialism justifies an assimilation policy. The upshot of the argument is that an interconnected world makes it difficult to resist assimilation, and that cultural change, caused by economic development, is a central human condition. All cultures have undergone great transformation. Some historical communities have been extinguished, while others have survived. The traditions and customs of those which have survived have been changed and for some partly lost.

The Marxist tradition has, however, been developed in other directions. The Soviet model, developed by Lenin, endorsed the idea of national self-determination and multinational federalism. The Soviet Constitution even legitimated the right to secession by national minorities.

Mao Zedong

Following Marxist theory, Mao Zedong maintained the view that the nationality question is by nature a question of class and that nationality and ethnicity will wither away after the end of class conflict. Mao also held that class division is much more important than ethnic division, that the majority of any nationality are peasants and workers, and that working classes across different nationalities could and should be unified against their common enemy, the exploiting class (Chen, Liu & Qiao 1998: 33–8; Yang & Wang 1994: 1–8).

The Chinese Communist Party (CCP), in the beginning, agreed with and supported Lenin's policy on the right of self-determination by national minorities, as evident in motions passed by the 1st Chinese Nationalist Congress (Mao 1966: 1033). Article 14 of the Constitution of the Chinese Soviet Republic declared in November 1931:

> The Soviet government in China recognizes the right of self-determination of the national minorities in China; the Mongols, Moslems, Tibetans, Miao, Li, Koreans and others inhabiting the territory of China enjoy the complete right to self-determination, that is, they may either join, or secede from, the Federation of Chinese Soviets, or form their own state as they may prefer. (Central Data Library 1991: 775–6)

Later this policy of self-determination was completely abandoned by the CCP. Mao Zedong abandoned it on the following grounds: (1) Lenin's theory of self-determination was used by Japan to support the independence of Mongolia; (2) The right to self-determination only properly applies to the case of oppressed nations casting off the rule of imperialism and colonialism to fight for independence, and hence does not apply to minorities within a socialist state; (3) The right to self-determination is not feasible in China, where different nationalities overlap and are interdependent (Yang & Wang 1994); (4) The self-determination of China's nationalities had been decided, once and for all, by their common revolutionary struggle and voluntary incorporation in the PRC (Smith 1990: 78).

The CCP not only rejected the principle of national self-determination, it also rejected the idea of federalism. Originally, Soviet-style multinational federalism was favoured by the CCP to accommodate the aspirations and needs of minorities. Nevertheless, Mao thought that federalism was not applicable in China because: (1) Marx, Engels and Lenin all supported a unitary centralised system; and (2) China, as a unitary country in which many nationalities have lived together for centuries, is different from Europe in general, and Russia in particular, where federalism was adopted in the wake of communist revolution (Ma & Zhong 1998: 29–38).

In place of federalism, a weaker system of regional autonomy was established. It applies in areas where a minority nationality lives in a compact community. Article 30 of the 1982 Constitution states that

> the administrative division of the People's Republic of China is as follows: (1) The country is divided into provinces, autonomous regions and municipalities directly under the Central People's Government. (2) Provinces and autonomous regions are divided into autonomous prefectures, counties, autonomous counties and cities. (3) Counties and autonomous counties are divided into townships, minority townships and towns. Autonomous prefectures are divided into counties, autonomous counties and cities. All autonomous regions, autonomous prefectures and autonomous counties are minority autonomous areas. (*Zhonghua renmin gongheguo xiafa* 1997: 9)

Deng Xiaoping

To a large extent, Deng Xiaoping continued to follow Mao's theory of minority nationality. Like Mao, Deng asserted that the autonomous ethnic minority system is suited to the Chinese situation and works much better than federalism. He claimed that the Chinese unitary system, comprising many autonomous minority regions, could not be given up, for it has many advantages (Deng 1993: 257). He argued that it is better than a federal system as demonstrated by the fact that the federal system of the former Soviet Union and Yugoslavia promoted localism and ethnonationalism and finally led to the collapse of the socialist system. In Deng's theory, a unitary system with autonomous regions for ethnic minorities is the best system to defend the unity of the nation-state against secessionism, and therefore works best for China (Chen & Wei 1998: 39–44; Sun Yi 1998: 43–8).

Deng emphasised the implementation of 'genuine autonomy' in terms of the rule of law. He said clearly that genuine autonomy involves putting into effect all self-governing rights according to the law, that is, all the autonomous rights as defined by the Constitution and the Autonomy Law (*Guojia minwei zhengce yanjiushi* 1997).

Traditional Marxist and Maoist class analysis of the ethnicity question and of the 'vanishing' of ethnicities had no place in Deng's pragmatism. But he shared with traditional Marxism, or perhaps Adam Smith, a form of economic determinism or reductionism regarding the minority question. While Deng repudiated the importance of class background, he emphasised the market and economic development as a way of dealing with the ethnicity question. For him, without economic development, autonomy is an empty word (Deng 1993: 167). Deng stressed the economic prosperity of ethnic minorities. For Deng, economic development is the way to prosperity, and prosperity will provide the ultimate resolution to the ethnic minority question. Deng said, for example, that 'Tibet is so big but has a small population. Developing Tibet only by Tibetans is not enough. It is not bad for Han Chinese to help them to speed up economic development' (Wang and Huang 1995: 3). Accordingly, the influx of Han Chinese into Tibet's minority areas was seen as a necessary step in assisting economic development. For example, Deng (1993: 246–7) told the then US President Jimmy Carter that 'it is not a bad thing if the number of Han population increases in minority areas; the key issue is whether the economy has developed there.'

Deng's theory of modernisation requires economic development to override any consideration of ethnic identity. Deng therefore highlighted the centrality of 'stability' (that is, the absence of conflict) in the autonomous regions. For him, the maintenance of stability is a precondition for economic development and the improvement of the autonomy system (*Guojia minwei zhengce yanjiushi* 1997). In order to maintain this stability, any form of minority autonomy that might generate conflict was overridden.

Jiang Zemin and Hu Jintao

The former general secretaries, Jiang Zemin and Hu Jintao have followed Deng's economic approach to the minority question. In 1992, Jiang Zemin stated that there is nothing trivial in the affair of ethnicity at the 1st National Conference on Ethnic Affairs. He called for a special emphasis and concern with minority issues. In the late 1990s, the Greater Western Development Plan was formulated and implemented in association with the need to speed up the economic development in minority areas. Jiang held the view that the key to solving the minority issue lies in speeding up economic development. In Maoist language, Jiang regarded the minority problem as 'the problem within people', not that of 'enemy versus friend'. In September 1990, Jiang Zemin articulated the notion of 'the three unbroken relations' (*sanbufenli*), that is, the Han cannot do without minorities, minorities cannot do without the Han, and minorities themselves cannot do without each other. Through such a formulation, Jiang again stressed the importance of national unity (Zhou 2010: 491).

Hu Jintao built up these ideas. For Hu, minority relations should be based on common grounds, that is, all nationalities must work together in solidarity, and must achieve co-prosperity. He defines the socialist nationality relations as 'equality, solidarity, mutual aid and harmony'; equality is the foundation stone, solidarity is key, mutual aid is guarantee, and harmony is the essence of all nationality relations. In 2009, Hu Jintao formulated the four 'never giving-up' or 'four sticking-to' policy: stick to the socialist road, stick to the minority policy of the Party, stick to the working together and solidarity principle, and stick to the unity of nation. His minority policy is also based on the notion of 'two hands': one hand on development, and the other hand on stability (Xie and Ji 2012).

In short, the Marxist legacy is a mixed one regarding minority issues. On the one hand, due to the influence of the Soviet model of multinational federalism, ideas of 'minority autonomy' have been a familiar and acceptable part of political discourse in China since the 1930s, long before they became popular in the West. On the other hand, these ideas of minority autonomy have clearly been subordinated to centralised Party rule and the imperatives of economic development.

7.4   CONTEMPORARY DEBATE ON LIBERAL MULTICULTURALISM IN CHINA

Liberalism, with its rich experience in confronting the minority question, has developed different systematic theories of minority rights. Will Kymlicka (1989, 1995), for example, persuasively argues that democratic institutions should include minority rights, in particular the right of national minorities not to be assimilated into a larger community. His interpretation of liberal theory justifies and defends the institutionalisation of internal boundaries between communities within a nation-state, and fundamentally challenges the Confucian approach to the minority question. Moreover, Western liberal theories of minority rights have quickly penetrated into

Asian studies. Thomas Heberer, for example, applies a liberal idea of minority rights and social justice in his study of the minority issue in China. He criticises China's immigration policy and argues that 'in the long run such a hard line and its effects may be the ultimate block to the unity of the country' (Heberer 1989: 131; B. He 1998: 20–44; Kymlicka & He 2005). Kymlicka (1995: 194–5) himself has also raised the issue of whether his theory can be extended to address ethnic problems in Africa and Asia. Moreover, according to Kymlicka's model of liberal multiculturalism, the idea of assimilation should be rejected, at least for national minorities, who should be accorded the right to maintain themselves as distinct societies alongside the majority culture. This right includes, if necessary, defining internal political boundaries that enable a minority group to live and interact primarily among themselves, and reduce their need to interact with members of the larger society.

In the intellectual context of liberal multiculturalism, many scholars, inside and outside China, have argued that a liberal multicultural approach is needed for Tibet. It is argued that Confucian sources can be used to support minority rights and implement liberal minority rights. In this process of the appropriation of Confucianism, is it possible to retain some Confucian cultural characteristics? Is Western-style liberal multiculturalism the only or best alternative to the status quo in China? The crucial issue concerns the use of internal territorial boundaries to prevent or reduce the intermingling of different groups. The Confucian discourse of *ronghe* is likely to play a role in the politics of minority issues, and it will continue to push China in the direction of ethnic intermingling.

In modern China, Sun Yat-sen advocated an assimilationist policy to achieve national unity, using both the terms *ronghe* (intermingling) and *tonghua* (assimilation) (Yang, Wang & Siu 1998: 11). In 1957, the then Chinese Prime Minister Zhou Enlai rejected 'reactionary' assimilation – where one group destroys another by force – and encouraged the 'progressive' assimilation or national merging of ethnic groups in advancing towards prosperity (Grunfeld 1996: 262).

Today, leaders in Beijing prefer the word *ronghe* to the term *tonghua*. In the official Chinese theory of minority rights, the term *minzu zizhuquan* is used to express the right to self-government by the minority group, but such a term does not accept the idea of non-assimilation, nor does it tolerate the attempt to institutionalise an internal boundary through any sort of system of territorial reservations. China's constitution says nothing about the right of minorities not to be assimilated. In fact, refusal to assimilate is usually interpreted as undermining national unity and the state's stability.

Beijing leaders prefer *ronghe* (intermingling) to *tonghua* (assimilation) for a number of reasons. Philosophically, the former term assumes equality between two parties, while the latter assumes a superior position of one party over the other. Liu Xigan (1984: 183) explains the distinction between assimilation and *ronghe* in the following: ethnic assimilation is imposed by force by an outside ethnic group; the assimilated ethnic group is in a passive position and is not consciously and willingly complying but rather is being forced or bullied into changing their ethnic characteristics and giving up their original way of life and beliefs. *Ronghe*, in contrast, is the fusion or amalgamation of majority and minorities in a self-voluntary process.

In an ideal Confucian world, to harmonise the relations between different ethnic and cultural groups and communities is a top priority. This harmonisation approach recognises differences while not imposing conformity, and minimises conflicts while not undermining autonomy. It stresses mutual respect and responsibility (Bodde 1967: 46–7). Under the umbrella of *ronghe*, minorities are encouraged to maintain and develop their cultures insofar as they do not constitute a political threat to the unity of the state, and they contribute to diversity, aesthetics and tourism.

Ethnic *ronghe* (intermingling or integration) occurs in two forms according to Liu Xigan (1984: 180–1). One form is the intermingling between each ethnic minority and the Han ethnic group. For example, through the 'tribute system' or intergroup trade, some members of ethnic minorities resided in central China, married and had children, produced descendants, flourished, and gradually lost their original ethnic characteristics and integrated among the Han people of the central plains. There were also some Han workers who moved to border regions, either to open up new farming areas or to escape from famine and conflict, who engaged in joint production with the ethnic minorities of those regions, exchanged expertise, intermarried, and gradually lost their original Han characteristics. The second form of *ronghe* is where different ethnic people unite together as a major ethnic group and engage in action in the name of that ethnic group, moving towards integration for unity. This often takes place in border regions due to ethnic cohabitation and intimate economic and cultural contact. China's ancient ethnic groups, such as Xiongnu, Rouran, Tujue, Huihe, Yue and Qiang, were produced under this kind of *ronghe*.

Ronghe is thus a natural integration between ethnic groups. It is the result of intimate inter-ethnic contact in the economy, culture and daily life, and does not involve force or pressure. Instead it is built on a base of mutual equality, mutual understanding, and playing to the strengths of each group (Liu 1984: 181).

Ronghe is not equal to sinicisation, and it is different from absorption. For example, let us suppose A and B are ethnic groups. Absorption means that either A absorbs B, which then loses its identity, or B absorbs A, which loses its identity. By contrast, *ronghe* has three patterns or processes of intermingling A and B:

1. A and B form a hybrid entity and create new properties.
2. A and B coexist and both of them maintain their crucial separate identities.
3. A and B coexist and some major properties of A and B are lost.

There are numerous historical instances illustrating these three models that have provided cultural and historical grounds for *ronghe* policy in China. These examples will help to explain the persistence of China's *ronghe* policy and will demonstrate the reasons for preferring it to the institutionalised internal boundaries for minority groups.

An instance of the first model was the formation of Han ethnicity, which was the product of the intermingling of numerous ethnic groups in the Chinese history. It is now difficult to make a distinction between A and B and others.

The second model was represented by the relationship between the Han and Yi. The Yi ethnic group has lived in Yunnan Province for around a thousand years. Today, younger generations of the Yi, whom I asked in my field trip in 1996, surprisingly know nothing about a huge tomb where 10,000 Han Chinese were buried. They were killed by the Yi in a battle that took place during the Tang dynasty. Intermingling and cultural assimilation has occurred and both Han and Yi now coexist while the Yi still maintain a distinctive cultural identity.[1] Another example is the relationship between Buddhism and Confucianism. Buddhism was sinicised when introduced into China, and was interpreted from a Confucian perspective. At the same time, neo-Confucian philosophy in the Song dynasty was deeply influenced by Buddhism. Nevertheless, both maintained their distinctive features and have coexisted for more than two thousand years.

The intermingling of the Manchu and the Han is the example of the third model. The Manchu used force to conquer Han areas and adopted Confucianism in order to rule the Han people. In 1723, Emperor Youzheng praised Confucius as the 'ancestor king'. In 1727, he regarded the birthday of Confucius as sacrosanct as that of Emperor Kang Xi, a founding father of the Qing dynasty. When the Manchu established their empire, both Manchu and Chinese were official languages. After more than three hundred years, both ethnic groups were integrated. The Manchu language influenced Beijing's vocabulary and pronunciation, but today only a few people can speak this language. It should be pointed out that the key elements of this successful intermingling include the ruling Manchu adopting Confucianism as an official ideology, and the Han Chinese, albeit subject to 'foreign' political rule, maintaining a cultural leadership role in sustaining and developing Confucianism and changing its cultural practice.

These historical precedents provided a strong incentive for the Chinese government to continue to support the *ronghe* policy towards ethnic minorities, in particular in Tibet. Han Chinese and Tibetans belong to the same race; Buddhism and Confucianism have coexisted for a long time; and Tibetan Buddhism has had close relations with other branches of Buddhism in the rest of China. Confucian scholars would argue that Confucianism constitutes a counterbalance to Kymlicka's non-assimilation policy, for the latter has practical problems such as the misuse of minority rights to maximise self-interests, the institutionalisation of separate communities, the violation of individual rights, and the intensification of ethnic conflicts, such as in India.

Confucianism emphasises great unity and harmony, and is hostile towards Kymlicka's argument for non-assimilation. The Confucian central aim is to achieve *ronghe* and harmony between the majority and minorities, prevent conflicts between the majority and minorities (or among minorities), maintain stability and order in the context of a diversity of races and ethnicities, and promote the coexistence of plural ethnic identities.

China's *ronghe* policy encouraging intermingling is a major challenge. Beijing believes that *ronghe* is workable in Tibet, and that it will be more successful in the next few decades. *Ronghe* puts into question whether it makes sense to view certain multi-ethnic regions as having a specific ethnic identity. Chinese scholar Zhou Yong questions the usefulness of ethnic autonomy in situations where a region is multi-ethnic. It is unclear who is autonomous, and 'ethnic' in the term 'ethnic autonomy' loses relevance, for example, in some multi-ethnic autonomous areas (Shih 2002: 254-5).

Professor Ma Rong (2009), at Peking University, has been calling for the scrapping of ethnic autonomy and preferential policies, suggesting that the systematic segregation of ethnic groups and institutions in China has rendered the Chinese nation (*Zhonghua minzu*) an empty concept, and that the assimilation, or literally Hanification (*Hanhua*), of minorities is an inevitable process of modernisation. In a similar vein, Hu Angang (a professor and policy entrepreneur at Qinghua University who has influenced many national policies) and Hu Lianhe (2012) called for a 'second generation of ethnic policies': one that would remove barriers to 'ethnic contact, exchange and mingling' and bring China in line with global standards. Hu calls on the government to adopt an 'apolitical' approach to ethnic relations and implement a range of urgent and radical reforms. These include the abolition of regional autonomous units; a shift from ethnic- to regional-based preferential policies; the removal of ethnic status from identification cards and other official documents; the removal of barriers to ethnic migration, intermarriage and market flows; and the strengthening of Putonghua and bilingual education. In a February 2012 front-page article in the Party School's *Study Times* (*Xuexi shibao*), Zhu Weiqun (2012), a Central Committee member and long-time Executive Director of its United Front Department, echoed many of the same sentiments as Ma and Hu. Zhu admitted the serious problems in the Party's ethnic and religious work. Suggesting that the current focus on state-guided development will not solve these problems on its own, he called for more emphasis on voluntary, self-initiated, ethnic fusion, arguing that ethnic blending and mixing is not the same as Hanification. Zhu thus suggests policies such as the removal of ethnic status from identification cards; a freeze on the creation of autonomous regions; the strengthening of Putonghua; and ethnically mixed schooling (Leibold 2012a, 2012b).

Similar trends are also observed in the West, where multiculturalism has been criticised as it undermined national unity and integration. Scholars such as Meer and Modood (2012a, 2012b) and Kymlicka (2012) have noted that there appeared to be a shift away from multiculturalism towards 'interculturalism' within Europe, reflected particularly in the Council of Europe's 'White Paper on Intercultural Dialogue' (2008) and the UNESCO world report on cultural diversity (2008). Advocates of 'interculturalism' promote its elements of dialogue, communication and interaction in a positive contrast with multiculturalism. Cultural and moral relativism – seen as a negative component of multiculturalism – are dismissed in interculturalism in favour of the notion of respecting diversity within universal values. However, as both Meer and Modood (2012a, 2012b) and Kymlicka (2012) argue, the differences are more rhetorical than analytical. Indeed, Kymlicka perceptively notes:

> The 'interculturalism as a remedy for failed multiculturalism' trope is not really intended to offer an objective social science account of our situation, but rather, . . . is intended to serve as a new narrative, or if you like, a new myth. (Kymlicka 2012: 213)

In contrast, Chinese discussion of the second generation of ethnic policy can be seen as a kind of public justification for the pre-existing changes to the minority policy which have undermined the autonomy of minority rights in recent decades. It is not yet clear whether this will lead to a shift away from ethnic autonomy and towards a more assimilationist policy, or a distinct new Chinese approach to ethnic relations. It is important to note that if minority policy follows the direction suggested by the advocates of the 'second generation of ethnic policies', this will change the nature of the Chinese state in terms of its ethnic configuration.

These second-generation ethnic policies have, however, come under criticism from other Chinese scholars. Jin Binggao, director of nationality theory at the Central Nationality University and a scholar of Korean minority background, argues that: (1) it violates the socialist theory of minority relations; (2) it is a misunderstanding, as Hu Jintao emphasised 'in favour of exchange, communication and intermingling of all peoples', not just 'intermingling into one'; (3) it violates the law of nationality; (4) it violates the socialist principle of equality; (5) it violates the fundamental policy of the prosperity of all nationalities; (6) it violates the socialist autonomy principle and institutional arrangements as 'de-politicisation' is in fact designed to introduce a unitary administrative system in minority areas, thus undermining and destroying the existing autonomy system. Thus, Jin argues, the second-generation ethnic minority policies ignore the reality of the one-sided willingness to do the intermingling; it is a 'leftist' line of thinking (Jin and Xiao 2012).

Ethnic Mongolian scholar Hao Shiyuan also criticises these second-generation ethnic policies. Hao (2012a) argues that the core principle of China's ethnic policies is genuine ethnic equality, which involves all ethnic groups enjoying equal rights in the political, economic, cultural and social spheres. He uses Classical Marxist principles to argue that genuine ethnic equality requires the protection of minority rights in accordance with the different conditions, such as geographic or historical conditions, that might have led to inequality. Hao also takes issue with the claim by proponents of the second-generation ethnic policies that minorities have been the greatest beneficiaries of previous ethnic policies. He argues that this claim is misleading because policies to develop ethnic minority areas are the second part of a broader development plan in which the eastern part of the country has already undergone great development. Hao (2012b) also points out that proponents of second-generation ethnic policies are being misleading when they use growth statistics to claim that minorities are the greatest beneficiaries of economic growth, because they conflate 'minority regions' with 'minorities'. For example, although Inner Mongolia is officially a 'minority region', 79.53 per cent of people living in the region are Han Chinese.

Interestingly, different ideologies play different roles with regard to the question of intermingling versus an internal boundary. Scholars like Hao Shiyuan and Jin Binggao use Marxist doctrine to defend the autonomy system, while the Confucian legacy has been used to argue for a pro-intermingling ethnic policy or even subconsciously to provide support for assimilation. Liberal theory could play a significant role in defending minority rights. However, liberal theory such as that put forward by Will Kymlicka has not been fully understood or employed by Chinese liberals to defend the idea of the internal boundary. When I gave a lecture on minority issues at the Mizu University of China in Beijing on 21 October 2012, only two out of 220 PhD students knew of Will Kymlicka's writings.

It should be pointed that Ma Rong's view of the United States model is misleading. Ma views the USA as a model of cosmopolitan ethnic relations – the immigrant 'melting pot' – that emphasises the individual, in contrast to a pluralist model that emphasises the collective rights of different ethnic groups. In fact, it contains both cosmopolitan and pluralist elements. As Kymlicka (2000) points out, the USA contains distinct nations, such as Puerto Rico or various Indian nations, which, unlike new immigrants, are not expected to be part of the 'melting pot'. Although initially suppressing claims for autonomy, the government now treats these ethnic groups as possessing group rights and grants them autonomy in a way that it does not for other ethnic groups that have arrived through immigration. Moreover, the idea of intermingling implies bringing civilisation to marginalised or 'backward' people – a colonial sentiment or mentality. The 'civilising' approach is problematic for a number of reasons. It often creates and deepens conflicts and presupposes an ethnic hierarchy, which is unacceptable today. It also assumes a kind of paternalism, which is equally unacceptable.

7.5   CONCLUSION

China's minority policies have been shaped primarily by a mixture of Confucianism, Marxism and a pragmatic focus on economic development. Today's leaders prefer to talk about the intermingling (*ronghe*), rather than assimilation, of ethnic groups; and their understanding of autonomy is narrower than the liberal interpretation.

Confucian minority rights legacies are complex and diverse. Confucianism did recognise and promote the autonomy of minorities and their customary rights. Confucian scholar Han Jin's interpretation of Confucian Yi-Xia doctrine implicitly contained the idea of minority rule and minority rights, and transcended Confucianism beyond Han Chinese (also see Neville 2000). Minority rights of Confucian style have such Chinese characteristics as: customary rights of autonomy, duty-deriving minority rights, minorities' entitlement to certain benefits, paternalistic affirmative traditions, communitarian support for collective rights, and above all, instrumental minority rights for the purpose of great unity and harmony. All of these constitute the basis for Confucianism to support and promote minority rights (Cheng Chung-Ying 1998).

Nevertheless, Confucianism has its internal limits. Confucian customary rights, ethnic autonomy, paternalistic affirmative policies and minorities' entitlements are often compromised in reality. Confucian communitarianism fails to recognise equality between different cultural communities and cannot guarantee its full protection of minority rights. Fang Xiaoru, a great Confucian scholar in the Ming dynasty, held a conservative Yi-Xia doctrine of unequal approach towards minorities, which is still an obstacle to the implementation of genuine autonomy in China's minority areas.

The Confucian rejection of non-assimilation constitutes a theoretical obstacle to the implementation of genuine autonomy in Tibet, and may therefore exacerbate the ethnic minority problem. Confucian legacies inhibited new thinking. China so far has failed to develop a *ren*-based approach to the Tibetan people. The ultimate solution to the Tibet problem in China is dependent upon a constructive critique of Confucian traditions. Some scholars have argued that China needs a new framework for discussing relations among ethnic groups. Ma Yang (2002: 103–11), for example, argued strongly that the foundation of state unity and the harmony of all nationalities must be based on respect for human rights. Thus, state unity is not the highest goal if it does not promote human rights.

The human right discourse sets up a new framework in which Confucian normative terms such as 'brotherly love', 'the family-like state' and paternalism have limited value and cannot even get on the table for public reason or justification (B. He 1996, 2001c). The most significant challenge is that China lacks the negotiation mechanisms through which a consensus may be reached between the central state and the ethnic minority regions. Also lacking is democratic verification for minorities to be associated with the Chinese nation-state. While what Kymlicka advocates – polyethnic rights and special representation rights – have been written into the Constitution and have already been partially implemented in China, the question of whether minority rights have been internalised as a part of Chinese culture and collective psychology remains to be seen. China desperately needs democratic governance in dealing with minority issues.

NOTES

1. 'Law of the People's Republic of China on Regional National Autonomy', 1 October, accessed 31 October 2012: <http://www.china.org.cn/government/laws/2007-04/13/content_1207139.htm>.
2. This depends on how minorities see their belonging, and their perceptions of the relationship between national and minority identities. Ma Chunwei, an official cadre in charge of minority matters in Yunnan, whom I interviewed on 23 January 1996 in Kunming, said he was clearly conscious of being a member of the Chinese community and a member of a minority when he was an undergraduate. He thought both could coexist.

8 Beyond Socialist Autonomy in Tibet

In 1987 and 1988, the 14th Dalai Lama proposed that the government of the People's Republic of China would remain responsible for Tibet's foreign policy while Tibet would be governed by its own constitution or basic law, and that the Tibetan government would comprise a popularly elected chief executive, a bicameral legislature and an independent legal system. Ten years later, in 1998, the Dalai Lama expressed his great disappointment. 'Sadly, the Chinese government has not responded positively to my proposals and initiatives over the past 18 years for a negotiated resolution of our problem within the framework [apart from the question of total independence of Tibet all other issues could be discussed and resolved] stated by Mr Deng Xiaoping' (Shiromany 1998: 144).

Over the years, Western leaders and governments have pressed the Chinese leadership to talk with the Dalai Lama. In October 2001 the US Congress passed the Tibetan Policy Act initiated by Dianne Feinstein, the US Senator from San Francisco, and Tom Lantos, Representative of San Mateo County. EU External Affairs Commissioner Chris Patten and Indian Defence Minister George Fernandes also called on China to begin dialogue with the Dalai Lama in March 2002 (*Tibetan Bulletin*, Jan-Apr 2002: 9). A twenty-strong European delegation to China in July 2002 urged dialogue between Beijing and the exiled government of the Dalai Lama, but was told by China's leader Li Peng and Vice-Premier Qian Qichen that Beijing was not ready for talks with the Tibetan leader (Canada Tibet Committee 2002). In response to the March 2008 Tibetan uprising and Chinese government crackdown, some Western leaders as well as influential celebrities boycotted the Beijing Olympic Games, while others conditioned their attendance on progress being made in talks between China and the Dalai Lama's envoy (Traynor and Watts 2008). In recent years Western leaders have also been meeting with the Dalai Lama, including the US President in February 2010 and the UK Prime Minister in May 2012, despite protests from Beijing.

So far Beijing has not accepted the Dalai Lama's proposals but has allowed visits to China led by the Dalai Lama's special envoy, Lodi Gyari. Gyari led the first delegation to China and Tibet in September 2002. A year later, Lodi Gyari and

Kelsang Gyaltsen, accompanied by Sonam N. Dagpo and Bhuchung K. Tsering, visited the provinces of Jiangsu, Zhejiang and Yunnan from 25 May to 8 June 2003. These visits have given Tibetans in exile the opportunity to re-establish contacts, and to engage extensively with the Chinese leaders and officials responsible for the Tibet–China relationship. They aimed to build mutual trust but touched little on the real question of autonomy. The fact that the Chinese host institution for these visits was the Department of the United Front indicates that the Chinese leadership was interested in winning the hearts of Tibetan people in order to oppose separatism, rather than in coming to the negotiating table to discuss the Dalai Lama's autonomy proposal. On 20 August 2003, Chinese authorities rejected a visit request from the Tibetan government in exile for a group of prominent exiled Tibetans, including former Tibetan exile government ministers Sonam Topgyal, Tenzin Namgyal Tenthong and Alak Jigme, the former head of the Tibet Fund in New York, Princhen Dharlo, and former head of the Office of Tibet in Tokyo, Pema Gyalpo (Canada Tibet Committee 2003).

In 2008, in response to international pressure after the March Tibetan uprisings, the Chinese government held an informal meeting with the Dalai Lama's representatives in Shenzhen in May, and formal dialogues in July and October (Davis 2012: 432). The Tibetans then presented an official 'Memorandum on Genuine Autonomy for the Tibetan People', which outlined their position for autonomy within the framework of the Chinese Constitution. 'The Chinese response was quick and harsh' (Davis 2012: 434), accusing the Tibetans of seeking 'covert independence' at a State Council press conference in November 2008. The last time they met was in January 2010, and in mid-2012, citing frustration with the lack of progress and deteriorating situation in Tibet, the two lead envoys, Gyari and Gyaltsen, resigned (Yee 2012).

In the West, people tend to think that the Dalai Lama's autonomy proposal provides a sound solution to the Tibet question, that the Dalai Lama has already met China's precondition for dialogue, and that the real problem lies in the Chinese leadership's negative perception of the Dalai Lama. In this view, if the Beijing leadership changes its view on the Dalai Lama, the Tibet problem can be solved easily. For example, Professor Orville Schell (2001), Dean of the Graduate School of Journalism at the University of California, Berkeley, in his 'letter' to the Standing Committee of the Central Committee of the Chinese Communist Party's Politburo in June 2001, advised Beijing to view the Dalai Lama as an asset who could serve the interests of Han Chinese and Tibetans alike, rather than a die-hard 'splittist'. Schell argues that it is in China's interest to settle the Tibet issue and to implement full autonomy in Tibet because 'China's impasse with His Holiness significantly harms China's acceptance as a great and respected power.'

The question is, however, why did Jiang Zemin and Hu Jintao fail to take Schell's advice, thus losing an opportunity to leave a 'political legacy . . . [of] a Tibet at peace and a more unified China' (Schell 2001)? Is it the case that some Western commentators are too naïve to understand the complexity of the issue?

This chapter aims to address the following essential questions: To what degree can the Dalai Lama's autonomy proposal provide a solution to the Tibet question?

How does Beijing react to the Dalai Lama's autonomy proposal? Why does Beijing reject the autonomy proposal? To address these specific questions, the chapter will examine in detail Chinese official documents and academic articles in Chinese journals. Chinese documents and articles are often dismissed by Western commentators as 'propaganda', and indeed in many cases they are. Nevertheless, to understand Beijing's refusal of the Dalai Lama's autonomy proposal, it is essential to examine the Chinese theory and practice of autonomy. Chinese cadres in charge of the autonomy matter are informed by the Chinese official theory of autonomy. Indeed, in his visits to China, Lodi Gyari has confronted a substantial question, that is, Chinese officials always stress that China has already developed a sound system of autonomy, implying that China does not need the Dalai Lama's autonomy proposal.[1] My detailed documentary presentation of the Chinese official theory of autonomy in the previous chapter and Beijing's view on the actual status of autonomy in Tibet can help us to understand the substantial difference between Beijing and Dharamsala and the obstacles to implement the Dalai Lama's autonomy proposal. It should be noted that my documentary presentation and summary does not suggest that I share and accept the Chinese official theory and view.

The structure of this chapter is as follows. It first examines the current minority policy in relation to Western liberal minority rights models. Then it describes the current Chinese official practice of autonomy, followed by a discussion on the Dalai Lama's proposal on the Middle Way to achieve genuine autonomy. It then discusses and explains why Beijing rejects the Middle Way proposal and offers several explanations for the current deadlock. Finally, it offers some suggestions on how to make a breakthrough; in particular, the chapter discusses the future prospects of consociational arrangements.

8.1   CURRENT POLICIES ON MINORITY NATIONALITIES IN RELATION TO WESTERN MODELS

Current Chinese policies on ethnic minorities are called, in Chinese terminology, *zhongguo minzu zhengce tixi* (the Chinese system for ethnic minority groups). Insofar as Confucianism and Marxism have shaped this minority system, with liberalism having only a minimal historical influence, one would expect China's policies to differ significantly from those of the Western democracies. And indeed there are important differences, discussed below. But it is worth noting that there are also significant areas of overlap.

According to Kymlicka, Western liberal democracies have recognised three broad categories of minority rights: (a) self-government rights; (b) special representation rights in the legislature or bureaucracy; and (c) accommodation rights, providing legal recognition to particular customs or practices (Kymlicka 1995: 27–33). We can find elements of all three in contemporary China, although not in quite the same way as they are recognised in the West. I will briefly discuss each in turn.

(a) Self-government: As noted in the previous chapter, Mao ultimately rejected the Soviet idea of multination federalism in favour of a system of regional autonomy.

This system of regional autonomy comprises three elements: the Constitutional framework, laws governing autonomy, and government policies (Li 1997). The implementation of autonomy rights is a top-down process from the Constitution to laws and concrete policies, and from the central government to autonomous local governments. In the articulation of minority rights in the Chinese Constitution, autonomy rights flow from, and are subordinate to, state sovereignty, rather than reflecting any pre-existing sovereignty on the part of minorities.

The Preamble of the 1982 Constitution of the PRC recognises the historical contribution of all nationalities to the PRC, and the responsibility of the unitary multinational state to promote the unity of nationalities (*Zhonghua renmin gongheguo xiafa* 1997: 1–4). Unlike the Soviet system, which nominally recognised the right of self-determination and the right to secede, China stresses that all territories of the national minorities are integral parts of the land of China. Article 4 of the 1982 Constitution states: 'All the ethnic minority autonomous areas are inseparable parts of the People's Republic of China' (Ibid.: 5).

Article 4 of the 1982 Constitution of the PRC recognises the equality of ethnic minorities, prohibits discrimination and oppression, and respects minorities' customs and use of their own languages (Ibid.: 4–5). Articles 114, 117, 118, 119, 120, 121 and 134 of the 1982 Constitution specify the following autonomous powers for minorities: local administrative leaders from their own ethnic group; financial autonomy; independent administration of economic development; independent administration of culture; use of a local public security force; use of their own language in government; and use of their own language in court. All nationalities have the freedom to use and develop their own spoken and written languages, and to preserve or reform their own customs and ways (Ibid.: 26–8).

The Law on Regional Autonomy for Minority Nationalities (LRAMN) was adopted on 31 May 1984 and amended in 2001. It provides a wide range of autonomy rights. Administration must (or should) be in the hands of functionaries from the minority population. The regions can promulgate their own laws and regulations, draw up their own production plans (within the bounds of the central state plan), and choose their own path towards economic and cultural development (within the parameters of the constitution). The law allows autonomous regions to change or modify, or even stop, the directives and policies from the central government if they find these are not suitable for the local situation (Zhou 1993: 37–8). For example, in Daili, Yunan Province, minority law has softened the central government's tough punishments against drugs and hunting wild animals. Furthermore, the autonomous regions can administer local finances themselves (within the framework of financial planning for the state as a whole), and have their own local security forces (Heberer 1989: 41). According to Ghai et al. (2010: 153), the 2001 amendments are significant as they include market-oriented economic development, and as such, 'commits autonomous areas, as other parts of the country, to the modernisation of the economy'. This is designed to improve living conditions in autonomous areas and, importantly, to integrate them into the economy and more strongly within the central administration.

(b) *Special representation rights*: Article 59 of the 1982 Constitution requires appropriate representation in the National People's Congress (NPC) and in the

NPC standing committee. A quota system allocates 12 per cent of the NPC seats to minorities, although the population of minorities constituted only 6.7 per cent of the total population of China in the 1980s, 8.98 per cent in 1995 and about 10 per cent now. These national-level quotas are in addition to guarantees of representation within each minority's autonomous region, discussed earlier.

There are also various affirmative action programmes in place to improve minority representation in the education system. For example, Tibetans can enter universities with lower points (210 for liberal arts and 170 for sciences) than their Han counterparts (250 points for admission) when they pass the entry examination. Hui applicants are given 10–20 added points as minorities. Yi applicants receive 40 added points for being a minority and have their score on the Yi language exam (50 points possible) added to their total score. Barry Sautman concludes that 'most beneficiaries of preferential admissions will become the professionally-competent and politically-loyal graduates that the policy is designed to produce. This alone may guarantee the future of affirmative action in higher education in China' (Sautman 1997: 40).

(c) Accommodation rights: The Chinese state has also provided legal protection for certain practices associated with particular ethnic or religious groups. For example, male or female Muslim students are allowed to wear their white caps or headscarves in schools, although they are often discouraged and even discriminated against by a Han-dominated society.

The state also adopts a differentiated preferential policy (youhui zhengce) for ethnic minorities with regard to birth control. Minorities are effectively exempted from the 'one-child' rule. While Han Chinese are allowed to have only one child, Tibetan cadres, workers and staff members are encouraged to give birth to only two children, but no limit is set for the broad masses of Tibetan farmers and herdsmen in the number of children they may have (Luo 1991: 20).

In all of these respects, we see some important areas of convergence with liberal theories of minority rights. Moreover, it is worth emphasising that the Chinese state's policy on the identification of one's ethnicity or 'nationality' is that it should be by free choice (Zhou 1998: 39–42). A couple in a mixed marriage can choose the ethnic identity of their children. Their children can make a choice again when they reach eighteen years old.

And yet there are also important areas of divergence between China's current approach and Western models. One problem is that the actual practice of minority rights often fails to live up to the promises made in the Constitution and in laws pertaining to ethnic minorities. It seems that rights that are recognised on paper are sometimes ignored in practice. The question of whether legally mandated minority rights have been internalised as a part of Chinese culture and collective psychology remains to be seen.

But even if we focus on the laws, and assume that they are being (or can be) implemented in practice, there are still four serious problems associated with the Chinese laws and constitutional provisions on minority rights.

First, the Constitution and the LRAMN constrain autonomy rights in several ways. They state that autonomy should be under a unified state leadership. Self-governing organs must implement the laws and polices of the state (Art. 4 of

LRAMN) and 'place the interests of the state as a whole above anything else' (Art. 7 of LRAMN). Article 118 of the Constitution defines the role of higher bodies such as the National People's Congress to approve the statutes and regulations that govern the exercise of autonomy rights. For example, the standing committee of the Chinese National People's Congress has ultimate power over interpretation of the Hong Kong Basic Law; and the substance and processes of democratisation in Hong Kong have to be approved by the central government.

Second, China lacks a democratic verification mechanism for minorities. An independent constitutional court is absent, and the Party dominates the decision-making on minority policies. The chairperson of the autonomous region is chosen by Beijing, and the party secretaries and military commanders are usually Han Chinese. These practices have violated the true meaning of self-government in that leaders should be chosen by the people themselves through elections. Elected leaders should serve to represent the interests of ethnic minority groups and to balance local minority interests with state and majority interests. No wonder the Tibetan government in exile has often accused the Chinese government of lacking sincerity – Beijing has never appointed a Tibetan as the party secretary for the Tibetan Autonomous Region.

Similarly, the fact that 12 per cent of the seats in the National People's Congress are reserved for minorities does not guarantee the effective representation of national minorities, because in most cases there are no competitive elections for people's deputies and minority representatives are 'hand-picked' by the Party.

Third, the economic power of minority groups is circumscribed in a very funda-mental way. There is no concept of 'ethnic' land in China. The state has appropri-ated the historical lands of ethnic minorities, made them a common asset of the state, and denied any ethnic affiliation to them. Chinese minorities, as is the case for all Han people, only have usage not ownership rights; by contrast, Canadian Indians have their collective land rights constitutionally protected.

Fourth, in social life, ethnic organisations with political agendas at the local grass-roots level are forbidden, thus constraining ethnic people in being able to organise themselves and defend their minority rights when they are violated. This lack of the freedom of association casts doubt about the genuineness of the regional autonomy system. The political autonomy rights of ethnic minorities are seriously deficient due to the lack of basic political and civil rights.

8.2   THE PRACTICE OF AUTONOMY IN TIBET

A brief history of Tibet's autonomy since the 1950s

From the CCP's perspective, the agreement concerning the peaceful 'liberation' of Tibet, reached in 1951 between the central government and the Tibetan govern-ment, established the sovereignty of China over Tibet. For example, it established that China was to be responsible for the foreign affairs and national defence of Tibet. However, the Dalai Lama offers a different interpretation. His view is that Tibet was an independent state when the Communist Chinese army invaded in 1950/51, in direct violation of international law. It was the newly installed Communist government in Beijing that had forced Tibetans to sign a treaty for the 'peaceful liberation of Tibet' and which had then proceeded to occupy Tibet (Dalai Lama 1995: 4).

Article 3 of the Agreement stipulated that the Tibetan people have the right to establish regional autonomy under the guidance of the central government. The Agreement gave Tibet a high degree of autonomy: the position and authority of the Dalai Lama and Panchen Lama would be maintained, and the existing political system (the unity of politics and religion) would not be changed. This political accommodation in Tibet was different from the so-called 'democratic reform' established in other areas of China at that time. Such an arrangement can be seen as 'one-country-two-systems'. However, in 1959 the People's Liberation Army clashed with what the CCP called a 'rebellion led by the Dalai Lama', and the 'one-country-two-systems' for Tibet became 'one-country-one-system'. In September 1965, the Tibetan Autonomous Region was formally proclaimed.

During the Cultural Revolution (1966–76), autonomy existed in name only. The 1975 Constitution even deleted the provisions concerning nationalities' rights to develop their languages and maintain their cultural customs and traditions (Yao 1995: 18).

After 1978, the Chinese government tried to re-establish and improve regional autonomy. In the 1980s, the State Council abolished the people's commune system and admitted that its policy of forcing Tibetans to raise wheat rather than the barley they preferred had been not only a cultural mistake, but an ecological disaster as well (Dreyer 1989). With the arrival of Wu Jinghua as regional party secretary of the Tibet Autonomous Region (TAR), and with Dorje Tsering as regional government leader, a limited cultural liberalisation took place between 1985 and 1988 (Karmel 1995: 486). This provided, for example, increased freedom of speech for the Panchen Lama (Karmel 1995: 488). Wu Jinghua dressed in Tibetan clothing for his first speech as Party secretary, and Dorje Tsering promoted the training of more minority cadres, and an end to 'leftist' mistakes (Karmel 1995: 489).

However, since 1989 the CCP has adopted a tough policy towards Tibetan secessionism, which has undermined efforts to implement true autonomy. The break-up of the Soviet Union and 'peaceful evolution' in Eastern Europe were alarming precedents for China. Chen Kuiyuan, the former Party secretary of the TAR, explained changes in China's policies towards Tibet by referring to international changes in the post-Cold War era: 'Especially under the influence of the international macroenvironment, separatist activities have intensified in Tibet and the situation of the anti-separatist struggle has sharpened. These factors are causing political instability' (Karmel 1995: 494). China's official press also claimed that the Dalai Lama's supporters harboured 'a hidden motive': 'They want to take advantage of [turmoil] to split China. To be frank, they want to bring about another "Bosnia-Herzegovina" in China! But China is not Yugoslavia' (Karmel 1995: 494).

The focus in the 1990s and early 2000s to suppress separatism and economic development was seen as the best solution to deal with unrest (Ghai et al. 2010: 144). The 2000 'Open up the West' campaign was a key initiative in this regard.

However, increasing dissatisfaction led to intense protests in the TAR and other Tibetan autonomous regions – at least eighteen country-level areas in total – beginning in March 2008. These protests led to heightened military and police involvement, the most extensive within China since the 1989 Tiananmen Square crackdown (Henders 2010: 195). A Human Rights Watch 2010 report details the violence and subsequent restrictions (Human Rights Watch 2010). Arrests and illegal detentions have increased since then, frequently spiking in the lead-up to sensitive anniversaries. Other measures include security raids, increased surveillance of monasteries, arbitrary detentions of monks, restrictions on movement, and permanent police presence in some monasteries to monitor religious activities (Human Rights Watch 2011). Self-immolations by monks, nuns and laypersons have occurred in protest. This in turn has resulted in increased security in the TAR and other Tibetan autonomous areas. In July 2012, reports emerged of bans of public gatherings of more than three people in Lhasa, leading to the cancellation of daily group exercises (Human Rights Watch 2012b).

Areas of autonomy practice

We will briefly examine the Chinese practice of autonomy in four areas: politics, law, culture and the economy. First, in the area of political autonomy, according to Chinese sources, the growing ranks of minority nationality cadres constitute an important milestone in national autonomy (Luo 1991). In the 1980s, a large number of ex-serfs and their children took up leading posts at various levels of government in Tibet, including chief leaders of the people's congresses, governments, courts and procuratorates at various levels (Luo 1991). In 1982, all Party first secretaries and government leaders at prefectural and city level were members of ethnic minorities; and at county level, minorities accounted for 86 per cent of first secretaries, county chiefs and people's congress standing committee chairmen. By 1994, there were 37,000 Tibetan cadres, or 66.6 per cent of the total number of cadres in the region, and in September 1994 Tibetan cadres were reported to account for 71.7 per cent of all cadres at the regional level, 69.9 per cent at prefectural (di) levels, and 74.8 per cent at the county (xian) level (Liao 1995). According to the Chinese government's 2009 White Paper on 'Fifty Years of Democratic Reform in Tibet' (Information Office of the State Council of the PRC 2009), in 2007 Tibetans and other minorities held 94 per cent of local people's congress seats, and 77 per cent of the staff positions at the regional, prefectural and county level state organs were held by Tibetans and other ethnic minority deputies. In addition, twelve of the twenty TAR deputies in the National People's Congress were Tibetan. However, according to the Central Tibetan Administration (2005), the percentage of Tibetan cadres actually shrank from 72 per cent of the total in 2000 to less than 50 per cent in 2003.

In addition, the Election Law (1979, amended 1995) states that four rural votes are equal to one urban vote. In Tibetan areas this has the effect of increasing Han influence, as the Han population predominantly resident in cities have greater voting weight than the predominantly rural Tibetans (Ghai et al. 2010: 163).

In terms of the representation of women within the TAR, in 1994, Tibetan women accounted for 10.2 per cent of officials at the county level and above (Liao 1995). According to a 2012 Xinhua report, 'women account for 41 per cent of all cadres in Tibet, 22 per cent of deputies to the TAR People's Congress, and 20 per cent of the TAR's committee of the Chinese People's Political Consultative Conference' (Fang 2012). However, these figures are not broken down by ethnicity so the numbers of Tibetan women within these statistics is not known.

Table 8.1 demonstrates how the percentage of Tibetan cadres varies in different areas. The percentage of Tibetans is lower in the most powerful institutions such as party and government, but higher in those with the least power such as culture and religion.

In recent years, the percentage of Tibetan cadres has dropped further. According to Fischer (2005), the proportion of Tibetan cadres fell to less than 50 per cent by 2003. Among the fifteen standing members of the Party Committee in the Tibetan Autonomous Region, only six are Tibetans; and in Lhasa city there are only nine standing members out of nineteen Party standing Committee members. At the county level, the percentage is much lower. Langxian city has only three Tibetan standing members in a thirteen-member Party Committee; and even then they only hold symbolic posts like the vice-chairperson of the Langxian People's Congress, or the vice-chairperson of the Lianxian Political Consultation Conference. It is amazing that like the rest of China the Chinese government also sent newly gradu-ated BA students to Tibetan villages to be village cadres. In Langxian, for example, twenty-four 'student cadres' in total each received special supervision from three senior cadres.[2]

In June 1956, only seven Tibetans were admitted into the CCP. In 1963, the CCP had about 3,000 ethnic Tibetan members. The number increased to 40,000 by 1988. By 1991, the CCP had over 57,000 Tibetan and other minority members. By the end of 1989, it is reported that there were about 1,000 Tibetan officers in leader-ship posts in the PLA, of whom sixteen were commanders and 164 held the rank of major (Liao 1995).

There are at least two interpretations of the above figures. The first interpretation

Table 8.1: The percentage of Tibetan cadres in different areas

Institution	Tibetan cadres (n)	Total cadres (n)	Tibetan cadres (%)
Tibetan Party Committee	43	195	22
Tibetan People's Congress	53	98	54
Tibetan government	88	216	40
Tibetan political consultation	139	164	85
Tibetan Nationality and Religion Committee	36	60	60
Tibetan Buddhist Association	51	52	98
Tibetan Institute of Social Science	100	122	82
People's Bank	69	146	47

Sources: Tibet Autonomous Region Bureau of Statistics, pp. 189–90; the table has been shortened by the author; Tibet Autonomous Region Bureau of Statistics (2003); Tibetan Commission on Human Rights and Development (2000)

is that they show a level of power-sharing and limited autonomy. The second inter-pretation, the official one, is that the data demonstrate self-rule by Tibetans. This is highly problematic as most high-ranking Tibetan cadres wield only titular power. Candidates for the chairpersons of the TAR are chosen by central leaders, while TAR Party secretaries are appointed by central Party leaders and are non-Tibetans, such as Wu Jinghua (Yi nationality) (1985–8), Hu Jintao (Han Chinese) and Chen Kuiyuan (Han Chinese). Only regional government leaders are Tibetans, such as Dorje Tsering (1985–8) and Gyaincain Norbu (Karmel 1995: 494).

In the area of legal autonomy, Tibet had enacted more than 160 special sets of rules and regulations, local laws and legal resolutions by the end of 2001 (Information Office of the State Council of the PRC 2001). They involve such areas as the structure of political power, social and economic development, marriage, education, written language, the legal system, natural resources and environmental protection. The government issued regulations banning the presence of outsid-ers at the traditional Tibetan sky burial ritual when the Tibetans took offence at groups of tourists (Dreyer 1989: 281). Nevertheless, most local laws passed by local people's parliaments are, as in the rest of China, formalistic in that they only repeat national laws. Local laws can modify national laws but cannot override the authority of national law which emanates from the centre. In addition, regulations developed in autonomous regions 'shall be submitted to the Standing Committee of the National People's Congress for approval before they go into effect' (Article 116, Constitution). This in practice limits any autonomous legislative power. Ghai et al. (2010: 175) explain that although all five autonomous regions have drafted autonomy regulations, none has had an autonomy or special regulation enacted.

In the area of cultural autonomy, the 1980s heralded a resurgence in the pro-tection of Tibetan culture. It became possible for Lamaist Buddhists to make the pilgrimage to Lhasa again. Monasteries and temples destroyed during the Cultural Revolution were rebuilt and expanded (Dreyer 1989: 281), and young men were again permitted to become monks if they so desired (Dreyer 1989: 281).

For Tibetans, a fundamental part of their cultural autonomy relates to religion. In September 1988, a committee established under the leadership of the late Panchen Lama called for 'self-government of religion' in Tibet in order to preclude adminis-trative interference in the religious affairs of all Tibetans in China (Heberer 1989). Ironically, when Panchen Lama died, Beijing initiated its own search for his reincar-nation while denying the Dalai Lama's findings.

The inability to practice religious autonomy and the corresponding restriction of religious practice by the Chinese government in Tibet is a root cause of dissatisfac-tion among Tibetans. Beginning in the 1980s, the central government placed limits on the number of people who could become monks (Dreyer 1989: 283). Restrictions have increased since then. Regulations are in effect in the TAR, and some autono-mous areas in Gansu, Qinghai and Sichuan, that prohibit the promotion of religion in schools (Sorensen & Phillips 2004, cited in Ghai et al. 2010: 180). There is also a ban on displaying images of the Dalai Lama, installed in 1996. According to Human Rights Watch, in 2003 Tibetan government workers were told they 'were in danger of losing their pensions and even their jobs if they traveled to Mount Kailash', one of the sacred sites in western Tibet. In the period since the 2008 protests, monasteries are forcibly searched for evidence of images of the Dalai Lama, with reports of arrests of those monks found contravening the ban (Human Rights Watch 2010). In June 2008, the People's Government of the Ganzi Tibetan Autonomous Prefecture in Sichuan issued the 'Measures for Dealing Strictly with Rebellious Monasteries and Individual Monks and Nuns', which further curtail religious observance (Human Rights Watch 2010: 43). And in January 2012 the TAR Party Secretary announced that senior-ranked party or government officials would be permanently placed inside almost all monasteries, under a regulation known as the 'Complete Long-term Management Mechanism for Tibetan Buddhist Monasteries' (Human Rights Watch 2012a). This is a dramatic change from the policy allowing nominal self-rule of monasteries, which was introduced in 1962 and reinstated in the early 1980s after the Cultural Revolution. The new policy also establishes 'management committees' of up to thirty people stationed in every monastery in the TAR.

The government also controls pilgrimage both to and from the TAR and to India. Previously one had to receive permission to travel from one's work unit. Sometimes permission was denied for purely economic reasons: the absence of a large number of people at the same time could affect production. At other times, the motivation for refusal was connected with social control (Dreyer 1989: 283), as pilgrims had raised banners calling for independence, hoisted Tibet's 'snow mountain and lion' flag (banned by government authorities), and distributed anti-Chinese leaflets in the past (Dreyer 1989: 283). Since the mid-1990s permits to travel to the TAR from other Tibetan autonomous prefectures must be obtained through the government, often at the village, township and county levels. Since 2002, permits have been required to go to Mount Kailash. In some years the Chinese authorities have granted permission for pilgrimages to India for special Buddhist festivals. However, in 2012 a number of the Tibetan pilgrims were detained and subjected to 'political re-education' upon their return (Wong 2012).

As Chapter 9 will explore in more detail, the use of Tibetan language has also been subject to diverse regulations. In 1987, the Tibet Autonomous Regional People's Congress adopted the Regulations on the Study, Use and Development of the Written Tibetan Language (for a trial implementation). At the same time, it articulated the principle of attaching equal importance to both written Chinese and Tibetan languages (with the emphasis laid mainly on the latter), and established a committee in charge of the use and development of the written Tibetan language. The people's government of the TAR promulgated, in October 1988, rules for the implementation of these regulations. These rules clearly stipulate that all conferences of the autonomous regional government and all official documents should use both Tibetan and Chinese languages; all newspapers, radio, TV and other mass media should use the two languages; all units, streets, roads, and public facilities should be marked in both Tibetan and Chinese languages; schools should gradually establish an educational system centred around Tibetan language education; and the judicial organs, while examining and trying cases, must guarantee that Tibetan citizens have the right to legal proceedings in their own language (Luo 1991: 20).

These regulations were amended in 2002, stating 'equality' between Tibetan and Chinese and setting out measures that prioritise bilingual skills. As Ghai et al. (2010: 182) argue, however, 'in practice the legal equality of minority languages with Chinese is a fiction'.

The Chinese government has extended significant effort to increase the educational levels of Tibetans, including through the transfer of resources. By 1990, college-educated students in Tibet stood at 5.7 per thousand of population, compared to 4.2 per thousand in 1982. The figures for high school education were 21.2 per thousand in 1990 and 12.1 per thousand in 1982. According to the central government, the enrolment rate for junior high school was 92.2 per cent in 2008, for senior high school it was 51.2 per cent, and for higher education it was 19.7 per cent. The proportion of illiterates and semi-literates in the Tibetan population has dropped from more than 90 per cent in the 1950s to 46 per cent in 1982, and further to 44 per cent at the end of 1994 (Liao 1995: 60–1; Luo 1991: 20–2). According to the central government, the illiteracy rate had fallen to 2.4 per cent in 2008 (Information Office of the State Council of the PRC 2009).

The Chinese government has also launched 'patriotic education campaigns', which began in 1994 and intensified in 2008 and again in 2012. These have expanded beyond monastic institutions to encompass government officials, party cadres and educational institutions, as well as farmers and entrepreneurs. According to TAR governor Pema Thinley, the implementation of these campaigns, designed to foster national identity and love for the motherland, has 'contributed to the protection of long-term stability in the region' (Tibetan Centre for Human Rights and Democracy 2012).

In the area of economic autonomy, Tibet has technically been permitted to make its own decisions concerning the development and exploitation of resources, which are to be used to benefit the local population (Heberer 1989: 46). Hu Yaobang's 1980 'six point directive' included 'the right to decide for oneself', referring to economic de-centralisation (Norbu 2001). However, the economic powers of minority nationalities, as one Chinese scholar acknowledges, are very limited because the centre does not want to give up its power. There is no legally defined boundary of economic power between Beijing and the autonomous regions. In all existing laws there is no provision for the financial aspect of autonomy rights (Dai 1997).

The Law on National Regional Autonomy stipulates that localities may, in accordance with state stipulations, carry out foreign trade activities and, with the approval of the State Council, open foreign trade ports. At the Second Session of the 4th People's Congress of the TAR in July 1985, Tibetan government leaders issued a series of preferential policies on Tibet's foreign trade activities. Tibet opened the Zham Port, abutting Nepal, for the development of border trade. In 2001, 95 per cent of Tibet's trade was with Nepal (Sautman and Dreyer 2006: 142), and total trade with Nepal reached US$542 million in 2010. In order to promote the development of Tibet's foreign trade activities, the central government has adopted special policies that specify lower rates for import and export duties, and has allowed the autonomous region to retain all of its export earnings (100 per cent for Tibet, 50 per cent for other autonomous regions) (Luo 1991: 22; Li 1997: 91).

Tibet's total imports and exports have increased from US$180 million in 1997 to US$390 million in 2007, and reportedly reached $US1 billion in 2011 (China Tibet Online 2012).

To encourage economic development in Tibet, Beijing had exempted Tibet from the general rule that one must be a permanent resident of a given area to start a business there. The result was that Tibetan cities, Lhasa in particular, were inundated with a so-called 'floating population' of Han Chinese from other provinces (Dreyer 1989: 282). Typically having better linguistic and technical skills than the locals, the Han Chinese tended to take business away from native Tibetans (Dreyer 1989: 282). A relocation campaign to (forcibly) settle Tibetan herders and rehouse 80 per cent of the rural population was instigated in the mid-2000s. There is also a widespread feeling that it is the Han Chinese, and not the local people, who profit from tourism (Dreyer 1989: 282; Henders 2010: 193).

There is thus a concern that the economic policies have been predominantly determined by external priorities and the solutions designed with the Han-majority provinces in mind (Henders 2010: 193). 'State economic development policies and spending actually contribute to economic dependence on central authorities, whatever their intent' (Fischer 2005, cited in Henders 2010: 195).

Evaluation of the Chinese practice of autonomy

The following section deals with issues that are often subjective and biased. Beijing emphasises the sacrifices made by a significant number of Chinese aid cadres who come to Tibet to provide their selfless services to Tibetan economic and cultural lives. By contrast, Kalon T. C. Tethong, the *kalon* for the Department of Information and International Relations of the Tibetan Government in Exile, regards the increasing number of these 'aid cadres' as a move 'to rule Tibet directly from Beijing' because they are directly appointed to sensitive and important posts in Tibet and are accountable to Beijing and not to the TAR authorities in Lhasa (*Tibetan Bulletin*, July–August 2001: 10).

Chinese theories and the criteria they utilise present an official picture of the 'great achievement' of Chinese autonomy. The record, however, has been unimpressive indeed, if Chinese practice were to be compared with the practice of autonomy in other parts of the world (Herzer 1999). Nevertheless, due recognition of the *limited* achievement of Chinese autonomy is needed.

It is difficult to fully confirm the claim that the record of the Chinese practice of autonomy in Tibet is merely a 'paper autonomy'. 'Cultural genocide' is not an intellectually appropriate conceptual framework for assessing PRC state policy, because it is politically charged and biased (Sautman 2003: 177). Clearly, minority rights are exercised and protected much more in the 'soft' areas such as the economy, health and culture than in the 'hard' area of political rights. Certainly, autonomy in culture and economy has often been undermined whenever the Party/state sees some practices threatening the unity of the Chinese nation-state. The limited practice of Chinese autonomy operates under a unitary state. Chinese autonomy lacks an internal boundary and an independent local judiciary with full responsibility for interpreting local laws and whose exercise of power is generally not subject to veto by the central government.

When an issue arises that is perceived to represent a challenge to stability, autonomy is restricted or reduced. In 1994, Beijing circulated a resolution reaffirming the leading position of Han Chinese cadres in the Tibetan government and Party organisation, and demanding Tibetan cadres cut their links with the Dalai Lama (Liao 1995: 59–60). As examined earlier, the protests and riots in Tibet in 2008 were perceived and presented as a threat to the security of the Chinese nation, and thus the Chinese government instigated measures that further curtailed autonomy in the region. In China, the concept of a unitary multinational state is underpinned by a consensus that stability overrides any other considerations.

Ethnic minority groups and the practice of multiculturalism are facing a number of major challenges in China. Significant among them is the commercialisation of multiculturalism, which might lead to the vulgarisation and fundamental alteration of minority cultures. While multiculturalism became a buzzword of the 1990s from boardroom to classroom throughout America, Europe and Australia, it has become an instrument of economic development in China. As Kristi Heim, a freelance writer based in Hong Kong, observed: 'Distinct from the majority Han Chinese, ethnic minorities are now the main attractions in some of China's most popular tourist sites. Their cultures – displayed through costumes, artifacts, performances, festivals and replica villages – have become valuable commodities in China's growing market economy' (Heim 1995). Tourism has been a mixed blessing in Tibet, as in other minority areas in China. While generating much-needed economic inputs, the benefits are tempered by the concerns regarding the influx of Han migrants, and the exploitation and degradation of Tibetan culture.

Chinese-style multiculturalism is strictly limited to the soft area of cultural production, distribution and symbol formation. As soon as we move to the political institutions of multiculturalism, national security considerations take precedence over consideration of minority rights. The Party/state allows cultural autonomy as long as it does not threaten the unity of China. The process of gaining political autonomy and self-government for ethnic minority groups is often compromised due to the priority given to the unity of the state and societal stability. While the overriding Chinese concern for national unity is, according to Mackerras (2003b: 43), 'a legitimate one', the overriding national security concern has blocked the development of a reasonable and healthy discussion forum on ethnic issues because those who even raise ethnic issues, for example in Tibet, are under suspicion and invite public security scrutiny.

8.3   THE DALAI LAMA'S PROPOSAL AND BEIJING'S RESPONSE

An ideal model of autonomy in Tibet

The Dalai Lama's Proposal was first presented on Capitol Hill during his visit to Washington in 1987 and was presented a year later at the European Parliament.

Under what came to be known as the Strasbourg Proposal, the government of the People's Republic of China would remain responsible for Tibet's foreign policy while Tibet would be governed by its own constitution or basic law, and the Tibetan government would comprise a popularly elected chief executive, a bicameral legislature and an independent legal system (Dreyer 1989: 284). Because religion constitutes the source of Tibet's national identity, and spiritual values lie at the very heart of Tibet's rich culture, it would be the special duty of the government of Tibet to safeguard and develop its practice (Rinpoche 1996: 47). The government of Tibet would also develop and maintain relations, through its own Foreign Affairs Bureau, in the fields of religion, commerce, education, culture, tourism, science, sports and other non-political activities. Tibet would join international organisations concerned with such activities (Rinpoche 1996: 48). The Proposal contains what the Dalai Lama (1995: 5) regards as 'maximum' concessions by the Tibetans, which provides that Tibet would not be fully independent of China.

Beijing rejected the Dalai Lama's Proposal for fear it would create an internal boundary and an 'independent kingdom'. For Beijing, Chinese autonomy is characterised by a combination of political 'self-rule', economic integration, cultural exchange and ethnic intermingling. Beijing is also reluctant to accept the idea of the chief executive in Tibet being elected rather than appointed. With regard to the return of the Dalai Lama to Tibet, China has said that the Dalai Lama may return as spiritual head of the Lamaist faith, but not as a secular leader (Dreyer 1989: 284). For his part, the Dalai Lama maintains that he does not desire any political position in Tibet.

Beijing also has different views on the issue of federalism. While the Dalai Lama advocates a loose federal system, Beijing is reluctant to adopt the idea of federalism. Both Mao Zedong and Deng Xiaoping rejected federalism.[3]

More recently, the Dalai Lama's envoy presented the 'Memorandum on Genuine Autonomy' during discussions in Beijing in early November 2008. It outlined 'aspirations' for genuine autonomy in eleven policy areas: education, religion, culture, language, environmental protection, economic development and trade, public health, use of natural resources, migration, internal public security, and religious, cultural and educational exchanges with other countries. Due to the Chinese government's outright dismissal of the proposal, a follow-up note was presented in February 2010, addressing the concerns and objections that the Chinese authorities had raised.

The borders of an autonomous Tibet

The extent of Tibet's border is one of the most sensitive and highly controversial issues contained in the Dalai Lama's Proposal. According to the Dalai Lama, Tibet comprises some areas now in Qinghai, Gansu, Sichuan and Ningxia; the areas that were part of the Tibetan Kingdom. Under the Dalai Lama's Proposal, the whole of Tibet, which is known as Cholka-Sum (U-Tsang Kham and Amdo), would become a self-governing democratic political entity, founded on laws by agreements of the people for the common good and the protection of themselves and their environment, in association with the People's Republic of China (Rinpoche 1996: 47). The conceived Greater Tibet includes most of Qinghai, and parts of Gansu, Ningxia,

Sichuan and Yunnan, where the remaining 51 per cent of the Tibetan population inhabits with Han Chinese and other ethnic groups. The idea of a Greater Tibet constitutes the core of modern Tibetan nationalism, which has been committed to a pan-Tibetan identity since 1959 and will continue to be on a collision course with Chinese nationalists over the sensitive internal boundary question.

In 2003, the Dalai Lama stopped using the concepts of 'greater Tibet' or 'smaller Tibet'. Instead, he has emphasised the protection of Tibetan culture within a Tibetan cultural zone.[4] For Beijing, however, Tibet is confined to today's TAR. Even Chinese dissidents, such as Yan Jiaji, who are sympathetic to the Dalai Lama, share this view. According to Yan, in a future federal China, the border of the Tibetan member state would encompass what it does now within the TAR.[5] By contrast, the Dalai Lama does not recognise the border of the TAR. When Beijing celebrated the twentieth anniversary of the creation of the autonomous region of Tibet, the Dalai Lama commented, 'it is a very bitter anniversary. . . . It is the beginning of enslavement' (Shiromany 1996: 81).

Conditions for negotiation

The Dalai Lama's Proposal sets up some preconditions for any negotiations. First, it demands the withdrawal of Chinese troops before a genuine process of reconciliation could commence (Rinpoche 1996: 52). China can have the right to maintain a restricted number of military installations in Tibet solely for defence purposes until a peace conference is convened and demilitarisation and neutralisation achieved. Second, for the Tibetans to survive as a people, it is imperative that Chinese immigration to Tibet stop and Chinese settlers be repatriated (Rinpoche 1996: 53) Later, the Dalai Lama removed some of his earlier conditions. In 2003, the Dalai Lama stated that the number of the People's Armed Police should be reduced in Tibetan cities, implying his acceptance of the stationing of Chinese troops.

The former Chinese President Jiang Zemin stated firmly in 1998 that before a dialogue could begin, the Dalai Lama must 'publicly make a statement and a commitment that Tibet is an inalienable part of China' and 'must also recognize Taiwan as a province of China' (Ching 1998: 37). Per Gahrton, a Swedish parliamentarian, thought that the Dalai Lama met these conditions when he gave a speech to the European Parliament in Strasbourg on 24 October 2001 (Canada Tibet Committee 2002). Beijing did not think so. This is because the Dalai Lama stated, 'Tibet was an independent country before its occupation by China. It had its own government, now in exile . . .There is no justification claiming that Tibet was "part of China" as Peking claims today' (Shiromany 1998: 60). In 2002, in reacting to the latest Chinese offer to the Dalai Lama – that he is welcome to return to Tibet if he meets two conditions – Mr Sonam Dagpo, the secretary in the Department of Information and International Relations of the Government in Exile, said the preconditions laid down by China, including accepting Tibet as part of China and Taiwan as its province, were just not acceptable, since Tibet had always been an independent nation until China occupied it forcibly (*Tibetan Bulletin*, January–April 2002: 10).

Beijing sees the Dalai Lama's public advocacy of autonomy for Tibet as little more than a smokescreen for independence because he failed to stop all independence activities. The Tibetan Youth Congress (TYC) is one example. The TYC clearly stated that its mission is to build an independent state of Tibet whose head is the Dalai Lama. The size of an independent state of Tibet would be 2.5 million square kilometres, with 6 million people and three provinces: U-tsang (Central), Dhotoe (Eastern) and Dhome (Northeastern). The national flag of Tibet would be twelve red and blue rays with two snow lions in the lower centre. The TYC promotes and protects Tibetan national unity and integrity by giving up all distinctions based on religion, region or status; works for the preservation and promotion of religion and Tibet's unique culture and traditions; and struggles for the total independence of Tibet even at the cost of one's life. It has launched campaigns like *Boycott Made in China* and *No Olympic-2008 in Beijing.*[6]

Tibetan youth organisations and their supporters launched an international *Boycott Made in China* campaign designed to create economic pressure on the Chinese government to end its occupation of Tibet on 7 December 2002. Simultaneous demonstrations in front of toy stores and shopping malls in cities across Canada, the United States, New Zealand, Europe and India marked the beginning of long-term and coordinated efforts to urge people to stop buying goods made in China. The Dalai Lama's oldest brother, Professor Thupten Norbu, sent a blessing message: 'I am confident that the campaign to boycott Chinese products will gain the support of freedom loving people around the world, and will eventually succeed in forcing China to respect the rights of its own people and acknowledge Tibetan independence.'[7]

Can the Hong Kong model of autonomy be applied to Tibet?

The Dalai Lama and many Western commentators have raised the question of whether China should apply the Hong Kong model of autonomy to resolve the Tibet question (Sautman & Lo 1995). It has been suggested that, following the Hong Kong model, Beijing would be responsible for Tibet's foreign affairs and defence but, in other areas, including issues of religion and culture, the Tibetans would be free to make their own decisions. Hong Kong commentator Frank Ching argued in 1998: 'It will take an act of statesmanship for China to offer this special status to an area already under its control. But such an offer, at a time when China is basking in the world's approval for its handling of Hong Kong, will be welcomed by the international community as a genuine attempt to resolve an issue that has proven to be intractable for almost four decades.' In 1992, the President of Qinghua University in Taiwan raised the issue to President Jiang Zemin, citing his 'layman's viewpoint' and asking if the 'one-country-two-systems could be applied to Tibet'. Jiang Zemin answered, 'It is right to say this, but we have gone so far already, and cannot go back to apply one-country-two-systems in Tibet' (Song 1997). In the eyes of Beijing, a 'one country, one system' relationship between the PRC and Tibet has already been in place for several decades, thus rendering the 'one country, two systems' inapplicable to Tibet (Sautman & Lo 1995). As Ghai et al. (2010: 158) explain, the Chinese government's position is that Article 31 of the Constitution – the 'one country, two systems' notion – can only apply to areas that were 'taken away from the "motherland"' and thus cannot be utilised for Tibet.

Beijing adopts a pragmatic attitude towards Taiwan and Tibet. While Beijing offers Taiwan a Hong Kong model of autonomy, and in fact a much higher degree of autonomy than Hong Kong's because Taiwan can maintain its own army, it rejects the Dalai Lama's Proposal. The Chinese practice of autonomy is apparently largely dependent on the power relations in each situation. Beijing thinks that the Hong Kong model of autonomy characterised by judicial independence, Hong Kong's own currency, an internal border with China and representatives in international organisations with regard to economic and cultural matters would be offering too much to Tibet.

Beijing has in mind several rather than one single model of autonomy to meet the needs of different circumstances. While Hong Kong enjoys a higher form of autonomy, Tibet should enjoy much less autonomous power than Hong Kong but higher autonomous power than that for Xinjiang and Inner Mongolia. The Hong Kong model of autonomy could not be applied to Tibet because Hong Kong then had to be united with the Mainland while Tibet has already been under China's control.

Summary

Beijing rejects the Dalai Lama's autonomy proposal as a solution to the Tibet question on the ground that the Dalai Lama has 'internationalized' the Tibet question. In addition, the proposal is rejected for the following reasons: (1) Beijing thinks that the acceptance of the proposal would create an internal boundary and an 'independent kingdom', which would eventually lead to Tibet's full independence; (2) Beijing is reluctant to accept the idea of the chief executive in Tibet being elected rather than appointed; (3) the Dalai Lama's demands that the territories of Tibet's autonomy should comprise some areas now in Qinghai, Gansu, Sichuan and Ningxia are totally unacceptable to Beijing; (4) Beijing will not accept the Dalai Lama's precondition for negotiation: a withdrawal of Chinese troops from Tibet. At the same time, the Dalai Lama refuses to satisfy Beijing's demand that he should 'publicly make a statement and a commitment that Tibet is an inalienable part of China'; (5) Chinese leaders reject the proposal because it entails the right to self-determination. While the Dalai Lama's *genuine* autonomy proposal draws on liberal principles of autonomy, Chinese theories of *regional* autonomy, derived from Marxist principles, reject the right of self-determination being applied to Chinese minorities. Chinese theories of autonomy are not based on rights, but on pragmatism and a combination of Marxism and Confucianism; and (6) according to the Chinese leadership, China has already established the Chinese system of regional autonomy for minority nationalities, which comprises three elements: a constitutional framework, laws governing autonomy, and government policies. Above all, Hu Jintao, the former General Secretary and the President of China, stated clearly that 'it is essential to fight unequivocally against the separatist activities by the Dalai clique and anti-China forces in the world, vigorously develop a good situation of

stability and unity in Tibet and firmly safeguard national unity and state security'
(*Tibetan Bulletin*, July–August 2001: 10).

8.4   UNDERSTANDING THE STALEMATE OF DIALOGUE

Talks between Chinese and Tibetan authorities have reached an impasse. Hardliners
on both sides of the conflict seem to be increasingly unwilling to compromise. The
dilemma lies in that while the Dalai Lama demands a Greater Tibet, Beijing refuses
it. In 1988, the Dalai Lama put forward the Strasbourg Proposals in which he asked
for a unified self-government for Tibet. In August 2009, Tibetan government in
exile *Kalon Tripa* (prime minister) Samdhong Rinpoche enunciated the current
position. He said:

> Since 1979, His Holiness the Dalai Lama has adopted the Middle-Way
> Approach of not seeking separation but for Tibet to remain within the People's
> Republic of China . His Holiness the Dalai Lama has repeatedly requested for
> the implementation of National Regional Autonomy provisions to the entire
> Tibetan nationality in order to preserve and promote Tibet's cultural and spir-
> itual heritage and identity. [Since] 2002 . . . we have further clarified how the
> entire Tibetan nationality can be brought under one autonomous administra-
> tion within the provisions of constitution and autonomy law and what are the
> advantages by doing this. (The Department of Information & International
> Relations 2009)

All past dialogues broke down when facing this tough issue. The main cause of
this breakdown is rooted in the dispute as to whether or not Tibet was ever an independent state. There are cogent arguments on both sides. Barry Sautman (2009),
Professor at Division of Social Science, Hong Kong University of Science and
Technology, utilising international law, particularly the Montevideo Convention
on the Rights and Duties of States, makes an argument that Tibet has always been
an integral part of China and has never qualified as a state according to either the
declaratory or the constitutive theories of statehood. On the other hand, Lobsang
Sangay (2012), from the East Asian Legal Studies Program at Harvard Law School,
now the elected Prime Minister of the Tibetan government in exile, also using
the Montevideo Convention, makes equally cogent arguments that Tibet was a
state from the eighth century until 1950. Although it can be argued that both
writers are operating from entrenched and biased perspectives, this is the very
nature of the dilemma. It is a dilemma which cannot be solved by further or more
detailed argument along the same lines. Every argument, however scholarly or
well researched, merely serves to deepen the chasm between the two protagonistic
views.

The following section surveys some of the factors that are contributing to the
reinforcement and exacerbation of these hardline attitudes. Several logic systems
are self-closed and prevent political compromise from occurring. My examination of

the position adopted by the Chinese government from the perspective of a number of different logic systems, however, does not provide an apologetic, but rather seeks to open up otherwise entrenched positions for deeper understanding.

Historical logic

Every dynasty in the history of China has faced challenges in reconciling the needs and demands of various minorities and these often involved uprisings and bloody suppressions, for example in the Han and Tang eras. Compared with these, the current Han–Tibet conflict is relatively minor. The uprisings and suppressions in terms of frequency, numbers and levels of violence are much smaller in scale compared with what has happened before and it is likely that many officials in China's central government regard the Tibet issue as inconsequential and the conflict as a completely normal state of affairs.

The normal historical policy response to minorities in China has been to integrate them into the mainstream population. This policy was known as *gaitu guiliu*. As discussed in the previous chapter, the policy converted the law and cultural customs of any minority into a unitary system of administrative control. This cultural assimilation completely disregarded minority rights. Behind China's current policy towards Tibet is the belief that because in the past *gaitu guiliu* was relatively successful in Yunnan and Guizhou, in the long term it can prevail in today's Tibet.

Political logic

China will not give up what it has controlled, and aims to get more control over Tibet. This is about power, the power of the CCP. For the CCP, it, and it alone, is the Party that represents Tibetans. In the eyes of the CCP, therefore, the Tibetan government in exile has no legitimate representative political role. Such a view is clearly presented in Beijing's response[8] to the Dalai Lama's 'Memorandum on Genuine Autonomy for the Tibetan People'.[9] By contrast, the Dalai Lama has undoubtedly enjoyed very high legitimacy among Tibetans, and this constitutes the major source of the Dalai Lama's power. International support and sympathy with the Dalai Lama's cause is another source of the Dalai Lama's power. This is the reason why Beijing does not like the so-called 'internationalization of the Tibet issue', as discussed later. The political logic poses the question of how it is feasible and realistic for the Dalai Lama to ask for political autonomy in Tibet when the CCP's power extends everywhere. Given the economic rise of China, Beijing perceives that it has greatly increased political resources and bargaining power to resist international pressure. If a compromise were made under international pressure, it would be regarded as a symbol of weakness according to this power logic. It is this increase in international political leverage which Beijing perceives as flowing from increased economic power which is likely to cause the CCP to make a grave error in failing to develop a Tibet policy that aims to make a compromise.

Behind the idea of a Greater Tibet is that all Tibetans are the same nationality and share culture and identity, and it is therefore legitimate to demand the redrawing of boundaries to provide strong administrative protection for Tibetan culture. Beijing rejects such an idea simply because it believes it will undermine the CCP's power. In the history of Chinese empires, divide and rule has been the common policy. Beijing does not accept that Tibet has ever been a united polity, arguing that it had been divided and ruled by several religious leaders. Beijing draws a parallel between this understanding of Tibetan history and the historic divide and rule policy of China in order to maintain Tibet in the unitary system. In a unitary system, the centre *delegates* its power to an autonomous region, but does not *share* power with it.

In some respects, the continuation of the conflict with Tibet is in the political interest of the CCP. The Tibetan issue has promoted and cultivated nationalist sentiment in China to unprecedented levels. Chinese nationals who previously felt no strong allegiance towards the CCP are suddenly rallying around its cause and uniting against a common enemy – the Tibetan 'separatists'. The CCP has seized on the opportunity to exploit the conflict in order to further inflame Chinese nationalism and loyalty towards the party.

Moreover, intelligence and security agencies in China see the prolongation of the conflict as a sure way to guarantee the continuation of current levels of government funding. It is feared that any signs of a resolution or even progress will lead to budget cuts. These agencies, in China, as elsewhere, have a strong incentive to sustain any conflict, or at least to create an exaggerated impression of its intractability. Even local governments will receive more funding from the central government to provide social services such as health and education.[10]

Political fear is arguably contributing to the stalemate. Chinese hardliners have routinely used the 'slippery slope' argument, pointing to the risks associated with compromise: concessions, no matter how modest, will be met with demands for further concessions, up to and including demands for independence. Hardliners can claim that their approach is preferable insofar as it does not carry the same risks. Additionally, the fact that China has lost so much of its moral credibility in the course of the conflict may be further diminishing its willingness to compromise. The less hope the Chinese have of gaining the moral high ground, the less likely they are to even bother competing in moral terms, and instead rely exclusively on force.

Economic logic

In the politics of the developmental state, rapid economic development has overshadowed any consideration of minority rights. State funding for minority areas is not so much for the purpose of progressing or strengthening minority rights as it is for promoting the penetration of state power. By contrast, in identity politics, the protection of cultural identities necessitates the enhancement of minority rights. In the developmental state, ethnic rights and identity are often secondary matters so the government is caught between identity demands and economic logic.

Economic development has reshaped ethnic relations. It has been used to justify the domination of state administrative power. Under the banner of development, the state has appropriated minority lands. Subsequently, it has developed policies to attract capital flow and encourage migrant labour into these areas, and favoured voluntary assimilation whereby minorities 'choose' to study and use the majority language in order to advance career prospects. Economic development has promoted a common market and integration. Even ethnic cultures have become commercialised products, which has degraded their cultural and ethnic significance.

The logic of internationalisation

Things have been made more complicated by the perceived 'internationalisation' of the conflict by the Tibetans. It is a striking fact that the majority of Tibetan organisations in Western societies are white-Westerners, with just a few Tibetans, while the majority of members in Chinese democratic opposition organisations in Western societies are Han Chinese. Given the overwhelming financial and military superiority of the Chinese state, the Dalai Lama has been forced to appeal to international actors to garner support for the Tibetan cause. But in China this has created the perception that the conflict is no longer purely domestic. It is now between China and a coalition of Tibet and its foreign sponsors, especially the US. It is believed in China that the Tibet issue is a manufactured problem and that without foreign involvement China could deal with it easily (He Liangliang 2004). Not only has this further inflamed nationalist zeal and extremist elements in China, it has also transformed the internal conflict into a national security issue and a perceived threat to China's political sovereignty. What is more, these feelings are only likely to intensify. As long as there is an asymmetric power relationship between China and Tibet, the Dalai Lama will continue to seek the involvement of foreign powers. This, in turn, will fuel perceptions of treacherous collusion between Tibet and its international supporters, further stiffening the resolve of Chinese hardliners. This vicious cycle threatens to obstruct any progress from being made in the near future. In short, the internationalisation of the Tibetan issue makes it one of the top national security issues in China, which further strengthens the centralised power. Human Rights Watch (2010: 4) perceptively notes the government's characterisation of unrest in Tibet as 'a conspiracy orchestrated by the Dalai Lama' and 'hostile foreign forces' that threatens the territorial integrity of the PRC and restricts its ability to respond in a balanced way and address the root causes of the unrest.

The logic of human rights

The idea that hosting the Olympic Games would encourage China to move towards improving human rights and increasing democracy, as it did in South Korea after the 1988 Seoul Olympics, was very much wishful thinking. China does not have a history of responding favourably to international censure. The sanctions against China after 1989 did not work effectively at all. Nowadays, using international public opinion to contain China is unworkable. The situation in China today is quite different from the one which prevailed in South Korea in 1988. As it remains to this day, in 1988 South Korea was an ally of the US, while China, although having status as a trading partner, cannot be thought of as a US ally.

In addition, it was widely supposed in China that the actions of the US House of Representatives in passing a resolution[11] condemning Beijing's human rights abuses was the politicisation of the Olympics. At the same time, sixty US senators signed a letter critical of Beijing's bid for the 2000 Olympics on the same grounds. The letter was sent to each of the ninety-one IOC members, and it is widely perceived in China that this action caused China to lose to Sydney in the bid to host the 2000 Olympics (Harvey 1993). China viewed this as a humiliation, with the human rights issue being used from the very beginning to curtail China's power (Wang 2008). Beijing believes it has the economic strength, political capability and sufficient soft power to disregard the US and resist Western pressure. More importantly, the slogan of 'resisting the Olympics' was built on an assumption that links human rights with sports (Zhang Bo 2008). This linking may have worked to some degree in forcing the South African government to change its apartheid policy but the situation is different in China. South Africa was a minority-dominated country so there was not the overwhelming sense of national pride which prevails in China. The attempt to link sport with human rights issues in China is seen by the vast majority of ordinary Chinese people as an affront to their national pride in hosting the Olympics and consequently it is counter-productive (Editorial 2008). When the West blurs the issues of human rights and democracy with sport to put pressure on China, disregarding this sense of pride, it only serves to undermine the human rights and democracy cause in China, and political reforms in China will consequently go backwards.

Yet another factor which is contributing to the stalemate is the perceived impracticality of the Dalai Lama, whose '5 Point Peace Plan for Tibet'[12] appealed to a combination of abstract moral values (human rights, democratic freedoms, the environment) rather than addressing itself to the practicalities of the situation on the ground, and suggesting feasible options for a resolution. As a result, the plan was dismissed out of hand, rather than being embraced as a genuine, realistic proposal for bringing the conflict to an end. In addition to this, the 5 Point Plan added to perceptions that the conflict was being deliberately internationalised by the Tibetan government in exile. For example, it is not clear whether 'Greater Tibet' is a genuine demand or an ambit claim, as Tibetans in exile were advised that they should demand more to increase their bargaining power.[13] There is an impasse on the issue because it is political suicide for the Dalai Lama to give up the Greater Tibet claim as his supporters come from all over the Tibetan areas and it is difficult for Beijing to accept this idea for the reasons discussed earlier.

The Dalai Lama is a religious leader who has to be honest and upright. Such a moral and religious role makes it difficult for him to 'play politics' by balancing different forces and factions. His advantage in the eyes of the world community is his moral behaviour, but his weakness in negotiating the issue is his lack of real politics. (Beijing plays on this dilemma, accusing the Dalai Lama of duplicity – questioning his moral authority when he acts politically and disputing his political legitimacy by pointing to his religious authority.)

Equally, there is a Tibetan establishment that benefits from the continuation of conflicts in terms of funding. It is difficult for them to take flexible and compromising steps. The more intractable the stalemate with China is made to appear, the more donations the Tibetan cause is likely to receive from abroad. And to the extent that hardliners seem to be more adept at rallying public support, Tibetan moderates are invariably squeezed out of the picture, marginalised and rendered politically impotent.

8.5   HOW TO BREAK THE STALEMATE?

How can the stalemate be broken? The most important thing is to reflect upon and critique the domination of the power approach. The power struggles between the Tibetan government in exile and the PRC and the internal conflicts in both camps need to be scrutinised and studied if there is to be a lasting and peaceful solution. The moderate faction within the CCP is a driving force for developing a compromise policy. It is important to somehow shift the balance of power from hardliners towards Chinese and Tibetan moderates, though admittedly this is easier said than done. Unfortunately the radicalisation of Tibetans in exile is often used to give sustenance to the hardline position and undermines the efforts of the moderate faction in the CCP.

It is imperative for both parties to move away from their old logics and find a new paradigm of understanding. Some Chinese have searched for and developed a new logic and new thinking. In the 1989 Tanner Lecture at the Chinese University of Hong Kong, Fei Xiaotong coined the term 'plurality in an organic whole', in which Tibet is placed under a unitary system but enjoys multicultural rights and institutions (Zhou 2007). Yan Jiaqi (1992) has been promoting the idea of federalism since the later 1990s to solve the Tibet issue. More than twenty-eight famous scholars, writers and filmmakers signed a petition to ask the Chinese government to abandon its propaganda-based approach and find a reason-based solution to the Tibet issue on 19 April 2008. (This can be seen as a part of public deliberation. See Chapter 10.)[14]

Below, I review some concrete proposals to address the predicament. Huang Jing, Professor at the National University of Singapore, suggests that Beijing should establish a National Committee on Tibet Affairs, an administrative body to deal with all Tibetan cultural matters. The proposal is that the Dalai Lama would play a critical role in this body, while leaving all other existing arrangements as they now stand (Huang 2009). This proposal, however, needs to be couched in different terms, giving the role not to the Dalai Lama himself but to legitimate representatives, acceptable to the Tibetan people. The Dalai Lama has consistently said that the issue should not be focused on his role but on the future of the Tibetan people.

Zheng Ge, professor of law at the University of Hong Kong, proposes a special cultural zone for Tibetans. This proposal recognises Tibetan culture as a special area deserving protection and enjoying the highest autonomy possible in a unitary system. Zheng argues that geographically Tibet is contiguous with Tibetan areas in Gansu, Qinghai, Sichuan and Yunnan provinces, shares the same culture with them, and that these four provinces already enjoy a considerable degree of local autonomy. Zheng proposes that these four provinces should be united with Tibet to form a 'Tibetan Special Cultural Region', which recognises and protects Tibetan culture, education and religion.

Zheng's idea derives from China's economic reform, in which the Chinese government has set up many Special Administrative Regions, Special Economic Zones and Nature Reserves in different areas. Flexible regional institutional arrangements have given these regions autonomy in some aspects. Within China's constitutional framework, perhaps as Zheng asserts, it is possible to explore a new institutional arrangement, namely the Special Cultural Region, in which a united policy on culture, religion and education will be implemented. For example, they could be policies relating to bilingual education, weekly working hours (extension of the policy of thirty-five hours of weekly work to the whole Tibetan Special Cultural Region), and special recognition for exclusively Tibetan holidays like the Tibetan New Year and Yogurt Festival (Zheng 2009).

This proposal has some merit in that it partially satisfies the aspirations of the Tibetan government in exile, while maintaining the existing administrative system in Tibetan areas and promoting economic integration. It conforms to Article 4 of the Chinese Constitution that all national autonomous areas are integral parts of the People's Republic of China, and that all nationalities have the freedom to use and develop their own spoken and written language and to preserve or reform their own folk traditions and customs.

Zheng's proposal occupies a middle ground in that it satisfies some of the demands for a Greater Tibet on the one hand and yet satisfies the ideal of a great union of China on the other hand. Of course, such a proposal invites criticism that it is too little to meet the interests of Tibetans and that it is difficult to separate politics from culture. It may be difficult but it is not impossible and there is room in both Chinese politics and culture for adjustments to be made.

Another critical question is about the multi-layer autonomous governing structure. One idea is that in the core area where most Tibetans live there could be self-government by Tibetans; and where Tibetans and Han Chinese live together there could be a co-governing structure or co-decision-making mechanism involving both Tibetans and Han Chinese. The Dalai Lama considered power-sharing institutions back in 1996, but is currently not willing to address this critical issue.

Zhu Lun (2001), Professor at the Institute of Nationality Studies at the Chinese Academy of Social Sciences, advocates a system of ethnic co-governance. There are two levels of ethnic co-governance. One is all ethnic groups' co-governance of the state. The other is the relevant ethnic groups' co-governance of an area of mixed habitation. Zhu claims that ethnic co-governance is under the precondition of national unity and has the republic as its goal. It is oriented towards the equal development of rights and benefits, and has positive ethnic interactions as its core political composition, operating mechanism and tool for implementation. Zhu also argues that although both China and the former Soviet Union used 'autonomy' to express and embody their promise of political rights to ethnic minorities, China's system of ethnic autonomous areas was under the precondition of a unified state and a republican style of co-governance of all ethnic groups. In contrast, the former Soviet Union's ethnic federation allowed the right to secede from the federation (Zhu 2001). Zhu's idea of ethnic co-governance can be seen as a Chinese modern search for consociationalism.

Consociationalism offers an institutional solution to the problem of communal conflict. According to Arend Lijphart (1984), the consociational model has four defining features: 1) a 'grand coalition', referring to power-sharing institutions; 2) mutual veto, meaning that issues must be settled by consensus between the different groups; 3) proportionality, whereby 'representation is based on population'; and 4) segmental autonomy. It was practised in Lebanon between 1943 and 1975, Malaysia between 1955 and 1969, Cyprus between 1960 and 1963, and Nigeria between 1957 and 1966. For the most part, however, particularly in the last two cases, earlier forms of consociationalism failed (Lijphart 1984: Chapter 5). Northern Ireland, however, can be cited as an example of successful consociationalism – although it is perhaps exceptional in its success; and this success can be attributed to the positive role played by public deliberation and dialogue (see Chapter 11).

A co-governing institution is one realist solution for places with a mixed population, such as Tibet. It has historical roots in China – the practice of co-governance in the Ming dynasty could be considered a quasi from of consociationalism – but it involved power distribution among majority and minorities. Consociationalism also helps to address the question of how to treat Han Chinese migrants in Tibet, as it does not adopt the policy that Han Chinese should be sent back where they come from.

There are, however, problems with this notion of consociationalism. It would entail a big compromise for Tibetans, particularly as the autonomy would not be authentic. It also legitimises the central government's settlement policy (the sheer number of Han Chinese moving to Tibetan areas has dramatically increased and is projected to continue into the future).

Despite these problems, consociationalism is likely to be a critical issue in the process of Chinese democratisation within which the Chinese liberals attempt to find an institutional and realistic solution. A number of other countries could point to potential success here. For example, the lesson from Northern Ireland is that the idea of self-rule was eventually abandoned and a power-sharing mechanism adopted. On the other hand, Greece is against power-sharing for migrant settlers from Turkey, which is a fundamental obstacle to the peace settlement in Cyprus.

8.6 CONCLUSION

Through an understanding of the current stalemate and logic systems behind the Chinese and Tibetan positions, this chapter has revealed the difficulty in developing democratic governance. The existing autonomy arrangement falls short of true autonomy; therefore democratic governance should focus on the true implementation of the autonomy principle. The idea of consociationalism should be further considered as one democratic mechanism that offers a realist solution.

NOTES

1. The author's interview with Lodi Gyari on 31 August 2003 in Washington, DC.
2. www.langxian.gov.cn, accessed 10 May 2013.
3. China would be more likely to adopt a territorial-based federalism than a multinational federalism. In the former, such as that in Australia, Austria, Germany and the USA, the political boundaries between the component units cut across the social boundaries between religious or ethnic groups. Such a system has not been challenged by any serious secessionist movements. In the latter, such as those of Belgium, Canada and Switzerland, political, cultural and social boundaries tend to coincide, and strong secessionist movements can occur as in Belgium and Canada.
4. *Open Magazine*, August 2003.
5. But Yan concedes that the federal parliament would ultimately decide on the scope of the Tibetan border and other border changes. Yan (1995: 14–16) argues that the concept of 'Greater Tibet' has yet to take shape among Tibetans in Qinghai, Gansu, Ningxia, Sichuan and other provinces, and the influence of the concept of 'Tibetan independence' among them is extremely limited. On this matter, Sautman and Lo (1995: 48–9) suggest a solution to this dispute: 'While present administrative borders might be kept in place during a trial period of enlarged TAR autonomy, there could be negotiations over issues affecting Tibetans outside the TAR, and rights provided within the TAR for all ethnic Tibetans, irrespective of their residency.'
6. More details can be found at the Tibetan Youth Congress website: http://www.tibetanyouthcongress.org/homepage.htm.
7. http://www.sft-canada.org/campaigns/economic/boycott-made-in-china/.
8. A summary of Beijing's response to the Memorandum can be found at http://news.xinhuanet.com/english/2008-11/21/content_10391968.htm, accessed 19 October 2009.
9. Full text can be found at http://www.tibetoffice.ch/web/mwa/memorandum/english.pdf, accessed 19 October 2009.
10. Statistics showed that the central government's transfer payments to Tibet amounted to 201.9 billion yuan (US$28.8 billion) between 1959 and 2008. Between 1959 and 2000, only 47.8 billion yuan was spent, while from 2001 to 2008 the figure increased to more than 154.1 billion yuan, making up 93.7 per cent of Tibet's financial revenue in the same period. Press Release, 31 March 2009 from Embassy of the People's Republic of China in Australia: http://au.china-embassy.org/eng/zt/zgxz/t554941.htm, accessed 19 October 2009. The funding from Beijing has directly impacted the GDP and lives of Tibetans (Yang & Sun 2009).
11. Full text of Resolution 1370, passed on 30 July 2008, can be found at: http://www.govtrack.us/congress/bills/110/hres1370/text.
12. Outlined in Address to Members of the United States Congress, Washington, DC, 21 September 21 1987. Full text can be found at: http://dalailama.com/messages/tibet/five-point-peace-plan, accessed 17 August 2012.
13. Interview with Lodi Gyari Rinpoche, the Dalai Lama's chief negotiator and Special Envoy in Washington, DC, at: http://www.phayul.com/mobile/?page=view&c=5&id=12253, accessed 17 August 2012.
14. http://wlx.sowiki.net/?action=show&id=31. A translation of this petition can be found at: http://www.englishpen.org/usr/translation_of_petition_by_chinese_writers_on_tibet_2.pdf, accessed 12 November 2009.

9   Beyond Chinese Linguistic Imperialism: Multi-linguistic Policy

9.1   INTRODUCTION: LINGUISTIC TRENDS

In recent years, Tibetans have engaged in a series of protests to defend their increasingly marginalised language. In October 2010, more than a thousand Tibetans in Qinghai protested against reports that the government was planning to put in place policies that would limit the use of the Tibetan language in schools by teaching all subjects except for English and Tibetan in Putonghua (BBC 2010). These protests spread to Beijing, where Tibetan university students also protested their concern about the proposed policies (Wong 2010). The European Parliament has supported Tibetans in defending the status of their language. It adopted a resolution in support of a language policy in which all subjects can be taught in the Tibetan language and condemned the Chinese government for its use of Putonghua as the main medium of instruction in Tibet.[1]

China was, and still is, a multi-lingual society, and has practised multi-lingual teaching for many centuries. The fifty-five recognised minorities in the PRC use more than 120 different languages (Sun Hongkai 2004). Officials in ethnic autonomous regions are encouraged to speak multiple languages, including both Putonghua 普通话 (common speech, mandarin) and local languages (Zhou 2004). The National People's Congress uses seven different languages in its work, and five different scripts appear on Chinese bank notes. Among the Han Chinese majority there is also great linguistic diversity, with a number of spoken Chinese language groups, such as the Wu, Yue and Min, having tens of millions of speakers. The expansion of Chinese state power and the power of the market into all corners of China has, however, witnessed the dramatic spread of Putonghua across China, which has slowly diluted the importance of minority languages.

There now seems to be a tendency towards the strengthening of Putonghua, as indicated by a number of factors:[2] the decline in the use of minority languages; the increasing use of Putonghua as an official teaching language in minority areas; the use of Putonghua in official meetings involving minorities; and the lack of incentives for those Han Chinese who work in minority areas to study minority languages (see Evans 2010; Feng 2009; Lin 1997). In 1992, the Ministry of Education issued the *Method for Practising Chinese Proficiency Test* (the Hanyu Shuiping Kaoshi, HSK) *in National Minorities Schools* to standardise the test for non-Chinese speakers, and in 1997 the Education Commission issued another official document on trial implementation of the HSK in national minorities schools (Bilik 2010).

Chinese oral languages have always been fragmented. The Chinese imperial script of *hanzi* has coexisted alongside, but separate from, numerous oral languages. One may argue that plural dialects in fact accommodate the needs of different people in different regions. There has been, however, a trend towards unifying oral and written languages in China. Standardising spoken language, in order to facilitate not only written but also oral communication, has been an important part of building a modern nation-state in China, particularly since the May Fourth Movement in 1919. The efforts to unify the oral and written languages through the spread of Putonghua constitute an ongoing political project in China's process of modernisation (DeFrancis 1950; Tai 1988). This project has developed very rapidly in recent decades, creating the possibility that for the first time Chinese language might achieve unification between written script and oral language. A survey of 500,000 people in thirty-one provinces in 2007, for example, found that 53 per cent of the population could effectively communicate orally in mandarin, and nearly 70 per cent of urbanites were fluent in mandarin; as a result the government has worked hard to improve the rate of mandarin in rural areas.[3]

China's language practices and policies have been shaped by the dominance of the Chinese *hanzi* (汉字) script, and the state's desire to create and maintain Great Unity (*da yitong* 大一同) built on linguistic imperialism. The principle of Great Unity is the first priority of political rule and language policy follows this principle. Linguistic justice is a secondary consideration when compared to the goal of national unity and development.

In contrast, within Europe states have developed policies to promote teaching in the mother tongue with the aim of increasing student attendance and classroom participation. In this framework, linguistic diversity is similar to biodiversity – some languages are endangered and require protection if they are not to become extinct. The preservation of linguistic diversity is seen as an indicator of social justice (Skutnabb-Kangas et al. 2009; Mohanty 2009; Perez 2009).

While I concur with the European moral position on linguistic issues, I argue that current Chinese linguistic policy in Tibet must be understood as an extension of Chinese linguistic imperialism. A long-term historical perspective makes it possible to trace the history of the Chinese language situation and linguistic policy, providing a key to understanding current educational and linguistic policy in Tibet, and offering us insight into the likely future direction of linguistic trends. It should be acknowledged that this historical approach is more concerned with *political* history than linguistic history.

The chapter draws on the Chinese concept of *gai tu gui liu* (改土归流 replacing native chieftains with state officials) to develop a Chinese experience-based argument, that is, the current language policy and practice in Tibet is a modern form of the historical practice of *gai tu gui liu*. The *gai tu gui liu* policy embodies a linguistic imperialism that has existed throughout a long period of Chinese history.

Borrowing the term 'linguistic imperialism' from Robert Phillipson (1992, 2009), I use it to describe a hierarchic linguistic structure where the dominance of the Han written language has been unchallenged and other minority languages are secondary. According to Phillipson, linguistic imperialism is a form of linguicism, a favouring of one language over others. It often entails hierarchic order and unequal rights for speakers of different languages. I use the term linguistic imperialism as an empirical and analytical tool to depict a historical pattern, that is, how the imperial status of *hanzi* was formed and developed, and then consolidated.

The chapter has five sections. The first section provides an introduction to linguistic policy in China. Section 2 depicts the Chinese history of linguistic imperialism. This is followed, in Section 3, by an explanation of the domination and historical force of Chinese linguistic imperialism and the reasons why this linguistic imperialism continues in contemporary China. These two sections examine the historical processes by which Chinese linguistic imperialism originated, formed and was consolidated. Section 4 discusses the prospects for China's multi-lingual education, and Section 5 presents some normative concerns with linguistic imperialism.

9.2   HISTORY OF LINGUISTIC IMPERIALISM

Qin and Han dynasties

The unification of the Chinese written language *hanzi* taking the form of *xiaozhuan* (小篆) can be traced back to China's unification under the Qin Empire in 221 BC. The varieties of Chinese script that had developed in the different warring states were standardised by the Qin government so as to facilitate communication between the centre and periphery, while the continued use of non-standard scripts was banned (Zhou & Ross 2004: 2).

Under the rule of the Wudi Emperor (汉武帝) during the Han dynasty, *xiaozhuan* was replaced by *lishu* (隶书), which was easily written and used widely by both the government and *mingjian* (non-government domain). The Wudi Emperor also elevated Confucianism to the status of exclusive official doctrine while abandoning all other doctrines, for the first time in Chinese history. Paper was invented and produced during the Eastern Han dynasty, which helped to spread the Chinese language and culture to local elites and ordinary people on a large scale.

Writing had a crucial role in the power of the Chinese empire. In his study of writing in early China, historian Mark Edward Lewis describes how the imperial canon was created, beginning with the early Qin policies such as a unified script that, along with the standardisation of weights and measures, was linked back to the *Yi* hexagrams; the stone-carved inscriptions by Qin Shihuang on the sacred mountains (Lewis 1999). He also discusses the state's attempt to ban certain private texts and to create a monopoly on official writing. Lewis's study draws our attention to the role of the Han emperor Wu in the creation of the Confucian canon, arguing that this establishment of a Confucian canon can be seen as involving a shift, over a period of three centuries, from the warring states model of political organisation to a new, unified imperial polity (Lewis 1999: 339–60).

According to Lewis, the importance of writing to the Chinese empire was not simply due to its administrative role, but also to the way that texts created an imaginary realm that produced an ideal model of society that could be used to judge actual institutions. It was the foundation of an education programme that created a collective vision of empire among local elites. The shared commitment of local elites to these texts, argues Lewis (1999: 4), was more important than the bureaucratic administration in creating links between the centre and local areas, and therefore helping to maintain the imperial system.

Xi Xia dynasty and Jin dynasty

The imperial status of Chinese *hanzi* was challenged by foreign conquerors and their new imperial rules. The Xi Xia (西夏 Western Xia) dynasty (AD 1038–1227) imitated *hanzi* and created its own written script, which was both an official and private language. *Hanzi* was still widely used in Han areas but was not an official language and it was limited to communication between the Xi Xia and Song dynasties. The Xi Xia imposed its language upon minority peoples (Cai et al. 1979: 159, 214).

After the Nüzhen (女真) established the Jin (金) dynasty (1119–38) the need to create a native ethnic script was more and more pressing. Under the influence of the neighbouring Han and Khitan scripts the Jurchen (Nüzhen) script was born. The Jurchen borrowed some forms of Han and Khitan script and imitated their methods, completing the creation of the basic script and words in a short period of time. In the first year of the *Tianjuan* (天眷) period of the Xizong Emperor (熙宗) (1138), a Nüzhen small script was created. In 1145, the fifth year of the *huangtong* period of the Xizong Emperor, imperial orders began to be recorded using the small script, which explains how the general use of the Nüzhen small script began among society at this time (Jin 2009). The Jin used the script in official documents (Kane 1989; Franke & Twitchett 1994). Eventually, following the evaporation of Jin political power, the influence of Nüzhen script began to fade away. By the end of the Ming period, Nüzhen script was disappearing and Nüzhen tribes began to use Mongolian script (Bao 2003). It has now passed out of human knowledge (Jin 2009).

The Xi Xia and Jin were a historical turning point in the history of Chinese linguistic imperialism in the sense that the *hanzi* script survived and continued to develop under the foreign rulers. Later, the Yuan and Qing dynasties created new written scripts backed by their political power, which led to rivalry between these scripts and *hanzi*. None of the new scripts lasted long and *hanzi* emerged as the final winner of the linguistic battle. This marked a fundamental difference between the ancient Egyptian and Chinese scripts. Both are made up of pictographic characters and both ancient Egypt and China were conquered by foreign powers. The former script disappeared, however, and its meaning became inaccessible until rediscovered in the late nineteenth century; today Egyptians use the Arab language. In contrast, the latter not only survived under a series of foreign rulers but evolved into the dominant script in a system of linguistic imperialism and became a form of soft power.

Yuan dynasty

The imperial status of Chinese *hanzi* hit a critical historical juncture under the Yuan. Kublai Khan (忽必烈) (1215–94) raised the importance of language and written script to the highest level, giving them a place in his unified strategy for political power and domination. Kublai Khan faced a number of language choices. The first was to use the Uyghur (畏兀儿) Mongolian script that had been used since Genghis Khan's time and would therefore only require the standardisation and expansion of its use. This option would meet the needs and tendency towards cultural inertia of the nobles and would involve the least effort and trouble. The second option was to use or borrow Han script, or Khitan (Liao) script, or Nüzhen (Jin) script, which at the time had a widespread social and cultural foundation. But Kublai Khan chose a third way – he created a new script. He wanted to create and use a transcendent new script to support the workings of a new dynasty, symbolising the beginning of a new period. To be the ruler of an empire of different ethnic groups using many different kinds of languages, Kublai Khan hoped to have a script that could record all of these different languages. Kublai Khan hoped to use his newly fixed-upon script to help unite his domain and ensure total rule. He hoped that the new script would triumph over that era's written languages of *hanzi* and the Uyghur Mongolian script (Zhang Jun 2008).

Kublai Khan appointed a Tibetan scholar, Basiba (八思巴, 1235–80), to draw up a new script that could supersede all kinds of spoken languages and be used throughout the empire. Basiba took a Tibetan script to act as the foundation for the alphabetic writing and created Basiba script.

Considering the reality of the social and cultural conditions he was facing, Kublai Khan first developed a 'bilingual script' system in government documents; that is, the newly created Basiba script was the dominant language but the languages of other states or ethnicities were also used alongside it. Later he used Basiba script widely on stele inscriptions, public notices, and plaques and signs dealing with political, religious and social affairs (Zhang Jun 2008).

In order to unite his domain and maintain his rule over diverse territories, Kublai Khan proclaimed Basiba script to be the new Mongolian script, and issued a warning that the old Mongol script should not be used and should be replaced by the new script in 1271. From then on, imperial edicts were in Basiba script, and Basiba script became the only legal national script. Kublai Khan established mechanisms to educate using Basiba script such as national script study in the capital and Mongolian script study in the regions, and made Basiba script the language of instruction for all levels of schooling. He also appointed special officials who were responsible for promoting the new script, selecting talented people who were proficient in the new script, and used the new script to translate the Han script classics. In order to encourage people to study and master the language he even exempted students of the new language from having to provide bonded labour and offered them official positions (Zhang Jun 2008).

During the Yuan period, a small group of Han Chinese, most from northern China, had learnt and mastered the new language and had adopted Mongolian names and cultures. In contrast, the majority of Han people in southern China still used *hanzi* and successfully resisted the new language (Li 2009). Despite the great efforts made by Kublai Khan, the Chinese intellectual elite and some sections of the Mongolian people, particularly the more independent Khan states, resisted the use of Basiba script. With the collapse of the Yuan dynasty, Basiba script was abandoned. The Mongolian script returned to the traditional Uyghur system and developed into a stable symbolic form of Mongolian identity. Mongolian spoken language also developed in different places, forming different dialects (Zhang Jun 2008).

Ming dynasty

In the wake of the demise of Yuan, the Ming dynasty restored *hanzi* as the official language. It also promoted it in minority areas. One example is the Buyi minority (布依族) in Guizhou province. While previous dynasties before the Yuan had adopted a *jimi* (羁縻 control and harness) policy in this ethnic minority area, the Ming established the status of province in 1481 and ordered every *tusi* official to enter their eldest son into the Imperial College, where they would study *hanzi*. The children of Buyi *tusi* who entered the Imperial College had not only their lodgings supplied by the state but even their clothing, hats, shoes and socks. (In contrast, during the mid–late Qing period the law required *all* children of *tusi* to be sent for Confucian instruction at all levels, and if they did not successfully complete their Confucian studies they were not able to serve as *tusi*.) In the early Ming, the law stated that the recipients of special policies in the Guizhou ethnic areas did not need to pass tests and could directly enter the Imperial College to study. Community schools (社学) were also established in all Buyi areas. In 1475, in all of Guizhou there were thirty places of Confucian study, among them more than ten that were in Buyi areas. In 1505, the Guiyang region had twenty-four community schools with 700 students. The funds for building schools were provided by the central government (Zhao 2008). All of this was designed to increase the use of *hanzi* in ethnic minority areas.

Qing dynasty

In the Qing dynasty both *hanzi* and Manchu language were used and promoted. In 1599, Nurhaci (努尔哈赤) ordered the creation of a Manchu language based on Mongolian script (Jin 2009). The codifying of Manchurian script promoted the work of translating the Han script classics, speeded up the Sinification of the late Jin rulers, and created the conditions for the establishment of the Qing dynasty and its move into the Central Plains (Bao 2003). While the Manchu rulers insisted on using the Manchu language as the official language, they had learnt a lesson from the failure of the Yuan dynasty's new language. As such, they adopted a policy of ruling subjects in their native language (同文之治) and used *hanzi* in the administration of the territories of the Ming. Through this policy the Qing dynasty was able to provide a way for Han subjects to accept its rule. As new dynasties overthrew old ones, their legitimacy depended on the continuing use of Han Chinese cultural practices, particularly *hanzi* and Confucian rituals. The Kangxi (康熙) Emperor (1661–1722) set up schools for Manchu elite to study both *hanzi* and Manchu language, and ordered Chinese scholars to compile the Kangxi Dictionary (康熙字典) as well as the Manchurian Dictionary. The Yongzheng (雍正) Emperor (1722–35) required Chinese officials from Fujian and Guangdong provinces to speak the official language and set up schools there to teach the officials how to speak it. In 1872, the Tongzhi (同治) Emperor demanded all official documents submitted to the court be written in *hanzi*. Around 1845, the spoken language used in Beijing formally became the national official spoken language; this was the origin of today's Putonghua (Zhang 1998).

It is remarkable that the Manchu language has slowly faded away and that many Manchu elites and common people converted to learning *hanzi* over a period of three hundred years (from Nurhaci's creation of a Manchurian language in 1599 to about 1899). This voluntary linguistic conversion was due to the following factors. Manchu rulers advocated the learning of *hanzi*, and several emperors themselves mastered Chinese language and literature at a high level. The examination system also speeded up the process of Sinification. The Manchu shifted from fishing and hunting to an agricultural economy; in this process they gave up many terms used specifically for hunting, and wrote Chinese poems and novels that described their new way of life (the best example is Chao Xueqing and his famous book, *Dream of the Red Chamber*). In addition, a significant number of Han Chinese flooded into the traditional Manchu territory due to natural disasters in 1792 (Zhang Jie 1995), outnumbering the Manchu people there, and so slowly the Chinese language replaced the Manchu language. Mixed marriages also led to the adoption of the Chinese language and the abandonment of the Manchu language (D. Zhang 2002; Dai 2007; Feng 2010; Zhang Lei 2008).

While Chinese language slowly became the dominant language, the Qing continued to employ other languages, cultural traditions and forms of governance in their rule over the frontier, as explained by the so-called 'New Qing historians' such as Elliott, Crossley, Purdue and Millward (see Rawski 1996). In their analyses, however, the New Qing historians have led us to overlook the power and hegemony of the Chinese language. We thus need to revisit and rebalance this debate (see Ho 1998). The Chinese language finally absorbed the Manchu language; the newly created Manchu language – like its predecessor the Basiba script – lost the battle with a Chinese script. Moreover, the Qing continued and strengthened Chinese linguistic imperialism through its education policy in minority areas.

Inheriting the Ming dynasty education policy, the scale and depth of policy during the Qing dynasty underwent comprehensive development. The Qing dynasty established a policy known as *gai tu gui liu*, which replaced local rulers with official representatives and promoted Confucian culture and the *hanzi* writing system in ethnic minority areas.

In Guizhou province, for example, the Qing established free community schools for ethnic minorities. The increase in formal education promoted the imperial examinations among ethnic minorities. In the years of the Qing dynasty, Guizhou had more than five thousand examination candidates and more than six hundred who held the *jinshi* degree (进士). There was an increased study quota and selection quota for Guizhou minorities, in particular, and there was a special category for *Miao* people (苗科) (Zhao 2008).

The Qing dynasty also promoted and implemented the *gai tu gui liu* policy in Hunan and Sichuan provinces. The majority of Tujia people (土家族) in Western Hunan Province could not converse in the Han language before *gai tu gui liu*. They spoke the Tujia language as the main tool for social interaction, and they did not have their own written script. After *gai tu gui liu* large numbers of Han moved into areas occupied by Tujia people and the Tujia language was subject to the influence of Han language. When Han-language schools were widely established and the numbers of Tujia entering these schools gradually increased, the use of Han script in the Tujia area of Western Hunan Province continually expanded and the Tujia language underwent great changes in pronunciation and vocabulary.[4]

The development of Confucian schools and education similarly promoted the transmission of Han spoken language and script among the Ba people (巴人) in the Eastern part of present-day Sichuan and Chongqing. This was the most externally obvious characteristic of the Confucianisation of the upper classes in society. When Ba society received Chinese Confucian schools and education, Han language and script took over, using Confucian culture as a carrier. Education was not limited to the upper stratum of society; the children of common people could receive educational opportunities, and so Confucian thought and culture began to completely permeate Ba society (Huang Xiu-Rong 2010).

The Naxi people (纳西族) are another useful example. From the Tang and Song until the Ming dynasty, *tusi* in Lijiang promoted the transmission of the culture of China's Central Plains, especially that the upper levels of society study Han script, shaping the bilingual social organisation of the traditional ruling class. After the Qing's *gai tu gui liu* policy, the establishment of official and private Han script education spread further among the people.

A cautious note on spatial distinction is needed. Historically, *gai tu gui liu* was more dominant and ultimately successful in the south of China where one encountered *tusi* chieftains and often there was no strong or pre-existing written language.[5] In the northern regions, however, the Qing maintained the *jimi* system and autonomy system.

Republic of China era: comparison with European linguistic shifts

Hanzi suffered a series of crises in the early modern period. This was surprising, given it had consolidated its imperial status in the late Qing period. Initially, Korea, Japan and Vietnam developed their national language scripts. Then in the early period of the May Fourth Movement, several radical Chinese scholars like Wu Zhihui called for the abandonment of *hanzi* script because it was regarded as backward, difficult to learn and unsuitable for science. In the 1930s, a romanisation (*pinyin*) movement emerged (Wang 2004). Nevertheless, the national oral language (*guoyin*) movement and vernacular writing (*baihuawen*) movement strengthened Chinese linguistic imperialism (Wang 2004).

In the process of modern nation-building on China's periphery, Vietnam and Korea moved away from using Chinese script and developed their own written languages. This was similar to the process that occurred in Europe, where different countries developed written forms of their own national languages. Benedict Anderson (1983: 44) writes that through print-languages, 'Speakers of the huge variety of Frenches, Englishes, or Spanishes, ... gradually became aware of the hundreds of thousands, even millions, of people in their particular language-field, and at the same time that *only those* hundreds of thousands, or millions, so belonged. These fellow-readers, to whom they were connected through print, formed, in their secular, particular, visible invisibility, the embryo of the nationally imagined community.' His analysis reveals how European nation-building was tied to print-language, and more specifically to print capitalism.

The European linguistic transformation in modern times involved two separate but related processes. One was the process of various local (spoken) dialects evolving into a national language. This involved standardised written texts in national languages combined with education systems that taught many more common people to read. The other process was the replacement of the written use of Latin with English, German, French, Italian, etc., promoted by nationalists and backed up by print capitalism. Before this, at one end of the scale there was the various local dialects, which were spoken in geographically restricted areas but not often written down, and at the other end was Latin, which was written (not generally spoken) and used by a transnational class of educated people. The development of national languages served to both *unite* local spoken dialects into commonly spoken languages and *divide* written language from Latin into national written languages.

There were two similar processes in China and the surrounding region: the division of a standard (transnational) written language/script into different national written languages/scripts, and the unification of locally spoken dialects into commonly shared national spoken languages. Japan, Korea and Vietnam previously used the *hanzi* script but developed their own national languages. In the formation of their national written languages the *hanzi* script was either changed, added to or abandoned completely. Vietnam, Indonesia, Japan and Korea have also mapped their vernacular languages onto new imagined national communities.

There are differences, however. The relationship between Chinese characters and Chinese spoken languages is different from the relationship between romanised writing systems and European languages. The vernacular languages of many of the non-Han frontier regions and various Chinese local dialects of the Republic and PRC have failed to develop into modern written languages; Chinese *hanzi* has instead remained dominant. The Chinese modern linguistic transformation moved in a cosmopolitan (or imperial), rather than local, direction (Anderson 1983: 74–83).

In comparative terms, the European linguistic transformation in modern times witnessed the decline of the written language of Latin and the emergence of various national languages. In contrast, the Chinese written language was revived and reformed and moved in a cosmopolitan (or imperial) direction in modern times.

Moreover, in modern times Indonesia based its official language on Malay rather than on Javanese, the language spoken by the largest number of people. Vietnam chose to use the roman alphabet to develop a new writing system. In both cases, the younger generations in Indonesia and Vietnam cannot read their classics, and their modern languages cut off the links with their ancestors' languages. Such a phenomenon has also occurred in many other countries. In contrast, Chinese graduates are able to read and understand their classics like *The Shiji* , 史記 'Records of the [Grand] Scribe', written by Sima Qian 司马迁 (145–86 BC), more than two thousand years ago.

9.3 TIBETAN LANGUAGE DURING THE IMPERIAL ERAS

The history of the Tibetan language differs from that of ethnic minority areas that were more formally part of the Chinese empire. The kingdom of Tibet began about the time of the Tang dynasty, in the late sixth–early seventh centuries (Pan 1992: 117). In the seventh century, borrowing from the Indian Gupta and Brahmi alphabets, Thomi Sambhota invented the written script. Tibet had the first official contact with China during Emperor Taizong's reign (627–649). The first Manchu mission to Tibet was in 1709, and 1720 marked the first time in Tibetan history that forces from China entered Lhasa (Kolmas 1967: 39). The territory of Qinghai was separated from Tibet in 1724 and a new boundary between Sichuan and Tibet drawn in 1727 (Kolmas 1967: 41). The Tibetan areas within these provinces were subject to the *tusi* system, as per other ethnic minority areas, while the Tibetan territory continued to be ruled under the Tibetan administrative system.

The Tibetan script came from India and thus the Tibetan language does not use *hanzi*. The autobiography of Rdo-ring Bstan-'dzin dpal-'byor [Rdo-ring], a Tibetan minister from 1783, reveals that neither the Chinese nor Mongol languages were well known among the Tibetan elites. In an account of his meeting with the Qing grand council (regarding the Gurkha wars), Rdo-ring states:

> He [the Emperor] looked closely at me and said, 'Do you understand Chinese and Mongol?' I stated that, aside from a few nouns, I did not know how to make sense of things in Chinese and that my understanding of Mongol was weak. (Cited in Sperling, 1998: 331)

The Manchu policies during the Qing dynasty were to maintain the native languages of the boundary regions, cementing their rule through cultural preservation. Thus, the Qing used the Tibetan language to rule over Tibet, the Uyghur language to rule in Xinjiang, and Mongolian in Mongol areas.

Monastic education was traditionally the main form of education in Tibet, with some private schools established in the eighteenth century that were open to both rich and poor children (Johnson 2000: 597). The Tibetan language was the mode of instruction.

9.4 LANGUAGE POLICIES IN TIBET IN THE PRC ERA

Ethnic minority language policies have been subjected to various changes throughout the PRC era. The right to use minority languages is enshrined within the Chinese Constitution (Article 53) and numerous laws. In addition to the 1995 Chinese Education Law (Article 12), the 2005 Regional Autonomy for Ethnic Minorities in China White Paper states in Article 33:

> According to the provisions of the self-government regulations for ethnic autonomous areas, the organs of self-government of such areas shall use one or more commonly used local languages when they are performing official duties. If more than one language can be used for such official duties, the language of the ethnic group exercising regional autonomy should be used primarily. (Information Office of the State Council, 2009)

And in Article 37:

> Organs of self-government of autonomous areas determine the educational plan, the establishment of schools, school system, the forms by which schools are run, curricula, language of teaching and method of instruction . . .
> . . . Schools [classes] and other educational institutions whose students are predominantly from ethnic minority families should, if possible, use text-books printed in their own languages, and lessons should be taught in those languages. Chinese language courses shall be offered at different times of the primary school period depending on the particular situation, to propagate the use of Putonghua. (Information Office of the State Council, 2009)

During the early days of the PRC the CCP demonstrated an intention to enhance language diversity and multi-lingualism in China. When the PRC was formed, eleven minority groups already had their own writing systems, and the government began to assist other minority groups, such as the *Tujia* minority, to develop their own scripts, so that now there are more than thirty kinds of scripts in use by minorities (Anderson 1983: 181). In these early years, minority policies were influenced more by the Soviet experience and ideology than the traditional Chinese imperial policies.

China developed and promoted the national unified, simplified *hanzi* system throughout China.[6] This process involved many more considerations than just relations between minorities and the centre, such as improving education levels and simplifying the characters to make it easier for everyone (not just minorities) to learn. Of course, the process of creating a simplified *hanzi* system created a cultural divide between the areas that were under CCP political control and Hong Kong, Macau and Taiwan, where the traditional complex characters were still used.

In the 1960s, China adopted assimilation policies to eliminate the 'dangers' posed by minorities like Tibetans and to consolidate the domination of *hanzi*. Tibet did not escape the attacks of the Cultural Revolution, with many important religious and cultural sites destroyed and their minority customs labelled as 'backward'. Mandarin continued to be the required language of instruction.

Limited cultural liberalisation occurred during the 1980s under the leadership of CCP General Secretary Hu Yaobang and Wu Jinghua as regional party secretary of Tibet. According to Karmel (1995: 487), they advocated the use of Tibetan language in educational programmes and by regional government leaders. Local governments were given more autonomy regarding cultural, religious and educational affairs (Schiaffini 2004: 82).

In the 1990s, the Chinese state had to deal with the challenges that sprang from ethno-nationalism and calls for democratisation on China's periphery. In response, the state reinforced the long historical tradition of the unification of language as the foundation of Great Unity. In minority areas/autonomous regions, it is possible to use local languages in primary and secondary schools, but at universities most of the instruction is in Putonghua.

Thus, as Kormondy (2002: 398) argues, the 'Cultural mutilation' of the 1950s to 1970s has 'been replaced by more subtle but profound means of cultural change: Han immigration, urbanisation, and manipulation of the educational system, all part of a general program of societal transformation of China as a whole.' Tibetan writer Dorjee Tsering also explains, 'when schools began teaching in Tibetan, there were no teaching materials in the Tibetan language' (cited in Schiaffini 2004: 82).

Tibetan language has been deliberately linked (by the Chinese government) to Tibetan nationalism and thus is viewed as a threat to the national unity of the Chinese state (Johnson 2000: 600; Wangdu 2011: 19). As Wangdu argues, the Chinese government's language and cultural policies in Tibet (and other areas such as Xinjiang) have, instead of diminishing ethnic nationalism, 'increased alienation and sense of exclusion' (Wangdu 2011: 22). Thus, the current status of the Tibetan language is a cause for concern. 'In the more remote areas, the language of instruction for the first three years of primary school is the native tongue, after which instruction is almost entirely in Mandarin, with English begun in some schools in the fourth grade' (Kormondy 1995, cited in Kormondy 2002: 385). Only within some Tibetan regions within Qinghai Province is the Tibetan language used beyond primary school (Wangdu 2011: 19).

The CCP's policy towards Tibetan culture and language can be seen as a modern version of *gai tu gui liu*, in the sense that in terminating the Dalai Lama's rule in Tibet, Beijing established a direct administrative system, appointed the party secretary of Tibet Autonomous Region, and implemented and promoted national educational and cultural policies there. Chinese became the official language used in schools. This practice, however, was mixed with the teaching of Marxism and socialism, which included political and legal commitments to multiculturalism and the protection of ethnic diversity and minority rights. Consequently, there was a tension between the traditional *gai tu gui liu* policy and modern socialist policy towards minorities.

It is a great tragedy that Tibetan language, which is over a thousand years old, has so radically lost its primacy within a short time span of four or five decades. The Tibetan language has become increasingly marginalised and downplayed as merely an instruction language for primary and secondary education.

The history of Tibetan–Chinese relations has featured numerous protests and demonstrations – in 1959, 1988, 1989, 1993, 2008, etc. While protests have been triggered by various concerns, education policy – and language policy in particular – is a core issue of conflict between the Tibetans (and other minority groups) and the Chinese government (Wangdu 2011: 19). In addition to the specific language protests such as the 2010 Qinghai protest mentioned earlier, since 2009 Tibetans have been resorting to self-immolation as a form of protest against the Chinese government's policies, particularly the increased restrictions on religious practices. Many of these have occurred in the Tibetan autonomous prefectures outside of the TAR (i.e. in Sichuan and Qinghai). Robbie Barnett, a Tibet scholar at Colombia University, fears that although language protests have thus far been treated as local issues resulting from 'misunderstandings', 'it is only a matter of time . . . before these issues will be treated in a much more serious way' (Radio Free Asia 2012).

9.5   THE DETERMINANTS OF THE CONTINUATION OF LINGUISTIC IMPERIALISM

Throughout China's process of dynastic change over thousands of years, *hanzi* has played a continuing role as the written form used by the elites across East Asia. It spread across the region, reaching Japan in the fifth century. *Hanzi* constituted the linguistic foundation of East Asian civilisation, including China, Japan, Korea and Vietnam. This is in contrast with India, where political dynasties were shorter-lived and more geographically fragmented, and where there was a diverse range of writing systems. In Europe, Latin played a role in unifying the educated elite across the continent. It was tied to the role of the church, and scientific communities who used Latin for their published works for a period during the Enlightenment before they shifted to using national languages. In China, the written script remained linked to secular authority, whereas the Tibetan and Arabic scripts used in peripheral areas in China were linked to religious authorities and religious texts. The Chinese script was consolidated through a series of long-lived empires and still enjoys 'imperial status' of domination today. Five factors account for the continuation of Chinese linguistic imperialism in contemporary China.

First, Chinese script is a kind of soft power. This soft power is a public good that different kinds of people can share and use to communicate with each other. It is a 'container' for cultural and material achievements. It is a cultural system through which political administration is able to exercise power. Jenner remarks: 'Chinese high culture generally, and the Chinese written language in particular, have had an amazing power to standardize or to play down quirkiness, unorthodoxy and difference' (Jenner 1992: 5). This linguistic dimension of soft power differs from a strategic conceptualisation of soft power developed by Nye, who sees soft power as an attractive power and strategy to get others to do what you want, and the ability to co-opt people and manipulate the agenda of political choice (Nye 2004).

Of course, the imperial status of *hanzi* has depended on political power and still does so today. Historically, Qin and Han emperors endorsed and supported *hanzi*, and Ming and Qing promoted the spread of *hanzi*. However, *hanzi* as a kind of soft power is, in my opinion, sometimes much more powerful than hard political or military power. Foreign dynasties like the Qing conquered China in political and military terms, but failed to resist the linguistic power of *hanzi* and had to accept its continued use as a core official language. There was even a very slow and gradual process of voluntary conversion to Chinese script. Several factors account for the voluntary conversion to Chinese script by foreign rulers. First, instrumentally they had to use it to rule the vast land and large population who had used *hanzi* for centuries. Second, generations of Chinese and many other peoples have improved the *hanzi* language system over at least three millennia. It is a civilisational product that has constantly adapted and changed its written forms, characters, and methods of how to express and distinguish meanings efficiently. In short, *hanzi* has a number of comparative advantages over minority languages in China, some of which do not have a writing system. Third, path dependence is also a factor. It is often easier to adapt the Chinese language rather than create a new language from scratch. A politically constructed language often has a short life, for example the language of Basiba. A language can be created by a strong military and political power, but often is unsustainable in the long term. The failure of the Basiba language may have contributed to the short political life of the Yuan dynasty, while the adoption of *hanzi* may have contributed to the longevity of the Qing dynasty.

The second important factor is *the choice of modern polity structures*, which has impacted on the political, cultural and linguistic life of minorities. Take the contrasting histories of India and China as an example. In India, there has never been a strong empire which lasted for more than a hundred years. Indian history is characterised by fragmentation into a number of rival kingdoms, and numerous linguistic worlds; even within the two major linguistic blocs, Dravidian and Aryan, there are many geographic and linguistic sub-groups (Amritavalli & Jayaseelan 2007). The short-lived empires in pre-colonial India did not have time to develop assimilation policies; and its history of the caste system reinforced group politics and tribal languages. A federal form of polity was chosen for the fledgling nation-state, at least in part because of this historical pattern. What has evolved is a relatively successful multinational federalism under which the rights, cultures and languages of India's minorities flourish for the most part.

In China, on the other hand, since the Qin dynasty (221 BC), a number of powerful empires, some lasting several hundred years, were established. China has continued this unitary tradition with a strong power at the centre controlling fragmental minorities at the periphery. In the long history of Chinese empires, there have been uninterrupted leadership periods of at least three decades, which has allowed for greater assimilation or intermingling. This historical difference helps explain the difference in linguistic policy. India has a Linguistic Commissioner, and India has often redrawn boundaries along linguistic and cultural lines. China has had a unified written language for a thousand years; it remains a unitary system. The boundary of provinces is never defined by language, although the boundary of major ethnic groups, like Tibetans, is related to, but not defined by, language. In this context,

Beijing does not recognise the internal border which the Dalai Lama's Greater Tibet implies.

The third factor is *the state's continuing use of a unified language to promote national political unity*. Throughout Chinese history, there has been an overarching concern for the greater union, and the unified language policy has been a major binding force. A unified language was the foundation of the Chinese political concept of Great Unity. Unification of the written language was seen to be an important factor in unifying the country politically. The linguistic imperialism of *hanzi* has interlocked with bureaucratic structures and institutions (such as the post-station system, civil service exam, and history-writing) across the dynasties in China. It is held that it was linguistic unity that prevented China from breaking apart in modern times.

Fourth is *the force of unified Chinese markets*. Most of the scholarship on linguistic questions has focused on the role of politics and culture rather than the economy. In the pre-modern market, Skinner noted that the boundaries between Chinese dialects could usually be found to follow the boundaries between markets: '. . . when my informants in Szechwan used to discourse on the peculiarities of speech characteristic of the different markets, that the minimal unit of significance to the dialect geographer of China is precisely the standard marketing area' (Skinner 1964: 44). In modern markets, however, economic development has promoted a *common* market and economic integration. In this process, even ethnic cultures have themselves become commercialised products, which has degraded their cultural significance. As more national markets develop within China, this trend towards viewing ability in Putonghua as necessary for economic prosperity can be seen in many places, including Shanghai, where the desire to sell products to outsiders has led to increasing use of Putonghua, and Yunnan, where similar national markets in areas including tourism have developed.

More parents in China are now encouraging their children to speak Putonghua at home, rather than their local dialect, because of the educational and career opportunities it is seen to provide. Internal migration has also fuelled the spread of Putonghua, with the development of internal transport networks encouraging interaction between people who previously would have been unlikely to leave their local area. Interestingly, the force of the market is sometimes much more influential than administrative power in promoting a unified language. In some minority-dominated enterprises, some Han Chinese are employed to deal with technology and market issues despite the owners' preference towards employing people of their own ethnicity.

It can be hypothesised that under market mechanisms ordinary minority people are generally the first to study the dominated language voluntarily and the first to be assimilated. In contrast, under traditional administrative mechanisms in the practice of *gai tu gui liu* (that is, the state setting up schools and offering incentives for minorities to study the dominated language), the local elite were the first to study the dominant language and to be assimilated. Today, it seems that ordinary people from minority areas are more interested in studying Chinese and/or English than their political elites who might be resistant to it, or argue for the protection of minority languages. For example, some Uyghur elites have argued against bilingual teaching. In this context, Ma Rong has argued that it is best to let the market decide what language is best. For him the spread of Putonghua leads to greater equality of opportunity for ethnic minorities within China.[7] Ordinary minority people might benefit from the new opportunities provided by the spread of Chinese linguistic imperialism, while some elites might lose out. The Chinese government often points out that the Dalai Lama's advocacy for Tibetan culture is a disguised attempt at maintaining a feudal power base that disadvantages ordinary Tibetans. The big question that is usually overlooked, however, in my opinion, is what exactly do ordinary minority people want? How can minorities become empowered in relation to both their cultural systems and economic life?

The fifth factor involves *the growing global status of the Chinese language and China's imitation of the imperialism of English*. With the rise of China, the Chinese government has taken steps to strengthen the international position of the Chinese language, such as by establishing more than six hundred Confucius Institutes around the world and pushing for international recognition of the use of *hanzi* in internet domain names. China is pushing the international expansion of Putonghua and the kind of *hanzi* used on the Mainland but not other Han dialects or non-Han spoken languages or scripts.

Chinese language policy exists between two linguistic worlds: the global dominance of the English language and the European world of language plurality. In many international organisations the parallel use of languages is the norm – the EU has twenty-three official languages (Phillipson 2003; Extra & Gorter 2008), the African Union operates using four ex-colonial languages, but ASEAN has adopted English as its working language (Kirkpatrick 2010).

While China certainly will continue to maintain its linguistic plurality and diversity as a political necessity, it has followed the example of English linguistic imperialism, which seems to provide the Chinese state with normatively legitimate justification. English is being spread through market forces and appeals to a mass market around the world (by contrast, Latin was promoted by the church and remained the property of elites). English is not only a tool for conducting international business; it is also in demand around the world and has become a commodity in its own right (Kachru & Nelson 2007; Murata & Jenkins 2009; Tam 2009; Vaish 2010; Pingali 2009; Seargeant 2009; Setter et al. 2010; Stanlaw 2004; Bautista 2008; Bolton 2002; Deterring 2008; Lim et al. 2010). Being able to speak English is a form of cultural capital and a path to a better economic future in many countries, and so the teaching of English has become a valuable export commodity for countries such as Australia, where schools and universities take on large numbers of international students keen to improve their English skills. The Chinese state has also developed and promoted the linguistic capital of Putonghua so that individuals will view learning the language as an investment in their economic future.

As China's international power rises, the Chinese language could be considered a potential rival to the global use of English. The history of Chinese linguistic imperialism goes back at least three millennia, much longer than that of English linguistic imperialism which has only been around for several centuries. Currently China is part of a globalised English world, and the Chinese language is not currently in a position to challenge the global dominance of English. Nor does the Chinese state have any desire to establish a closed linguistic world excluding English; rather it aims to build an open linguistic world (Xu 2010; Liu Jun 2007). Interestingly, many Tibetans, Uyghurs and Mongols in China are learning English but through the intermediary language of Putonghua and *hanzi*.

9.6   CHINA'S LINGUISTIC WORLD OVER THE COMING CENTURY

While I do not adopt historical determinism, the history of Chinese linguistic impe-rialism tells us that the force of *hanzi* is greater than the force resisting it. The force is cultural soft power, which at times and in some areas is much more powerful than that of the CCP. Much more intense violence took place in response to the *gai tu gui liu* policy under the Yongzheng Emperor, and there was even a revolt (Feng 1992). Today's protests mentioned earlier are much smaller in terms of scale and much less intense in terms of the level of violence. It is expected that in the future these pro-tests will continue alongside the implementation of *gai tu gui liu*.

The long-term impact of *gai tu gui liu* should not be underestimated. Behind China's current linguistic policy towards Tibet is the belief that because in the past *gai tu gui liu* was relatively successful in Yunnan and Guizhou, in the long term it may have reasonable success in today's Tibet, in the sense that Putonghua and *hanzi* are accepted as the dominant languages in the Tibetan region but the Tibetan lan-guage and Buddhism remain an integral part of Tibetan life. Tibetan leaders in exile, including Samdhong Rinpoche, the former Tibetan government in exile's *Kalon Tripa* (prime minister), seem to be unaware of this possibility.[8]

While China remains a multi-lingual society, and multi-linguistic and bilingual practice is likely to continue, there will be different patterns of bilingual education and practices which are likely to follow previous historical patterns. Often this process would begin with the minority language being dominant over the Chinese language. Then in the next stage both Chinese language and minority language would be equally important. Then slowly this would evolve into the next phase in which the Chinese language became dominant while the minority language became secondary. Finally, bilingual practice would disappear and Chinese language would become the only written and spoken language. This is the historical pattern of Chinese linguistic imperialism. It is likely that this history will replay again in many areas of China in the near future.

By the end of 2115, around one hundred years from now, Tibetan Buddhism and language will certainly remain but are likely to play much less important roles than today. Both Tibetan and Uyghur languages may be pushed into the private sphere. It is more likely that the spread of *hanzi* and Putonghua will be more successful in the areas where the Tibetan Autonomous Region borders neighbouring provinces than in remote and isolated Tibetan areas. Following regional differentiated policy in the later Qing, the Chinese state is likely to develop a new differentiated regional policy in terms of spreading *hanzi* and Putonghua. Chinese linguistic imperialism is likely to be more successful in Tibetan areas than in Xinjiang. This is because Chinese and Tibetans belong to the same larger ethnic group that shares certain cultural characteristics such as the Buddhist tradition and history. Uyghurs are much more ethnically distinct from Chinese and use a language that is part of a Turkic language group that is used in a number of different countries outside China.

9.7 CONCLUDING REMARK: BEYOND LINGUISTIC IMPERIALISM

Now I will break from the previous analysis to address some normative issues inherent in the empirical discussion of linguistic imperialism. First, to describe the historical formation and consolidation of Chinese linguistic imperialism is not to internalise and naturalise it as 'normal'. I have no intention of glorifying the dominant language and rationalising the linguistic hierarchy. On the contrary, I am aware of the criticism and concern from minorities and understand their uncomfortable feelings towards Chinese linguistic imperialism. This can be found in the popular culture of minorities. For example, they often accuse current bilingual teaching of being fake, laugh at those they label *minkaoban* (members of ethnic minorities who finish their schooling in *hanzi*/Putonghua), despise those who speak good Putonghua for not maintaining their cultural tradition, and regard their own language as best. To understand their feelings is to respect their cultural integrity.

Perhaps we should make a policy recommendation that the Chinese state needs to promote minority language teaching to Han Chinese as a counter to Han language dominance and encourage Han students to learn minority languages as an appreciation for cultural and linguistic diversity. In sharp contrast to today, the Qiaolong Emperor studied Tibetan language and communicated to Tibetan nobles in their language. It goes without saying that no Chinese General Party-Secretaries from Mao Zedong to Xi Jinping have ever attempted to learn Tibetan as a mode of communication. The Chinese government should make a legal requirement that all employees in the state administration of autonomous regions (*zizhiqu*) speak, read and write the language of the autonomous region. This is an institutionalised way to build up an incentive structure for Han to learn a minority language. Both majority and minorities must realise the value of multiculturalism.

Second, we must have an accurate and proper understanding of Chinese linguistic imperialism. It has been associated with bilingual or multi-lingual teaching. While *hanzi* remained the core language of the empire, a plurality of other written forms persisted in peripheral areas such as Tibet, which developed and maintained its language throughout most of Chinese history. The Chinese script provided a standard written form that could be used for communication between elites, but this was also accompanied by a plurality of Chinese spoken language groups across the country.

A benign emperor often tries to achieve a balance between Chinese linguistic imperialism and multi-lingual practice and teaching. It is recommended that the Chinese state continues this plural practice to craft policies that find a balance between the forces of economic development and modernisation that are driving the expansion of Putonghua, and the desire for the preservation of language plurality and cultural difference. In the modern world, the Chinese state has to take seriously the dangers of an unjust way of managing language diversity. The process of policy-making should involve the participation, consultation and deliberation of those groups who are affected by linguistic policy. Policies should be made according to the principle of equal access to education and economic opportunity. Any sizable ethnic group must have its higher education taught in its own language; without it, this group is culturally disadvantaged.

Third, there is an emergent mixed regime where Confucianism, the socialist culture of equality, and liberal multiculturalism interact and play competing roles in constructing the modern discourse on linguistic policy. While they give rise to inter-nal tensions between unity and plurality, equality and hierarchy, as well as between linguistic justice and administrative control, they also create new and open spaces, dual identities and hybridity. Developments in this direction are likely to become the new norm. While *hanzi* expands and prevails, it ought to leave space for minority people to continue their own language practices. Nevertheless, an unspoken factor behind many cultural policies is the fear of ethnic separatism. The puzzle for the government is how to promote minority culture and language without promoting a separatist form of minority nationalism at the same time. This is a delicate problem in that while assimilation might be more politically convenient for the government than genuine multiculturalism, it is also a risky strategy that plays into the hands of those who accuse the government of trying to suppress minorities. In the end, it is a moral issue; to respect one's language is to respect one's dignity and the value of one's culture. Cultural equality has assumed increasing importance in the normative discourse of multiculturalism. When cultural superiority plays a part in the domina-tion of the weak by the strong, as seen in Tibet today, the idea of cultural equality is challenging this form of political and cultural power.

NOTES

1. http://www.tibet.net/en/index.php?articletype=flash&id=2007&rmenuid=morenews&tab=1, accessed 30 May 2011.
2. See the interesting article about how one should refer to this language. Zhang Wenmu advocated 'Chinese language' (中国语, Zhōngguó yǔ) at http://www.danwei.org/language/chinas.
3. http://news.xinhuanet.com/english/2007-03/07/content_5812838.htm, accessed 19 October 2011.
4. http://www.xxz.gov.cn/goxx/situation.php?id=13.
5. I would like to thank James Leibold for this point. Leibold (2007) has discussed the work of C. Pat Giersch, John Herman, Donald Sutton, William Rowe and others working on the late imperial frontier in the South.
6. Of course, one can argue that the primary reason for adopting simplified *hanzi* was for educational proliferation.
7. Ma made such a remark in the workshop on 2–3 December 2010 at La Trobe University, Australia.
8. The author's talk with Samdhong Rinpoche on 10 December 2009 in Melbourne.

10 A Deliberative Approach to the Tibet Autonomy Issue

10.1 INTRODUCTION: SEARCH FOR AN ALTERNATIVE TO OVERCOME THE CURRENT STALEMATE

The Tibet issue has remained intractable for at least fifty years (Sperling 2004; Sautman & Dreyer 2006). Several dialogues between representatives of the exiled Dalai Lama and the Chinese government in the last few years have produced no tangible results (Rajan 2005; *The Nation* 2005; Rabgey & Sharlho 2004). The 2008 Tibetan protests against Chinese rule in the run-up to the Beijing Olympics, and the counter-protests by Chinese students in major cities around the world, inflamed mistrust and suspicion between the Tibetan and ethnic Chinese communities. This discord tarnished China's credibility as a global power (Economy & Segal 2008: 47).

Over the next few years, increased radicalisation in both Tibetan and ethnic Chinese communities is anticipated. This highlights the need for initiatives that would build up mutual understanding and trust at a grassroots level, as well as within the leaderships. Given how hard it is now to rebuild trust between the Chinese government and the Tibetan government in exile, it is vital to promote mutual understanding and trust between the two communities of people through a process of citizens' deliberation.

A deliberative approach to minority rights issues in Xinjiang Province was called for by Justin J. Stein (2003), who argues: 'CCP rhetoric regarding the unity and apparently utopian quality of interactions between various nationalities should be replaced by a more genuine discourse reflective of vying interests and preferences.' In the past decade, the Dalai Lama himself has made a number of significant efforts to talk with Han Chinese scholars in the US and beyond (Zhang Weiguo 1999). Even earlier, in 1988, Wu Jinghua, the former party secretary of the Tibet Autonomous Region (TAR), organised a series of 'heart to heart' meetings with representatives of the major monasteries to hear their grievances. Wu paid a price, becoming dubbed a 'Lama Secretary' (Bahl 1989) and being removed from his position a few months later.

Between 2009 and 2012, Beijing sent a number of official delegations to major international cities to host a series of talks on China's Tibet policy. (A quick online search for the term 'Sino–Tibetan dialogue' on 10 August 2012 brought up a list of 533,000 items.) Such meetings could potentially reduce mutual distrust, explore new thinking and initiatives, and provide a basis for the development of a deliberative approach. Nevertheless, most of the dialogues ended in rhetorical stalemate (Rabgey & Sharlho 2004). Some were designed to promote and reinforce the fixed view of one side.[1] Others remained consultative and were oriented towards elites rather than citizens.

The genuine deliberative approach is foreign to Chinese officials and scholars, and no doubt will be regarded by some with intense suspicion. However, the limitations of elite dialogue give rise to a need for public deliberation in which critical intellectuals and scholars, ordinary citizens and students can consider and perhaps change their views and follow reason-based argument. Elsewhere I have examined the extent to which some dialogues are deliberative (B. He & Hundt 2008). Here I stress that dialogue can and should be made deliberative through well-designed public discussion. Moreover, the deliberative approach is currently favoured in conflict resolution studies (see Chapter 11), and has been applied to the national identity conflict issue in China in recent years. The application is innovative in that it attempts to change the Chinese political culture by developing the deliberative forum in a civil society context (B. He 2004c; Leib & B. He 2006).

In collaboration with Alex Butler and Simon Bradshaw, I organised a three-day deliberative workshop in late November 2008 in Melbourne, Australia. This was a pilot deliberative forum on the Tibetan autonomy question, Sino–Tibet relations, and the disputed history of Tibet. The academic aims of the workshop were to test whether deliberation promotes mutual understanding, leads to value change, polarises the participants, or produces moderating effects. Its practical purposes were to promote greater mutual understanding and tolerance between ethnic Chinese and Tibetan groups, and to enhance the deliberative capacities of both ethnic Chinese and Tibetan students.

The deliberative workshop had mixed results. The recruitment of participants was difficult and therefore disappointing, and the question of its value remains unchanged. The small sample size in this study means that the results are best considered as indicative and may therefore act as pointers for further confirmatory work. Nevertheless, the experiment validated two claims. First, a *citizen-initiated* deliberative forum moves away from, and is more effective than, those of state institutions in terms of creating a public space, challenging narrow official lines of thinking, and moderately changing people's opinions. Second, a deliberative forum is able to reduce the level of mutual distrust and build up mutual understanding and trust despite its inherent limits.

This chapter examines the achievement and limits of this innovative experimental deliberation. The structure of the chapter is as follows. It first examines the reasons and background for applying the deliberative approach to the Tibet issue, followed by a discussion of the design of a deliberative forum on the Tibet autonomy question. The results of the deliberative forum are examined in detail in the last two sections. A study of how deliberative democracy can be combined with referendum is discussed in Chapter 11.

10.2   DESIGN AND SAMPLING OF THE DELIBERATIVE EXPERIMENT

The deliberative experiment on the Tibet issue explored whether deliberation can help deal with the problem of Tibetan autonomy. The experiment aimed to implement Habermas' (1996a) principle that argumentations are factually true, normatively right and expressively sincere. The participants were asked to critically reflect on the two competing official discourses on the Tibet issue, that of the Chinese government and that of the Tibetan government in exile (TGIE). Alternative views and approaches were to be explored. The deliberative workshop attempted to democratise the state's discourses on the Tibet issue and to create a considered public sphere in which ethnic Chinese and Tibetans could engage in serious discussion.

The workshop was intended to involve real people in the real world, allowing them to engage in real dialogue. Fishkin's experimental study of deliberative polling in Northern Ireland (discussed in Chapter 11) was limited in that it dealt with 'easy' issues like education policy. One could argue that when it comes to the most difficult issues like autonomy, deliberation alone cannot solve the problem. Our deliberative workshop put this argument to the test. We focused on a number of tough political questions regarding the issue of Tibetan autonomy and examined whether deliberation enhances mutual understanding and trust. Would the participants change their value position in the course of deliberative process? Would considered opinion prevail, and if so, how?

A public deliberation that meets the requirements of deliberative democracy must be well designed to ensure that it fulfils the principles of representation, openness, transparency, equality and fairness. To ensure equitable representation, random selection is the best method. Originally I thought this could be done easily, given the vast number of Chinese students in Australian universities. It soon turned out to be impractical and disappointing. In major cities around the world, including Canberra, thousands of Chinese students participated in what they regarded as the patriotic cause of defending China against the Dalai Lama and his supporters in March and April 2008. But when they were offered an opportunity to explore the reasons why Tibetans protested against the Beijing Olympic Games and to participate in finding a solution to the Tibet problem, they showed indifference. This indifference can be explained in a number of ways. It might have been because of the mutual suspicion that built up around the conflicts during the Olympic Torch relay. Fear of consequences for participating in the project, which might occur when they returned to China, also likely played a part. So did political propaganda casting the Dalai Lama as an 'enemy' and the Chinese political culture, which tells students not to discuss sensitive issues like Tibet during their time abroad. The indifference from many Chinese students gives rise to a

Table 10.1: Demographic information (from Survey Questions 1–6)

	Ethnic Chinese (%)	Tibetans (%)
Q1 Gender – Male	75	79
– Female	25	21
Q2 Education – Secondary School	0	29
– Undergraduate degree	42	57
– Postgraduate degree	58	14
Q3 Visited Tibetan Area before	0	46
Q4 Visited Han Chinese Area before	100	23
Q5 Speak Mandarin	100	92
Q6 Speak Tibetan	8	69

Source: By author

worrying concern that Chinese students are more or less emotional but non-rational nationalists.

After the impossibility of random selection became clear, I called for volunteers and was able to find fourteen Tibetan students and twelve ethnic Chinese students who came from major universities in Australia. These included the Australian National University, the University of Adelaide, the University of Sydney, the University of Technology of Sydney, Monash University and The Royal Melbourne Institute of Technology. All were aged between 19 and 33, with the average age being 27. The demographic information about the participants is provided in Table 10.1.

A few of the Chinese participants have lived in minority areas and a couple could speak a little bit of Tibetan. Six Tibetans were recently arrived, young exiles from Tibetan areas of China, while three were born of mixed marriages of Tibetan and Australian parents. This explains why most of the Tibetan participants were able to speak Chinese at the level of basic conversation. It was interesting to observe that most of the volunteer Chinese participants showed a great interest in developing their knowledge. The survey result showed that they made more changes in their opinions than their Tibetan counterparts. By contrast, the newly exiled Tibetans tended to want to 'teach Chinese [persons] about the real situation'; they were more radical in demanding complete independence than other Tibetans. Interestingly, the three second-generation Tibetan exiles from the mixed marriages were more moderate and tended to change their opinions in the process of thinking critically and reflectively. Nevertheless, they shared with the rest of the Tibetans the aspiration for the preservation and development of Tibetan culture. Certainly there appeared to be two different levels of knowledge, language and experience in the Tibetan group. But given the anonymity of the data, it is impossible to disaggregate the data to isolate and reflect upon the differences between second-generation Tibetans and China-educated Tibetans.

To ensure frank deliberation, anonymity was guaranteed. Most Chinese participants are going back to China (three had returned by the time of writing). In order to ensure that the Chinese (as well as Tibetan) students could speak out freely without fear of political risk, all their names were kept private and they filled out the survey questionnaire anonymously.

To ensure high-quality deliberation, it is necessary to give participants as much information as possible. All participants were provided with a 275-page reading packet a month prior to the workshop and encouraged to read as much of the material as possible before their arrival. The packet contained a mixture of sixteen scholarly articles, official government documents and newspaper stories – an *equal* number from both Tibetan and Chinese sources, with detailed and balanced perspectives on the Tibet issue. The items were carefully selected by the organisers who consulted with the affected groups in the selection exercise.

Discussions about sovereignty and the national boundary question often trigger fury, and face-to-face interactions, in particular, can become volatile. To try to control these negative effects, we introduced a carefully moderated form of deliberation. Importantly, to meet the fairness and equality principles, two facilitators were chosen, Baogang He, who has a Chinese background, and Lobsang Sangay, who has a Tibetan background. They were not to put forward their own ideas but were to make sure that all participants had equal time to speak and to prevent domination by one or two persons. They were required to lead the participants to appreciate the perspectives of others, give reasons in good faith, and implement the following rules: 'Listen to others carefully'; 'Don't interrupt when others are speaking'; 'Everyone has a chance to talk and must express his/her view sincerely'; 'Be fully committed to rational discussion and avoid an emotional attack on others'; and 'Try to give concrete examples and evidence'. Most of the time, the two facilitators maintained neutrality in leading the discussions and presenting both sides of the argument, which the survey results confirm. Occasionally, however, one facilitator did put forward his own view, which may have affected the process.

In order to identify and measure whether the participants changed their opinions, two surveys were carried out. Before the deliberation, the participants were asked to complete a questionnaire to record their opinions and positions on a number of issues. After the deliberation, the participants were asked to complete the same questionnaire once more and to answer a few new questions about the *process* of deliberation.

The deliberative workshop began with a general introduction by Professor Baogang He, followed by an address by Professor Damien Kingsbury, who talked about how Indonesia managed the issues of East Timor and Aceh. Then the participants were divided into two groups, each made up of half Tibetans and half ethnic Chinese. The two facilitators led the groups through a series of sessions designed to give the participants greater knowledge and understanding of each other, of their personal and family backgrounds, and of the historical events and leaders who have shaped those backgrounds.

The first day focused on Tibetan and ethnic Chinese perspectives on the Tibet situation. The uses and limitations of history in resolving conflict and the myth of objective historical 'truth' were examined. The second day focused on the Dalai Lama's 'Middle Way' policy. The workshop concluded with an intellectual exercise in which Tibetan students were asked to imagine what they would recommend to Chinese President Hu Jintao on handling the Tibet issue, if they were his policy advisers. Ethnic Chinese participants, on the other hand, were required to consider how they would act if they were policy advisers to the Dalai Lama. This exercise was intended to force the participants to look at the issue from the perspective of others.

To enhance the deliberative capacities of the participants, Baogang He suggested three 'ladders' for them. The first ladder related to their ability to express and reflect each of their views critically. The second ladder required the participants to go beyond their own perspectives in search of a diversity of opinions. In placing oneself in the position of another, it is important to consider whether the views of others are convincing and whether one should modify his/her own views as a result. The third ladder involved the synthesis of competing views in a systematic manner, in order to develop a balanced view on the complexity of the Tibet issue. Throughout the deliberative process, the participants engaged factual truths about certain historical events, asked many normative questions concerning human rights and moral responsibility, and expressed their views sincerely.

10.3   RESULT AND DISCUSSION

Knowledge gain

In comparing the results of the first and second surveys, it can be seen that both the ethnic Chinese and Tibetan students increased their level of knowledge substantially (see Table 10.2).[2] This knowledge gain might be an indicator of improving mutual understanding, which in turn helps to increase the level of mutual trust. However, both ethnic Chinese and Tibetan knowledge dropped slightly for two questions, which might be accounted for by lapses in memory.

Increased mutual trust

Both the ethnic Chinese and Tibetan students increased the level of mutual trust, even when discussing the controversial issue of Tibetan autonomy. The ethnic

Table 10.2: Knowledge gained (based on Survey Questions 8–11)

	Chinese		Tibetans	
	1st survey	2nd survey	1st survey	2nd survey
Q8	8.3	50	92.9	85.7
Q9	75	91.7	92.9	85.7
Q10	83.89	78.6	75	92.9
Q11a	66.7	91.7	64.3	78.6
Q11b	58.3	91.7	35.7	64.3
Q11c	66.7	58.3	50	71.4

Source: By author

Chinese participants were asked whether 'most Tibetans are trustworthy'. On a scale where 0 is 'strongly disagree', 5 is in the middle, and 10 is 'strongly agree', the mean value increased from 4.5 in the first survey before the deliberation to 6 in the second survey after the deliberation. The mean value for the Tibetan respondents on the question of whether 'most Chinese are trustworthy' increased from 4.5 to 6. The mean value for the Tibetan respondents improved from 5 to 8 regarding the statement that 'Most Chinese I have met are trustworthy' (see Table 10.3 in the Appendix at the end of this chapter). This closely mirrored the results of the deliberative poll in Northern Ireland, as discussed in Chapter 11.

When we examined the transcript of the group discussion, it became clear that throughout the process, almost all participants expressed a view on the importance of trust. What we, the researchers, believe to have been the enhancement of mutual trust came through the recognition of the reasonableness of the other party. Anecdotal evidence showed that in the beginning, some ethnic Chinese students were angered by the 'unbelievably unreasonable' Tibetan protests over the Beijing Olympics. Likewise, some Tibetans felt that the ethnic Chinese students did not understand the Tibetans' quest for justice and that their actions were intended to deliver a strong message to the world. After three days of contact and deliberation, each side found the other side equipped with reasoning capacity.

The result was very positive. At the end of the event, each side found that the other side had a reasonable argument. With regard to the question of whether 'most Tibetans are open to reason', the mean value of the ethnic Chinese respondents increased from 2.7 in the first survey to 7 in the second. In contrast, the mean value of the Tibetan respondents increased from 4.4 to 6, a rather small indicator of change, on the question of whether 'Most Chinese are open to reason' (see Table 10.3).

Moderating effect

The deliberation workshop produced a moderating effect. When two groups in a divided society are separated, their emotions are fully charged and they see things through a fixed viewpoint without considering the perspectives of others. When the ethnic Chinese and Tibetan groups came together in small group discussions, however, an immediate moderating effect became apparent. The use of English as the communicative language also promoted moderation because neither group was communicating in its native language. Many participants thus were unable to express their anger and emotions easily (of course, one could also argue that this would have made people suppress their feelings). The facilitators played a role in controlling any extreme behaviour and in encouraging a greater understanding of others.

One example of the moderating effect was the discussion about competing interpretations of history. While the Tibetan participants held the view that China invaded Tibet and carried out a colonisation policy, the ethnic Chinese participants clung to the idea that China liberated Tibet from the serf system and carried out socialist reform there. These two views possibly, but not necessarily, were the product of official indoctrination, and were likely to be reinforced if one group had no contact with the other group. Consequently, this kind of knowledge was reproduced within an isolated and closed environment.

When the two groups were put together to exchange opinions, however, members of each recognised alternative views immediately and the matter became much more complex than was originally thought. As a result, five or six students did critically examine two interpretations of the disputed history and questioned the role of history. When it was recognised that each interpretation contains partial truth, it became more difficult to make a strong and exclusive argument. As a result, a compromise was preferred, which tends to soften radical political positions. In this way, deliberation was able to reduce the level of radicalisation and achieve a middle ground.

Enhanced deliberative capacities

The deliberative workshop succeeded in enhancing deliberative capacities. Quite a few participants from both sides agreed that a power-sharing mechanism might be a realistic solution to deal with the current predicament. The participants were able to develop a diversity of views, considering the perspectives of others and changing their own positions and opinions. For example, there was a convergence on policy issues over the display of religious photographs and also over the language of school instruction. The participants were asked whether Tibetans should be allowed to display photos of the Dalai Lama in temples. Before deliberation, the ethnic Chinese participants scored a mean of 6.5. By contrast, the Tibetan participants scored the highest possible approval grade of 10. After deliberation, there was a clear shift in the approval of the ethnic Chinese participants, with the mean increasing to 7.6 (see Table 10.3).

With regard to the teaching of Tibetan in schools in Tibetan areas, the mean approval scores for both the ethnic Chinese and Tibetan participants dropped. While both strongly favoured Tibetan being taught in schools in Tibetan areas, the scores dropped slightly, from 9.67 to 8.5 for the ethnic Chinese and from 10 to 9.5 for the Tibetans (see Table 10.3).

Before deliberation, ethnic Chinese participants scored a mean of 6.3 when asked whether autonomy was the best option for Tibet (Tibet is still a part of China but enjoys full autonomous rights). After deliberation, the mean score dropped to 5.8. A similar trend emerged when considering whether independence (Tibet will gain independence from China) was the best option for Tibet. Initially, the ethnic Chinese participants recorded a mean score of 1.67 while the Tibetan participants scored 6.8. Subsequent to the deliberative workshops, the mean scores declined to 0.3 and 6 respectively (see Table 10.3). It is very interesting that the Tibetan students' support for both independence and autonomy decreased though they were still favoured strongly compared with the Chinese students' group.

Consensus and process

The deliberative workshop reached a consensus on a number of issues, including the undesirability of using force, the importance of establishing mutual trust, and the necessity of compromise: the Chinese and Tibetan students in their group discussion expressed the same view on these issues. Several participants said that despite the different perspectives, the future can be changed through mutual trust and compromise. Interestingly, both sides shared a similar mean value on a number of questions: whether they were optimistic about the future of China (Question 26) and the future of Tibet (Question 27), and if they thought that most people in Australia were open to reason (Question 28) and were trustworthy (Question 29) (see Table 10.3).

The participants said that they greatly appreciated the process. When asked a series of questions on a 0–10 scale, where 0 indicated 'generally a waste of time' and 10 meant 'extremely valuable', the participants gave the small-group discussions an average rating of 8.88 and the entire three days' deliberation an average rating of 8.31. They also thought the process considered their views very equally. On a 1–5 scale, where 1 is 'very equal' and 5 is 'very unequal', the average answer for whether the 'small group moderator provide[d] everyone with an equal opportunity for discussion' was 1.46 and the average for whether the group members were, in fact, equal in the discussion was 2.04 (see Table 10.3).

10.4   THE LIMITS OF DELIBERATION

Some aspects of deliberative results have fallen short of the ideal of deliberative democracy. They include the continuation of polarisation, the absence of change in the value issues, and the continual recitation of official views. With regard to a number of main issues such as cultural identity, foreign intervention and autonomy, there is a tendency for the two groups to polarise (see the results of Survey Questions 12, 13, 14, 15, 16, 18, 19, 20 and 22). Although the participants changed their opinions on policy and attitude issues between tests 1 and 2, value issues remained largely unchanged.

Tibetan participants insisted that the boundary of Tibetan autonomy should include all Tibetan areas, including those located in China outside the TAR, while the ethnic Chinese participants thought such a view unrealistic and likely to damage China's unity. The ethnic Chinese participants regarded Beijing's efforts in Tibet as laudable modernisation. One participant expressed the view that minorities should not feel pain about losing their cultural identity because Han Chinese cultural identity is also lost daily through globalisation. By contrast, some Tibetan participants asserted that unless the people of China recognise that China occupied Tibet, Tibetans will continue to feel patronised.

No change of opinion among the ethnic Chinese participants was recorded on the question of regarding autonomy as a disguise for independence. Two reasons account for this. First, the Tibetan participants failed to convince the others during small-group discussions with their explanations on the involvement of the US Central Intelligence Agency (CIA) in Tibet.[3] Rather, one Tibetan recounted the story of India's transition from self-rule to independence. This only served to strengthen the view of the ethnic Chinese participants that autonomy is a camouflage for independence. Second, the Tibetan participants associated autonomy with independence. This is demonstrated by the fact that the questions 'Is autonomy the best option for Tibet?' and 'Is independence the best option for Tibet?' received similar scores: the mean value for the former was 7.6 and for the latter 6.8.

The deliberative workshop reveals that the nature of the issue itself has an impact on the deliberation process and outcome. The national identity issue is different from social policy issues. The former is concerned with sovereignty and nationalism; the latter is about the preferences, needs and demands of daily life. Value and identity attitudes are difficult to change quickly through deliberation, while social policy preference can be changed through public deliberation and consultation.

Although quite a few participants did move away from the official line, some Tibetans and ethnic Chinese continued to repeat the official views. The opinions of individuals are sometimes shaped by the communities or social positions to which they belong. One ethnic Chinese participant articulated this well: 'I fully understand and support the principle of self-determination from my personal experience of being a Han Chinese, a member of minority in Russia, Xinjiang, and Australia, but I will not support the Tibetan cause.'[4]

The examination of historical evidence and competing claims proved to be difficult. These complicated historical disputes have not been solved by historians and scholars after years of research, let alone by Tibetans and ethnic Chinese students after one weekend of deliberation. It is unrealistic for students to solve all the problems associated with the Tibet issue, and it is impractical to expect change in value and full development of deliberative capacity within two or three days. The restricted timeframe for the workshops meant that participants were unable to fully synthesise the intellectual arguments.

The fundamental limitation is the application to nationality conflict issues of the deliberative approach, since it is alien in the Chinese context. The central government has been the dominating and sole arbiter on nationality questions. A pessimist might hold that the nature of authoritarianism is hostility towards deliberation and truthfulness; radical Tibetans may see deliberation as empty talk.[5] Deliberative democracy requires a strong commitment to the freedom of speech and the freedom of association, and currently the Chinese political system falls short of these democratic criteria. In this context, the practice of deliberative democracy has been constrained by the absence of the freedom of speech and associations in China. An officially sponsored workshop between Canada and China on human rights held in the Central Party School also experienced this limitation. When Will Kymlicka raised the Tibet question in the workshop, the organiser announced a tea break!

10.5 CHALLENGES TO DELIBERATIVE DEMOCRACY

In order to make deliberative conflict resolution mechanisms effective and powerful, deliberative democracy must sharpen its tools and meet the following challenges.

Unpack deliberation

A critical issue is to detect what kinds of deliberation have impact on processes and outcomes. Most public deliberations are consultative, in the sense that citizens' opinions are heard, but the final decision is still in the hands of the elites like the head of state or the members of the parliament. In contrast, empowered deliberation, combined with a referendum mechanism, is democratic deliberation in which citizens have direct input in the collective decision-making process.

Elite deliberation played a much more decisive role than citizens' deliberation in the former Soviet Union. In elite negotiation or parliamentary deliberation, it is not clear whether reason-based arguments or the strategic use of debate prevail. However, in communal deliberation in the case of Northern Ireland, the question was how community dialogue could be translated into state institutions and the decision-making process, and as an extension of this how public deliberation could manage differences in the conflict of interests among citizens or groups.

Liberal deliberation is usually an open process whereby any issue can be discussed. However, in Singapore public debate on racial questions is discouraged. Even in its consociational democracy some highly contentious issues are excluded from the public debate. This, in effect, leads to a form of authoritarian deliberation whereby elites select and manage the topic and timing of discussion, and decide which issues are put on the table, declaring at the same time that citizens should be involved in open deliberation (B. He & Warren 2011). Authoritarian deliberation has historical roots in China. For example, there were debates in the imperial Tang dynasty in China over how to treat other races and minorities and how to bring different communities into the mainstream. In the history of India, territorial unity often involved a princely dialogue.

The question of how deliberative democracy can draw on its historical experience to enrich deliberative projects and at the same time overcome the fundamental limit of historical courses of deliberation is a challenging one.

Two versus multiple parties

There is also the question of how many parties to involve in the deliberations in order for them to be both effective and democratically legitimate. In explaining the resolution of the Northern Ireland conflict in 1998, Horowitz claims that 'the narrowing of the process to two internal parties, one of which proposed and the other of which disposed, was conducive to adoption of a coherent plan' (Horowitz 2002: 218). Previous negotiations resembled a 'convention', whereas the 1996–8 negotiations were a 'tete-a-tete' involving only two major actors. Horowitz suggests that if negotiations in divided societies are to achieve results, 'the multiplicity of parties, espousing a mélange of approaches and provisions, will somehow need to be reduced' (Horowitz 2002: 220).

The notion that the number of active parties should be reduced might seem to contradict the deliberative approach that has emphasised the involvement of civil society groups and ordinary citizens in the public sphere. The involvement of a plurality of actors certainly makes the issue even more complex. Noel (2006: 425) observes: 'first debated among the few, Canadian constitutional politics finally had reached the many, but only to end up being for nobody, that is, closed for all political purposes'. The wider the scope of the problem that needs addressing, the more participation of citizens is required by the deliberative approach; the higher the number of influencing factors the deliberative approach faces, the more complex the situation becomes. Deliberation is a long process and does not promise an easy solution. Deliberative theorists have to develop complex strategies of dealing with such complexity.

The two-party and deliberative democracy, however, can be reconciled in a number of ways. One way, as Dryzek suggests, is the bottom-up process in which informal discourse influences public opinion, which in turn infiltrates the political sphere and with this places constraints on policy options. The other way is the top-down process in which the elites strike political deals behind closed doors, but their successful implementation relies on the involvement of civil society. Byrne argues that 'the complementarity of both the elite power-sharing and grass-roots participatory approaches is critical to building a sustainable peace' (Byrne 2001: 328). The latter is needed to create a 'culture of peace' – where stereotypes and negative attitudes are broken down, a shared identity is created, and local populations are willing to accept and abide by the settlements reached by their elites.

Avoiding the sovereignty question and how to influence state policy?

Dryzek argues that deliberation in divided societies should not be focused on questions of political sovereignty and constitutional politics. Indeed, our deliberative forum on the Tibet autonomy issue revealed that there was little change in the attitude towards sovereignty by either the Chinese or Tibetan students. This raises an important question: how will deliberation have any impact on the decisions and actions of the state? Dryzek's response is that discursive engagement in the public sphere can influence state action in an informal and indirect way. These deliberations introduce or develop a public discourse such as new terms, concepts and a new rhetoric. This becomes part of the public consciousness, and is eventually able to infiltrate and permeate, and in turn influence, the political sphere (Dryzek 2005).

It is, however, doubtful whether public-sphere deliberation can be abstracted from sovereignty issues. Noel argues that this is simply not feasible. In practice, deliberation cannot proceed in isolation of the realities of power politics. Political deliberators cannot check their political interests, identity and advantages at the door. Noel acknowledges that, in so far as this is true, deliberation can never occur under conditions that meet the demanding normative standards of democratic political theory (Noel 2006).

Thus, it seems clear that public deliberation must involve the state. However, it is not enough for a political authority to host a dialogue. At the end of the day, referendums are still needed to deal with sovereignty issues directly and decisively.

Semi-detached?

According to Dryzek (2005), engagement in the public sphere ought to be semi-detached from the state, or dissociated from sovereign authority. This idea of 'semi-detached' has a number of advantages. It can move away from, and even challenge, the state's monopoly of sovereignty. It is able to allow citizens to defend their right to discuss the sensitive matter that will impact their life. When keeping distance from the state, it enables a search for diversity of opinion and plural options, can facilitate the formation of public opinion, and can create reason-based legitimacy.

Nevertheless, 'semi-detachment' is temporary; the final resolution is ultimately a process of moving from 'semi-detached' to 'complete engagement', a higher level of interaction between the state and civil society. As deliberative conflict resolution still relies on the state, civil society must engage with the state. What is missing in Dryzek's discussion is precisely this shift from 'semi-detachment' to 'complete engagement'.

Impact of political culture

The biggest challenge to deliberative democracy in divided societies is the fact that deliberative democracy seems to be absent from most, if not all, such societies. The problem may run deeper still. Deliberative democracy requires a certain kind of political culture – a culture which seems to be weak or non-existent in most divided societies. In a culture where the political process has been dominated by the state, the idea of 'semi-detachment' is very problematic. In the first instance, any attempt to organise a deliberative forum will be dismissed as ineffective and futile if the state is not directly involved. Where force and violence are widely seen as the most effective political tools, it is difficult to invite disputing parties to engage in dialogue. The conflict between Israel and Palestine is a case in point. In a popular culture where emotion and nationalist sentiment are prevalent, reasoned argument is difficult to achieve. Expatriate Chinese students are another example of this. Many such students virulently defended the Olympic Torch Relay in April 2008, but few were willing to discuss the sensitive topic of Tibet. Some of them regarded the issue as a sovereignty question and, as such, a matter for the state; not a subject for individuals to discuss.

Unfavourable to the disadvantaged groups?

A common objection to the deliberative model of democracy is that individuals who are lacking a 'sophisticated political vocabulary' are at an inherent disadvantage. They are unlikely to prevail over their more articulate counterparts, no matter the strength of their argument. Indeed, our deliberative forum demonstrated that the Chinese participants commanded more analytical skill in the discussion than the Tibetans. However, this deficiency can be addressed by deliberative institutional design. For example, the random selection of participants can recruit marginalised people. Political equality and equal deliberative influence can be achieved through facilitators who ensure a fair exchange for all. Experts can also play an important role in helping to articulate the voice and arguments of the disadvantaged groups.

More importantly, allowing narratives and personal stories is another useful instrument (O'Flynn 2006). Indeed, the stories told by the Tibetans during our deliberative experience were striking and impressive. One Chinese participant claimed that he was inclined to sympathise with the Tibetans as a result.

The problem with randomised deliberative assemblies

The random selection of participants is an effective mechanism to try to ensure full representation that is statistically valid. Nevertheless, it is very difficult to introduce this method in a divided society, due to political sensitivities as demonstrated by this experiment; and it is also very expensive to attract a group that can be considered at all random. J. Fishkin and B. Luskin pay their participants, try to hold the deliberative exercise in attractive locations, and go to some length to induce members from lower socio-economic groups and other disadvantaged populations to participate. It would likely be extremely difficult to expand this technique to a deliberative forum on a sovereignty, boundary or identity issue. Nevertheless, a modified version of deliberative polling should be one critical device being employed in the proposed deliberative referendum in next chapter.

10.6   CONCLUSION

This chapter has examined the case of a deliberative workshop on the Tibet issue and highlighted the achievements and limits of deliberative conflict resolution mechanisms. Deliberative dialogue improved knowledge and mutual understanding, enhanced mutual trust and deliberative capacities, and produced moderating effects. It provided quantitative evidence that Han–Tibetan mistrust can be significantly reduced through deliberative discussion and reflective interaction, and offered *some* potential for repairing a distrusting relationship between the ethnic Chinese and Tibetan communities. The participants may still be locked in polarised positions on independence and sovereignty issues, but the level of polarisation over social and cultural policies can be reduced.

Despite the fact that daily encounters between Han and Tibetans do indeed exist, they are not necessarily deliberative: some are 'propaganda' aimed at educating or civilising Tibetans; many involve prejudice. The experiment of public deliberation based on social science methods discussed in this chapter sets up an ideal criteria, and steers the daily practice into a more deliberative and democratic direction.

Citizen deliberation would be in the interest of both the Chinese government, which needs to develop its soft power and improve its international reputation, and the Dalai Lama, who has called for Tibetans to befriend the ethnic Chinese to gain more supporters among them. Moreover, local governments within China under pressure to heal the social rift have been introducing a variety of deliberative forums to address local policy issues (B. He 2006a; Fishkin et al. 2010). It is imperative and possible for the Chinese government to employ more heart-to-heart forums that would help ease ethnic tension and build a harmonious society.

In addition, citizen-initiated deliberative forums can take place outside the existing institutions of the nation-state (Rabgey 2004). Small talks with limited numbers of people can begin with friendship associations or local communities such as those in Australia, Canada, the US and many European countries. One dialogue forum in Hong Kong has already produced a number of innovative ideas such as a 'Tibetan Special Cultural Zone' to address the current stalemate (see Chapter 8).[6]

Ideally, talks would naturally progress into the Tibetan region itself, where the daily practical needs of citizens can be more directly addressed (Rabgey & Sharlho 2004). In the short term, 'irrelevant discussions' are not geared at all towards finding resolutions for complicated issues. Rather, they break down barriers and resentment, encourage mutual understanding, trust and cooperative behaviour, and lay the ground work for more official work. Deliberative workshops can break down self-closed knowledge-production systems while fostering a new flexible, critical generation. Deliberations practised widely in the public sphere can produce new terms and concepts, create discourses favourable to resolution, raise public consciousness, and eventually penetrate the political sphere, influencing state policy and action in an informal, indirect way (Dryzek 2005). Deliberative democracy can help China to address the dilemma of the empire thesis discussed in Chapter 3. It would enhance public capacities, build mutual trust and avoid polarisation, and could lead to the moderation of policy responses. Suppressing public debate on the Tibet question only exacerbates the problem. Political rule over minority areas, and over Tibetan areas in particular, must be based on public reason and consent, and must avoid one-sided nationalism.

NOTES

1. This is the personal experience of this author from several workshops and conferences.
2. The questionnaire had six factual questions to test the knowledge level of the participants.
3. The CIA encouraged, trained and controlled Tibet's resistance movement (see Conboy & Morrison 2002).
4. The note taken by Baogang He.
5. Lobsang Yeshi of the pro-independence Tibetan Youth Congress complains that Tibetans are allowed 'talks about talks', but when they finally explain their position they are condemned (Davis 2008).
6. I was invited to participate in this dialogue forum organised by the University of Hong Kong on 29–30 July 2009.

APPENDIX

Knowledge questions

8. In which year did the Dalai Lama propose the Middle Way policy?
A. 1957; B. 1987–8; C. 1996; D. 2008; E. Don't know.
9. Did Chinese leader Deng Xiaoping say that apart from the question of total independence, all other issues could be discussed and all problems can be resolved?
A. True; B. False; C. Don't know.

10. Under the Dalai Lama's autonomy proposal, which of the following areas of government would remain the responsibility of the central Chinese government? (Note: this is a multiple choice question and you can choose a few)
A. Foreign affairs; B. Defence; C. Education; D. Language; E. Religion; G. Health.
11. China's Law on Regional Autonomy for Minority Nationalities adopted on 31 May 1984 provides a wide range of autonomy rights:
a. Administration must or should be in the hands of functionaries from the minority population.
A. True; B. False.
b. The regions can promulgate their own laws and regulations, draw up their own production plans (within the bounds of the Central State Plan), and choose their own path of economic and cultural development.
A. True; B. False.
c. Autonomous regions cannot change or stop the directives and policies from the central government.
A. True; B. False.

Table 10.3: Mean value of the Survey

	Chinese students		Tibetan students	
	before	after	before	after
12. China should allow Tibet to have autonomy, in order to preserve its traditional culture and allow the Dalai Lama to return to Tibet. (Strongly agree – 0, Strongly disagree – 10)	4.3	4.08	2.8	1.4
13. Tibet has long been part of China, Tibet has benefited from modernisation, and the Dalai Lama should not be allowed to return because he aims to split Tibet from China. (Strongly agree – 0, Strongly disagree – 10)	3.83**	5.83**	8.4	7.57
14. Is the Dalai Lama's autonomy proposal sincere? (Where 0 is not at all sincere, 5 is median level, 10 is the most sincere)	5.42	4.75	9.7	10
15. Do you believe that the Chinese government is serious about the Dalai Lama's autonomy proposals? (Not serious – 0, Serious – 10)	5.25**	7.08**	1.2	2.29
16. Do you believe that the Dalai Lama is seeking independence in the guise of autonomy? (Where 0 is to seek independence, 5 is median level, 10 is not to seek independence)	3.92	3.92	9.9	9.3
17. Is autonomy the best option for Tibet? (Where 0 is the worst, 5 is in the middle, 10 is the best)	6.33	5.8	7.7	7.4
18. Is independence the best option for Tibet? (Where 0 is the worst, 5 is in the middle, 10 is the best)	1.67*	0.3*	6.8	6
19. Is the current situation the best option for Tibet? (Where 0 is the worst, 5 is in the middle, 10 is the best)	4.5	3.5	0.4	1
20. Should Tibetans be allowed to display photos of the Dalai Lama in temples? (Where 0 is strong disapproval, 5 is in the middle level, 10 is strong approval)	6.5	7.58	10	10
21. Should schools in Tibetan areas be encouraged to teach Tibetan? (Where 0 is strong disapproval, 5 is in the middle, 10 is strong approval)	9.67*	8.5*	10	9.5

Table 10.3 (*continued*)

	Chinese students		Tibetan students	
	before	after	before	after
22. Should schools in Tibetan areas be encouraged to teach in Tibetan rather than in Mandarin? (Where 0 is strong disapproval, 5 is in the middle, 10 is strong approval)	5.58	3.92	9.4*	7.5*
23. Tibetans don't understand the Chinese perspective on Tibet. (Where 0 is strongly agree, 5 is in the middle, 10 is strongly disagree)	2.58	3.17	6.6	6
24. Westerners don't understand the Chinese perspective on Tibet. (Where 0 is strongly agree, 5 is in the middle, 10 is strongly disagree)	3.8	2.5	5.9	6
25. Chinese don't understand the Tibetan issue. (Where 0 is strongly agree, 5 is in the middle, 10 is strongly disagree)	5.3	6.33	2.2	2
26. Are you pessimistic or optimistic about the future of China? (Where 0 is very pessimistic, 5 is neither pessimistic nor optimistic, 10 is very optimistic)	8	7.7	6	6
27. Are you optimistic or pessimistic about the future of Tibet? (Where 0 is very pessimistic, 5 is neither pessimistic nor optimistic, 10 is very optimistic)	7	6	8.2	7
28. Most people in Australia are open to reason. (Where 0 is strongly disagree, 5 is neither agree nor disagree, 10 is strongly agree)	7.5	6.4	7.6	8
29. Most people in Australia are trustworthy. (Where 0 is strongly disagree, 5 is in the middle, 10 is strongly agree)	6.67	7	6	7
30. Most Tibetans are open to reason. (Where 0 is strongly disagree, 5 is in the middle, 10 is strongly agree)	2.67*	6*	8.7	8.5
31. Most Tibetans are trustworthy. (Where 0 is strongly disagree, 5 is in the middle, 10 is strongly agree)	4.25**	6**	7.9	9
32. Most Chinese are open to reason. (Where 0 is strongly disagree, 5 is in the middle, 10 is strongly agree)	5.3	6	4.4*	6*
33. Most Chinese are trustworthy. (Where 0 is strongly disagree, 5 is in the middle, 10 is strongly agree)	6.7	7	4.5	6
34. Most Tibetans I have met are reasonable. (Where 0 is strongly disagree, 5 is in the middle, 10 is strongly agree)	3.75*	7*	10	8
35. Most Chinese I have met are trustworthy. (Where 0 is strongly disagree, 5 is in the middle, 10 is strongly agree)	7.5	7	5**	8**

Source: By author

Note: 'Before' refers to the mean scores of the first survey before deliberation, 'After' the mean scores of the second survey after deliberation. T-tests of the difference in mean scores on the above questions at the two stages showed that while some with mark * were significant at the $p=0.15$ level, others with mark ** achieved p scores of 0.05, and many remain unchanged.

11 The Idea of Deliberative Referendum: Synthesis and Conclusion

This concluding chapter not only aims to provide a summary of the democratic approaches discussed in the book, but also seeks to present an integrated theory of democratic governance which is centred on deliberative referendum. It presents a synthesis of the theory and case studies in the book, focusing on the idea of deliberative referendum and how it can improve democratic governance mechanism.

This book has examined a number of democratic devices: referendums, autonomy and minority rights, consociational arrangements and deliberative forums (Chapter 1); the referendum as a conflict resolution mechanism (Chapter 5); liberal multiculturalism's system of minority rights that protects the interests of Tibetans (Chapters 7–9); consociational democracy and the building of complex power-sharing mechanisms (Chapter 8); deliberative democracy and its offer of a talk-centric approach as better management of the conflicts of divided societies (Chapter 10). Each of these devices has been applied throughout the world with varying degrees of success and failure.

In the specific context of China, this book has sought to develop an anti-empire thesis that articulates how democracy can address the national identity issue (Chapter 3); it has discussed a federalism solution to the Taiwan question (Chapter 4); it has examined the case of the 2004 referendum in Taiwan and attempted to derive lessons from it so as to improve referendum mechanisms and processes through public deliberation (Chapter 5); it has discussed Taiwan's bid for a UN seat, and examined questions concerning political representation and equality (Chapter 6); it has examined three competing discourses on the Tibetan question, calling for a dialogue and engagement between Confucianism and liberalism (Chapter 7); it has dealt with the autonomy issue in Tibet and makes a number of mini-proposals to overcome the current stalemate (Chapter 8); it has addressed China's language policy in Tibet, and called for the return to the multi-linguistic policy of the Qing dynasty (Chapter 9); and it has examined and tested the idea that the Tibetan autonomous question could be addressed through a deliberative experiment

(Chapter 10).

To this point, our ideas about democratic approaches have been treated separately in different chapters. It is useful now to combine these democratic approaches in both theory and practice; to forge a synthesis of them in a spirit of holism. Here I attempt to develop a hybrid theoretical argument about the integration of the principles of history and democracy, majority rule and minority rights, consociational and deliberative democracies, and referendums and public deliberation; an integrated theorisation that is centred on deliberative democracy.

Deliberation-centred democratic governance is deeply rooted in what John Dryzek calls a 'deliberative turn'. A close examination of existing democratic mechanisms points to the emergence of a normative condition of deliberation. This deliberative condition refers to the modern condition of complexity, in which most complex public policy issues – in particular the boundary question discussed in this book – increasingly require public input, dialogue and deliberation. It includes the available deliberative tools like deliberative polling, and it entails the supposition that conflict resolution must be done through public reasoning rather than force.

The chapter proceeds with the theoretical synthesis of three deliberative approaches and a theoretical discussion of the need to develop an integrated theory of democratic governance. This is followed by a proposal for improving democratic governance through a combination of referendum and deliberation. It then outlines a number of the strategies and conditions under which a referendum can be held successfully.

11.1 A SYNTHESIS OF DELIBERATIVE APPROACHES TO CONFLICTS

The theory and practice of deliberative democracy was first developed in Western societies in the political science disciplines in the 1990s (Cohen 1989; Dryzek 1996), then spread to Asia and even to China (Leib & B. He 2006). Deliberative democracy prioritises reasoned argument and discussion in which 'interests' are recognised but do not dominate. The cogency and force of argument should prevail over political power. Communications work to ensure that arguments and statements are *factually true, normatively right, and expressively sincere* (Habermas 1996a). Deliberation examines the merit of an argument and evidence at a reflective and rational level, leading to changes in opinion and policy attitude. Deliberation requires that reason and truth predominate, and that emotion, bias and social prejudice must give way to reason and substantive argument. The deliberative capacity can be measured by the existence and development of diverse views, the willingness to change one's view, and the respect for reason and the production of the best argument.

Deliberative democratic theorists also stress the capacity, right and opportunity of ordinary citizens to participate in public deliberation. The developed and varied forums of public deliberation include citizen juries, focus groups, consensus conferences, deliberative polling and town meetings (Fung & Wright 2003). The deliberative approach to national identity conflicts has been introduced and examined by

O'Flynn, Dryzek, Fishkin and others, as will be discussed later. Here I would like to review, compare and synthesise their deliberative approaches.

Scholars offer different evaluations of the effects of deliberation in different contexts and dynamics. Cass Sunstein (2000, 2003) shows that in groups formed from populations where the mean differs on policy issues – without any conscious effort by the facilitators to intervene in the natural dynamics – participants will shift towards the extremes in a dynamic of 'group polarization'. James Fishkin (2009) shows that when groups are more balanced from the outset, are provided with balanced materials and are moderated by facilitators trained to bring out minority opinion, no such polarisation occurs. These results should be taken into consideration by anyone planning a deliberative intervention. Ackerman and Fishkin's (2004) 'Deliberation Day', as an example, would probably not be able to be facilitated in every precinct by trained facilitators, hence the outcome might well be greater polarisation. So too, we might view the support for democratisation in the Taiwan and Tibetan exile communities as a potential effect of group polarisation. Any effort to combine referendums with deliberation should factor in and seek to minimise the group polarisation effect.

The deliberative approach can be seen as a form of Interactive Conflict Resolution (ICR). ICR involves problem-solving discussions between unofficial representatives of groups or states engaged in protracted violent conflict. The objective is to rehumanize the enemy, foster positive attitudes, and create agreement on the source and nature of the conflict (Fisher 2007). Fisher (2007: 229) explains that 'the rationale is to provide an informal, low risk, noncommittal, and neutral forum in which unofficial representatives of the parties may engage in exploratory analysis and creative problem solving, free from the usual constraints of official policy and public scrutiny'.

ICR might include highly influential representatives from the conflicting groups, ordinary members, and also representatives of the diaspora communities (Fisher 2007). In some cases, the aim of ICR is primarily educational: to provide insights and change perceptions. But in other cases the aim is to transfer the solutions suggested in the informal interactions to official decision-making bodies via the influential participants. ICR workshops can also indirectly contribute to an official solution by 'legitimizing problem-solving interactions between adversaries and the accumulation of public opinion supporting negotiation' (Fisher 2007). Furthermore, 'grassroots reconciliatory dialogue across adversarial lines can . . . help counteract the influence of pressure groups working to block conciliatory policies' (Fisher 2007).

The deliberative conflict resolution can be further broken down into the following three approaches that can be derived from the available literature and should by no means be treated as exhaustive. All three are not by and large contradictory.

The theoretical principle of deliberation

Following John Stuart Mill, Ian O'Flynn is adamant that a stable democracy cannot exist without a sense of common identity. He builds his argument around two key norms of deliberative democracy: reciprocity and publicity. The requirement of reciprocity states that, in seeking to justify proposals, citizens must appeal to reasons that *all* parties to the discussion can appreciate, not to reasons reducible to the interests of one ethnic group. By publicity, O'Flynn (2006) means that the process by which representatives arrive at decisions should be open and transparent. He claims that a proper respect for these norms can help the citizens of divided societies develop and sustain a stronger sense of common identity, without discarding their ethnic affiliations.

O'Flynn also stresses the importance of fostering a strong civil society in which individuals can engage each other in non-ethnic terms, and which allows space for the emergence of identities that cut across ethnic lines. It is essential to allow alternative forms of political engagement and expression, or reasoned political argument. A common objection to deliberative democracy is that those without a sophisticated political vocabulary are at an inherent disadvantage. They are unlikely to prevail over their more articulate counterparts, no matter the strength of their case. This deficiency can be partly addressed, says O'Flynn, by allowing narratives and personal stories to be included in deliberations.[1]

Discourse in the public sphere

The public sphere, the conditionality of sovereignty and the transnationalisation of political discourse feature prominently in John S. Dryzek's version of deliberative democracy in divided societies (Dryzek 2006). Dryzek argues that contending discourses (sets of concepts, categories and ideas that provide ways of understanding the world) underlie many of the world's conflicts. These discourses can, however, open the way to greater dialogue across state boundaries and between opposing factions in societies divided by ethnicity, nationality or religion. The argument is that engagement among discourses that is not geared towards building sovereign authority or making political decisions can help to resolve many of the most intractable conflicts.

Dryzek's aim is to determine how deliberative procedures can yield results on contentious issues where the fundamental values and beliefs that participants bring to the table are diametrically opposed or contradictory. Dryzek offers a number of recommendations for deliberative democracy in divided societies.

Firstly, deliberation should be focused not on values or ideals, but on specific *needs* – such as the need for education or for adequate sustenance. Since such needs can be appreciated by all parties to the deliberation, focusing the discussion on them will make divisions seem less intractable.

Secondly, there should be periods of 'small talk' that are not geared towards resolving any issues at all. Dryzek makes this recommendation on the basis of research showing that periods of 'irrelevant discussion' can help to foster subsequent cooperative behaviour.

Third, Dryzek argues that deliberation should not necessarily occur primarily within the existing institutions of the nation-state, and should not be directly connected to political decisions, especially not those regarding sovereign authority. Dryzek maintains that people involved in deliberative procedures are unlikely to change their minds or to admit that they have changed their minds, where the deliberation is intended to produce a political decision – particularly one that has some bearing on who controls the state and its resources. The 'deadly contest for sovereignty' inhibits people from opposing factions from making concessions. Furthermore, individuals are typically reluctant to admit that they have changed their minds 'under the gaze of both opponents and those with a shared identity'. Personal pride and credibility play an important role here.

For these reasons, Dryzek recommends that deliberations should occur within an 'informal communicative realm' that takes place over time, such as a public network, deliberative poll or policy dialogue. This would afford participants the opportunity to admit having been persuaded by the other side. If the deliberations are not directly linked to political decisions, the contest for power is less likely to prevent people from openly changing their minds.

Experimental approach

James Fishkin and his colleagues have developed an experimental study on the effectiveness of grassroots deliberation in managing and de-escalating identity conflicts. In 2007, Fishkin organised a 'deliberative poll' in Omagh, Northern Ireland. One hundred and twenty-seven Protestants and Catholics were asked to answer a series of questions relating to children's education policy in the region. After the poll, the participants were invited to deliberate in small-group discussions and plenary sessions. The original questionnaire was then put before the participants once more. The results indicated that the perceptions of the participants changed significantly in the course of the dialogue. The proportion of Catholics who believed Protestants were 'open to reason' increased from 36 per cent to 52 per cent, while the proportion of Protestants believing that Catholics were 'open to reason' increased from 40 per cent to 56 per cent. There was also a dramatic increase in the proportion of each community that viewed the other as 'trustworthy'. For Catholics, the proportion rose from 50 per cent to 62 per cent, and for Protestants it rose from 50 per cent to 60 per cent. The experiment suggests that citizens are open to rational discussion and willing to change their opinions, and that deliberation can enhance mutual trust in divided societies (Fishkin 2009).

Comparing the three approaches

O'Flynn's approach is characterised by its emphasis on principles of reciprocity and publicity. For O'Flynn, deliberations should take place between elite representatives as well as ordinary citizens. The aims of deliberation should engage major political issues, create an overarching civic identity and resolve seemingly intractable political problems. Dryzek, by contrast, situates deliberation entirely in the public sphere, and insists that deliberation should be 'semi-detached' from the state, focusing on specific needs, not issues of sovereignty and constitutional essentials. The aim is to create shared discourses in divided societies. The experimental approach developed by Fishkin similarly sees deliberation taking place at the grassroots level, but in a controlled setting where all the relevant information for decision-making is provided and there is input from experts and facilitators. One would think that to have any noticeable impact, such experiments would need to be replicated on a large scale.

The three approaches offer different accounts of how deliberation is supposed to confer legitimacy upon the solutions. For O'Flynn, legitimacy is achieved by the satisfaction of reciprocity and publicity. These principles ensure that the solutions reached take account of the interests of all involved and treat persons as equals. According to Dryzek, a resolution is legitimate if it can be justified in terms of a shared discourse that has arisen through public-sphere deliberation, including a plurality of voices. Meanwhile, for Fishkin, a resolution is legitimate if it is reached by participants who have been given all of the relevant information and the opportunity to deliberate.

The three approaches aim at different but related outcomes. O'Flynn aims to treat all participants as equals and does not marginalise extremist elements. As a result, the outcome is more likely to be accepted by all involved, and the prospect of a backlash from extremist groups is minimised. For Dryzek, informal deliberation in the public sphere is supposed to create a new discourse that is favourable to a resolution. In the long term, this new discourse infiltrates the political sphere and influences official decision-making. For Fishkin, the aim of deliberation is to build tolerance and trust by breaking down stereotypes and negative attitudes, and to rehumanise the other.

The three approaches differ in their methods of enhancing the deliberative capacities of citizens. Fishkin's approach seems to be strongest in this regard, in so far as participants in his experimental deliberative polls are provided with balanced materials and an excellent selection of the relevant information and there is input from experts and facilitators. O'Flynn, by contrast, does not provide mechanisms for enhancing the deliberative capacities of citizens. Those citizens with limited deliberative capacities are simply encouraged to rely on narratives rather than on reasoned argument. Having said this, O'Flynn's publicity principle does ensure that citizens are given an insight into the reasoning employed by representatives in their decision-making. In a similar vein, Dryzek focuses on specific needs rather than issues of sovereignty and constitutional essentials; this arguably makes the deliberative process more accessible to ordinary citizens.

Regarding the degree of interaction required, O'Flynn stresses that within civil society, high levels of interaction are needed to create overarching civic identity. The interaction between civil society and the state is ensured via the principle of publicity. By contrast, Dryzek emphasises extensive interaction within civil society but only a 'loose' connection between the state and the public sphere, where the former is 'semi-detached' from the latter. Fishkin limits deliberation to isolated experiments involving a relatively small sample of participants.

The empirical testability of the three approaches varies. It is difficult to see how O'Flynn's proposal might be tested for effectiveness. And in relation to Dryzek's approach, determining whether a public discourse has changed the public consciousness and infiltrated the political realm is no easy feat. Only Fishkin's approach seems to be empirically testable: the impact of deliberation is rigidly tested through pre- and post-deliberation polling, and the results are quantifiable.

The effectiveness of the three deliberative approaches is subject to interpretation. According to Dryzek, the Canadian experience demonstrates that when deliberation is focused on sovereignty and the constitution, the likely outcome is 'deadlock, frustration, and failure' (Dryzek 2005). But public-sphere informal deliberation has helped make Canada 'such a generally successful society' (Dryzek 2005). Alain Noel (2006), however, points out that the 'deepening of democracy' in Canada – the greater inclusion of the masses in the political process – has led to an impasse. Ajzenstat and Cook (1994) further argue that public participation has worsened the divisions in Canadian society.

Take another example: Northern Ireland. Dryzek lists the case of Northern Ireland in the 1990s among his 'three kinds of failure' (Dryzek 2005). He says that the relationship between the public and political spheres is too 'tight'. Those involved in the public deliberation had close links to the political leadership on both sides. Deliberation thus tended to degenerate into a 'contest over sovereign authority'. By contrast, Sean Byrne seems to think that the public deliberation in Northern Ireland has been quite successful. The interactions among local historical societies and churches/clergymen have created forums for joint problem-solving in and between local neighbourhoods (Byrne 2001: 339).

In summary, the three deliberative approaches examined above are complementary. They can be synthesised into a coherent scheme where deliberation takes place through a shared discourse, in a controlled experimental setting and is guided by the dual principles of reciprocity and publicity. This synthesised deliberative approach serves as a foundation for the idea of deliberative referendum.

11.2   AN INTEGRATED ARGUMENT ABOUT DEMOCRATIC GOVERNANCE

I will now examine the argument about the combination of the principles of history and democracy, majority rule and minority rights, consociational and deliberative democracies, and referendums and public deliberation.

The complex combination between history and democracy

I have examined a number of non-democratic approaches to the boundary issue, pointing out the conflict between historical principle and democracy principle (Chapter 1); investigated the impact of Chinese imperial history on the current national boundary problem (Chapter 3); and discussed the historical force of Han linguistic imperialism and the legacy of the *gai tu gui liu* policy (Chapter 9). It is unrealistic to reject the force of history completely. Now it is time to examine an overlooked issue, that is, the possibility of the complex linkage between democracy and history.

First, we have to acknowledge the problem of the historical principle. Take the example of the Chinese government's sovereign claim over Taiwan on the grounds that Taiwan has been a part of China for centuries. But there are various competing accounts of Taiwan's history. Taiwanese nationalists reject the view that Taiwan shares a 5,000-year history with China, and assert that Taiwan is no more than four hundred years old, beginning with Holland's colonisation. In this version of history, Taiwan began as a colony of Holland, was subsequently ruled by Zheng (1662–83), then by Qing (1683–1893), then by the Japanese (1895–1945), and finally by the KMT from 1945 onwards. Thus, while Taiwan was part of China for hundreds of years, for several decades of its history it was under Japanese rule. If disputes over sovereignty and national boundaries are to be settled by history, as the nationalist insists, how are different historical periods to be weighed against one another? Equally, we should not overlook the impact of hundreds of years of Chinese rule over Taiwan; this historical legacy will continue to play its critical role in the politics of reunification or independence.

Democracy and history are inextricably linked. Although the democratic principle holds that contemporary people are not bound by the decisions of the past, history has clearly influenced the shape of modern democracies, as well as the decisions reached by democratic means. A common history and language create a context in which democratic decision-making is possible. In any democracy a circumscribed group of people enjoy suffrage and exercise the right to vote. But suffrage is determined by membership, which is typically decided by non-democratic criteria such as history, birth, nationality and political geography. Consider the demographical legacy of colonialism: the domination of whites in the USA, Canada, Australia and New Zealand. This historical legacy impacts upon the composition of population, and consequently determines who is the majority and who is the minority. This in turn impacts democratic decisions. In short, democratic politics cannot abstract themselves from the influences and constraints of history.

History and collective memory as well as democracy have all also played a major role in the politics of secession and unification. Norway's secession from Sweden, for example, was motivated by the distinct histories of the two nations, but ultimately brought about via referendum. German reunification was regarded as a historical necessity by German nationalists, because the country was arbitrarily divided in the wake of the Second World War. But again the democratisation of Germany made the achievement of this aspiration possible. History seems to provide the impetus for secession and unification movements. A successful reunification is often associated with the past history of unity, while a successful secession with the past history of independence.

Kymlicka makes a history-based normative argument that indigenous communities have the minority rights to autonomy due to their place in historical occupation, but immigrant communities do not have due to their voluntary migration. He argues that these rights are the result of historical agreements, such as the treaty. For example, Quebecois leaders agreed to join Canada on the condition that jurisdiction over language and education be guaranteed to the provinces, not the federal government. To respect such agreements is to respect the self-determination of minorities, and to ensure that citizens have trust in the actions of government.

Therefore, the history of cultural communities should be a basis for the internal boundaries of communities (Kymlicka 1995: 116–19).

It seems that the best, perhaps the only feasible, solution to ethnic disputes over territory is not to replace the historical principle with a democratic principle. History cannot be denied a role in resolving such issues. To deny the role of history is to deny the emotional linkage between ancestors and current generations. Furthermore, where there are competing historical claims to territorial integrity, a democratic referendum cannot deny their legitimacy completely. The historical claims will remain to forever challenge the justice of decisions reached through democratic means if it fails to take account of historical fact. The historical and democratic principles must therefore be reconciled and combined through deliberation. Historians and democrats should not compete, but cooperate. The deliberative model of democracy has the potential to achieve this, as it encourages dialogue between the present and past: historical issues are settled by deliberation in the present, but the present deliberations are at the same time shaped and informed by history. In this way, deliberative democracy closes the gap between majoritarian and historical approaches to resolving identity conflicts in divided societies.

Given Kosovo has been part of Serbia since the fourteenth century, and given the contested nature of history, Alterman (1999) imagines a perfect world where the warring sides in ethnic disputes over territory lay down their arms and submit themselves to a panel of historical experts. In the case of Kosovo, these experts would study the historical record of a battle that occurred more than six hundred years ago in Kosovo and determine which side's claims had greater merit. There would be a ruling, and each side would give up its historically unjustifiable demands in the face of superior historical documentation. This would allow reason and intellectual power to decide the matter. Alterman's approach is deliberative, but not democratic. For a deliberative democrat, the judgement of historical experts is insufficient; a sufficiently broad public consensus is also necessary to confer legitimacy upon a settlement.[2] History provides no more than *provisional* legitimacy. Nationalism 'is inconceivable without the ideas of popular sovereignty preceding – without a complete revision of the position of ruler and ruled, of classes and castes' (Emerson 1960: 214).

The combination of majority rule, minority rights and deliberation

A desirable democratic mechanism is to combine the majority rule inherent in referendum, autonomy and minority rights with public deliberation. Democracy as majority rule could support winners; those, for example, who have their nation-state. Democracy as self-determination, however, may support losers, like those who fail to establish a new state. One cannot reject one and accept the other in an arbitrary way. We need to view the key components of democratic management of the boundary issue, discussed in Chapter 1, as a *system* of ideas and arrangements. We cannot pick one mechanism, such as majority rule, while rejecting others such as minority rights. We need to balance majority rule with minority rights, as well as the state's right to national sovereignty with the right to autonomy by minorities. Democratic governance requires normatively that power and resources are distributed in a fair way, through a balance of minority rights and majority rule, and a balance of the unity of the nation-state and genuine autonomy.

These balances touch upon the question concerning the fairness of democratic management. Without fairness democratic management could otherwise become a tyranny of the majority. Democratic management requires fair procedures, the protection of minority rights, the voice of opposition, the participation of civil society and public deliberation, and finally a just balance between majority rule and minority rights. In particular, a majority cannot decide the fate of minorities through a simplistic referendum, as will be discussed later on.

It is also vital to consider the combination of public deliberation and minority rights, in relation to the practice of multiculturalism. Chapter 7 has shown how three different theories of multiculturalism – liberal, Confucian and Marxist – exhibit serious theoretical tensions and constitute an obstacle to addressing the Tibetan question. It calls for discourse dialogue and engagement between Confucianism and liberalism; the success of this kind of dialogue will lay down a solid foundation for public deliberation on the question of autonomy for Tibet. Chapter 8 examined the current state of Tibetan autonomy and explained the stalemate that exists; it has also suggested several ways out of that stalemate, such as ideas of a cultural autonomous zone, consociational arrangement and a deliberative approach. Chapter 9 discussed the Tibetan language issue, explaining the penetration of Han language into Tibet as a historical phenomenon of linguistic imperialism. It calls for a multi-linguistic policy through pluralism. Chapter 10 discussed a deliberative experiment and its dialogues in a real-world setting. All four chapters point to deliberative multiculturalism which emphasises rational dialogue and mutual respect with firmly guaranteed political rights, especially for minorities (Kim 2011). All parties involved should listen to one another, engage in serious dialogue, and reach mutual compromise with sincerity. While public deliberation cannot solve the sovereignty problem directly, it can help to enhance trust and develop mutual tolerance, thus fulfilling one crucial condition by which the boundary-related problem can be managed.

The combination of deliberative democracy and consociationalism

The device of consociationalism was introduced in Chapter 8 to address the Tibet question. Here I would like to extend the discussion to argue that a power-sharing mechanism, if it is to succeed, needs communal support and public deliberation which factors for inter-ethnic group discussions. Take the example of the power-sharing arrangement in Northern Ireland. It was a puzzle that a Protestant majority in Northern Ireland agreed to a power-sharing arrangement in 1998, which deviated from the rule that 'majorities [that] have power do not wish to share it', especially not with minority groups they resent (Horowitz 2002: 197). What convinced that majority to give up on its demand for majoritarian institutions?

Horowitz claims that leaders of the Ulster Unionist Party were willing to accept the power- sharing arrangements that were designed to benefit nationalists because they thought that these arrangements would be beneficial to Protestants in the future when they found themselves in the minority.

The answer lies in dialogue, public deliberation, negotiation, and the participation of civic groups: all played their due roles in favour of an agreement in 1998.
First, the Catholic and Protestant factions in Northern Ireland have tried count-
less times before to negotiate and to find a resolution to their dispute. Often the
negotiations have failed to yield tangible results. However, each of these attempts
'left a residue of general ideas and concrete proposals'. It was not necessary to start
from scratch in 1996. The parties were able to build on the foundations laid in previous negotiations. Horowitz (2002: 193–220) explains: 'It was possible to achieve
agreement in the last 24 hours because so much had been done in the last 24
years.'

Second, deliberation between Catholics and Protestants at the grassroots level
also played a role in the success. Pearson (2001: 274) suggests that informal discussion between elites, as well as interaction between ordinary citizens, is essential
if formal political negotiations are to produce a lasting settlement. Byrne (2001)
observes that previous attempts to resolve the Northern Ireland conflict prior to
1997 failed because they did not engage the masses, only elites. The failed agreements include the Sunningdale Agreement, the 1976 Constitutional Convention,
the 1978 Recognisation Policy, the 1979 Consultative Document, the 1981 Rolling
Devolution Policy, the 1985 Anglo-Irish Agreement, the 1991 Peter Brooke
Initiative, the 1993 Downing Street Agreement and the 1995 Frameworks Proposal.
Elite negotiation tends to focus on interests and resources. But for a lasting settlement to be achieved, the civic culture needs to be transformed: the people need to
be made more 'deferential'. Elite bargaining cannot achieve this, only grassroots
participation and inter-group contact can.

Rothman and Olson also claim that political bargaining by elites which focuses
on economic, territorial and military interests cannot deal with the underlying identity-based tensions behind a conflict. Therefore, where a conflict is settled through
elite bargaining alone, there is a good chance that the underlying tensions will have
cause to flare up again before too long. The 1995 Dayton Peace Accords are given
as an example – the Bosnian conflict was settled through interest-based bargaining,
but the ethnic/identity issues at the root of the conflict were not addressed, and so
an even more virulent conflict erupted in Kosovo a few years later. Rothman and
Olson argue that, in order to avoid this, it is necessary to deal with the underlying
identity-based tensions, and this can only be achieved through the 'interactive
conflict resolution' method formulated by Ronald Fisher. This involves informal
dialogue between conflicting parties at the grassroots level (Rothman & Olson
2001; Pearson 2001).

George Mitchell, US envoy to the Northern Ireland peace talks, adopted a deliberative approach in an effort to get both sides to work together in implementing the
settlement. He asked the parties:

> merely to sit down and mutually discuss their 'hopes and fears' for the future.
> He reasoned that they had never been through such a venting, visioning,
> and listening process, and that only through an icebreaker of this sort could a
> perception of common concern and trust begin to seep into their relationship.

(Pearson 2001: 276)

This process seems to have worked. The next stage of the implementation of the 1997 accord was agreed upon shortly after the deliberation. The IRA agreed to decommission its weapons while the joint executive was taking office. Thus it seems that informal discussion was essential even *after* the peace plan had been agreed upon! It was essential for the plan to actually be *implemented*.

Third, the 1997 Good Friday Agreement worked because hardline and paramilitary groups were engaged, and 'modes of community peace building' have evolved in Northern Ireland in more recent times. A number of non-governmental organisations, such as local historical societies, have been working to build bonds across the two communities. The churches have set up prayer groups for members of both communities, and clergymen have attended funerals of murder victims from both communities. The Community Relations Council (CRC) and other bodies have created forums for joint problem-solving in and between local neighbourhoods (Byrne 2001: 339). Nevertheless, the consociational model imposes significant restrictions on the deliberation. As Dryzek (2005: 222) claims, the consociational condition of 'segmental autonomy' involves excluding highly contentious issues from the public debate.

11.3 DELIBERATIVE REFERENDUM: IMPROVING DEMOCRATIC GOVERNANCE MECHANISM

Here I would like to develop the argument about why and how referendums should be combined with deliberation in an ideal situation (in a non-ideal situation, there will be potential conflict between referendum and deliberation); it is a theoretical attempt at an integrated theory that explains how deliberative referendums can address and manage national boundary issues successfully.

The major problem with the referendum process held in 2004 in Taiwan was its deliberative deficit. This deliberative deficit, borrowing the words from Uhr (2002: 179–80), is 'the imbalance between, on the one hand, resources available to strengthen community deliberation and, on the other hand, the deceptions and misrepresentations of many referendum activists which weaken the deliberative process'. This kind of referendum undermined the deliberative process because the lack of flexibility tends to discourage people from participating in deliberation. In the absence of public deliberation, referendums are easily manipulated by extremist politicians who don't represent the true opinions of people.

To ensure the success of a referendum, any referendum must be preceded by a period of consultation and dialogue of all the competing sides. Disputants are more likely to accept the results of a referendum that has taken place following some such deliberative process. A multilaterally agreed secession is better than a unilaterally agreed one precisely because the former involves negotiation and deliberation. In the same vein, a deliberatively driven referendum is better than a manipulative one because it is open, rational and fair. A closely fought referendum that is preceded by genuine deliberation can be more legitimate than a referendum that includes little deliberation, even when the latter results in a larger majority vote (Chambers 2001: 242–3). This is because in the former case the majority is forced to come up with reasonable arguments rather than just relying on superior numbers. The legitimacy of the outcome does not rest solely on the size of the majority when the votes are counted. Deliberation must therefore be seen as a crucial element of any successful and effective referendum: 'For strong democracy, public talk and political judgment are the goal, not plebiscitary willfulness' (Barber 2003: 288).

If Taiwan is to hold successful referendums on issues of national identity and national boundaries in the future, it is necessary to rewrite the rules to strengthen the deliberative potential of referendums so as to generate a greater sense of public legitimacy. Increasing the deliberative component of referendums as discussed below will increase the likelihood they will make a productive contribution to resolving Taiwan's national identity issues. Through a synthesis of the previous studies on referendum with a modification, I propose the following procedural steps towards achieving a deliberative referendum for both Taiwan and Tibet in the future.

Set up the referendum Commission

The parliament should establish a dedicated all-party committee on referendums, and a broadly representative referendum Commission should be established to 'manage the conduct of referendums, including the prior organization of national plebiscites where appropriate, followed by popularly elected constitutional conventions to work through the details of possible constitutional changes' (Uhr 2002: 177).

Citizens' initiative

In the 2004 referendum, the DPP proposed it while the KMT opposed it; the division between political parties on whether a referendum should be held indicated that the referendum was a political game. A new referendum should come from citizens' initiative. Citizens can submit a petition for a legislative referendum on the national boundary/identity question and collect signatures from registered voters within twelve to eighteen months. The number of signatures would have to equal 5 or 10 per cent of the national voting tally in the last presidential election (Barber 2003).

Setting up a consultation and negotiation mechanism and process

The consultation and negotiation mechanism has been set up in Canada. In 2008, the Canadian Supreme Court issued an important ruling on the issue of Quebec and secession. It determined that constitutional amendments would be required in order to enact secession. Thus, while a first step towards secession would be 'a clear expression of the people of Quebec of their will to secede from Canada', that is, through a successful referendum, this would not have any legal effect. It would, however, compel the federal government 'to negotiate constitutional changes to respond to that desire' (Radan 2012: 16–17). In a similar vein, while Taiwanese have a right to hold referendums, the Beijing government has a right to consultation and negotiation over the future of Taiwan. In particular, Beijing needs to agree with the wording of the proposed referendum with regard to the change in the national identity status, and negotiates with the term of conditions. Only through this balanced check system can a referendum be held meaningfully. In summary, Radan (2012: 18) explains that the legal requirement of holding a referendum occurs in only two situations: 'in cases of a secessionist claim where the relevant parties enter into an agreement that requires a referendum to be held as a means of resolving the secessionist claim'; and in cases where there are 'explicit provisions in a parent state's constitution that mandate the holding of a referendum has part of the process of secession'.

Civil education through a series of public deliberation

Local and national discussions and debates on specific boundary-related issues are mandatory throughout the local and national assemblies and in the print and broadcast media (Barber 2003: 285). Mandatory also is a 'Deliberation Month', during which citizens are encouraged to engage in deliberation, facilitated by an independent body.[3] Apart from debates in assemblies, many other forms of public deliberation are encouraged, such as citizen juries, town meetings and national televised debates. In particular, deliberative polling techniques (as developed by Fishkin) can be employed: they generate reliable, genuine and high-quality public opinion and provide a reliable democratic basis in the random selection of community representatives. Considered public judgement emerges from reason-based public deliberation which truly reflects changes in public opinion. It meets the ideals of democratic rule and procedure: inclusive participation, equal influence, true representation and considered public judgement. However, the randomly selected participants in deliberative polling do not have the authority to make a decision with regard to the national identity question because they are not legitimate representatives of the populace; they cannot speak for, let alone make a decision on behalf of, those who were not randomly selected citizens. In the absence of a due voting process, the public forum cannot translate into authoritative decision-making. Even the best argument generated through public deliberation will not win over all citizens; it is the nature of public opinion that people will be divided on controversial national identity issues. Consequently, referendums are still needed.

Multiple-choice format

In conventional referendums, choices are generally limited to exclusive either/ or questions, leaving little space for public deliberation. By contrast, deliberative democracy explores different options for deliberation, not constrained by either/ or questions. When options for expanded public deliberation are inserted into the referendum process, participants do not see the vote as an 'all or nothing' proposition but rather as an ongoing consultative process (Chambers 2001: 250–1). A multiple-choice format, as suggested by Barber (2003), can be employed to replace the conventional 'yea/nay' option. The actual questionnaire of multi-choices ought to be discussed and debated through public deliberation and elite negotiation.

Two-stage votes

Barber (2003: 288) suggests there would be 'two voting stages, separat[ed] by six months of deliberation and debate'. The first vote is non-binding but intended to provoke deliberation. The second vote is 'to take full advantage of the educational benefits of the multi-choice referendum, and at the same time to guard against a too-impetuous citizenry or a too-powerful elite gaining temporary control of public opinion' (Barber 2003: 288). It would in effect revaluate the result of the first vote.

The role of China in promoting deliberative referendum

If China had the right to consultation on the referendum process and the design of the multiple-choice questionnaire, it would have a duty in return to promote genuine deliberation. This is the lesson from the 2004 referendum held in Taiwan. In 2004, China's external pressure had a chilling effect on genuine deliberation over Taiwan's national identity. The fact that Chen Shuibian referred to the referendum as a 'defensive referendum' indicates the important role the threat from the Mainland played in framing the debate. Beijing can have a major influence on any deliberation that takes place in Taiwan on the question of national identity due to the coercive threat it wields over the participants. Taiwanese may feel they are under duress and not able to consider all options openly and honestly while they face a potential military attack from the Mainland. One option might be to enlarge the deliberative process surrounding future referendums by actively inviting participants from the Mainland. There would be strong resistance to this, both from Taiwanese who feel that only they have the right to decide Taiwan's future and from the Mainland government, which would be reluctant to lend any legitimacy to the referendum process if it could result in an outcome that it sees as undesirable. The possibility of such cross-Straits deliberation might be greater, however, if it were to occur as part of an ongoing discussion without the pressure of a looming referendum. Although he condemned Taiwan's referendums as 'provocations', State Councillor Tang Jiaxuan has also said that the Mainland is 'ready to have contact and interaction with [Taiwanese] for increased understanding and greater identity of views' (Shangwu Sun 2004: 1).

11.4   HOW TO ACHIEVE A SUCCESSFUL REFERENDUM

Full realisation of a people's self-determination is dependent upon true respect for the rights and freedoms of the individuals who make up the people. Beran (1998: 42–53) lists conditions that may *disallow secession*: (1) secessionists cannot assume the responsibilities of independent states; (2) they will not recognise the right of secession for others; (3) they wish to exploit or oppress a group within their jurisdiction; (4) secession would create an enclave; (5) the secessionists' territory is essential to the existing state; and/or (6) the territory has a disproportionately high share of the economic resources of the existing state.

For Buchanan (1991: Chapter 2), the good of cultural preservation justifies the right to secession only if five conditions are met: (1) the culture is threatened; (2) less disruptive ways of preserving the culture are unavailable or inadequate; (3) the culture is not 'pernicious'; (4) the secessionists are not seeking to establish an illiberal state; and (5) neither the state nor any third party has a valid claim to the seceding territory.

After his visit to the Soviet Union where he witnessed the referendum process first-hand, Dahl seems to have accepted the value of democratically managing the boundary question. But he has qualified this acceptance by stressing four conditions for political self-determination: (1) at a minimum, demands for political autonomy, whether for full independence or only partial autonomy, cannot be justified unless it can be shown that a majority of people in the proposed unit definitely want autonomy; (2) the people within the proposed unit intend to govern themselves democratically; (3) they will adequately protect minorities within the now autonomous unit; and (4) autonomy would not result in serious harm to people in the existing state (Dahl 1991: 491–6).

The normative requirement made by Dahl that the people within the proposed unit really intend to govern themselves democratically seems to be valid and reasonable. Take a pertinent example of the Inkatha Freedom Party (IFP), the ethnic Zulu nationalist party in South Africa. In the early 1990s, the IFP attempted to establish a sovereign Zulu King. At the same time it rejected the adoption of a democratic system for its proposed independent state because, it argued, a democratic national state was incompatible with 'traditional' Zulu society (Shapiro 1997: 315–25). The IFP won only 10.5 per cent of the total Zulu vote, about a third in the 1994 election, and ultimately failed to gain an independent state.

These checklists of normative conditions help to judge which group is right or wrong, or which group has convincing grounds to seek independence. However, checkpoints are easy to list but difficult to match in reality; they are often too subjective to be practically useful. As a remedy, through an empirical investigation this book has identified and examined the preconditions for a successful referendum.

The art of democratic management relies on a study of political science. Wilson's vision of a new political geography is not merely based on democratic principles, but scientific principles as well. In the same spirit, the project of democratic management of the boundary question discussed in this book is based on a science of politics, offering an empirical study of fundamental questions concerning the nature and features of the democratic governance project. Here I would like to examine the key question: to what degree and under what conditions can democracy manage the national boundary question, and to what degree and under what conditions is democracy inapplicable to the question?

Wambaugh (1933: ix, 506) sees referendum as a tool in the workshop of political science and summarises eighteen points concerning political techniques of referendums from the world referendum experience (1914–33). Following Wambaugh,

I would like to identify and examine the strategies and conditions for a successful referendum by drawing on the referendum experience around the world. The lessons concern: the acceptance of the referendum principle; the conduct of referendums free from manipulation; the protection of minority rights; and the importance of reasonable turnout rates and a sufficient cross-nationality vote.

The key is to accept the referendum principle

If a referendum is to settle the national boundary/identity question, the outcome of the specific referendum must be accepted as having binding force by the main political players. In Wambaugh's terms, 'the plebiscite must be held under the formal agreement of both parties' (1933: 506). Otherwise, the legitimacy of the referendum itself is questionable.

In the Yugoslav case, when both Serbia and Croatia held their own referendums and denied the outcome of the other, the referendums did not help to settle the national boundary/identity question. Instead, they made the situation worse because the conflicting results of the two referendums were used to support claims for both union with and independence from Yugoslavia in Croatia and Bosnia-Herzegovina.

The acceptance of democratic procedure to decide the boundary issue is related to the knowledge and calculation of the outcomes of those procedures. Catholic-nationalist groups boycotted the referendum of 1973 (popularly called the 'border poll') because they constituted around a third of the population in Northern Ireland. The secessionist Moro National Liberation Front (MNLF) boycotted the 1989 referendum over the autonomy question, which deeply affected the turnout in areas of Sulu and Tawi-Tawi in the Philippines. In contrast, the three Baltic states held their own referendums over independence in 1991 because they were overnumbered in their republics, but boycotted the Union referendum because they were outnumbered in the former Soviet Union. Slovenia went to referendum because its leaders knew the positive result.

The referendum can be forced to be employed if a greater power has the capacity to impose democratic procedures on weaker or smaller nation-states, as Western democratic countries did to Indonesia, which held a referendum for East Timor after it suffered economic crisis in 1999. The greater powers, as Cobban observes, are one of the ultimate determining factors that decide the fate of small nation-states and their boundaries (Cobban 1969: 18–19, 289).

In the case of Taiwan, nevertheless, it would be highly dangerous to carry out a referendum with the US's support but without China's endorsement. Chai Trong and many others worked hard to induce the US's support for referendum but were denied by China.[4] If it were taken, this would be a risky move towards a war.

A successful referendum requires a civic culture in which the result of the vote is respected. If the community is divided along ethnic or partisan lines then a referendum can crystallise differences between groups and generate further conflict. In Taiwan, there was insufficient civic unity to prevent attitudes to the referendum splitting along party political lines. At the same time, there was no cross-Straits consensus that could have reduced the external coercion that distorted the vote.

The policy initiatives and responses in China were important. The National People's Congress has passed the anti-secession law, which mandates the use of force should Taiwan secede. It has also been proposed that China could hold a referendum to decide whether China should use force to reunify with Taiwan (*Lianhe Zaobao*, 5 June 2003). The prospect of holding two different referendums on both sides of the Taiwan Straits should not be excluded. Chinese scholars suggest that China should draft a referendum law and hold a referendum on the Taiwan question. If the majority of Chinese voters accept Taiwan's separation, the Chinese leadership would not be regarded as 'treacherous' and they would not need to take responsibility. If the referendum denies Taiwan's separation, the Chinese government has a legal basis to use force against Taiwanese separatism (*Lianhe Zaobao*, 26 June 2003). Of course, one may wonder how likely it is that the Chinese government will set a precedent of allowing the whole country to vote on such an important political question.

Ensuring free and fair referendums

The manipulation of referendums by elites undermines the trust of the people and the legitimacy of referendums, and thus tends to lead to the failure of the democratic management of the boundary question. For instance, the question of the 1991 Union referendum reads as follows: 'Do you consider it necessary to preserve the Union of Soviet Socialist Republics as a renewed federation of equal, sovereign republics in which the rights and freedoms of people of any nationality will be guaranteed in full measures?' (White, Gill & Slider 1993: 88). This is an extremely ambiguous formulation of the question. And voters were asked to approve the 'preservation' of 'a renewed federation' which did not yet exist. During the referendum, Gorbachev used state-run television and Communist party newspapers to rally support, while the 'no' campaign was dispersed and uncoordinated (Butler & Ranney 1994: 141). It is not surprising that 93.3 per cent of the voters in Azerbaijan, 97.9 per cent in Turkmenia, 93.7 per cent in Uzbekistan and 70.2 per cent in Ukraine supported the union. However, a few months later, in the republic referendums on independence, 99.58 per cent of the voters in Azerbaijan, 94.1 per cent in Turkmenia, 98.2 per cent in Uzbekistan and 90.3 per cent in Ukraine supported independence (White, Gill & Slider 1993: 89). This volatile electoral behaviour casts doubt on what appears 'democratic' and indicates the undecided binding power of referendums over the boundary question. Nevertheless, one may argue that the shifting figures reflect the bias of the question of the Union referendum and the unstable vote was due to manipulation.

A majority alone cannot decide the fate of minority communities through referendums

Majority rule can be misused to legitimate the dominance of one majority and to serve the majority group that claims to represent the whole nation-state and is therefore 'democratically' free to ignore the interests of minorities. This was the case with the Union referendum of 1991 in the former Soviet Union where the Russian majority had decisive influence. However, the Union referendum was considerably overshadowed by the larger victories of the supplementary pro-independence vote. For example, 80 per cent of the voters supported an independence proposal in some areas of Ukraine (Butler & Ranney 1994: 142). Moreover, the Union referendum did little to defeat the secessionist attempts of the three Baltic states and failed to hold the union together, even though the result of the vote supported the maintenance of the union. The lesson is clear: a referendum over the boundary issue should allow a minority community to decide its political future. Moreover, a normative implication of this lesson is, as Beran (1998: 39) argues, 'The right of a smaller community always overrides the right of the larger community of which it is part, if there is a conflict of wishes regarding political boundaries.' It seems that a large community does not have the right to veto the secession issue, as in the case of the former Soviet Union, although it has the right to be consulted as its interests are likely to be influenced by secession. This lesson has direct political implications in the Taiwan Straits. Even if Taiwan held a referendum over its national status, China should not hold a referendum to decide the Taiwan question, because the vastly greater population of China cannot rightfully decide the future of the smaller Taiwan, although China does have a right to be consulted.

Protection of minorities

Referendums over the boundary question tend to subject the minority to the rule of the majority without properly protecting them. Majority rule may be considered a crude device by minorities (Freeman 1998: 19). Whatever flaws majority rule has, however, it cannot be completely rejected. What we need is to combine majority rule with minority rights. The right to secede should not be exercised in referendums over the boundary question if minority rights are not protected. As Dahl insists, secessionists should adequately protect minorities within any new autonomous unit. In short, the project of democratic management must protect minorities, resist majority tyranny, correct the misuse of majority rule, and achieve a workable balance between majority rule and minority rights.

Failure to maintain such a balance will have dangerous consequences. Minority Serbs in the proposed independent state of Croatia, for example, foresaw that they would become a minority and be disadvantaged; thus they held a referendum for a union to protect their interests. Croatia, on the other hand, held another referendum to support its independence. Both employed majority rule without adopting an appropriate programme to protect minority groups.

In the 1991 referendum over the independence of the Baltic states, Russian speakers had voting rights. Many advocates of independence convinced ethnic minorities that citizenship would be extended to them in their new countries. However, subsequently the Baltic states imposed tough conditions for them to become citizens. This became a source of tension between the new states and Russia, and for the further secessionist movements of Russian speakers in the newly independent countries.

While majority rule may become tyrannical, so minority terrorism becomes tyran-

nical. A minority group of extreme nationalists may reject democracy and use terrorism to achieve their independence. Terrorists fought for their political causes, for
example in Chechnya, Northern Ireland, Spain and the Philippines. These terrorist
activities constitute an obstacle to democratic management of the boundary question and reduce the peace effect of referendums.

Sufficient approval rate

A referendum over the boundary issue implies majority rule, which gives rise to the
question of how strong a majority should be required: simple majority, two-thirds,
three-quarters or seven-eighths? The requirement of majority rule varies in the politics of referendums. In the UK, for example, the 40 per cent rule stipulated that in
order for the devolution proposal to pass, the number of 'yes' votes had to be equal
to or greater than 40 per cent of all registered voters. Although the 1979 referendum
over the autonomy question in Scotland gained a 51.6 per cent approval rate with
a 63.6 per cent turnout rate, that 51.6 per cent represented only 33 per cent of the
region's total electorate (Butler & Ranney 1994: 134).

The question then, is what is an appropriate requirement for majority rule? This
is a difficult question. If the approval rate of a referendum is too low, it ought to be
discredited. The Ukrainian government, for example, refused to accept the outcome
of the 1991 referendum over Crimean independence, which won a 54.2 per cent
majority (Anderson 1996: 70–1). Even considering a Crimean population of about
90 per cent Russian speakers, there were a significant number of Russian speakers
who did not want to reunify with Russia. It is conceivable that one reason for the
Ukrainian government's refusal to accept the outcome of the 1991 referendum was
that a 54.2 per cent majority was not considered sufficient for the return of Crimea
to Russia.

Arguably, if one raises the procedural hurdle too high, it will create other difficulties. Gorbachev, for example, insisted that a two-thirds majority should be required
for secession in Latvia. This requirement seems unreasonable, because the Russian
population accounted for 34 per cent of Latvians at that time. The case of Belau
(Palau) also illustrates that a 75 per cent majority requirement was too high, and
finally it was dropped down to a simple majority.

In history, the lowest approval rate recorded in a referendum was 2.5 per cent
in the Mayotte referendum of 1976. The highest approval rate was 100 per cent in
referendums held in Nice in 1792 and Rome in 1870. In the referendum over the
question of autonomy for Southern Mindanao in the Philippines in 1977, a 97.9 per
cent vote rejected the autonomy proposal. Such high rates have now been totally
discredited.

Sufficient turnout rate

The turnout rate is extremely important in assessing the true level of support. The
highest referendum turnout rates recorded, for example, are 99.7 per cent in the referendum over Austrian union with Germany in 1938, and 99.5 per cent in the

Savoy referendum of 1792 over its union with France. These high rates have been discredited as coercive and manipulative.

Low turnout rates also raise the question of legitimacy. Take the example of the Basque Country, where 68.8 per cent of voters approved the constitution but the voter turnout was only 45.5 per cent. This was below the Spanish and Catalan level of 67 per cent (Linz & Stepan 1996: 100). Such a low turnout raised the question of the degree to which the Basque people actually endorsed the constitution.

To take another example, New Caledonia held a referendum in 1987 to decide whether it should remain part of France. After the pro-independence Kanak Socialist National Liberation Front (FLNKS) called for a boycott of the referendum, 98.3 per cent of voters, with a 59 per cent turnout rate, supported continued union with France. The FLNKS claimed success for its boycott call because only 59 per cent of the 85,200 registered voters took part. Ninety per cent of those who abstained from voting in the referendum resided in constituencies inhabited largely by Kanaks, whose population made up only about 43 per cent of New Caledonia's population (*Far East Economic Review* 1987: 34). Bob Hawke, the then Australian Prime Minister, said this kind of low turnout 'is not going to settle the issue' (*Far East Economic Review* 1987: 34).

Here I propose a legitimacy index which combines approval rate and turnout rate. This is calculated through the following equation. First, an approval rate is multiplied by a turnout rate. Second, the sum of the multiplication is then divided by 100. This index gives us an indicator of the level of general support. It might be hypothesised that the higher the legitimacy index score is, the higher will be the chance of a successful settlement of the national identity question, except in a few cases with dubiously high legitimacy index scores.

The mean legitimacy index score for all referendums from the 1790s to the 1990s all over the world on the independence question is 68.49; the mean for referendums on union is 67.69; for referendums on the EU, 41.69; and for referendums on autonomy, 42.37. These figures demonstrate that, generally speaking, referendums on independence questions gain the highest support, followed by referendums on union, while referendums on the EU gained only around 42 per cent support (B. He 2002d). This low legitimacy index score for the EU question seems to statistically support the thesis of democratic deficiencies: the EU is not democratically set up (Pogge 1997). The score for referendums on autonomy is also low. This is understandable in that autonomy is often introduced where communities are deeply divided; such conditions tend to divide the vote and produce a low legitimacy index.

Sufficient cross-nationality vote

The level of cross-nationality or cross-ethnicity support is another indicator of a high level of legitimacy that a referendum can deliver. The more cross-ethnicity/nationality the vote is, the higher the level of legitimacy. In the 1921 referendum in Upper Silesia, for example, 59.6 per cent of voters with a 97.5 per cent turnout rate supported union with Germany rather than Poland. About 200,000 Polish-speaking or bilingual Upper Silesians chose to remain in Germany. This 'cross-voting' of Upper Silesian Poles constituted 30 per cent out of a pool of about 675,000 electors (Tooley 1997). The fact that a significant number of Russian speakers supported independence in the 1991 referendum in Latvia offers a convincing endorsement of the independence cause: 73.7 per cent of voters, with an 87.6 per cent turnout, favoured independence in Latvia. Given that 54 per cent of the population is ethnic Latvian and 34 per cent is Russian, this approval rate provides sufficient legitimacy for independence because a significant number of Russian speakers cast a cross-ethnicity vote in favour of independence.

11.5   CONCLUSION

As discussed above, each of the traditional approaches to conflict resolution discussed here – history, liberal multiculturalism, consociationalism and referendum – require some degree of grassroots deliberation in order to reliably achieve lasting results. Deliberation is crucial to any method of conflict resolution, and complements other democratic mechanisms and institutions. One might go so far as to say that resolving ethnic conflicts through the historical principle, referendums or power-sharing institutions is inconceivable without according some role to deliberation.

Deliberative democracy as a conflict-resolution mechanism offers several advantages. Foremost, by its nature it is against any use of violence and war. It addresses historical injustices through reconciliation and deliberation. It can avoid the vicious circle of authoritarian repression that leads to violent struggle, which in turn leads to further suppression and mistrust. It moves heated discussions of national and ethnic identity forward, preparing the groundwork for reconciliation through the fostering of mutual trust. It also improves the existing elite negotiation by developing and promoting open and transparent public deliberation.

The three deliberative democracy approaches I have examined above are complementary and can be synthesised in real-life application; referendum and public deliberation can be synthesised into a coherent scheme that affords a new device for deliberative referendum, with built-in rigorous procedures to ensure the maximum degree of public deliberation. This significantly improves the existing referendum mechanism and helps to solve some of the problems associated with the conventional practice of referendums, such as symbolic, manipulative, mobilised and purely emotional processes. The well-designed procedures of deliberative referendum, prescribed above, can achieve Habermas' (1996a) criteria that arguments and statements are *factually true, normatively right, and expressively sincere*. In short, this book brings together the democratic theories of the national boundary question with the development of empirical and normative analysis of public deliberation. It confronts the difficult challenges of divided societies where there is no apparent answer, and offers to them new tools of public deliberation. While this model has great promise in practice and in academe, it does have its own limits and a set of unresolved problems (Chapter 10), and still needs to be improved to be a feasible and practical conflict-resolution mechanism. This ought to be the focus of future research in the field.

China provides a fascinating window on the boundary issue. Through an analysis of China's troubled relations with Taiwan and Tibet, this book demonstrates that democracy offers a valuable approach to the national boundary question that has long haunted China. In modern times, China has tried to apply democratic devices to address the boundary question, but it has thus far failed. The past failure of the democratic approach should not, however, be an excuse to reject democratic governance today. With improving democratic mechanisms and procedures, China may be successful in settling and/or managing its national boundary/identity question through successive democratic attempts.

This book differs from predominant Chinese nationalist, socialist or Confucian discourse in that it articulates a liberal, democratic and deliberative argument about boundary questions. It develops and builds a democratic discourse and a systematic way of thinking on boundary questions: why democracy is required and desirable; what is democratic governance; how deliberative referendum and procedures can be employed; and under what conditions referendum can be successful.

When the right conditions arise, the Chinese public and China's leadership will have to give consideration to democratic governance for Tibet and Taiwan. This democratic governance project is rooted in the historical Enlightenment tradition, the age of democratisation, the contemporary world of the 'deliberative turn', and the paradox of China's politics of national boundary. China cannot evade the democratic challenge on this important issue; it must welcome democratic governance sooner rather than later and use it judiciously.

NOTES

1. Lynn Sander (1997) made this point first, and Jurg Steiner (2012) provides some evidence on the usefulness of stories. Millett (2000) also argues that the exclusion of 'anecdotal' argument from academic discourse has been a way of excluding women's experience.
2. Of course, defining the relevant public remains hard; and international legal legitimacy is also needed. For example, Aceh's status of autonomy may gain its support from the fact that it has been self-governing; still, Aceh resolution needs to be approved by the Indonesian parliament and international community.
3. Bruce Ackerman and James Fishkin (2004) proposed a Deliberation Day for each presidential election year. Given the national boundary question is always a historically embedded contentious issue, an extensive month of deliberation is definitely required.
4. Chai Trong argued that the US's support is primary while China's rejection is secondary in the author's interview in Taipei on 14 April 2002.

References

Ackerman, Bruce and Fishkin, James S. (2004). *Deliberation Day*, Yale University Press, New Haven.

Ahmad, F. (1993). *The Making of Modern Turkey*, Routledge, London.

Ajzenstat, J. and Cook, C. (1994). 'Constitution Making and the Myth of the People', in C. Cook (ed.), *Constitutional Predicament: Canada after the Referendum of 1992*, McGill-Queen's University Press, Montreal, pp. 112–26.

Alterman, E. (1999). 'Untangling Balkan Knots of Myth and Countermyth', *New York Times*, 31 July.

Amritavalli, R. and Jayaseelan, K.A. (2007). 'India', in A. Simpson (ed.), *Language and National Identity in Asia*, Oxford University Press, Oxford, pp. 56–9.

Anand, D. (2009). 'Strategic Hypocrisy: The British Imperial Scripting of Tibet's Geopolitical Identity', *Journal of Asian Studies*, vol. 68, no. 1, February, pp. 227–52.

Anderson, B. (1983). *Imagined Communities*, Verso, London.

Anderson, M. (1996). *Frontiers: Territory and State Formation in the Modern World*, Polity Press, Cambridge.

Ardley, J. (2003). 'Learning the Art of Democracy? Continuity and Change in the Tibetan Government-in-Exile', *Contemporary South Asia*, vol. 12, no. 3, pp. 349–63.

Bao, Yuzhu (2003). 'Qingdai menggu shehui zhuanxing yanjiu: Houjin jiqi qingchu mengguzu diwei jiqi yuyan wenzi' ('The Study on Mongolian Social Changes in Qing Dynasty: The Mongolian Social Status and its Language and Script in the Late Jin and the Early Qing'), *Neimenggu minzu daxue xuebao-shehui kexue ban (Journal of Inner Mongolia University for Nationalities: Social Sciences)*, vol. 29, issue 3, pp. 16–22.

Bahl, S.K. (1989). 'China's Failure in Tibet: Pulls and Pressures in Domestic Politics', *China Report*, vol. 25, no. 3.

Baldwin, Thomas (1992). 'The Territorial State', in Hyman Gross and Ross Harrison (eds), *Jurisprudence: Cambridge Essays*, Clarendon Press, Oxford, pp. 207–30.

Banks, A.S., Day, A.J. and Muller, T.C. (1997). *Political Handbook of the World 1997*, CSA Publications, Binghamton University, New York.

Barber, Benjamin R. (2003). *Strong Democracy: Participatory Politics for a New Age*, University of California Press, Berkeley.

Baum, J. (1999). 'Fat and Happy: Has Democracy Cooled Ardour for Independence?', *Far Eastern Economic Review*, 29 April.

Bautista, M.L.S. (ed.) (2008). *Philippine English: Linguistic and Literary Perspectives*, University of Hong Kong Press, Hong Kong.

BBC (2000). 'Chinese President Calls for Mobilizing Armed Forces to Settle Taiwan Issue', *BBC Summary of World Broadcasts*, 6 January (FE/D3730/F2).

BBC (2010). 'Tibetan Students in China Protest Over Language Policy', *BBC News Asia Pacific*, 20 October (accessed 7 November 2012), <http://www.bbc.co.uk/news/world-asia-pacific-11581189>.

Beran, H. (1998). 'A Democratic Theory of Political Self-determination for A New World Order', in P.B. Lehning (ed.), *Theories of Secession*, Routledge, London, pp. 33–60.

Bilik, N. (2010). 'How Do You Say "China" in Mongolian?: A Deeper Understanding of Popular Educational Thinking in China', paper presented at *Multicultural Education and The Challenges to Chinese National Integration Conference*, 2–3 December, La Trobe University, Melbourne, Australia.

Bockman, H. (1998). 'The Future of the Chinese Empire-State in a Historical Perspective', in K.E. Brodsgaard and D. Strand (eds), *Reconstructing Twentieth-Century China: State Control, Civil Society, and National Identity*, Clarendon Press, Oxford.

Bodde, D. (1967). 'Harmony and Conflict in Chinese Thought', in A. Wright (ed.), *Studies in Chinese Thought*, University of Chicago Press, Chicago.

Boggs, W. (1966). *International Boundaries: A Study of Boundary Functions and Problems*, AMS Press, New York.

Bolton, K. (ed.) (2002). *Hong Kong English: Autonomy and Creativity*, University of Hong Kong Press, Hong Kong.

Boyd, H.R. (2004). *The Future of Tibet: The Government-in-Exile Meets the Challenge of Democratization*, Peter Lang, New York.

Brahm, L. (2005). 'Conciliatory Dalai Lama Expounds on Winds of Change', *South China Morning Post (SCMP)*, 14 March.

Buchanan, Allen (1991). *Secession: The Morality of Political Divorce from Fort Sumter to Lithuania and Quebec*, Westview Press, Boulder.

Bush, R.C. (2005). *Untying The Knot: Making Peace in The Taiwan Strait*, Brookings Institute Press, Washington, DC.

Butler, D. and Ranney, A. (1994). *Referendums Around The World – The Growing Use of Direct Democracy*, AEI Press, Washington, DC.

Byrne, S. (2001). 'Consociational and Civic Society Approaches to Peacebuilding in Northern Ireland', *Journal of Peace Research*, vol. 38, no. 3, May, pp. 327–52.

Cai, M., Zhou Q., Wang Z., Zhu R. and Ding Z. (eds) (1979). *Zhongguo tongshi di liu ce (The 6th Volume of History of China)*, Renmin Press, Beijing.

Calhoun, John (1953). *A Disquisition on Government and Selection from the Discourse*, The Bobbs-Merrill Company, New York.

Canada Tibet Committee (2002). *China Says No to Dialogue with the Dalai Lama (AFP)*, 15 July (accessed 5 November 2012), <http://www.tibet.ca/en/newsroom/wtn/archive/old?y=2002&m=7&p=15_2>.

Canada Tibet Committee (2003). *China Cancels Long-Planned Visit by Tibetans (Radio Free Asia)*, 21 August (accessed 5 November 2012), <http://www.tibet.ca/en/newsroom/wtn/archive/old?y=2003&m=8&p=21_1>.

Carpenter, T.G. (2005). 'Taiwan's Troubles', *Harvard International Review*, vol. 27, issue 3, October.

Central Data Library (1991). *Selected Documents of Central Committee of the CCP*, vol. 7 (1931), The Central Party School Press.

Central Tibetan Administration (2005). *Dramatic Decrease in No. of Tibetan Cadres in 'TAR'*, *Statistic Show*, 27 January (accessed 5 November 2012), <http://tibet.net/2005/01/27/dramatic-decrease-in-no-of-tibetan-cadres-in-tar-statistics-show>.

Chambers, S. (2001). 'Constitutional Referendums and Democratic Deliberation', in M. Mendelsohn and A. Parkin (eds), *Referendum Democracy: Studies in Citizen Participation*, Palgrave Macmillan, New York, pp. 231–55.

Chan, Joseph (1999). 'A Confucian Perspective on Human Rights for Contemporary China', in J.R. Bauer and D.A. Bell (eds), *The East Asian Challenge for Human Rights*, Cambridge University Press, Cambridge, pp. 212–37.

Chang, Bi-Yu (2004). 'From Taiwanisation to De-sinification: Culture Construction in Taiwan since the 1990s', *China Perspectives*, vol. 56, November–December, pp. 34–44.

Chang, F. (1998). 'ROC Monitors Mideast Tensions', *The Free China Journal*, vol. XV, no. 51, 25 December.

Chang, Hui-Ching and Holt, R. (2007). 'Symbols in Conflict: Taiwan (Taiwan) and Zhongguo (China) in Taiwan's Identity Politics', *Nationalism and Ethnic Politics*, vol. 13, pp. 129–65.

Chang, Ya-Chung (1999a). 'The Identity and Integration of Taiwan and Mainland China: Reflections on the EU Model', *Issues and Studies*, vol. 38, no. 10, pp. 1–25.

Chang, Ya-Chung (1999b). 'The "Cross-Taiwan Strait Basic Agreement" and The Future of Taiwan and Mainland China', *Issues and Studies*, vol. 38, no. 8, September, pp. 1–29.

Chao, L. and Myers, R.H. (1998). *The First Chinese Democracy: Political Life in the Republic of China on Taiwan*, The Johns Hopkins University Press, Baltimore.

Chen, Ming-Tong (2012). 'Taiwan in 2011: Focus on Crucial Presidential Election', *Asian Survey*, vol. 52, no. 1, January/February, pp. 72–80.

Chen, Qimao (1996). 'The Taiwan Strait Crisis: Its Crux and Solutions', *Asian Survey*, vol. 36, no. 11, November, pp. 1055–66.

Chen, Qinghua and Wei, Yingxue (1998). *Deng Xiaoping minzu lilun yanjiu huigu (Review of the Studies on Deng Xiaoping's Theory about Nationalities)*, Heilongjiang minzu congkan (Heilongjiang Nationality Series), Ha'erbin, no. 4, pp. 39–44.

Chen, Yan and Ordeshook, P.C. (1994). 'Constitutional Secession Clauses', *Constitutional Political Economy*, vol. 5, no. 1, pp. 45–60.

Chen, Yanbin, Liu, Jianzhong and Qiao, Li (1998). *Mao Zedong sixiang minzu lilun yanjiu huigu (Review of the Studies on Mao Zedong Thought about Nationalities)*, Heilongjiang minzu congkan (Heilongjiang Nationality Series), Ha'erbin, no. 4.

Chen, Yangbin (2014). 'Towards Another Minority Educational Elite Group in Xinjiang?', in James Leibold and Chen Yangbin (eds), *Minority Education in China: Balancing Unity and Diversity in an Era of Critical Pluralism*, Hong Kong University Press, Hong Kong, pp. 201–19.

Cheng, Chung-Ying (1998). 'Transforming Confucian Virtues into Human Rights', in de Bary and Weiming Tu (eds), *Confucianism and Human Rights*, Columbia University Press, New York, Chapter 7.

Cheng, Yishen (1989). *Dulipinglun de minzhu sixiang (The Democratic Ideas of the Journal of Independent Forum)*, Lianjing chuban Gongsi, Taiwan.

China Daily (2003). 'Taiwan's Referendum Attempt Provokes Response', 27 March (accessed 30 August 2012), <http://www.china.org.cn/english/2003/Mar/59919.htm>.

ChinaReviewNews.com (2012). *Cong lijie dao huajie: Zhengqu Taiwan minyi chuyi (From Understanding to Resolution: Observations on the Struggle for Taiwan's Public Opinion)*, 27 August (accessed 26 November 2012), <http://www.chinareviewnews.com/doc/1021/8/3/8/102183844.html>.

China Tibet Online (2012). *2011 Top Economy Numbers in Tibet*, 12 January (accessed 5 November 2012), <http://en.tibet328.cn/02/02/201201/t1080328_1.htm>.

Ching, F. (1998). 'Hong Kong Solution for Tibet?', *Far Eastern Economic Review*, vol. 161, no. 31, 30 July.

Chiou, C.L. (1986). 'Dilemmas in China's Reunification Policy Toward Taiwan', *Asian Survey*, vol. 26, April, pp. 467–82.

Chou, Yujen (1997). 'The Impacts of Taiwan's National Identity and Democratisation on its International Stance and East Asia's Security', paper presented at the XVIIth World Congress of the International Political Science Association, 17–21 August, paper no. SS-61, pp. 1–39.

Christie, C. (1996). *A Modern History of Southeast Asia: Decolonization, Nationalism and Separatism*, Tauris Academic Studies, London.

Chu, Yun-Han and Lin, Jih-Wen (2001). 'Political Development in 20th-Century Taiwan: State-Building, Regime Transformation and the Construction of National Identity', *China Quarterly*, vol. 165, pp. 102–29.

Chun, A. (1994). 'From Nationalism to Nationalizing: Cultural Imagination and State Formation in Postwar Taiwan', *The Australian Journal of Chinese Affairs*, no. 31, January, pp. 49–69.

Chung, O. (1999). 'Neither Yam Nor Taro', *Free China Review*, vol. 49, no. 2, February.

Clark, Robert P. (1989). 'Spanish Democracy and Regional Autonomy: The Autonomous Community System and Self-government for the Ethnic Homelands', in Joseph R. Rudolph and Robert J. Thompson (ed.), *Ethnoterritorial Politics, Policy, and the Western World*, Lynne Rienner Publishers, Boulder.

Cobban, A. (1969). *The Nation State and National Self-Determination*, Collins Clear-Type Press, London, pp. 18–19, 289.

Cohen, J. (1989). 'Deliberative Democracy and Democratic Legitimacy', in A. Hamlin and P. Pettit (eds), *The Good Polity*, Blackwell, Oxford, pp. 17–34.

Conboy, K. and Morrison, J. (2002). *The CIA's Secret War in Tibet*, University Press of Kansas, Lawrence.

Copper, J.F. (2003). *Taiwan: Nation-State or Province?*, 4th edn, Westview, Boulder.

Copper, J.F. (2005). *Consolidating Taiwan's Democracy*, University Press of America, Lanham.

Cooper, J.F. (2009). *Taiwan: Nation-State or Province?*, Westview Press, Boulder.

Cough, R. (1978). *Island China*, Harvard University Press, Cambridge, pp. 153–4.

Council of Europe (2008). *White Paper on Intercultural Dialogue: Living Together as Equals in Dignity*, 7 May, 118th ministerial session, Strasbourg (accessed 29 October 2012), <http://www.coe.int/t/dg4/intercultural/Source/Pub_White_Paper/White%20Paper_final_revised_EN.pdf.

Cuevas, B.J. and Schaeffer, K.R. (eds.) (2003). 'Power, Politics, and The Reinvention of Tradition: Tibet in the Seventeenth and Eighteenth Centuries', *Proceedings of the Tenth Seminar of The International Association for Tibetan Studies*, Oxford, vol. 3.

Dahl, Robert A. (1964). *A Preface to Democratic Theory*, University of Chicago Press, Chicago.

Dahl, Robert (1989). *Democracy and Its Critics*, Yale University Press, New Haven.

Dahl, R.A. (1991). 'Democracy, Majority Rule, and Gorbachev's Referendum', *Dissent*, Fall, pp. 491–6.

Dahl, R. (1998). *On Democracy*, Yale University Press, New Haven and London.

Dai, Guang-Yu (2007). 'Manzu jiqi xianshi de yuyan wenzi' ('The Manchus and Its Ancestors' Language and Writing System'), *Yuncheng xueyuan xuebao (Journal of Yuncheng University)*, vol. 25, issue 1, pp. 46–8.

Dai, Xiaoming (1997). 'Guanyu minzu zizhi difang caizheng zizhi jiqi falu wenti' ('On Financial Autonomy of National Autonomous Regions and Related Legal Issues'), *Minzu yanjiu (Nationality Studies)*, no. 6, pp. 8–17.

Dalai Lama (1995). 'Statement by His Holiness The XIV Dalai Lama on His September 1995 Visit to the United States', *Tibet Press Watch*, vol. 7, no. 5, October.

Davis, M.C. (1999). 'The Case for Chinese Federalism', *Journal of Democracy*, vol. 10, no. 2.

Davis, M.C. (2008). 'Establishing a Workable Autonomy in Tibet', *Human Right Quarterly*, vol. 30, no. 2, pp. 257–8.

Davis, M.C. (2012). 'Tibet and China's "National Minority" Policies', *Orbis*, vol. 56, no. 3, Summer.

De Bary, W.T. and Tu, Weiming (eds) (1998). *Confucianism and Human Rights*, Columbia University Press, New York.

Deepak, B.R. (2011). 'India, China and Tibet: Fundamental Perceptions from Dharamsala, Beijing and New Delhi', *Asian Ethnicity*, vol. 12, no. 3, pp. 301–21.

DeFrancis, J. (1950, reprinted 1975). *Nationalism and Language Reform in China*, Princeton University Press, Princeton.

DeLisle, Jacques (2002). 'The China–Taiwan Relationship: Law's Spectral Answers to The Cross-Strait Sovereignty Question', *Orbis*, vol. 46, no. 4, Fall, pp. 733–52.

Deng, Xiaoping (1993). *Deng Xiaoping Wenxuan: Volume 1 & 3*, People's Press, Beijing.

Deterring, D. (2008). *Singapore English*, Edinburgh University Press, Edinburgh.

Dion, S. (1996). 'Why is Secession Difficult in Well-Established Democracies?', *British Journal of Political Science*, vol. 26, April, pp. 269–83.

Dittmer, L. (2000). 'On The Prospect of an Interim Solution to The China–Taiwan Crisis', *China Information*, vol. XIV, no. 1, pp. 58–68.

Dittmer, L. (2005). 'Taiwan's Aim-Inhibited Quest for Identity and the China Factor', *Journal of Asian and African Studies*, vol. 40, nos 1–2, pp. 71–90.

Dreyer, J.T. (1976). *China's Forty Millions: Minority Nationalities and National Integration in the People's Republic of China*, Harvard University Press, Cambridge.

Dreyer, J.T. (1989). 'Unrest in Tibet', *Current History*, vol. 88, no. 539, September, pp. 281–4.

Dryzek, J.S. (1996). *Democracy in Capitalist Times: Ideals, Limits and Struggles*, Oxford University Press, New York.

Dryzek, J.S. (2005). 'Deliberative Democracy in Divided Societies: Alternatives to Agonism and Analgesia', *Political Theory*, vol. 33, no. 2, pp. 218–42.

Dryzek, J.S. (2006). *Deliberative Global Politics*, Polity Press, Cambridge, pp. 154–7.

Duara, P. (1990). 'Nationalism as The Politics of Culture: Centralism and Federalism in Early Republican China', The Woodrow Wilson Center, *Asia Program Occasional Paper*, no. 37, 11 June.

Duncan, C. (ed.) (2004). *Civilizing The Margins: Southeast Asian Government Policies for the Development of Minorities*, Cornell University, Ithaca, New York.

Dunn, J. (1979). *Western Political Theory in The Face of the Future*, Cambridge University Press, Cambridge.

Ebai, S.E. (2009). 'The Right to Self-Determination and The Anglophone Cameroon Situation', *International Journal of Human Rights*, vol. 13, no. 5, pp. 631–53.

Economy, E.C. and Segal, A. (2008). 'China's Olympic Nightmare: What the Games Means for Beijing's Future', *Foreign Affairs*, vol. 87, no. 4, July–August.

Editorial (2008). 'Pohuai Beijing Aoyun Shi Zuida de Qinfan Renquan' ('Sabotaging Beijing Olympic Games is the Biggest Violation of Human Rights'), *Observation Notes*, no. 4.

Eisenstadt, S.N. (1992). 'Centre–Periphery Relations in the Soviet Empire: Some Interpretative Observations', in A. J. Motyl (ed.), *Thinking Theoretically about Soviet Nationalities: History and Comparison in the Study of USSR*, Columbia University Press, New York, pp. 205–24.

Elazar, D.J. (1995). 'From Statism to Federalism: A Paradigm Shift', *Publius: The Journal of Federalism*, vol. 25, no. 2, Spring, pp. 5–18.

Elazar, D.J. (1996). 'New Trends in Federalism', *International Political Science Review*, vol. 17, no. 4, October.

Election Study Center – National Chengchi University. 'Changes in the Taiwanese/Chinese Identity of Taiwanese (1992~2012.06)' (accessed 12 September 2012), <http://esc.nccu.edu.tw/english/modules/tinyd2/content/TaiwanChineseID.htm>.

Emerson, R. (1960). *From Empire to Nation: The Rise to Self-Assertion of Asian and African Peoples*, Harvard University Press, Cambridge.

Evans, S. (2010). 'Language in Transitional Hong Kong: Perspectives from the Public and Private Sectors', *Journal of Multilingual and Multicultural Development*, vol. 31, no. 4, pp. 347–63.

Extra, G. and Gorter, D. (eds) (2008). *Multilingual Europe: Facts and Policies*. Mouton de Gruyter, Berlin and New York.

Fang, Yang (2012). 'Over 40% Tibetan Cadres are Women', *Xinhua*, 20 February (accessed 5 November 2012), <http://news.xinhuanet.com/english/china/2012-02/20/c_131420949.htm>.

Feder, D. (2003). 'Barring Taiwan From UN a Threat to Peace', *Human Events*, vol. 59, issue 32, September.

Feder, D. (2004). 'Taiwan's Exclusion From UN: Unjust and Perilous Treatment', *Human Events*, vol. 60, issue 30, September.

Feder, D. (2006). 'United Nations Again Slams Door on Taiwan', *Human Events*, vol. 62, issue 31, September.

Feng, Anwei (2009). 'Identity, "Acting Interculturally" and Aims for Bilingual Education: An Example from China', *Journal of Multilingual and Multicultural Development*, vol. 30, no. 4, July, pp. 283–96.

Feng, Erkang (1992). *The Biography of Yongzheng*, Taiwan Shangwu yinshuguan (The Commercial Press Ltd, Taiwan), Taipei, pp. 397–9.

Feng, Yunying (2010). 'Dongbei diqu manyu shuairuo yuanyin jianlun' ('Study on Manzu Language's Decline in Northeast Area') *Manzu Yanjiu* (*Manzu Minority Research*), issue 3, pp. 90–3.

Finane, A. (1994). 'A Place in the Nation: Yangzhou and The Idle Talk Controversy of 1934', *The Journal of Asian Studies*, vol. 53, no. 4, pp. 1150–74.

Fincher, J. (1972). 'China as a Race, Culture, and Nation: Notes on Fang Hsiao-Ju's Discussion of Dynastic Legitimacy', in D.C. Buxbaum and F.W. Mote (eds), *Transition and Permanence: Chinese History and Culture: A Festschrift in Honor of Dr Hsiao Kung-Ch'üan*, Cathay Press, Hong Kong.

Fischer, M. (2005). *State Growth and Social Exclusion in Tibet: Challenges of Recent Economic Growth*, NIAS, Copenhagen.

Fisher, R.J. (2007). 'Interactive Conflict Resolution', in I.W. Zartman (ed.), *Peacemaking in International Conflict: Methods and Techniques*, United States Institute of Peace, Washington, DC, pp. 227–72.

Fishkin, J. (2009). *When the People Speak: Deliberative Democracy and Public Consultation*, Oxford University Press, Oxford, Chapter 6.

Fishkin, J., He, Baogang, Ruskin, B. and Siu, Alice (2010). 'Deliberative Democracy in an Unlikely Place', *British Journal of Political Science*, vol. 40, no. 2, pp. 435–48.

Fitzgerald, J. (1996). 'The Nationless State: The Search for a Nation in Modern Chinese Nationalism', in J. Unger (ed.), *Chinese Nationalism*, M.E. Sharpe, Armonk, New York.

Fraenkel, J. and Grofman, B. (2006). 'Does the Alternative Vote Foster Moderation in Ethnically Divided Societies? The Case of Fuji', *Comparative Political Studies*, vol. 39, no. 5, pp. 623–51.

Franke, H. and Twitchett, D. (1994). *The Cambridge History of China: Volume 6 – Alien Regimes and Border States, 907–1368*, Cambridge University Press, Cambridge.

Frechette, A. (2007). 'Democracy and Democratization Among Tibetans in Exile', *Journal of Asian Studies*, vol. 66, no. 1, pp. 97–127.

Free China Review (1999). Editorial, vol. 49, no. 2, February.

Freeman, M. (1998). 'The Priority of Function over Structure: A New Approach to Secession', in Percy B. Lehning (ed.), *Theories of Secession*, Routledge, London, pp. 13–32.

Friedman, Ed. (1994). 'Reconstructing China's National Identity: A Southern Alternative to Mao-Era Anti-Imperialist Nationalism', *The Journal of Asian Studies*, vol. 53, no. 1, pp. 67–91.

Friedman, Ed. (1996). 'A Democratic Chinese Nationalism', in J. Unger (ed.), *Chinese Nationalism*, M.E. Sharpe, Armonk, New York.

Fukuyama, F. and Avineri, S. (1994). 'Comments on Nationalism and Democracy', in L. Diamond and M.F. Flattner (eds), *Nationalism, Ethnic Conflict, and Democracy*, The Johns Hopkins University Press, Baltimore.

Fung, A. and Wright, E.O. (2003). *Deepening Democracy: Institutional Innovations in Empowered Participatory Governance*, Verso, London.

Fung, Yu-lan (1952). *A History of Chinese Philosophy*, vol. 1, trans. Derk Bodde, Princeton

University Press, Princeton. English translation from James Legge (1970), *The Works of Mencius*, Dover Publications, New York.

Gai, Xingzhi and Gao, Huiyi (2008). 'Naxizu Hanyuzhongjieyu de Yuyin Tedian' ('Phonetic Features of Inter-language of Naxi Minority'), *Minzu Yuwen (Minority Languages of China)*, issue 6, pp. 39–41.

Gellner, E. (1987). *Culture, Identity and Politics*, Cambridge University Press, Cambridge.

Ghai, Y. (1991). 'The Past and Future of Hong Kong's Constitution', *China Quarterly*, vol. 128, December, pp. 794–813.

Ghai, Y., Woodman, S. and Loper, K. (2010). 'Is There Space for "Genuine Autonomy" for Tibetan Areas in the PRC's System of Nationalities Regional Autonomy?', *International Journal on Minority and Group Rights*, vol. 17, issue 1, pp. 137–86.

Gladney, Dru C. (1994). 'Representing Nationality in China: Refiguring Majority/Minority Identities', *The Journal of Asian Studies*, vol. 53, no. 1, pp. 92–123.

Glasner, B. and Billingsley, B. (2011). 'Taiwan's 2012 Presidential Elections and Cross-Straits Relations: Implications for The United States', *Center for Strategic and International Studies*, November, Washington, DC.

Gold, T.B. (1993). 'Civil Society and Taiwan's Quest for Identity', in S. Harrell and Chun-Chieh Huang (eds), *Cultural Change in Postwar Taiwan*, Westview Press, Boulder.

Goldsmith, B. and He, Baogang (2008). 'Letting Go without a Fight: Decolonization, Democracy, and War, 1900–1994', *Journal of Peace Research*, vol. 45, no. 5, pp. 587–611.

Goldstein, M.C. (1995). 'Tibet, China and The United States: Reflections on The Tibet Question', occasional paper, *The Atlantic Council of The United States*, April.

Goodhart, P. (1971). *Referendum*, Tom Stacey Ltd, London.

Gray, J. (1993). *Post-liberalism: Studies in Political Thought*, Routledge, New York.

Grunfeld, A.T. (1996). *The Making of Modern Tibet*, M.E. Sharpe, Armonk, New York.

Guo, Shuyong (2000). 'A Preliminary Study on Several Problems of The Democratization of International Relations' ('Shilun guoji guanxi minzhuhua de jigewenti'), *Pacific Journal*, no. 1, 15 March.

Habermas, J. (1996a). *Between Facts and Norms: Contributions to a Discourse Theory of Law and Democracy*, Polity Press, Cambridge.

Habermas, J. (1996b). 'National Unification and Popular Sovereignty', *New Left Review*, no. 219, September–October, pp. 3–13.

Hao, Shiyuan (2012a). 'Zhongguo minzu zhengce de hexin yuanze burong gaibian (yi)', ('The Core Principles of China's Ethnic Policy Must Not Change (One)'), *Zhongguo Minzu Bao (China Ethnic News)*, 3 February (accessed 31 October 2012), <http://www.mzb.com.cn/html/node/293027-1.htm>.

Hao, Shiyuan (2012b). 'Zhongguo minzu zhengce de hexin yuanze burong gaibian (er)', ('The Core Principles of China's Ethnic Policy Must Not Change (Two)'), *Zhongguo Minzu Bao (China Ethnic News)*, 10 February (accessed 31 October 2012), <http://www.mzb.com.cn/html/Home/report/293026-1.htm>.

Hao, Zhidong (2010). *Whither Taiwan and Mainland China: National Identity, the State and Intellectuals*, Hong Kong University Press, Hong Kong.

Harmstone, Teresa-Rakowska (1997). 'Soviet Nationalities and Perestroika', *Canadian Review of Studies in Nationalism*, vol. XXIV, nos 1–2.

Harvey, R. (1993). 'China's Olympic Bid Is an Explosive Situation', *Los Angeles Times*, 20 September (accessed 22 November 2012), <http://articles.latimes.com/1993-09-20/sports/sp-37315_1_national-olympic>.

He, Baogang (1996). *The Democratisation of China*, Routledge, London.

He, Baogang (1997). *The Democratic Implications of Civil Society in China*, Macmillan, Basingstoke and St. Martin's Press, New York.

He, Baogang (1998). 'Can W. Kymlicka's Liberal Theory of Minority Rights be Applied in East

Asia?', in Paul van der Velde and A. McKay (eds), *New Developments in Asian Studies*, Kegan Paul International, London and New York, pp. 20–44.

He, Baogang (1999). 'The Roles of Civil Society in Defining The Boundary of a Political Community: The Case of South Korea and Taiwan', *Asian Studies Review*, vol. 23, no. 1, March, pp. 27–48.

He, Baogang (2001a). 'The National Identity Problem and Democratization: Rustow's Theory of Sequence', *Government and Opposition*, vol. 36, no. 1, Winter, pp. 97–119.

He, Baogang (2001b). 'The Question of Sovereignty in the Taiwan Strait: Re-examining Peking's Policy of Opposition to Taiwan's Bid for UN Membership', *China Perspectives*, no. 34, pp. 7–18.

He, Baogang (2001c). 'Why Does Beijing Reject the Dalai Lama Autonomy Proposal?', *Review of Asian and Pacific Studies*, Seikei University, Japan, no. 22, pp. 61–3.

He, Baogang (2002a). 'Can Democracy Provide an Answer to the National Identity Question in China?: A Historical Approach', in J. Wong and Yongnian Zheng (eds), *China's Post-Jiang Leadership Succession: Problems and Perspectives*, The National University of Singapore Press, Singapore, pp. 163–88.

He, Baogang (2002b). 'Democracy and Civil Society', in A. Carter and G. Stokes (eds), *Democratic Theory Today: Challenge for the 21st Century*, Polity Press, Cambridge, pp. 203–27.

He, Baogang (2002c). 'Democratization and the National Identity Question in East Asia', in Yeung Yue-man (ed.), *New Challenges for Development and Modernization: Hong Kong and the Asia-Pacific Region in the New Millennium*, Chinese University of Hong Kong Press, Hong Kong, pp. 245–73.

He, Baogang (2002d). 'Referenda as a Solution to the National Identity/Boundary Question: An Empirical Critique of the Theoretical Literature', *Alternatives: Global, Local, Political*, vol. 27, no. 1, pp. 67–97.

He, Baogang (2003). 'Why Is Establishing Democracy So Difficult in China?: The Challenge of China's National Identity Question', *Contemporary Chinese Thought*, vol. 35, no. 1, pp. 71–92.

He, Baogang (2004a). 'China's National Identity: A Source of Conflict between Democracy and State Nationalism', in Leong Liew and Shaoguang Wang (eds), *Nationalism, Democracy and National Integration in China*, RoutledgeCurzon, London, pp. 170–95.

He, Baogang (2004b). 'Confucianism Versus Liberalism over Minority Rights: A Critical Response to Will Kymlicka', *Journal of Chinese Philosophy*, vol. 31, no. 1, March, pp. 103–23.

He, Baogang (2004c). 'Transnational Civil Society and the National Identity Question in East Asia', *Global Governance: A Review of Multilateralism and International Organizations*, vol. 10, no. 2, May, pp. 227–46.

He, Baogang (2005). 'Minority Rights with Chinese Characteristics', in W. Kymlicka and Baogang He (eds), *Multiculturalism in Asia*, Oxford University Press, Oxford, pp. 56–79.

He, Baogang (2006a). 'Participatory and Deliberative Institutions in China', in E.J. Leib and Baogang He, *The Search for Deliberative Democracy in China*, Palgrave Macmillan, New York, pp. 176–96.

He, Baogang (2008). *Deliberative Democracy: Theory, Method and Practice*, China's Social Science Publishers, Beijing, Chapter 4 on 'Deliberative Democracy and National Identity Question'.

He, Baogang (2010). 'A Deliberative Approach to the Tibet Autonomy Issue: Promoting Mutual Trust through Dialogue', *Asian Survey*, vol. 50, no. 4, pp. 709–34.

He, Baogang (2013). 'Working with China to Promote Democracy', *Washington Quarterly*, vol. 36, no. 1, pp. 37–53.

He, Baogang, Galigan, B. and Takashi, Inoguchi (2007). *Federalism in Asia*, Edward Elgar, Cheltenham.

He, Baogang and Goldsmith, B. (2008). 'Letting Go Without a Fight: Decolonization, Democracy, and War, 1900–1994', *Journal of Peace Research*, vol. 45, no. 5, pp. 587–611.

He, Baogang and Guo, Yingjie (2000). *Nationalism, National Identity and Democratization in China*, Ashgate Publishers, Aldershot.

He, Baogang and Hundt, David (2012). 'A Deliberative Approach to Northeast Asia's Contested History', *Japanese Journal of Political Science*, vol. 12, no. 3, pp. 37–58.

He, Baogang and Sautman, B. (2005–6). 'The Politics of the Dalai Lama's New Initiative for Autonomy', *Pacific Affairs*, vol. 78, no. 4, Winter, pp. 601–29.

He, Baogang and Warren, M. (2011). 'Authoritarian Deliberation: The Deliberative Turn in Chinese Political Development', *Perspectives on Politics*, vol. 9, no. 2, pp. 269–89.

He, Liangliang (2004). 'Zhongguo yu xifang zhenying dou er bupo, yirou kegang' ('China Contended the West without Being Contentious and Dealt with the West Gently'), *Wenhui Newspaper*, 24 April, available at <http://www.chinareviewnews.com>.

Heberer, T. (1989). *China and its National Minorities – Autonomy or Assimilation*, M.E. Sharpe, Armonk, New York.

Heim, K. (1995). 'Multiculturalism with Chinese Characteristics', *The Asian Wall Street Journal*, 20 December.

Henders, S.J. (2010). *Territory, Asymmetry, and Autonomy: Catalonia, Corsica, Hong Kong, and Tibet*, Palgrave Macmillan, New York.

Hertz, F.O. (1945). *Nationality in History and Politics: A Study of the Psychology and Sociology of National Sentiment and Character*, Kegan Paul, London.

Herzberg, Robert (1992). 'An Analytic Choice Approach to Concurrent Majorities: The Relevance of John C. Calhoun's Theory for Institutional Design', *The Journal of Politics*, vol. 54, no. 1, pp. 54–81.

Herzer, E. (1999). 'The Practice of Autonomous and Self-Government Arrangements', presented at *International Workshop on Tibetan Autonomy and Self-government: Myth and Reality*, Heritage Village, India, 10–12 November.

Ho, Ping-Ti (1998). 'In Defense of Sinicization: A Rebuttal of Evelyn Rawski's "Reenvisioning The Qing"', *The Journal of Asian Studies*, vol. 57, no. 1, February, pp. 123–55.

Holmes, S. (1988). 'Precommitment and The Paradox of Democracy', in J. Elster and R. Slagstad (eds), *Constitutionalism and Democracy*, Cambridge University Press, Cambridge, pp. 195–240.

Horowitz, D.L. (2002). 'Explaining the Northern Ireland Agreement: The Sources of an Unlikely Constitutional Consensus', *British Journal of Political Science*, vol. 32, no. 2, April, pp. 193–220.

Hu, Angang and Hu, Lianhe (2012). 'Dì èr dài mínzú zhèngcè: Cùjìn mínzú jiāoróng yītǐ hé fánróng yītǐ' ('Second Generation Ethnic Policies: Promoting Intermingling and Development'), *Xinjiang Shifan DaXue Xuebao (Journal of Xinjiang Normal University: Social Sciences)*, vol. 32, no. 5, pp. 1–12.

Hu, Shaohua (2000). *Explaining Chinese Democratization*, Praeger, Westport, Connecticut.

Huang, David W.F. (2006). 'Did The 2004 "Peace Referendum" Contribute to The Consolidation of Taiwan's Democracy?', *Taiwan Journal of Democracy*, vol. 2, no. 2, pp. 143–76.

Huang, Jing (2009). 'Beijing's Approach and Strategy Toward The Dalai Lama: Dilemma and Choices', paper presented at the *Roundtable on the Tibet Issue*, The University of Hong Kong, 29–30 July.

Huang, Xiu-Rong (2010). 'Lun rujia xuexiao jiaoyu yu baren' ('The Confucius School Education and Ba People'), *Xinan Minzu Daxue Xuebao, Renwen Shehui Kexue Ban (Journal of Southwest University for Nationalities: Humanities and Social Science)*, vol. 31, issue 10, pp. 26–30.

Human Rights Watch (2010). *'I Saw It With My Own Eyes': Abuses by Chinese Security Forces in Tibet, 2008–2010*, 21 July, Human Rights Watch, New York.

Human Rights Watch (2011). *China: End Crackdown on Tibetan Monasteries*, 12 October (accessed 5 November 2012), <http://www.hrw.org/news/2011/10/12/china-end-crackdown-tibetan-monasteries>.

Human Rights Watch (2012a). *China: Tibetan Monasteries Placed Under Direct Rule*, 16 March (accessed 5 November 2012), <http://www.hrw.org/news/2012/03/16/china-tibetan-monasteries-placed-under-direct-rule>.

Human Rights Watch (2012b). *China: Arbitrary Expulsions of Tibetans from Lhasa Escalate*, 19 June (accessed 5 November 2012), <http://www.hrw.org/news/2012/06/19/china-arbitrary-expulsions-tibetans-lhasa-escalate>.

Hwang, Kwan (1994). 'Korean Reunification in a Comparative Perspective', in Young Whan Kihl (ed.), *Korea and the World: Beyond the Cold War*, Westview Press, Boulder, pp. 279–99.

Information Office of the State Council of the PRC (2001). *Tibet's March Toward Modernization*, 1 November, Beijing (accessed 5 November 2012), <http://news.xinhuanet.com/zhengfu/2002-11/18/content_633165.htm>.

Information Office of the State Council of the PRC (2009). *White Paper on 'Fifty Years of Democratic Reform in Tibet'*, March, Beijing (accessed 5 November 2012), <http://www.chinadaily.com.cn/china/2009-03/02/content_7527376.htm>.

International Campaign for Tibet and the International Human Rights Law Group (1994). *The Myth of Tibetan Autonomy: A Legal Analysis of the State of Tibet*, Washington.

Jacobs, B. (1997). 'China's Policies Towards Taiwan', paper given at *Taiwan Update 1997: Taiwan, Hong Kong and PRC Relations*, Brisbane, Queensland, Australia, 14–15 August.

Jakobson, L. (2005). 'A Greater Chinese Union', *The Washington Quarterly*, vol. 28, no. 3, pp. 27–39.

Jansen, M. (1967). *The Japanese and Sun Yat-Sen*, Harvard University, Cambridge.

Jenner, W.J. (1992). *The Tyranny of History: The Roots of China's Crisis*, The Penguin Press, London.

Jeon, Jei Guk (1992). 'The Origin of Northeast Asian NICs in Retrospect: The Colonial Political Economy, Japan in Korea and Taiwan', *Asian Perspective*, vol. 16, no. 1, pp. 71–101.

Jiang, Yinliang (ed.) (1990). *Zhongguominzushi (The History of Chinese Nationalities)*, Nationality Publisher, Beijing, pp. 138–45.

Jin, B. (2009). 'Lun nvzhen wenzi yu jinyuan wenhua de guanxi' ('On the Relationship Between Jurchen Language and Jin's Culture'), *Jilin sheng jiaoyu xueyuan xuebao (Journal of Education Institute of Jilin Province)*, vol. 25, no. 9, pp. 151–2.

Jin, Binggao and Xiao Rui (2012). 'On Maintaining Socialist Ethnic Theory and Policy with Chinese Characteristics: Analysis of Second-generation Ethnic Policy', *Journal of Northwest University for Nationalities*, no. 4, pp. 12–19.

Johnson, B. (2000). 'The Politics, Policies, and Practices in Linguistic Minority Education in The People's Republic of China: The Case of Tibet', *International Journal of Educational Research*, vol. 33, issue 6, pp. 593–600.

Johnston, A. (1993). 'Independence Through Unification: On the Correct Handling of Contradictions across the Taiwan Straits', *Contemporary Issue*, no. 2, Harvard University, Cambridge.

Jones, S.B. (1967). 'Boundary Concepts in the Setting of Place and Time', in Haem J. de Blij, *Systematic Political Geography*, 2nd edn, John Wiley & Sons, Inc., New York, pp. 162–88.

Kachru, Y. and Nelson, C.L. (2007). *World Englishes in Asian Contexts*, University of Hong Kong Press, Hong Kong.

Kane, D. (1989). *The Sino-Jurchen Vocabulary of The Bureau of Interpreters: Uralic and Altaic Series*, vol. 153, Indiana University, Research Institute for Inner Asian Studies, Bloomington, Indiana.

Kant, Immanuel (1983). *Perpetual Peace and Other Essays on Politics, History and Morals*, trans. Ted Humphrey, Hackett Publishing Company, Cambridge.

Kao, Mily Ming-Tzu (2004). 'The Referendum Phenomenon in Taiwan: Solidification of Taiwan Consciousness?', *Asian Survey*, vol. 44, no. 4, pp. 591–613.

Karmel, S. (1995). 'Ethnic Tension and The Struggle for Order: China's Policies in Tibet', *Pacific Affairs*, vol. 68, issue 4, Winter, pp. 485–508.

Kaymak, E. (2012). 'If At First You Don't Succeed, Try, Ty Again: (Re)Designing Referenda to Ratify a Peace Treaty in Cyprus', *Nationalism and Ethnic Politics*, vol. 18, no. 1, pp. 88–112.

Kedourie, Elie (1960). *Nationalism*, Hutchinson University Library, London.

Kennedy Memorial Center for Human Rights and Institute for Human Rights Studies and Advocacy (1999). 'Rape and Other Human Rights Abuses by the Indonesian Military in Irian Jaya (West Papua), Indonesia', May (accessed 18 October 2012), <http://wpik.org/Src/vaw_report.html>.

Kim, Nam-Kook (2011). 'Deliberative multiculturalism in New Labour's Britain', *Citizenship Studies*, vol. 5, no. 1, pp. 125–44.

King, C. (1994). 'Eurasia Letter: Moldova with a Russian Face', *Foreign Policy*, Winter, pp. 106–21.

Kirkpatrick, A. (2010). *English as a Lingua Franca in ASEAN: A Multilingual Model*, University of Hong Kong Press, Hong Kong.

Knaus, J.K. (2003). 'China's Opportunity to Resolve Tibet Issue', *Boston Globe*, 8 December.

Ko, Shu-ling (2003). 'Referendum Map Detours Legislature', *Taipei Times*, 25 June.

Ko Shu-ling (2006). 'Chen Praises EU Integration Model', *Taipei Times*, 5 October (accessed 29 October 2012), <http://www.taipeitimes.com/News/taiwan/archives/2006/10/05/2003330482>.

Kolas, A. (2003). '"Class" in Tibet: Creating Social Order Before and During the Mao Era', *Identities: Global Studies in Culture and Power*, vol. 10, issue 2, April, pp. 181–200.

Kolas, A. and Thowsen, M.P. (2006). *On the Margins of Tibet: Cultural Survival on the Sino-Tibetan Frontier*, University of Washington Press, Seattle.

Kolmas, J. (1967). *Tibet and Imperial China: A Survey of Sino-Tibetan Relations up to the End of The Manchu Dynasty in 1912*, occasional paper, no. 7, Australian National University, Centre of Oriental Studies, Canberra.

Kormondy, E. J. (1995). 'Observations on Minority Education, Cultural Preservation and Economic Development in China', *Compare: A Journal of Comparative and International Education*, vol. 25, no. 2, pp. 161–78.

Kormondy, E. J. (2002). 'Minority Education in Inner Mongolia and Tibet', *International Review of Education*, vol. 48, no. 5, pp. 377–401.

Krasner, S.D. (1999). *Sovereignty: Organized Hypocrisy*, Princeton University Press, Princeton, pp. 3–12.

Kristof, L.K. (1969). 'The Nature of Frontier and Boundaries', in R.E. Kasperson and J.V. Minghi (eds), *The Structure of Political Geography*, Aldine Publishing Company, Chicago, Chapter 11, pp. 126–39.

Kuo, Tai-chun and Myers, R.H. (2004). 'Peace Proposal One: The China Commonwealth Model', in S. Tsang (ed.), *Peace and Security Across the Taiwan Strait*, Palgrave Macmillan, Basingstoke.

Kymlicka, W. (1989). *Liberalism, Community and Culture*, Clarendon Press, Oxford.

Kymlicka, W. (1995). *Multicultural Citizenship: A Liberal Theory of Minority Rights*, Clarendon Press, Oxford.

Kymlicka, W. (2000). 'American Multiculturalism and The "Nations Within"', in D. Ivison, P. Patton and W. Sanders (eds), *Political Theory and the Rights of Indigenous Peoples*, Cambridge University Press, Cambridge, pp. 216–36.

Kymlicka, W. (2001). 'Reply and Conclusion', in W. Kymlicka and M. Opalski (eds), *Can Liberal Pluralism be Exported? Western Political Theory and Ethnic Relations in Eastern Europe*, Oxford University Press, Oxford.

Kymlicka, Will (2012). 'Comments on Meer and Modood', *Journal of Intercultural Studies*, vol. 33, no. 2, pp. 211–16.

Kymlicka, W. and He, Baogang (eds) (2005). *Multiculturalism in Asia*, Oxford University Press, Oxford.

Larus, E.F. (2006). 'Taiwan's Quest for International Recognition', *Issues and Studies*, vol. 42, issue 2, June, pp. 23–52.

Lederer, I.J. (ed.) (1960). *The Versailles Settlement: Was it Foredoomed to Failure?*, D.C. Heath and Company, Boston.

Leib, E.J. and He, Baogang (eds) (2006). *The Search for Deliberative Democracy in China*, Palgrave Macmillan, New York.

Leibold, J. (2007). *Reconfiguring Chinese Nationalism*, Palgrave Macmillan, New York, Chapter 1.

Leibold, J. (2012a). 'Rethinking Ethnic Policy', *China Policy Brief*, 30 May (accessed 22 November 2012), <http://brief.policycn.com/rethinking-ethnic-policy>.

Leibold, J. (2012b). 'Towards a Second Generation of Ethnic Policies?', *China Brief*, vol. XII, issue 13, July, pp. 7–9.

Lewis, M.E. (1999). *Writing and Authority in Early China*, State University of New York Press, Albany, New York.

Li, Jianhui (1997). 'Luelun zhongguo minzu zhengce tixi' ('On the System of Nationality Policies in China'), *Dangdai zhongguoshi yanjiu (Contemporary Chinese History Studies)*, no. 5, pp. 85–103.

Li, Zhi-An (2009). 'Yuandai hanren shou menggu wenhua yingxiang kaoshu' ('Mongolian Influence on the Ethnic Han Chinese in the Yuan Dynasty'), *Lishi Yanjiu (Historical Research)*, issue 1, pp. 24–50.

Liao, Hollis S. (1995). 'The Recruitment and Training of Ethnic Minority Cadres in Tibet', *Issues and Studies*, vol. 31, no. 12, December, pp. 35–67.

Lieberthal, K. (2005). 'Preventing a War Over Taiwan', *Foreign Affairs*, vol. 84, no. 2, March–April, pp. 53–63.

Lijphart, A. (1984). *Democracies: Patterns of Majoritarian and Consensus Government in Twenty-one Countries*, Yale University Press, New Haven.

Lim, Benjamin Kang (2000). 'China Warns Taiwan Against Independence', *Reuters*, 28 January.

Lim, L., Pakir, A. and Wee, L. (eds) (2010). *English in Singapore: Modernity and Management*, University of Hong Kong Press, Hong Kong.

Lin, Gang (1996). 'The Conditions, Consequences and Prevention of Conflicts between Mainland China and Taiwan', *Modern China Studies*, no. 2, pp. 93–7.

Lin, Jing (1997). 'Policies and Practices of Bilingual Education for the Minorities in China', *Journal of Multilingual and Multicultural Development*, vol. 18, no. 3, pp. 193–205.

Lin, J. (2011). 'Is Taiwan Too Economically Dependent on China?', *Taiwan Business Topics*, vol. 41, no. 11, American Chamber of Commerce.

Lin, Qiumin (1991). *Documentary Collection on ROC and United Nations. Reparticipation (Zhonghua Minguo yu Lian he guo shi liao hui bian. Chong xin can yu pian)*, San Min Book Co. Ltd, Academia Historica (San min shu ju, Guo shi guan), Taipei.

Linz, J.J. and Stepan, A. (1996). *Problems of Democratic Transition and Consolidation: Southern Europe, South America, and Post-Communist Europe*, The Johns Hopkins University Press, Baltimore and London.

Liu, A.P. (1966). *Mass Politics in the People's Republic: State and Society in Contemporary China*, Westview, Colorado.

Liu, Houqing (1999). 'Confucianism and Han Wu Emperor's Nationality Policy', *Qinghai Social Sciences*, no. 2, pp. 98–102.

Liu, I-Chou (1998). 'The Taiwanese People's National Identity – A New Survey Method' ('Taiwan minzhong de guojia rentong – yi ge xin de celiang fanshi'), paper presented at the *1998 Annual Conference of the ROC Political Science Association*.

Liu, Jun (2007). *English Language Training in China: New Perspectives, Approaches, and Standards*, The Continuum International Publishing Group Ltd, London.

Liu, Xigan (1984). 'Analysis on Integration and Assimilation of Ethnic Groups' ('Shilun Minzu de Ronghe yu Tonghua'), in Dujian Weng (ed.), *An Outline History of Chinese Ethnic Relations (Zhongguo Minzu Guanxishi Gangyao)*, China Social Sciences Press, Beijing, pp. 178–87.

Liu, Zehua (ed.) (1996). *The History of Chinese Political Thought: Sui, Tang, Song, Yuan, Ming, Qing*, Zhejiang People's Press, Hangzhou, pp. 457–73.

Louis, V. (1979). *The Coming Decline of the Chinese Empire*, Times Books, New York.

Lu, Myra (1998). 'KMT Wins Taipei, Bolsters its Majority in Legislature', *The Free China Journal*, vol. XV, no. 49, 11 December.

Lu, Myra (1999a). 'DPP Opts Not to Revise Wording of Platform', *The Free China Journal*, vol. XVI, no. 2, 8 January.

Lu, Myra (1999b). 'Interior Ministry Approves Draft of Referendum Law', *The Free China Journal*, vol. XVI, no. 21, 28 May.

Lu, Myra (1999c). 'Legislature Again Shelves DPP's Bill on Plebiscites', *The Free China Journal*, vol. XVI, no. 16, 23 April.

Luo, Chih-Mei (2011). 'Modelling The Diversity of EU Members' Paths to European Integration and Policy Implications for Taiwan–China Relations', *Journal of Contemporary European Studies*, vol. 19, no. 2, pp. 273–91.

Luo, Qun (1991). 'The Autonomous Rights of Tibet', *Beijing Review*, vol. 34, no. 21, 27 May–2 June, pp. 20–2.

Ma, Rong (2009). 'Xiandaihua bushi hanhua, gengbushi Minzu Tonghua' ('Modernization is Not Hanification, Nor Ethnic Assimilation'), *Zhongguo minzu bao (China Ethnic News)*, 11 December.

Ma, Xing and Zhong, He (1998). 'Minzu quyu zizhi yanjiu huigu' ('Review of the Studies on National Regional Autonomy'), *Heilongjiang minzu congkan (Heilongjiang Nationality Series)*, Ha'erbin, March.

Ma, Yang (2002). 'Reconsideration on the Discourse on National Blending', *Strategy and Management*, no. 5.

Mackerras, C. (2003b). 'Ethnic Minorities in China', in C. Mackerras (ed.), *Ethnicity in Asia*, RoutledgeCurzon, London.

Makley, C.E. (2003). 'Gendered Boundaries in Motion: Space and Identity on the Sino-Tibetan Frontier', *American Ethnologist*, vol. 30, issue 4, November, pp. 597–619.

Mao, Zedong (1966). *Selected Works of Mao Zedong*, vol. 3, People Press, Beijing.

Mathou, T. (2005). 'Tibet and its Neighbors – Moving Toward a New Chinese Strategy in the Himalayan Region', *Asian Survey*, vol. 45, no. 4, July/August, pp. 503–21.

Mattlin, M. (2004). 'Referendum as A Form of Zaoshi: The Instrumental Domestic Political Functions of Taiwan's Referendum Ploy', *Issues and Studies*, vol. 40, no. 2, pp. 155–85.

Mayall, J. (1991). 'Non-intervention, Self-determination and The "New World Order"', *International Affairs*, vol. 67, no. 3, pp. 421–9.

Mayall, J. and Simpson, M. (1992). 'Ethnicity is Not Enough: Reflections on Protracted Secessionism in the Third World', *International Journal of Comparative Sociology*, vol. 33, nos 1–2, pp. 5–25.

Medani, Khalid Mustafa (2011). 'Strife and Secession in Sudan', *Journal of Democracy*, vol. 22, no. 3, July, pp. 135–49.

Meer, N. and Modood, T. (2012a). 'How Does Interculturalism Contrast with Multiculturalism?', *Journal of Intercultural Studies*, vol. 33, no. 2, pp. 175–96.

Meer, N. and Modood, T. (2012b). 'Rejoinder: Assessing The Divergences on Our Readings of Interculturalism and Multiculturalism', *Journal of Intercultural Studies*, vol. 33, no. 2, pp. 233–44.

Mill, J.S. (1947). *Utilitarianism, Liberty, and Representative Government*, J.M. Dent and Sons Ltd, London, pp. 366–7.

Miller, David (1995). *On Nationality*, Clarendon Press, Oxford.

Miller, D. (2006). 'Is Deliberative Democracy Unfair to Disadvantaged Groups?', in Maurizio Passerin d'Entrèves (ed.), *Democracy as Public Deliberation*, Transaction Publishers, New Brunswick, pp. 201–25.

Millett, K. (2000). *Sexual Politics: A Manifesto for Revolution*, University of Illinois Press, Urbana.

Minghi, J.V. (1970). 'Boundary Studies in Political Geography', in R.E. Kasperson and J.V. Minghi (eds), *The Structure of Political Geography*, pp. 140–60.

Mohanty, A.K. (2009). 'Multilingual Education – A Bridge Too Far?', in T. Skutnabb-Kangas, R. Phillipson, A.K. Mohanty and M. Panda (eds), *Social Justice Through Multilingual Education*, Multilingual Matters, Bristol.

Moon, E.P. and Robinson, J.A. (1997). 'Past Trends Show Election Results Not So Surprising', *The Free China Journal*, 5 December.

Moore, M. (1997). 'On National Self-determination', *Political Studies*, vol. XLV, pp. 900–13.

Morelli, V. (2012). 'Cyprus: Reunification Proving Elusive', *Congressional Research Service*, R41136, 13 August, CRS, Washington, DC.

Morgenthau, H.J. (1957). 'The Paradoxes of Nationalism', *Yale Review*, vol. XLVI, June.

Morgenthau, H.J. (2006). *Politics Among Nations: The Struggle for Power and Peace*, 7th edn, rev. K.W. Thompson and W.D. Clinton, McGraw Hill, New York, pp. 329–34.

Mountcastle, A. (2006). 'The Question of Tibet and the Politics of the "Real"', in B. Sautman and J. Dreyer (eds), *Contemporary Tibet: Politics, Development and Society in a Disputed Region*, M.E. Sharpe, Armonk, New York, pp. 85–106.

Murata, K. and Jenkins, J. (eds) (2009). *Global Englishes in Asian Contexts*, Palgrave Macmillan, Basingstoke.

Neville, R.C. (2000). *Boston Confucianism: Portable Tradition in the Late-Modern World*, State University of New York Press, Albany, New York.

Ni, Shixiong and Wang, Yiwei (2002). 'A Preliminary Study on the Democratization of International Relations' ('Shilun guoji guanxi minzhuhua'), *Journal of International Studies*, no. 3, 13 May.

Noel, A. (2006). 'Democratic Deliberation in a Multilateral Federation', *Critical Review of International Social and Political Philosophy*, vol. 9, no. 3, pp. 419–44.

Norbu, D. (2001). *China's Tibet Policy*, RoutledgeCurzon, New York.

Nye, J.S. Jr. (2004). *Soft Power: The Means to Success in World Politics*, Public Affairs, New York, pp. 2–5.

Offe, C. (1991). 'Capitalism by Democratic Design: Democratic Theory Facing the Triple Transition in East Central Europe', *Social Research*, vol. 58, no. 4, pp. 865–92.

O'Flynn, I. (2006). *Deliberative Democracy and Divided Societies*, Edinburgh University Press, Edinburgh.

Oklopcic, Z. (2012). 'Independence Referendums and Democratic Theory in Quebec and Montenegro', *Nationalism and Ethnic Politics*, vol. 18, no. 1, pp. 22–42.

Omestad, T., Saferstein, C. and Harper, L. (2012). *Former NSC Advisors Recall Nixon Trip – and the Making of China Policy*, 9 March, United States Institute of Peace (accessed 8 October 2012), <http://www.usip.org/publications/former-nsc-advisers-recall-nixon-trip-and-the-making-china-policy>.

Osborne, R. (1985). *Indonesia's Secret War: The Guerilla Struggle in Irian Jaya*, Allen & Unwin, Sydney.

Pakulski, J. and He, Baogang (1999). 'National Integrity, Elites and Democracy: Russia and China Compared', *Journal of Communist Studies and Transition Politics*, vol. 15, no. 2, pp. 69–87.

Pan, Yihong (1992). 'The Sino–Tibetan Treaties in The Tang Dynasty', *T'oung Pao*, vol. 78, pp. 116–61.

Payne, R.J. and Veney, C.R. (2001). 'Taiwan and Africa: Taipei's Continuing Search for International Recognition', *The Journal of Asian and African Studies*, no. 36, issue 4, pp. 437–50.

Pearson, F.S. (2001). 'Dimensions of Conflict Resolution in Ethnopolitical Disputes', *Journal of Peace Research*, vol. 38, no. 3, pp. 275–87.

People's Daily Online (2003). 'US, China Co-operate to Fight Taiwan Referendum Plan', 26 August (accessed 3 September 2012), <http://english.peopledaily.com.cn/200307/29/print20030729_121109.html>.

Perez, S.J. (2009). 'The Contribution of Postcolonial Theory to Intercultural Bilingual Education in Peru', in T. Skutnabb-Kangas, R. Phillipson, A.K. Mohanty and M. Panda (eds), *Social Justice Through Multilingual Education*, Multilingual Matters, Bristol.

Phillipson, R. (1992). *Linguistic Imperialism*, Oxford University Press, Oxford.

Phillipson, R. (2003). *English-Only Europe? Challenging Language Policy*, Routledge, New York.

Phillipson, R. (2009). *Linguistic Imperialism Continued*, Routledge, New York.

Pingali, S. (2009). *Indian English*, Edinburgh University Press, Edinburgh.

Pogge, T.W. (1997). 'Creating Supra-National Institutions Democratically: Reflections on the European Union's "Democratic Deficit"', *The Journal of Political Philosophy*, vol. 5, no. 2, pp. 163–82.

Qi, Dongtao (2012). 'Divergent Popular Support for The DPP and The Taiwan Independence Movement, 2000–2012', *Journal of Contemporary China*, vol. 21, no. 78, 1 November, pp. 973–91.

Qvortrup, M. (2012). 'Introduction: Referendums, Democracy, and Nationalism', *Nationalism and Ethnic Politics*, vol. 18, no. 1, pp. 1–7.

Rabgey, T. (2004). 'Newtibet.com: Citizenship as Agency in a Virtual Tibetan Public', conference paper presented at *Tibet and Contemporary World*, The University of British Columbia, 18–20 April.

Rabgey, T. and Sharlho, Tseten Wangchuk (2004). 'Sino-Tibetan Dialogue in the Post-Mao Era: Lessons and Prospects', *Policy Studies*, no. 12, East-West Center Washington, Washington, DC.

Radan, P. (2012). 'Secessionist Referenda in International and Domestic Law', *Nationalism and Ethnic Politics*, vol. 18, no. 1, pp. 8–21.

Radio Free Asia (2012). *Schools Closed, Teachers Detained*, 18 April (accessed 8 November 2012), <http://www.rfa.org/english/news/tibet/school-04182012152205.html>.

Rajan, D.S. (2005). 'Beijing and the Dalai Lama: Ice Melting?', *South Asia Analysis Group*, New Delhi, paper no. 1271, 28 February, available at the Observer Research Foundation (accessed 8 November 2012), <http://www.observerindia.com/cms/sites/orfonline/modules/analysis/AnalysisDetail.html?cmaid=2153&mmacmaid=83>.

Rawski, E.S. (1996). 'Presidential Address: Reenvisioning The Qing: The Significance of The Qing Period in Chinese History', *The Journal of Asian Studies*, vol. 55, no. 4, November, pp. 829–50.

Reilly, B. (2001). *Democracy in Divided Society: Electoral Engineering and Conflict Management*, Cambridge University Press, Cambridge.

Renen, J.E. (1882). 'Qu'est-ce qu'une nation?' ('What Is a Nation?'), *conférence faite en Sorbonne*, le 11 Mars 1882 (Lecture delivered at the Sorbonne on 11 March 1882), (accessed 18 October 2012), <http://fr.wikisource.org/wiki/Qu%E2%80%99est-ce_qu%E2%80%99une_nation_%3F>.

Reuters (2000). 'Beijing Tells US: We Are No Yugoslavia', 4 February (accessed 29 October 2012), <http://www.hurriyetdailynews.com/default.aspx?pageid=438&n=beijing-tells-us-we-are-no-yugoslavia-2000-02-05>.

Reuters (2000). *World Bank Rejects Settlement Loan to China*, http://ehis.ebscohost.com/eds/detail?sid=196b5204-0c84-4b4e-8a5b-c173ac5e274e%40sessionmgr14&vid=4&hid=115&bdata=JnNpdGU9ZWRzLWxpdmU%3d#db=n5h&AN=b4f3625827e414cab3b0ee005954a174.

Rigger, S. (1999–2000). 'Social Science and National Identity: A Critique', *Pacific Affairs*, University of British Columbia, vol. 72, no. 4, Winter, pp. 537–52.

Rigger, S. (2003). 'New Crisis in the Taiwan Strait?', *Foreign Policy Research Institute E-Notes*, 5 September (accessed 3 September 2012), <http://www.fpri.org/enotes/20030905.rigger.newcrisistaiwan.html>.

Rinpoche, S. (1996). *Tibet: A Future Vision*, Tibetan Parliamentary and Policy Research Centre, New Delhi, India.

Roberts, J.B. (1997). 'The Secret War over Tibet', *American Spectator*, vol. 30, no. 12, pp. 30–6.

Rosen, S.P. (2002). 'The Future of War and The American Military: Demography, Technology and The Politics of Modern Empire', *Harvard Magazine*, May–June (accessed 8 October 2012), <http://harvardmagazine.com/2002/05/the-future-of-war-and-th.html>.

Ross, R. (2006). 'Taiwan's Fading Independence Movement', *Foreign Affairs*, vol. 85, issue 2, March–April.

Rothman J. and Olson, M.L. (2001). 'From Interests to Identities: Towards a New Emphasis in Interactive Conflict Resolution', *Journal of Peace Research*, vol. 38, no. 3, pp. 289–305.

Rustow, D.A. (1970). 'Transitions to Democracy: Towards a Dynamic Model', *Comparative Politics*, vol. 2, pp. 350–1.

Sanders, Lynn (1997). 'Against Deliberation', *Political Theory*, vol. 25, no. 3, pp. 347–76.

Sangay, Lobsang (1999). 'China in Tibet: Forty Years of Liberation or Occupation', *Harvard Asia Quarterly*, Summer, pp. 23–31.

Sangay, Lobsang (2011). 'Inaugural Speech of Kalon Tripa Dr Lobsang Sangay', *International Campaign for Tibet*, 8 August (accessed 11 October 2012), <http://www.savetibet.org/media-center/tibet-news/inaugural-speech-kalon-tripa-dr-lobsang-sangay>.

Sangay, Lobsang (2012). 'Democracy in Exile: The Case for Tibet', available at http://www.youtube.com/watch?v=Obz-9Y3wwdQ.

Sautman, B. (1997). 'Affirmative Action, Ethnic Minorities and China's Universities', working paper in the *Social Sciences*, no. 13, Hong Kong University of Science and Technology, 20 May.

Sautman, B. (2003). '"Cultural Genocide" and Tibet', *Texas International Law Journal*, vol. 38, no. 173, pp. 173–240.

Sautman, B. (2009). *All that Glitters Is Not Gold: Tibet as a Pseudo-State*, monograph no. 197, University of Maryland School of Law Contemporary Asia Series, Baltimore.

Sautman, B. and Dreyer, J. (eds.) (2006). *Contemporary Tibet: Politics, Development and Society in a Disputed Region*, M.E. Sharpe, Armonk, New York.

Sautman, B. and Lo, Shiu-Hing (1995). 'The Tibet Question and The Hong Kong Experience', occasional papers/reprints series, *Contemporary Asian Studies*, no. 2, School of Law, University of Maryland.

Schell, O. (2001). 'Chinese Puzzle: Why Won't Beijing Make Peace with the Dalai Lama?', *San Francisco Chronicle*, 24 June (accessed 11 October 2012), <http://www.sfgate.com/opinion/article/CHINESE-PUZZLE-Why-won-t-Beijing-makepeace-2906341.php>.

Schiaffini, P. (2004). 'The Language Divide: Identity and Literary Choices in Modern Tibet', *Journal of International Affairs*, vol. 57, no. 2, pp. 81–98.

Scott, Ian (1989). *Political Change and the Crisis of Legitimacy in Hong Kong*, Hurst, London.

Seargeant, P. (2009). *The Idea of English in Japan: Ideology and the Evolution of a Global Language*, Multilingual Matters, Bristol.

Segal, G. (1996). 'Taiwanese Elections: Prospects for Stability', *China Review*, Summer, pp. 18–20.

Seshagiri, Lee (2010). 'Democratic Disobedience: Reconceiving Self-Determination and Secession at International Law', *Harvard International Law Journal*, vol. 51, no. 2, Summer, pp. 553–98.

Setter, J., Wong, C.S.P. and Chan, B.H.S. (2010). *Hong Kong English*, Edinburgh University Press, Edinburgh.

Shakya, Tsering (2008). 'Tibetan Questions', *New Left Review*, vol. 51, May–June.

Shapiro, I. (1997). 'Group Aspirations and Democratic Politics', *Constellations*, vol. 3, no. 3, pp. 315–25.

Shearer, I. A. (1994). *Starke's International Law*, 11th edn, Butterworths, Sydney.

Sheng, Lijun (1998). 'China Eyes Taiwan: Why Is a Breakthrough so Difficult?', *The Journal of Strategic Studies*, vol. 21, no. 1, March.

Sheng, Lijun (2001). 'Taiwan at a Crossroads', *Asian Perspective*, vol. 25, no. 1, pp. 195–227.

Sheng, V. (1997). 'Junior High Books Spark Controversy Over Content', *The Free China Journal*, 27 June.

Sheng, V. (1998a). 'DPP Election Win May Unite Opposition Forces', *The Free China Journal*, vol. XV, no. 26, 3 July.

Sheng, V. (1998b). 'DPP Factions United in Mainland Policy Meeting', *The Free China Journal*, 20 February.

Sheng, V. (1998c). 'DDP's Mainland Policy Exemplifies Party's Maturity', *The Free China Journal*, 27 March, p. 7.

Sheng, V. (1998d). 'DPP's Mainland Policy Sparks Intraparty Clash', *The Free China Journal*, 16 January.

Shih, Cheng-Feng (ed.) (1994). *Taiwan Nationalism*, Qianfeng Publisher, Taipei.

Shih, Cheng-Feng (1997). 'Emerging Taiwanese Identity', prepared for *Taiwan Update 1997: Taiwan, Hong Kong and PRC Relations*, Brisbane, Queensland, Australia, 14–15 August.

Shih, Cheng-Feng (1998). *Sub-ethnic Groups and Nationalism*, Qianfeng Publisher, Taipei.

Shih, Cheng-Feng (2000). 'Taiwan's Emerging National Identity', in C.L. Chiou and Leong H. Liew (eds), *Uncertain Future: Taiwan–Hong Kong–China Relations after Hong Kong Return to Chinese Sovereignty*, Ashgate, Aldershot, pp. 245–64.

Shih, Chih-Yu (2002). 'The Teleology of State in China's Regional Ethnic Autonomy', *Asian Ethnicity*, vol. 3, no. 2, pp. 249–56.

Shiromany, A.A. (ed.) (1996). *The Spirit of Tibet, Vision for Human Liberation: Selected Speeches and Writings of His Holiness The XIV Dalai Lama*, Tibetan Parliamentary and Policy Research Center, New Delhi.

Shiromany, A.A. (ed.) (1998). *The Political Philosophy of His Holiness The XIV Dalai Lama: Selected Speeches and Writings*, Tibetan Parliamentary and Policy Research Center, New Delhi.

Sina (2006). *Xianggang meiti cheng dalu dui tai zhengce chansheng juda citie xiaoying (Hong Kong Media States Mainland's Taiwan Policy Has Major Magnet Effect)*, 18 January (accessed 26 November 2012), <http://news.sina.com.cn/c/2006-01-18/13268018295s.shtml>.

Skak, M. (1996). *From Empire to Anarchy: Postcommunist Foreign Policy and International Relations*, Hurst, London.

Skinner, G.W. (1964). 'Marketing and Social Structure in Rural China: Part 1', *Journal of Asian Studies*, vol. 24, no. 1, pp. 3–44.

Skutnabb-Kangas, T., Phillipson, R., Mohanty, A.K. and Panda, M. (eds) (2009). *Social Justice Through Multilingual Education*, Multilingual Matters, Bristol.

Smith, W.W. (1990). 'China's Tibetan Dilemma', *The Fletcher Forum of World Affairs*, vol. 14, no. 1, Winter.

Song, Liming (1997). 'Minzu zhuyi yu xizang wenti' ('Nationalism and Tibet Problem'), *Modern China Studies*, no. 2, pp. 159–67.

Sorensen, T.C. and Phillips, D.L. (2004). 'Legal Standards and Autonomy Options for Minorities in China: The Tibetan Case', *Belfer Center for Science and International Affairs*, John F. Kennedy School of Government, Harvard University.

Sperling, E. (1998). 'Awe and Submission: A Tibetan Aristocrat at the Court of Qianlong', *The International History Review*, vol. 20, no. 2, June, pp. 325–35.

Sperling, E. (2004). *The Tibet–China Conflict: History and Polemics*, East-West Center Washington, Washington, DC.

Stanlaw, J. (2004). *Japanese English: Language and Cultural Contact*, University of Hong Kong Press, Hong Kong.

Stein, J.J. (2003). 'Taking the Deliberative Turn in China: International Law, Minority Rights, and the Case of Xinjiang', *Journal of Public and International Affairs*, vol. 14, Spring.

Steiner, Jurg (2012). *The Foundation of Deliberative Democracy: Empirical Research and Normative Implications*, Cambridge University Press, Cambridge.

Stepan, A. (1997). 'Toward a New Comparative Analysis of Democracy and Federalism: Demos Constraining and Demos Enabling Federations', paper given at XVIIth World Congress of the International Political Science Association, Seoul, 17–21 August, Footnote 27.

Stringer, K.D. (2006). 'Pacific Island Microstates: Pawns or Players in Pacific Rim Diplomacy?', *Diplomacy and Statecraft*, vol. 17, issue 3, September.

Su, Yung-Yao (2012). 'Big Majority Oppose Unification: Poll', *Taipei Times*, 15 April (accessed 8 October 2012), <http://www.taipeitimes.com/News/front/archives/2012/04/15/2003530364>.

Suettinger, R.L. (2003). *Beyond Tiananmen: The Politics of US–China Relations 1989–2000*, Brookings Institute Press, Washington, DC.

Sun, Hongkai (2004). 'Theorizing Over 40 Years' Personal Experiences with the Creation and Development of Minority Writing Systems of China', in Minglang Zhou and Hongkai Sun (eds), *Language Policy in the People's Republic of China: Theory and Practice Since 1949*, Kluwer Academic Publishers, Boston, pp. 179–99.

Sun, Shangwu (2004). 'Chen's Policies Endanger Peace Across Straits', *China Daily*, 20 January.

Sun, Yan (2011). 'The Tibet Question Through the Looking Glass of Taiwan: Comparative Dynamics and Sobering Lessons', *Asian Ethnicity*, vol. 12, no. 3, pp. 337–53.

Sun, Yi (1998). '1996–1997 nian minzu wenti lilun yanjiu zongshu' ('A Summary of the Theoretical Studies on Nationalities between 1996 and 1997'), *Heilongjiang minzu congkan (Heilongjiang Nationality Series)*, Ha'erbin, no. 3.

Sunstein, C.R. (2000). 'Deliberative Trouble? Why Groups Go to Extremes', *Yale Law Journal*, vol. 110, no. 71, pp. 71–119.

Sunstein, C.R. (2003). 'The Law of Group Polarization', in J.S. Fishkin and P. Laslett (eds), *Debating Deliberative Democracy*, Blackwell, Oxford.

Swaine, M.D. (2004). 'Trouble in Taiwan', *Foreign Affairs*, vol. 83, no.2, March/April, pp. 39–49.

Tai, James H.Y. (1988). 'Bilingualism and Bilingual Education in the People's Republic of China', in C.B. Paulston (ed.), *International Handbook of Bilingualism and Bilingual Education*, Greenwood, New York, pp. 185–202.

Tam, K. (2009). *Englishization in Asia: Language and Cultural Issues*, Open University of HK Press, Hong Kong.

The Department of Information and International Relations, Central Tibetan Administration (2009). 'Kalon Tripa Samdhong Rinpoche's Keynote Address on Round Table Discussion on "Greater Tibet"' (accessed 22 November 2012), <http://tibet.net/wp-content/uploads/2012/06/MIDWAY-ENGLISH.pdf>.

The Free China Journal (1997). 'New Trend Set in Party Politics', editorial commentary, 5 December.

The Nation (2005). 'Talks Progressing, Says Tibet's PM-in-Exile', Bangkok, 10 March.

Thurman, R. (2008). *Why the Dalai Lama Matters: His Act of Truth as the Solution for China, Tibet, and the World*, Atria Books, New York.

Tibet Autonomous Region Bureau of Statistics (1990). *Xizang shehui jingji tongji nianjian, 1990 (1990 Year Book of Social and Economic Statistics in Xizang)*, China Statistics Press, Shijiazhuang.

Tibet Autonomous Region Bureau of Statistics (2003). *Tibet Statistical Yearbook 2003*, China Statistics Press, Beijing.

Tibetan Centre for Human Rights and Democracy (2012). *China Re-launches 'Legal Education' Campaign in 'Tibetan Autonomous Region'*, 20 May (accessed 5 November 2012), <http://www.tibetcustom.com/article.php/20120520204936611>.

Tibetan Commission on Human Rights & Development (2000). *Impoverishing Tibetans: China's Flawed Economic Policy in Tibet*, Dharamsala.

Tien, Hung-Mao (1994). 'Toward Peaceful Resolution of Mainland–Taiwan Conflicts: The Promise of Democratization', in Ed. Friedman (ed.), *The Politics of Democratization: Generalizing East Asian Experiences*, Westview Press, Boulder, pp. 189–95.

Tien, Hung-Mao (1997). 'Taiwan's Transformation', in L. Diamond, M.F. Plattner, Yu-Han Chu and Hung-Mao Tien (eds), *Consolidating The Third Wave Democracies: Regional Challenges*, The Johns Hopkins University Press, Baltimore.

Tooley, T.H. (1997). 'The Polish–German Ethnic Dispute and the 1921 Upper Silesian Plebiscite', *Canadian Review of Studies in Nationalism*, vol. 24, nos. 1–2, pp. 13–15.

Traynor, I. and Watts, J (2008). 'Merkel Says She Will Not Attend Opening of Beijing Olympics', *The Guardian*, 29 March (accessed 5 November 2012), <http://www.guardian.co.uk/world/2008/mar/29/germany.olympicgames2008>.

Tsang, Steve Yui-Sang (1988). *Democracy Shelved: Great Britain, China, and Attempts at Constitutional Reform in Hong Kong, 1945–1952*, Oxford University Press, Hong Kong.

Tsang, Steve Yui-Sang (2000). 'China and Taiwan: A Proposal for Peace', *Security Dialogue*, vol. 31, no. 3, pp. 327–36.

Uhr, J. (2002). 'Rewriting the Referendum Rules', in J. Warhurst and M. Mackerras (eds), *Constitutional Politics: The Republic Referendum and The Future*, University of Queensland Press, Brisbane, pp. 177–80.

UNESCO (2008). *The 2nd UNESCO World Report on Cultural Diversity: Investing in Cultural Diversity and Intercultural Dialogue* (accessed 31 October 2012), <http://www.unesco.org/new/en/culture/resources/report/the-unesco-world-report-on-cultural-diversity>.

Vaish, V. (ed.) (2010). *Globalization of Language and Culture in Asia: The Impact of Globalization Processes on Language*, Continuum Publishing, London.

Verma, V.S. (2009). 'Post-Dalai Lama Situation and The Middle Path: Discussions with Chinese Scholars in Beijing', *China Report*, vol. 45, no. 1, pp. 75–87.

Wachman, A.M. (1994). *Taiwan: National Identity and Democratization*, M.E. Sharpe, Armonk, New York.

Waldron, A. (2004). 'How Would Democracy Change China?', *Orbis*, vol. 48, no. 2, Spring, pp. 247–61.

Wallace, R.D. (2007). 'The Two-China Crisis: Background, Implications and Outcomes', *Defense and Security Analysis*, vol. 23, issue 1, March, pp. 69–85.

Wambaugh, S. (1933). *Plebiscites since the World War*, Carnegie Endowment for International Peace, Washington, DC.

Wang, D. and Huang, X. (1995). 'Minzu quyu zizhi zhengce zai xizang de weida shijian' ('Great Practice of Regional Autonomy Policy in Tibet'), *Xizang ribao (Tibet Daily)*, 11 August.

Wang, Gungwu (1995). *The Chinese Way: China's Position in International Relations*, Scandinavian University Press, Oslo.

Wang, Gungwu (1996). 'The Revival of Chinese Nationalism', *International Institute for Asian Studies*, Lecture Series 6, Leiden.

Wang, H. (2004). *Xiandai zhongguo sixiang de xingqi- xia juan, di er bu (The Rise of Modern Chinese Thought: Volume 2, Part 2)*, Sanlian Bookstore, Beijing, pp. 1139–45 and Appendix 1.

Wang, Hui (2008). 'Dongfang zhuyi, minzu quyu zizhi yu zunyan zhengzhi' ('Orientalism, Regional Autonomy and Dignity of Politics: Some Thoughts on Tibet Issues'), *Tian Ya*, no. 4, pp. 173–91.

Wang, Lixiong (2002). 'Reflections on Tibet', *New Left Review*, NLR 14, March–April, pp. 79–111.

Wang, Pengling (1997). 'Zhongguo minzu zhuyi de yuanliu – jianlun cong geming de minzu zhuyi zhuanxiang jianshe de minzu zhuyi' ('Source of Chinese Nationalism – On the Transformation from Revolutionary Nationalism to Constructive Nationalism'), *Modern China Studies*, issue 2, pp. 101–27.

Wang, Weimin and Yi, Xiaohong (1996). 'Minzu yishi: lijie qiansulian minzu wenti de guanjian' ('National Consciousness: Understanding The Crux of the National Problem of the Former Soviet Union'), *Shanxi shida xuebao, Sheke ban (Linfen)*, no. 4, pp. 17–21.

Wang, Yizhou (2000). 'Rethinking The Concept of Sovereign', *Europe*, no. 6, pp. 4–11.

Wangdu, Kalsang (2011). 'China's Minority Education Policy with Reference to Tibet', *Tibetan Review*, June, pp. 19–23.

Whelan, F.G. (1983). 'Prologue: Democratic Theory and the Boundary Problem', in J.R. Pennock and J.W. Chapman (eds), *Liberal Democracy: Nomos XXV*, New York University Press, New York.

White, L.T. III (2000). 'War or Peace over Taiwan', *China Information*, vol. XIV, no. 1, pp. 1–31.

White, S., Gill, G. and Slider, S. (1993). *The Politics of Transition: Shaping a Post-Soviet Future*, Cambridge University Press, Cambridge, p. 88.

Wines, M. (2008). 'Malawi Cuts Diplomatic Ties with Taiwan', *The New York Times*, 15 January (accessed 29 October 2012), <http://www.nytimes.com/2008/01/15/world/africa/15malawi.html?ref=world>.

Wong, Ed. (2010). 'Tibetans in China Protest Proposed Curbs on Their Language', *New York Times*, 22 October (accessed 8 November 2012), <http://www.nytimes.com/2010/10/23/world/asia/23china.html?_r=0>.

Wong, Ed. (2012). 'China Said to Detain Returning Tibetan Pilgrims', *New York Times*, 7 April (accessed 5 November 2012), <http://www.nytimes.com/2012/04/08/world/asia/china-said-to-detain-returning-tibetan-pilgrims.html?_r=1>.

Wright, E. (2010). *Envisioning Real Utopias*, Verso, London.

Wu, Guoguang (2004). 'Passions, Politics, and Politicians: Beijing between Taipei and Washington', *The Pacific Review*, vol. 17, issue 2, pp. 179–98.

Wu, Naide (1993). 'The Sense of Provincialism, Political Support and National Identity', in *Zuqun guanxi yu guojiang rentong (Sovereign Relations and National Identity)*, Institute for National Policy Research, Chang Yung-Fa Foundation, Taipei.

Xie, Fenghua and Ji, Peng (2012). 'An Investigation of Hu Jintao's Idea of Minorities', *Forward Position*, no. 22, pp. 4–5.

Xin, Qiang (2009). 'Mainland China's Taiwan Policy Adjustments', *China Security*, vol. 5, no. 1, pp. 53–64.

Xu, Likun (1998). 'Brief Introduction of Chieftain System in The Ming Dynasty' ('Mingdai tusi zhidu shulue'), *Journal of Guangxi Institute of Socialism*, no. 3, pp. 16–22.

Xu, Mingxu (1999). *Intrigues and Devoutness: The Origin and Development of the Tibet Riots*, Mirror Books Ltd, Brampton, Ontario.

Xu, Zhichang (2010). *Chinese English: Features and Implications*, Open University of HK Press, Hong Kong.

Yan, Jiaqi (1992). *Disan gonghe – weilaizhongguo de xuanze (The Third Republic – A Choice for Future China)*, Global Publishing Co. Inc., New York.

Yan, Jiaqi (1995). 'Federalism and The Future of Tibet', *Tibet News*, no. 19, Autumn, pp. 14–16.

Yang, Jin (2009). 'Woguo de minzu quyu zizhi yu Dalai Lama "gaodu zizhi" de benzhi qubie' ('The Essential Difference between China's Regional Ethnic Autonomy and Dalai Lama's High Degree of Autonomy'), *Red Flag*, no. 2, pp. 12–14.

Yang, Jingchu and Wang, Geliu (1994). 'Woguo de minzu quyu zizhi: Mao Zedong dui Marxism's minzu lilun de gongxian' ('National Regional Autonomy in China: Mao Zedong's Contribution to Marxist Theory of Nationality'), *Minzu yanjiu (Nationality Studies)*, no. 1.

Yang, Minghong and Sun, Jiqiong (2009). 'Zhongyang caizheng buzhu dui xizang jingji fazhan he shouru feipei de yingxiang fenxi' ('Analysis of The Impact of Central Government Subsidies on Tibet's Economic Development and Income Distribution'), *Journal of Southwest University for Nationalities: Humanities and Social Science*, no. 7, pp. 1–5.

Yao, Junkai (1995). 'Shixing minzu quyu zizhi, cujin xizang fanrong changsheng' ('Implement Regional Autonomy, Promote Tibet's Prosperity'), *Xizang minzu xueyuan xuebao: shehui kexueban (Journal of Tibetan Nationality Institute: Social Sciences)*, no. 3.

Yee, A. (2012). 'Dalai Lama's Envoys to China Resign in Frustration', *The Christian Science Monitor*, 7 June (accessed 5 November 2012), <http://www.csmonitor.com/World/Asia-South-Central/2012/0607/Dalai-Lama-s-envoys-to-China-resign-in-frustration>.

Yin, Wan-Lee (1995). 'On "Taiwan in the China Circle"', *The Journal of Contemporary China*, vol. 4, no. 8, Winter–Spring, pp. 102–5.

Yu, Peter Kien-Hong (1998). 'Concept of New Taiwanese Foresees New, Unified China', *The Free China Journal*, vol. XV, no. 51, 25 December.

Zhang, Bo (2008). 'Lun zhengzhihua aoyunhui zai guoji renquanfa shang de feifaxing' ('On the Illegality of Politicized Olympic Games in International Human Rights Law'), *Probe*, no. 3, pp. 107–10.

Zhang, Dan (2002). 'Qiantan hanwenhua dui manzu yuyanwenhua xingshuai de yongxiang' ('Analysis of the Influence of Chinese Culture on the Rise and Fall of Manchu Language and Culture'), *Heilongjiang Shizhi (Heilongjiang History)*, issue 2, pp. 41–2.

Zhang, Fengshan (1999). 'On Taiwan's Independence Referendum', *Taiwan Studies*, no. 2, pp. 14–21.

Zhang, Jie (1995). 'Qingdai manzu yuyan wenzi zai dongbei de xingfei yu yongxiang' ('The Influence and Rise and Fall of Manzu language in the Northeast in Qing Dynasty'), *Beifang Wenwu (Northern Cultural Relics)*, vol. 1, no. 41, pp. 63–8.

Zhang, Jun (2008). 'Rentong yu jiangou, Meng yuan shiqi yuwen jianshe de lishi kaocha' ('Identification and Construction: Historical Research on Language Construction in the Mongolian-Yuan Period'), *Ningxia Shehui Kexue (Social Sciences in Ningxia)*, issue 4, pp. 135–6.

Zhang, Lei (2008). 'Manyu xiaowang de lishi beijing tanjiu' ('Explore The Historic Background on the Disappearance of Manzu Language'), *Liaoning Jiaoyu Xingzheng Xueyuan Xuebao (Journal of Liaoning Education Administration Institute)*, issue 3, pp. 76–8.

Zhang, Weidong (1998). 'Beijingyin heshi chengwei hanyu guanhua biaozhunyin?' ('When Did Beijing Sounds Become the Standard Sound System of Chinese Mandarin?'), *Shenzhen daxue xuebao, Renwen shehui kexueban (Journal of Shenzhen University, Humanities & Social Sciences)*, vol. 15, issue 4, pp. 93–8.

Zhang, Weiguo (ed.) (1999). *Icebreaking: Dialogue with the Dalai Lama*, Foundation for China in the 21st Century, Washington, DC.

Zhang, Wenmu (2002). 'China's National Interests in the Process of Globalization', *Strategy and Management*, no. 1, pp. 52–64.

Zhao, Quansheng (1988). 'A Proposed Model of Unification and Plural Politics', *China Forum*, vol. 26, no. 5.

Zhao, Quansheng (2005). 'Beijing's Dilemma with Taiwan: War or Peace', *Pacific Review*, vol. 18, no. 2, June, pp. 217–42.

Zhao, Yi-jun (2008). 'Mingqing shiqi buyizu diqu de xuexiao jiaoyu' ('School Education in the Region of Bouyei Nationality During the Period of the Ming and Qing Dynasties'), *Minzu Jiaoyu Yanjiu (Journal of Research on Education for Ethnic Minorities)*, vol. 19, no. 4, pp. 77–82.

Zheng, Ge (2009). 'Wenhua fazhan yu minzu quyu zizhi' ('Culture, Development and Regional Ethnic Autonomy'), paper presented at the *Roundtable on The Tibet Issue*, University of Hong Kong, 29–30 July.

Zhonghua renmin gongheguo xiafa (1997). (*The Constitution of People's Republic of China*). China's Law Press, Beijing.

Zhou, Chuanbin (1998). 'Minzu zhengce lilun yanjiu huigu' ('Review of the Theoretical Studies on Nationality Policies'), *Heilongjiang minzu congkan (Heilongjiang Nationality Series)*, Ha'erbin, no. 3.

Zhou, Minglang (2004). 'Minority Language Policy in China: Equality in Theory and Inequality in Practice', in Minglang Zhou and Hongkai Sun (eds), *Language Policy in the People's Republic of China: Theory and Practice Since 1949*, Kluwer Academic Publishers, Boston, pp. 71–95.

Zhou, Minglang (2010). 'The Fate of The Soviet Model of Multinational State-Building in the People's Republic of China', in T.P. Bernstein and Hua-yu Li (eds), *China Learns from the Soviet Union, 1949–Present*, Lexington Books, Plymouth.

Zhou, Minglang and Ross, H.A. (2004). 'Introduction: The Context of the Theory and Practice of China's Language Policy', in Minglang Zhou and Hongkai Sun (eds), *Language Policy in the*

People's Republic of China: Theory and Practice Since 1949, Kluwer Academic Publishers, Boston, pp. 1–18.

Zhou, Ping (1993). 'Minzu zizhi difang xingzheng guanli de teshuxing' ('Special Characteristics of The Administration in Autonomous Regions'), *Sixiang zhanxian (Thought Battlefield)*, no. 4, pp. 37–8.

Zhou, Wenjiu (2007). 'From "The Chinese Nation is One" to "The Plurality in an Organic Whole": An Historical Investigation of the Evolution of the Theories of Chinese Nation', *Journal of Peking University: Philosophy and Social Sciences*, vol. 44, no. 4, pp. 102–9.

Zhou, Yanshan (1995). 'New Thinking on the "Chinese Commonwealth"', *Modern China Studies*, no. 4, pp. 19–24.

Zhu, Lun (2001). 'On Ethnic Co-governance – A Study of the Political Realities in Ethno-National Communities in Contemporary States with Multiple Ethical Groups' ('Minzu gongzhilun – dui dangdai duominzu guojia zuji zhengzhi shishi de renshi'), *Social Sciences in China*, no. 4, pp. 95–105.

Zhu, Weiqun (2012). 'Dui dangqian minzu lingyu wenti de jidian sikao' ('Reflections on Current Ethnic Minority Issues'), *Xuexi Shibao (Study Times)*, 13 February (accessed 31 October 2012), <http://www.studytimes.com.cn:9999/epaper/xxsb/html/2012/02/13/01/01_51.htm>.

Index